# Giving the Church

# Giving the Church

*The Christian Community Through
the Looking Glass of Generosity*

Michael Moynagh

scm press

© Michael Moynagh 2024

Published in 2024 by SCM Press
Editorial office
3rd Floor, Invicta House,
110 Golden Lane,
London EC1Y 0TG, UK

www.scmpress.co.uk

SCM Press is an imprint of Hymns Ancient & Modern Ltd
(a registered charity)

Hymns Ancient & Modern® is a registered trademark of
Hymns Ancient & Modern Ltd
13A Hellesdon Park Road, Norwich,
Norfolk NR6 5DR, UK

All rights reserved. No part of this publication may be reproduced,
stored in a retrieval system, or transmitted,
in any form or by any means, electronic, mechanical,
photocopying or otherwise, without the prior permission of
the publisher, SCM Press.

Michael Moynagh has asserted his right under the Copyright, Designs
and Patents Act 1988 to be identified as the Author of this Work

British Library Cataloguing in Publication data
A catalogue record for this book is available
from the British Library

ISBN 978-0-334-06612-5

Typeset by Regent Typesetting
Printed and bound in Great Britain by
CPI Group (UK) Ltd

# Contents

| | | |
|---|---|---|
| *Foreword by Paul Avis* | | vii |
| *Acknowledgements* | | xiii |
| Introduction: Bringing Generosity into View | | 1 |

## Part 1 The Church's Identity

| | | |
|---|---|---|
| 1 | Called to Give? The Church's Vocation | 25 |
| 2 | What is the Gift? The Church's Nature | 53 |
| 3 | An Attractive Gift? The Four Marks | 75 |
| 4 | An Available Gift? The Hidden and Visible Church | 97 |
| 5 | A Gift for Everyone? The Socially Inclusive Church | 118 |

## Part 2 The Church's Self-donation

| | | |
|---|---|---|
| 6 | A Sociological Framework | 147 |
| 7 | A Liberating Purpose | 169 |
| 8 | A Conversational Manner | 191 |
| 9 | A Eucharistic Spirituality | 217 |
| 10 | Becoming an Attractive Gift | 239 |

| | |
|---|---|
| *Bibliography* | 261 |
| *Index of Names and Subjects* | 277 |

# Foreword

It is a pleasure and privilege for me to be asked by Michael Moynagh to contribute a Foreword to his latest work of applied ecclesiology and missiology, the third in a trilogy. In this short essay I aim to pave the way for his special contribution and also to continue the cordial dialogue which we have enjoyed for several years now with aspects of his argument in this book.

First, I want to note the sombre and troubling background against which Michael and I do our research, thinking and writing. It is not controversial to say that the context of his work and mine is one of overall church decline by almost every measure and across almost all Christian traditions. To be specific: in the Church of England the number of worshippers and clergy is steadily reducing; the take-up of the pastoral offices of baptism, confirmation, marriage and funeral services has plummeted; parish finances are often struggling and unable to meet the demands made on them; many church-based organizations and activities are now defunct; the social and cultural influence of the church in the nation is minimal; church leaders (bishops) are hardly visible and barely known, even within their own dioceses; the proceedings of the General Synod are generally ignored by the national media. So the context in which we must work is one of the acute marginalization, approaching invisibility and irrelevance, of the Christian church, especially in many densely-populated urban areas. The taxi driver who was taking me from the station to an institution of theological education in the north of England asked what the institution did and when I replied that it trained vicars, he commented, 'Are there any these days?' Taxi drivers don't miss much.

In the English countryside, every landscape seems to reveal a church tower or spire, the church and churchyard remain sacred sites to almost all and probably a majority of the inhabitants would recognize their parish priest, or at least know their name. Yet even here the planned starving of rural parishes of clergy is a major factor in the recent marked decline in the number of participating parishioners and therefore of church-based activities and so of the overall effectiveness of the church's gospel witness within the community. The rural heartlands of the Christian Church in England are crumbling in many places.

Some aspects of decline are the Church's own fault; they are self-inflicted. Some parishes have to put up with clergy (if they are fortunate enough to have them) who, rather than getting out into the thick of the community, creep about trying to remain inconspicuous and act merely like chaplains to their dwindling congregations. It is also obvious that a good many clergy have received an inadequate training, both before and after ordination; they don't understand their role and tasks and have very little theology to sustain them, in spite of noble efforts to raise the standard through the Common Awards programme based at Durham University. Clergy appointments are sometimes tainted with cynicism, quite often putting square pegs into round holes, especially urban clergy transplanted to rural communities that they don't understand. Above all, there are simply not enough good-enough clergy on the ground. One consequence is that we are being told that lay people can do most of the work traditionally undertaken by the ordained. Volunteers already take up much of the slack, including some responsibilities that are not appropriate or even legal, especially pastoral oversight by stealth.

But lay ministry is an estimable calling in its own right, a key expression of the baptismal mandate of all Christians. It should not be seen as a 'stop-gap' but rather as requiring rigorous calling, training and commissioning in ways that are theologically appropriate to the various lay roles. However, often enough these lay ministers, especially perhaps worship leaders, remain untrained, unsupervised and unsupported. That is asking for trouble in some cases. The Save the Parish movement is drawing urgent attention to these pastoral problems and is publicly challenging the prevailing high-level strategy in the Church of England which is a toxic mix of centralized control (national certainly, and diocesan in some cases) with its accompanying bureaucratization and the consequent drawing away of funds from the front line. That is not the case everywhere, but it is the overall trend. It is the antithesis of subsidiarity. What the reversal of that strategy and the replacement of its underpinning ideology with a more salutary ecclesiological mindset would involve is another story and we cannot embark on it here.

I believe that few, however, would deny the basic premise of my argument, which is this. It has been well said that 'Small is Beautiful' and that surely remains true in many contexts. To me that insight means that the local is beautiful. The local – and in church terms that normally means the parish – is beautiful in our eyes because it is the source and centre of all that counts most in Christian and community life. It is within the parish that energy, activity, motivation, service to others and fund-raising

# FOREWORD

are generated most successfully. The local (the parish in our terms) is where love blossoms and where trust can be built up over time between clergy and lay ministers, on the one hand, and parishioners, on the other. And without love and trust – the keys to the essentially personal and relational nature of ministry and mission – nothing for the Kingdom of Christ can be achieved. Love and trust cannot be transmitted from a distance – so not from remote clergy and lay ministers, operating from their centralized hubs or 'minsters' making forays into territory that they hardly know and trying to convert people who do not know them. The opposite of that mirage of mission is a ministry in every community and in every neighbourhood and that is precisely the vision that Michael Moynagh is pursuing in this book. He wants to make the Christian gospel, Christian worship and Christian fellowship available, visible and accessible in every place. But how, we may well ask, are we to achieve that ambitious missional and pastoral ideal?

First, Michael is looking for the kind of church that gives itself away to others. A self-giving church is a church that finds its *raison d'être* in serving others in the name of Christ. It expresses its God-given identity in reaching out to draw others into 'communion in Christ' (as he finely and consistently puts it). Modern scholarly studies of the concept of 'gift' help to resource this aspect of his argument. He recognizes that many parish churches are already energetic centres of voluntary service to those in the local community (and further afield) who are disadvantaged, sick, or suffering in other ways. But how can the church, with all its human flaws and shortcomings, ever be a self-giving, self-sacrificial body? The recent sexual abuse horrors in the major churches have once again put the spotlight on that aspect of the church's history that points to sin, error, oppression and crime. Some in our society, who have been wounded and traumatized by the church, would see the offer of the church as a toxic gift and one to shudder at; they want none of it. We must be acutely sensitive to that fact when we talk about the church and mission in our theology.

The church can only be the 'giving church' because the Christian God, the Holy Trinity, is a self-giving, gracious and generous God who has given and continually gives of Godself to the world and to the Church (John 3.16). The self-communication of God in love at all times and to all persons is the key to all the central biblical doctrines: creation, revelation, redemption and sanctification. Jesus Christ is the personal embodiment, the incarnation, of this divine self-giving love. Dietrich Bonhoeffer called Jesus the man who lived entirely for others. Jesus gave himself away out of love. Another thread in the tapestry of divine self-giving, as we learn from John 17, is that the Father has given believers to the Son from all eternity. They are his 'own', the gift of the Father to the Son. A theology of a self-giving church can rest only on a theology of a self-giving God. But that is not all.

In the church, God imparts the divine life to faithful disciples through the ministry of the word and the sacraments, underpinned by pastoral care. God gives Godself through the appointed means of grace. The content and meaning of word, sacrament and pastoral care is always Jesus Christ, the Word incarnate (John 1.1–14). Those who are called, trained and authorized to minister these precious means of grace are giving Christ alone, Christ and all his benefits; nothing else. God is giving Jesus Christ to the world, to the church, and to the world in the church through these means of grace which are also human practices. In response and in return, the church gives itself to God in adoration, service and mission, which are also human practices. The celebration of the Eucharist (thanksgiving) is at the very heart of this faithful response and is the primary and central practice of the Christian community. Eucharistic worship is trinitarian, offered by the church to the Father, through the mediation of the Son, in the life and power of the Holy Spirit. Individual Christians also give themselves to God and to others as a living sacrifice (Rom. 12.1) in worship, prayer, service and witness. So there is a glorious, constant, ceaseless exchange of giving and gifts in the relationship between God and the church, the church and God.

One expression of the self-giving of the church – and the one that Michael Moynagh particularly wants to bring to our attention – is the filling of the many gaps in the visible, available, accessible and local form of the church by means of new Christian communities. As he recognizes, they are not needed everywhere – to start up a new church in rural parishes, in villages and small towns, where the parish church is already the hub of Christian presence and worship, would be schismatic and would cause outrage. But who can deny that there are gaps enough to be filled in the fabric of Christian presence and witness throughout the land that existing structures do not and probably cannot meet? As an ecclesiologist and ecumenical theologian (as well as a priest and pastor), I am extremely wary of any moves that would further fragment the one church of Jesus Christ, which is already in pieces. and I have recently set out these convictions again in *Reconciling Theology* (SCM Press, 2022). Therefore we must tread carefully. It is axiomatic for me that no one, with a good conscience and theological integrity, can – or rather should – start their own church. A 'new' Christian community can be only an extension or offspring of the existing Christian community. Only God's church can spread God's church. New Christian communities cannot be set up at the whim of a freelance individual, however much they may

FOREWORD

claim that the Holy Spirit has prompted them to do so. There is no ego-trip to be had here. Mike Moynagh insists – though without going into the practical implications – that new Christian communities need to be authorized and to be part of the existing church as an ordered community (an institution); that they should be placed only where they are needed and not started in rivalry to existing forms of the Church on the same site; and that careful oversight is required, not least for safeguarding reasons (as some tragic, scandalous and avoidable developments in recent years have demonstrated). But are these new Christian communities to be considered as 'churches'? That would seem to be a major further step.

There is a succinct definition of the church that goes back before the Reformation and was reproduced in the Church of England's Thirty-nine Articles as Article XIX. This reads (and we need to make allowance for the sexist language of the time): 'The visible Church of Christ is a congregation of faithful men, in which the pure Word of God is preached, and the Sacraments be duly ministered according to Christ's ordinance.' We should note that the Article is not at all thinking in 'congregationalist' terms, of autonomous gathered communities of believers. 'Congregation' is used elsewhere in the Anglican formularies to refer to the whole nation, and in the Old Testament the equivalent term refers to the whole people of Israel. The 'congregation', large or small, is the total Christian community in its setting. But it is only when the Word is correctly ('purely') preached and the sacraments are properly ('duly') celebrated that a Christian community can be called a church. Now, it is not for any community to call itself a church on its own authority. Only the church can recognize a church. And that is where duly constituted authority, episcopal and synodical, comes into play. There are thus several threads that link and bind new Christian communities to the parent Church.

Mike Moynagh does not go deeply into these matters of ecclesiastical polity, of canonical and episcopal authority. There is more to be said and more work to be done. But what he has so valuably done is to provide a vision and a rationale for filling the gaps in the fabric of Christian presence and witness throughout the land. He has done that on the basis of wide reading, deep reflection, clear and accessible exposition and a concern for the mission entrusted to the church. I commend *Giving the Church* as a unique contribution to our thinking about the church and God's mission for our times.

*Paul Avis*
*Honorary Professor, School of Divinity, University of Edinburgh;*
*Editor-in-Chief of Ecclesiology; honorary assistant priest in the*
*Axe Valley Mission Community, Diocese of Exeter*

# Acknowledgements

Many conversations and different types of literature have helped shape this book, and I am grateful for them all. Though remaining shortcomings are mine, particular thanks are due to Revd Will Donaldson, Drs Erin Crider, Anne Richards and Clare Watkins, Revd Drs Michael Beck and Andrea Russell, Professors Andrew Bradstock and Stefan Paas, Rt Revd Graham Cray and Rt Revd Dr Mike Harrison, who commented on parts of the book and in some cases the whole of it. Revd Professor Paul Avis has been a particular source of encouragement and advice, and I owe him a great debt. Big thanks, too, to David Shervington, Rachel Geddes, Kate Hughes, Elizabeth Hinks and the team at SCM Press. I have continued to value my links with Wycliffe Hall, Oxford and my teaching sessions there. And as ever, my wife Liz has been unstinting in her support. Without her, *Giving the Church* would never have been written.

*Revd Dr Michael Moynagh*
*Oxford, February 2024*

# Introduction:
# Bringing Generosity into View

What might the Christian community look like if we put the church as a gift centre stage? Of course, the idea that the church is a gift is not new. The World Council of Churches' 'new affirmation on mission and evangelism' puts it plainly: 'The church is a gift of God to the world for its transformation toward the kingdom of God' (2013b, §10; see §56).[1] However, the gift idea is not developed. And that is typical of how theologians have treated the notion. They have widely recognized that the church is called to be one of God's gifts, but by and large have stopped short of exploring the logic of giving and its implications for the Christian community.

They have emphasized many other features of the church. The Roman Catholic theologian Avery Dulles famously condensed these into six models: the church as institution, as a communion joined to the Trinity, as sacrament, as creature of the Word, as servant and liberator, and as a school of discipleship (Dulles, 2002). But theologians have not paid equal attention to the church as a gift. True, giving is firmly implied in Dulles's models. When the body is faithful to its head, the church's organizational arrangements can be seen as gifts from God. So too can the church's communal life, God's sacramental presence through the church, the Word that gathers Christians together, the church's liberating service, and the ecclesial resources that enable discipleship. All are divine gifts. Giving is indispensable to these understandings of the church, but giving itself has been left in the background.[2]

This may appear surprising, because generosity is central to the Christian faith. Father, Son and Holy Spirit are revealed as givers – in the gift of life in creation, in Christ's self-giving to save creation, in the gift of the Spirit to bring creation to perfection through Christ, and in Christ's gift of the kingdom to the Father when God's reign is complete. From beginning to end, generosity is the story of God. In which case, might we not expect generosity to be the focus of Christian thinking about the church? Might we not suppose the church to be more than an institution, a communion and so on? Might not the church as Christ's body personify his generosity – be a gift that all these other descriptions point to?

The immediate response may be that the church lacks credibility as a gift. Recent clerical child abuse and its cover up, the church's involvement in religious wars and genocide, the brutal internal politics of the church and more cast a noxious shadow over the claim to generosity. The church's moral high ground has shrunk to a mole hill. I shall return to the church's sinfulness at various stages, but here it may be worth asking: if the idea of the church as a gift elicits incredulity, might this not challenge the Christian community to become more attractive to others and to God? Might the very call to be a gift invite the church to reflect critically on its life and prayerfully seek reform?

And might this self-critique prevent the church being given from a position of superiority? Instead, when it is offered to others, might the Christian community become a gift by standing with those outside the church who have been shamed because the church itself has been shamed; with those who have abused their power because the church has also abused its power; and with those who are anxious about their relevance because in many places the church, too, is anxious about its relevance? Just as friends may be gifts to one another by sharing their failures, might the church become a gift by standing in solidarity with others burdened by failure – 'You are not alone. We stand where you stand'?

In particular, might this realistic stance help commend the church to a post-institutional age? Many people are suspicious of the controlling tendencies of organizations. They want to be freed, valued and respected within supportive relationships. Can the Christian community be offered as the gift of such relationships? The church's manifold shortcomings may seem to say 'No'. Yet might a self-critical church, which admits its mistakes, become a trusted community because of its very transparency? Could part of the answer to 'Why bother with church?' lie in combining honesty about the gift's defects with ambitions to be a more compelling gift? Might *this* be a church worth striving for?

*Giving the Church* is wet cement. It is a trial run to see what might happen if we made generosity key to our thinking about the church. How might seeing the church as a gift change some of the ways we imagine the Christian community? Might it offer concepts and language to help the church navigate the complex world we now inhabit? Might the Christian community be enabled to see itself afresh as it seeks to be a twenty-first-century banner of Christ's reign? And might that jolt the church into becoming a more attractive gift? This is one hope: that a doctrine centred on generosity will encourage the Christian community to clean its Augean stable.

INTRODUCTION

Another hope is to sharpen the notion of mission, which is now de rigueur in understandings of the church. If it is true that lack of a target means you never hit it, can a goal for mission be described that is both broad enough to encompass the spectrum of mission and yet specific enough to focus the church's energies? And might this goal be the church's self-giving to others? A third hope is to offer a doctrine of the church that will resource today's worldwide constituency of church planters, now being swelled by the founders of new forms of Christian community. Driven sometimes more by evangelistic zeal than by a 'high' doctrine of the church, might their efforts be enriched by, and contribute to, a bigger vision of the Christian community? And might this vision encourage other traditions to embrace church planting, which is too often limited to evangelical churches?

This introduction begins with three recent and important developments in our understanding of the church. How does giving the church to others connect with them? Next, we relate the book's theme to the post-Christendom world in which the church finds itself. We then start to unpack what it means for the church to be a gift, especially when power abuses have made the gift unwelcome. Finally, we outline the book's argument.

## Three developments

### *Communion ecclesiology*

One recent development has become known as 'communion ecclesiology', which is a family of views. In the Roman Catholic Church communion ecclesiology was a reaction against over-identifying the Christian community with the Church's structures and teaching. By the mid-twentieth century, Roman Catholic teaching had become dominated by the role of priests, bishops and papacy and the infallibility of the Church's authority, the magisterium.[3] These emphases were so strong that the Christian community was in danger of becoming almost indistinguishable from the Church's hierarchy and authorized teaching.

The official reaction against this came at Vatican II when, between 1962 and 1965, Roman Catholic bishops met to discuss how their Church should engage with the modern world. Building on the insights of Johann Adam Möhler (1796–1838), George Tyrrell (1861–1909), Yves Congar (1904–1995), Henri de Lubac (1896–1991) and others, one conclusion was that the church was not only characterized by papal authority and hierarchy but was above all a 'holy People of God' in which the laity

3

have a key role. The Holy Spirit joins God's followers invisibly to Christ and each other, especially through the Eucharist, and this communion is expressed outwardly in the visible church.

Outside the Catholic Church, the influential Orthodox theologian John Zizioulas roots the church in the Trinity and in Christ. The Trinity is a communion (*koinonia*) of persons, relational in its very being, and the church likewise is relational by nature. The church also derives from Christ, who is head of the church and who was born and exists in the fellowship of the Spirit. By means of the Spirit, Christ becomes who he is by being in communion with the many who comprise his body; Christ would not be the Christ we know without this community, rather as you or I would not be who we are without our families. It is at the Eucharist that the fellowship of Christ and the Spirit is expanded to include members of the church. The church enables the Eucharist to exist and the Eucharist simultaneously enables the church to exist. 'Church and Eucharist are interdependent, they coincide, and are even in some sense identical' (Zizioulas, 2011, p. 105).

Protestant theologians too have developed versions of communion ecclesiology, again often rooted in the Trinity (for example, Volf, 1998; Fiddes, 2003). This has allowed communion ecclesiology to seize the limelight in ecumenical understandings of the church. In its important 2013 convergence statement, *The Church: Towards a common vision*, the World Council of Churches described *koinonia* as central to the ecumenical search for a shared understanding of the Christian community. This understanding is framed by the Trinity. 'In the Church, through the Holy Spirit, believers are united with Jesus Christ and thereby share a living relationship with the Father' (WCC, 2013a, §13).

The logic of communion ecclesiology is that the communal life of the church should be understood as a gift. Being community is a gift that is given through the Spirit supremely at the Eucharist. The Spirit is a gift (Rom. 5.5) who creates communion (2 Cor. 13.14), which includes the communion of saints. So when Christians are given the Spirit, they gain more than the Spirit alone. They receive the divine person who is always creating communion. The gift of the Spirit is rather like the gift of a club membership card; the card brings with it the community of other members.

The communion included in the gift of the Spirit involves participating in the giving nature of God, whose generosity is most revealed in the gift of the Son in Jesus. As the church is drawn into the life of the Godhead, its relationships are flavoured by this generosity. St Paul viewed the church as a community whose members are equipped with gifts for the good of all (1 Cor. 12.7ff.). When these gifts are not released within the body everyone is diminished. 'If one part suffers, every part suffers with it' (1 Cor. 12.26). This verse comes at the end of a passage emphasizing that each person and their gifts are indispensable. Paul seems to be feeling towards an understanding of how failing to give means somebody else's inability to receive, and how not receiving reduces the capacity to give; the person has less to offer (Williams, 2008b, p. 122). When a gift is shared, on the other hand, recipients are given resources that they can give in their turn (2 Cor. 8.14). Paul describes what a communion of people sharing in God's giving is like. Mexican waves of generosity are to course endlessly through the church.

To be consistent with this identity, the church must be a gift to people beyond the church. Having received the gift of communion in Christ, the Christian community must enable others to receive the gift too. They must stretch their internal giving to people outside. Otherwise a wedge would exist between the church's behaviour in the world and its participation in divine giving, between generosity within the church and a lack of generosity to people beyond. Just as God is consistent – God's relationships with the world flow out of God's being within the Trinity – so the church must also have integrity. Its relationships with others must flow out of its nature as a generous communion. The church as a gift with the character of giving resonates with the communal model of the Christian community.

## The mission of God

A second major development in understanding the church has been the rediscovery of the *missio Dei*, the mission of God. The evolution of *missio Dei* theology has been summarized by David Bosch (1991, pp. 389–93) and by Stephen Bevans and Roger Schroeder (2004, pp. 286–95). The modern idea of the *missio Dei* (though not the term) first surfaced clearly at the International Missionary Council's 1952 meeting in Willingen, Germany, and the concept has been developed in various ways since.

Central to the notion is that mission is foremost an activity of God. Old Testament scholar Christopher Wright maintains that the Bible reveals a personal divinity who has a missionary purpose, which is that the whole of creation should give glory to God. Scripture describes humanity with a mission, Israel with a mission, Jesus with a mission, and the church with a mission – all with that purpose in view and all sharing, therefore, in the divine mission (Wright, 2006, pp. 64–8). The activity of this missional God means, in Jürgen Moltmann's words, that it 'is not the church that "has a mission" but the very reverse: that the mission of Christ creates its own church' (Moltmann, 2000, p. 10). Rather than the church engaging in mission and asking God to bless it, God engages in mission and asks the church to join in. The focus shifts from the church to God.

This emphasis on God has helped draw together theologies of the church and theologies of mission. In the past, they tended to occupy different compartments. Doctrines of the church typically focused on what the church is; understandings of mission on what the church does. However, both disciplines are now bridging the divide that kept them apart. In each, the immediate starting point today is neither the church's nature nor its activity, but the missional reality of the triune God. Doctrines of the church pay greater attention to how God's mission calls the church into being; theologians of mission give more weight to the church as God's vehicle for mission (Bevans, 2005, pp. 45–9). *The Church: Toward a common vision* reflects this convergence. The two middle chapters, which address topics of typical concern to theologians of the church, are sandwiched between opening and closing chapters about mission. Church and mission are welded together. Church members are to tear down their Hadrian's Walls against others.

God's outward orientation is often described as 'the sending of God', one translation of *missio Dei*. The Father is not himself sent, but reveals a missionary heart by sending both Son and Spirit to work for the fulfilment of creation. The church is sent in their wake to participate in God's mission by means of the Spirit. However, as John Flett points out, sending is a thin notion. It has been interpreted in all sorts of ways. Flett argues that fundamentally God's orientation to the world involves self-giving: 'in his act of creation, reconciling, and redeeming, God gives himself [*sic*] entirely to humanity' (Flett, 2010, p. 202). Not least, God's Son dies for humanity. This makes divine giving, as the form in which sending occurs, the heart of mission. Rather than God's self-donation being an aspect of sending, sending should be seen as an aspect of divine self-giving. Sending is what happens when generosity overflows the Trinity and pours out in creating, sustaining and redeeming creatures beyond. The church is summoned to take part in this divine outpouring. Just as God's self was given to the world in Jesus, so the church's self – communion in Christ – is to be shared with others for the sake of creation. Giving is more fundamental to God's missionary act than sending.

## Liberation theologies

A third major development is theologies of liberation. These began in Latin America, where parts of the Roman Catholic Church had a long tradition of co-struggling with the poor. Vatican II's commitment to

# INTRODUCTION

social justice encouraged Gustavo Gutiérrez and others to argue that the Christian community evangelizes the world by joining the poor in battling for liberation (Gutiérrez, 1973). Liberation theology reflects on reality with a view to overturning the unjust structures of society; the weak and marginalized must be freed to flourish. The church undertakes this reflection not from an armchair, but by throwing itself into action to liberate the oppressed. Knowing God is to encounter God in the exertion for justice because that is where God is supremely present (Luke 4.18–19).

We can trace a progression of thought. In the hands of Latin American liberationists, Vatican II's emphasis on the people of God became an emphasis on *oppressed* people at the base of the church. Leonardo Boff (1986) described an 'ecclesiogenesis', in which a new kind of church was being born bottom-up from the faith of the poor. But of course people at the grassroots are not all the same. So, drawing on the insights of Latin American liberationists, theologians around the world and across the denominations have developed theologies tailored to the particular colours of the demographic spectrum. African, Asian, Black, feminist, LGBTQ+ and post-colonial theologies have mushroomed. Each asks how God can liberate the people in question, give them fuller lives within forms of church that reflect their social identities, and through them launch tornados of change against injustice elsewhere in the church. Focus has shifted from the ecclesial landscape as a whole to the church's foothills, to particular villages that have been trampled upon or ignored.

Historically, these groupings have been silenced mainly by male Western elites who have dominated the Christian community. Liberationists seek to give voice to muted groups, enable each to express in church their own particular experience of God, and encourage the wider church to pay attention to them. The key step is solidarity. The Christian community is to draw alongside those who have been marginalized by society and the church, identify with them, join in their struggles for a more fulfilling life, invite them to voice their Christian experience in their own fashion, and encourage them to share the whole church's life on equal terms to other groups.

This solidarity can be expressed in the language of giving. When the church dwells among people who have been denied their full rights and becomes 'their' church, it gives itself to them. Just as in the incarnation Christ joined himself to men and women by giving himself to humanity, the Christian community joins itself to an oppressed group by giving itself to it; it offers what it has and who it is to the group, and welcomes what the group gives back. This is not a giving that depletes the church. Christ did not lose anything by being joined to humanity. Instead, he gained a dimension of being that previously he had not directly experienced. Likewise, when the church gives itself to people who have been silenced it gains their voice. Its collective song is enriched as more voices take part and contribute their distinctive harmonies (Tanner, 2005, pp. 72–85). Thus, just as communion ecclesiology and the *missio Dei* can lead naturally to seeing the church as a gift, so it is with liberation theology: the church is to be a gift by standing alongside people on the social edge and giving itself to them.

## A new theological era?

The idea of the church as a gift, therefore, should attract our attention because it resonates with these theological streams. Might it also speak to the context in which the church now finds itself? Many think that the church is on a new threshold. Phyllis Tickle called this the Great Emergence – the latest in a series of seismic transitions that occur roughly every 500 years (Tickle, 2008). Though this has struck a popular chord, it is not clear why history's wheel should turn every half millennium. Why do 500 years have a revolutionary magic? More interesting is the Roman Catholic theologian Karl Rahner's suggestion that the church has entered a new theological era. Reflecting on the Second Vatican Council, Rahner argued (with qualifications) that the Council was the first major official event at which the church acted as a world church. Representatives from around the world began to influence each other. A process of de-centring the Western church had begun (Rahner, 1979). This trend has continued apace since. The dominance of the Western church has been eroded by the global South's growing economic weight, by the church's expansion in the South, and by calls to unshackle the church from its colonial legacy.

### A new context

At the same time, but not referred to by Rahner, there has been a second de-centring – of the church *within* the West, especially Europe. Often described as a shift to post-Christendom, the church has lost its central place in the society it did so much to shape. Now on the edge, it is called to serve people whose outlooks are very different to the 'Christian culture' that once prevailed. Church allegiance is declining, while those who do join come, like many in the global South, with new and distinctive expectations of God's family.

This double de-centring has ushered in what Rahner, speaking about

## INTRODUCTION

the emergence of a world church, described as a third theological epoch. The first was the short period of Jewish Christianity. The second, initiated by the conversion of the Gentiles, was the period when the church dominated a distinct cultural region: that of Hellenism and Europe. The third epoch is the arrival of the world church. Like the transition from Jewish to Gentile Christianity, today we are seeing an equally profound theological transition from a Christianity of Europe ('with its American annexes', Rahner, 1979, p. 722) to a fully world religion.[4] Just as the Jews lost their central place within Christ's visible body, so the European church is losing its central position. Religious forms are more diverse both on the world stage (Rahner's focus) and in the West (more evident since Rahner wrote).

Rahner argued that shifting to the second epoch required Jewish believers to revise sharply how they imagined their faith would be expressed in the church's life. The same must be true of the current shift. As the church responds to cultural changes throughout the world it must be willing to question its inherited practices and assumptions. Rahner asked whether, in this transition, 'The Church can legitimately perceive possibilities of which she never made use during her second major epoch because these possibilities would have been meaningless in that epoch and consequently illegitimate' (1979, p. 724). People for whom Christendom models of church seem like a foreign country are now exploring these alternatives.

One inkling of this is the new forms of church starting to emerge from the chrysalis of the old. For example, the Church of England's vision for the 2020s includes 'mixed ecology as the norm'. It calls for 10,000 new worshipping communities alongside existing congregations, so that God's people can more fruitfully serve today's smorgasbord of cultures and contexts.[5] Despite cutting other parts of its budget, in 2021 the Methodist Church of Great Britain substantially increased its financial commitment to encouraging new forms of Christian community. Each year the Church of the Netherlands (PKN) gathers the leaders of over 100 fresh expressions of church for mutual learning and encouragement.

In December 2019 *Christianity Today* reported the growth of micro-congregations in several US mainline denominations: 'These communities go by different names – fresh expressions, missional communities, micro-churches.' Their values 'include intentional focus on mission to a specific population, an emphasis on lay leadership, low costs, and a high rate of reproduction.' The Southern Baptist Convention's North American Mission Board president, Kevin Ezell, said that its model for church plants has shifted towards a 'blended ecology' approach; this builds a bridge between the new congregation and traditional church. Reggie

McNeal of North America's Leadership Network believed that these contextualized communities are a 'harbinger that something really big is underfoot,' which will undo the western church's 'single modality church expression'.[6]

## New imagination for a new age

On this changing landscape I want to plant a flag: in gratitude for grace, the church is called to a life of generosity. By sharing in the Abrahamic promise to be a blessing to all nations, the church is to be a constant gift. It will do this by giving itself through, for example, pastoral care, solidarity with the poor, care for creation, reconciliation and contributions to the creative arts, and especially through its ministry of word and sacrament to which others are invited. Almost all congregations do at least some of these things, often very well. However, the church always exists in some kind of institutional form and so these gifts inevitably arrive institutionally packaged. And the institution frequently fails people. The church's gifts, therefore, can be a mixed blessing, ambiguous gifts, sometimes even venomous (as in the case of the sexual abuse scandals).

As a thought experiment, could generosity be a theological map that helps the church navigate the transition to a new theological era? In particular, might giving enable the Christian community to become more attractive to others at a time when it is held in great suspicion? For example (as Part 2 explores):

- Generosity starts by paying attention. 'What sort of present would the recipient like?' The question requires the church to abandon its arrogant 'we know best' Christendom stance, to view itself from the standpoint of its critics (not least those it has hurt), and listen respectfully to others to discover how best to be a gift to them.
- Generosity demands that the gift be appropriate to the receiver, which means the gift must be contextualized. This fits a world that celebrates diversity.
- A gift is not a gift unless it is released, allowing recipients to receive it in their own way. This indigenizing possibility addresses post-colonial and post-Christendom resentment at external control in and by the church – whether from former colonial powers or, in the West, from ecclesial authorities with a history of superiority and entitlement.
- Giving is reciprocal. One gift brings forth another in response. As recipients of the church's generosity offer authentic return gifts from their different backgrounds, increasingly the church will be dominated less

# INTRODUCTION

by historic Western cultures and more by the world's cultural hetero-
geneity.
*   Gifts strengthen human relationships. When the church and the world
    give and receive from each other, the church's frequent separation
    from outsiders can be reversed.
*   Gifts change the people involved. Through the church's self-donation,
    the Spirit can reform the church in habits of generosity and expand the
    world's horizons through the church's gifts.

The idea of the church as a gift can be developed in a number of directions.
I have chosen to focus on how the church can give itself by offering new
Christian communities to people beyond its walls, where these communities are needed and are structurally connected to the ecclesial institution
or network within which they are embedded. This focus is partly because
starting such communities is a live and growing issue as the church moves
away from a 'single modality church expression'. More, it is because
this aspect of the church's generosity is deeply ingrained in the church's
history (see Chapter 3); yet it has been largely forgotten by much of the
church (especially in Europe and North America) and in many of the
doctrinal reflections on the church. Mostly, though, it is for the reasons
set out in Chapter 1: offering communion in Christ is the church's most
precious gift and for large chunks of the population today this gift is most
appropriately offered in an updated form of church multiplication.

As this dimension of the church's generosity begins to be rediscovered,
I would like to suggest that it should be seen as a normal part of the
church's whole life of giving. 'Normal' does not mean done by everyone (many people will not feel called to this ministry), nor does it mean
always (other missional challenges may have priority), nor will it be at
the expense of other missional tasks (new Christian communities cannot
be the only gift the church offers). But 'normal' does mean commonplace
(as part of the church's DNA), to be expected (such as having a place in
ministerial formation), and being intrinsic to the church's mission (an
aspect of the church's vocation but not the whole of it).

Offering new Christian communities can be seen as normal if we are
clear about what we have in mind. It includes traditional forms of church
planting, such as starting a church in an area of new housing. But it also
extends to a congregation's outreach initiatives, which are approached in
a new way. Imagine, for example, a luncheon club for older people. It is
valuable in its own right, but traditionally it would also have been seen
as a potential bridge to Sunday worship. Instead, in an approach that is
beginning to surface, a spiritual activity might be started alongside the
club as an optional extra. If participants in this spiritual extra were to

journey into Christ, they would become the equivalent of a new congregation *where they are*. A new initiative may be started in the prayerful hope that this will be the destination, or a spiritual extra may be added to an existing initiative (with the consent of those involved). Either way, what emerges will not be separate from its parent congregation or church but strongly linked to it, sharing in its governance structure and with proper oversight of safeguarding, data protection and other concerns.

This is not hugely different from what happens already or used to happen in some forms of outreach – a short devotional talk at the end of a youth club for instance. What is new (for reasons that Chapters 4 and 5 discuss) arises from the cultural gap between Sunday church and many people today: in today's 'third theological era', the talk would not be seen as an encouragement to attend church on Sunday but as a step to contextualized and fully Christian worship alongside the youth club, including authorized baptisms and Holy Communion where appropriate. How these new Christian communities are overseen and recognized will vary between Churches, denominations and networks, but they must be integrated into each tradition's institutional arrangements. They will not therefore spring up separately to the existing church, as some fear (see Milbank, 2023, p. 49), let alone in competition with the current church, but as part of the latter's outreach and ongoing life. Old and new will live together in mutual dependence, love and support, with deepening connections between the two (as discussed in Chapter 5). When understood in this way, the idea that starting new Christian communities ought to be normal for the church should not, I hope, raise too bushy an eyebrow.[7]

Could generosity as a theological canopy for the church's life help founders of new Christian communities to understand and articulate their vocation? Might self-giving, for instance, be more fruitful language than church planting with its imperialistic overtones ('we'll invade your territory and impose our version of the church')? Instead of outsiders replicating their model of church irrespective of the circumstances, church multiplication would be seen as a gift exchange emerging from the setting and building relationships. It would have a flavour of mutual generosity absent from the language of church planting. Not least, a theological framework of generosity would invite founders of new Christian communities to consider whether the latter are a welcome gift. Self-critique would be built in. In short, could giving the church arrest our attention because it helps to address today's missional situation?

INTRODUCTION

# The nature of giving

But is giving a healthy notion? It has often been criticized for diminishing recipients and creating dependence on the giver. So what does ethical giving look like, and might answering this be a third reason for considering our theme? The deceptively simple word gift is actually quite complicated. In popular use today, giving is often associated with altruism, which 'at its most basic simply means action for the sake of the other' (Barclay, 2018, p. 23). You give something – and almost any action or thing can be a gift[8] – to please the recipient without seeking a benefit in return.[9] Yet look more closely and you'll find that few gifts are without strings. Apart from anonymous gifts, giving usually creates an obligation to offer a return present. A gift from a friend leaves you wondering how to reciprocate at some point. Equally, it is impossible to be generous without getting back some benefit, not least feeling satisfied you have done the right thing. Swamped by commercially-driven promotion of products 'for free' ('buy one, get one free'), many people are aware of the self-serving potential of generosity and hence suspicious of the rhetoric of giving. In what sense therefore, if at all, is giving altruistic?

## *Self-interested or self-expressive?*

Remembering that giving differs between societies and has changed down the centuries, modern thinking about the subject began with the anthropologist Marcel Mauss's study *The Gift*, first published in 1925. Drawing from several cultures, Mauss explored how a gift prompts its inevitable repayment. In some primitive societies, he argued, the obligation to give back is based on the spirit of the gift. This is a power within the gift that requires it to be returned to its original owner by means of a counter gift; otherwise the recipient will suffer in some way. He also suggested that part of the personality of the giver is attached to the gift. This attachment becomes a kind of homing instinct that strives to return the gift to the person from whom it originally came. Again, the gift becomes dangerous if there is no return present.

Later anthropologists, such as Marshall Sahlins (2017), have disagreed. Instead of the gift's boomerang movement, they have focused on the central place of reciprocity in giving and the contribution of gifts to social cohesion.[10] To simplify, one approach – by sociologists as well as anthropologists – is to adopt a 'self-interested' model. Givers behave generously to get something in return, such as being well regarded by others, getting a favour, keeping a friend, or to avoid feeling indebted.

The receiver reciprocates for similar reasons. This to-and-fro maintains the relationship, while we fool ourselves with stories of altruism to hide the self-interest involved.

These stories have been 'deconstructed' by Jacques Derrida (1992), who points to the inner contradiction in the notion of gift. It is intrinsic to generosity that the gift is offered without the giver getting something back. If someone gives in the hope that they will be thanked or well regarded, or get a favour or present in return, this is not an act of generosity. It is the promotion of the giver's interests. Similarly, if the recipient recognizes what is offered as a gift, she will feel indebted and obliged to respond with a gift. Otherwise she will lose face. Her return gift, when made, would be an act of duty rather than an expression of generosity. Indeed, the moment anything is recognized as a gift, its gift character disappears. What is given becomes a debt to be repaid to retain the giver's respect. Derrida strips away the fig leaf of generosity, and reveals giving to be no longer giving because self-interest is involved. The gift dissolves into self-centredness.

But this assumes a narrow definition of giving; a gift is only a gift if it brings no benefit to the giver and places no obligation on the recipient. However, giving is like other virtues. It has intrinsic rewards, such as the joy of being thanked and the satisfaction of doing the proper thing. Giving would not be giving without these rewards. Yet Derrida peels the rewards away, as if serving a curry without the spices. He then confuses them with motivation; the rewards become the reason. Yet enjoying the grateful response to your present need not mean that you gave in order to be thanked. Perhaps you gave out of delight that she passed her exam. Likewise, giving inevitably creates obligations because it is a relational activity, reinforcing social ties based on mutuality. It does not follow that the only reason you gave was to strengthen a relationship. You might have given from a feeling of goodwill towards the person, as when a mother gives spontaneously to a newborn child (Cheal, 2016, p. 8).

An alternative to the 'self-interested' model is the 'expressive' one. Givers make a statement about their attitude and feelings towards the relationship and/or the recipient – they want a friendship with the beneficiary, they are grateful to her, they are thinking about her (when giving to charity) poverty is a blight on society and so on. Drawing on empirical research, David Cheal argues: 'Gift morality takes many forms, but there can be little doubt that one of the most common is the desire to give to others as an expression of love for them' (Cheal, 2016, p. 39).

Giving is a form of communication, an 'empathetic dialogue' (Fennell, 2002, pp. 93–6). As such, the giver hopes for a reply. But this reply is not a reward for giving. It is part of the exchange that keeps the dialogue going. Givers are rewarded by two by-products of the dialogue. One is a deeper relationship thanks to giving. The other is the intrinsic rewards of giving, such as the joy of pleasing the recipient, satisfaction from finding an appropriate gift, and feeling virtuous when supporting a charity. These rewards are not the prime motive for generosity but the inherent result of pursuing the recipient's welfare.[11] Giving 'is pleasurable precisely insofar as it is *not* egoistically motivated' (Osteen, 2002a, p. 26; italics original).

Though differing from Mauss, the 'self-interested' and 'self-expressive' models support his view that there is something more to gift exchange than an economic transaction. There is a surplus, an extra, about the gift that expresses relationship and generates an obligation to return the gift (not the original, but an equivalent). The obligation creates social solidarity. In the 'self-interested' model, altruism is a costume *hiding* our selfish motives. On the 'self-expressive' view, the costume *is* the motive. Altruism reflects the giver's favourable attitude towards the recipient and/or the relationship and it generates various rewards as a by-product.

## Christian giving

Within Christian theology, Kathryn Tanner (2005) upholds the possibility of giving with no strings attached. For her, typical human exchanges are characterized by obligation and competition. Givers assume that their resources are depleted by giving. So givers and recipients compete to protect what they have. The calculation, 'What should I give and what emotional and other rewards would I receive in return?', ensures that the giver does not miss out. But divine generosity is totally different. God's giving is free, unconditional and non-competitive. God's generosity is God's own free choice. God keeps loving even when there is no human response. God's grace cannot be earned or repaid since it hugely exceeds what humans can offer back. Moreover, God's resources are not depleted, so God has no need to protect them by getting something in return. The infinity of divine riches ensures that they are constantly replenished as God gives.

Women and men respond appropriately to grace by seeking to give, like God, unconditionally and non-competitively. Giving without strings allows resources to be pooled so that they are more equally distributed. More importantly, givers and receivers become joined to one another in relationships of solidarity, so that what benefits one also benefits the other. When recipients smile so do the givers, because they are one together. The gift's acceptance by the recipient is tantamount to its acceptance by the giver, because in solidarity what happens to one happens to all (Tanner, 2005, pp. 31–85). It is a bit like Christmas with young children. The child's delight in opening a present is mirrored in the mother's delight when seeing the present accepted. All share the fun. It would be absurd for the mother to expect a return gift of equal value. She doesn't need it because the child's joy is her joy. Everyone benefits even without the reciprocal obligation.

Though in many ways attractive, Tanner's view downplays the relational benefits of mutual obligation. Healthy relationships are built not by one-sided giving, but by giving and giving back. In her Foreword to the 1990 edition of Mauss's *The Gift*, anthropologist Mary Douglas wrote:

> There should not be any free gifts. What is wrong with the so-called free gift is the donor's intention to be exempt from return gifts coming from the recipient. Refusing requital puts the act of giving outside any mutual ties. Once given, the free gift entails no further claims from the recipient ... A gift that does nothing to enhance solidarity is a contradiction. (Mauss, 1990, p. x)

This applies also to our relationships with God. Though we have done nothing to deserve God's gifts, once we accept them and become friends with God (see John 15.15) we enter into a relationship with mutual obligations, as in the Scriptural notion of covenant. God keeps giving to us through the Holy Spirit and we respond with the gift of lives that seek to reflect God. Echoing God will include sharing our resources with others in a Godlike way, as Tanner suggests. But it will also involve mutual giving that grows human relationships through the to-ing and fro-ing of gifts.

This broadly is the view of John Milbank (1995), who underlines the reciprocal nature of relationships, including with God, and the role of obligated giving in strengthening them. Drawing on Pierre Bourdieu, he notes that, unlike economic exchanges, return gifts are delayed. If someone gives you a 'welcome home' present and you immediately give a present back, you devalue the original gift. It becomes like the quid pro quo of a contractual exchange.[12] Gifts are also returned non-identically. A birthday present is not reciprocated on a like-for-like basis. Giving is reciprocal, therefore, in a manner different to economic exchange. Because we cannot escape giving's obligatory nature, the challenge is to decontaminate the motives for giving so that a 'purified gift exchange' (or 'purified giving') can occur. At a human level, gifts are purified the more they are motivated by Christian love.[13]

One sign of this love is to give more than the receiver might reasonably expect (Hochschild, 1989) – hence the response, 'Oh, you shouldn't have!' The 'more' need not be monetary value but includes the effort and imagination put into selecting the gift. The birthday present is a delight

## INTRODUCTION

because it meets a need she had barely recognized. You gave your time generously because he could not have sensibly hoped you would spend the whole day fixing his laptop. A dinner guest bringing a bottle of wine goes beyond a formulaic exchange (everyone in those circles does this) if the wine is unusual or has a relevant story ('We visited the vineyard and thought of you because...'). Gifts become purified when the degree of attention to the recipient is unexpected. In the case of giving to God, creativity perhaps takes the place of the unexpected because – for many Christians – an all-knowing God cannot be surprised. We do not return God's gifts through a mechanical response but by using our imaginations to ask, 'What would most delight God?'

If return gifts are obligatory, does God's generosity put us in debt to God and if so does this make God's love unattractive, as Robyn Horner suggests? We *have* to respond, and so we lose our freedom (Horner, 2001, p. 17). The answer is that we are under an obligation only if we choose to accept a relationship with God in the first place. Having accepted the obligations that go with any friendship, we still have plenty of freedom to choose when and how to return God's gifts. This represents, in fact, an expansion of freedom. We have opportunities we previously lacked to please God. Far from being 'not particularly loving', as Horner suggests, God is exceptionally loving. He offers us a relationship with bounteous fruits that in our fallenness we did not deserve and he enables us to contribute to the friendship creatively. What sort of relationship would it be if it was entirely one-sided?

'Purified giving', therefore, can be understood as creative generosity when women and men give back to God, and as giving beyond what the recipient can reasonably expect in the case of human exchanges. 'Purified giving' is human generosity that seeks to thrill the recipient by putting the latter's interests before the giver's. The giving need not be completely disinterested, in the sense that there is no emotional return to the giver; giving may legitimately bring the giver joy and satisfaction. But the giving is pure when it happens in relationships of mutual generosity and when the giver puts the recipient first by giving over and above what could be fairly anticipated.

### A spectrum

Purified giving lies at one end of a spectrum. It is the moral cathedral of human generosity because, as an expression of the Great Commandment to love others, it is motivated mainly by the desire to please the recipient. By creating obligations to return the gift, it sustains and deepens relationships. Somewhere in the middle of the spectrum is 'ambivalent' generosity. The giver is motivated by self-centred concerns but also wants to gratify the recipient. An employer gives staff a Christmas party in the hope they will be pleased, but the motive is to encourage loyalty (the staff's return gift). The gift is both self-interested and altruistic. Again, the to-and-fro of gifts strengthens relationships. At the spectrum's other end are the ethical slums of 'contaminated giving'. Here, giving slides into abuse. Giving is used to demean the recipient or to manipulate the receiver's behaviour, as with a bribe. Recipients may be worse off because the humiliation or obligation to act against their preference exceeds the benefits of the gift. Once more giving creates and maintains relationships, but one party is exploiting the other. As is often pointed out, in some languages 'gift' and 'poison' have the same linguistic roots.[14]

Unfortunately, as we have noted, the church has all too often been experienced as poison. This does not negate the good the church also contains. Alongside an abusive minister in one place is a Mother Theresa in another. Beside Christians who have fomented religious conflict are saints who have sacrificed themselves for peace. At best, the church is a mixed gift, a combination of 'disordered failure and redemptive capacity' (Radner, 2012, p. 2). Amid the tragic malevolence of the institution, the church is still endowed by grace to transmit God's generosity. Like Hosea's loyalty to his faithless wife, Christ keeps loving his bride and working through her. Far from allowing complacency, this grace constantly beckons the church to repentance at every level, to the reform of its structures and processes so that it can be a better gift, and to the continuous development of doctrine and practice so that it can avoid contamination as new situations arise (Avis, 2021b, p. 249). The result is a hotchpotch of purified, ambivalent and contaminated giving. With God's help, the church is constantly called to reach for the 'purified' end of the spectrum and participate in divine generosity.

God's love infinitely exceeds human love. It is boundless and unmerited. It is beyond what humanity could reasonably expect. And it seeks the well-being of human beings and through them the rest of creation. It is from this love that God gives the church to the world, a claim Chapter 1 will unpack. God wants to gather men and women around Christ and be in communion with them. Divine joy from giving derives from the process of giving itself and from the loving relationships established, which include believers' grateful response. Because giving the church is the Spirit's work, we can prayerfully expect God to provide the replenishment that will empower the church's continued generosity. At the same time, the church as a gift will grow in value as the Spirit draws recipients into the giving God and expands their generosity.

INTRODUCTION

This is not, therefore, an exchange in which there are only two parties, God and the church. It becomes a three-part exchange as Christians respond to divine generosity by giving to people beyond the church. Perfect giving may be an ideal for humans (Belk, 1996, p. 76), but it is an ideal that can steer the church away from sin towards Christ, away from insensitive or coercive giving towards respectful and kind liberality. In other words, the church can give ethically. And this is a third reason why the church as a ('purified') gift should claim our attention.

## Outline

The church is called to a life of generosity – giving on a broad front but within that a particular giving in the form of new Christian communities. This theme invites our consideration because it emerges naturally from current understandings of the church, it suggests a way of being church that fits the unfolding post-Christian context, and it can be undertaken ethically as a participation in God's 'purified' generosity to the world. By reflecting on the nature of giving, the Christian community can become more self-critical about the manner in which it offers its gifts, which will help the church to scrub its gifts clean.

As a minister in the Church of England, I am writing from 30 years' experience of new forms of church – first as a naive practitioner then as a researcher, consultant and advocate. This gave rise to *Church for Every Context* (Moynagh, 2012), an academic textbook widely used in 'fresh expressions' circles, and to *Church in Life* (Moynagh, 2017); in dialogue with entrepreneurship literature, the latter suggests a emergent framework for innovating new Christian communities. *Giving the Church*, the third of the trilogy, is written for students and theologians of the church, of mission and of church planting. Written from an ecumenical perspective to embrace multiple understandings of the Christian community, it supports the earlier volumes by provisionally reworking some of the doctrines of the church so as to pay greater attention to church multiplication as an expression of divine generosity.

Without crowbarring all aspects of the Christian community into a single model, Part 1 describes the church's identity as gift:

- the call of the church to generosity in many ways, including its particular call to give away its self in the form of new Christian communities,
- the nature of the self that is offered,
- four marks that can make the gift of the church's self attractive,

# GIVING THE CHURCH

- the gift's availability (addressed through discussing the church's hiddenness and visibility),
- and how offering an exclusive gift can lead paradoxically to greater inclusion.

It follows that if generosity should be central to the church's vocation, how the Christian community gives should not be marginal in thinking about the church. It should be as high on the agenda of church doctrine as sacraments, ministry, ecumenical relations and other key practices of the church's life.

Part 2, therefore, seeks to purify the understanding of the church's giving by lifting the ethical cloud that might darken the notion. It uses the gift of new Christian communities as an example to argue that the church's generosity can be seen as a type of gift exchange in which mutual giving forms and deepens the Christian community's relations with the world. Drawing on how Christ is given to humanity and enriched by some of the literature on gifts, it describes a moral framework that can help the exchange to be healthy – receiving first, giving appropriately, letting go, accepting the gift, giving back, and mutual transformation.

It then brings that framework into dialogue with liberation theology (to describe the goal of giving away new Christian communities), with the herald model of the church (to describe the conversational manner in which they are offered), and with the sacramental model (to provide a eucharistic spirituality in support). As a result, we can begin to re-imagine these models and re-purpose them for understanding the church's entire life of generosity. The final chapter responds to the charge, addressed at various points in the book, that all too often the church has been an unwelcome gift. It claims that the Christian community can be made more attractive precisely by giving its self to others in the form of new Christian communities, as part of an ongoing gift exchange.

*Giving the Church* is not meant to be a 'blueprint ecclesiology', divorced from the muddy realities of church life (Healy, 2000). Rather, it arises from my experience of new Christian communities and from my prayerful hope that theological reflection on them can illuminate possibilities for action. Accordingly, most chapters conclude with implications for the church's mission and for church planting in particular. Thus the book seeks to go beyond a defence of new forms of Christian community. Arising from them, as a question from the edge, it asks whether God's people as a whole might think differently about the church in order to act differently.

# INTRODUCTION

## *Notes*

1 In 2022 the Church of England's 'Transforming Effectiveness' programme of work was described as being informed by four theological principles, the first of which was 'The Church is God's gift in Christ through the Holy Spirit for the salvation of the world and the healing of all creation' (General Synod, 'Transforming Effectiveness – An Introduction and Update', GS 2224).

2 The theme of gift comes most to the fore in discussions about means of grace in the church, not least the sacraments, but these discussions are a far cry from making gift or generosity a controlling framework for thinking about the church.

3 Throughout, I use lower case to denote the church in general and upper case when referring to the name of a particular Church, such as the Roman Catholic Church.

4 Rahner acknowledges his assumption that the contemporary transition is more *theologically* decisive than past transitions, such as from ancient Gentile Christianity in the Mediterranean to medieval and then modern European Christianity.

5 'Simpler, Humbler, Bolder', General Synod GS 2223, Church of England, June 2021.

6 Kara Bettis, 'Carving out a niche for micro-congregations', *Christianity Today*, December 2019, https://www.christianitytoday.com/pastors/2019/fall/carving-out-niche-for-micro-congregations.html (accessed 19.12.2023).

7 For more on this, see Moynagh 2012 and 2017.

8 'Almost anything can serve as a gift ... Gifts are endlessly variable resources that help us to express our feelings toward other people and, particularly, to inform them about the nature of the bond we have in mind' (Komter, 2005, p. 43).

9 For an outline of the historical context that has produced this modern idea of a 'pure' altruistic gift, see Barclay, 2015, pp. 54–63.

10 Highlights from the extensive literature on giving include: Berking (1999), Bourdieu (1990, 1997), Godbout (1998), Godelier (1999), Gregory (1982), Hyde (2012), Lévi-Strauss (1987 [1950]), Osteen (2002a), Weiner (1992).

11 The literature often uses one term, 'the return gift', to describe both a gift returned by the recipient and the giver's emotional rewards from giving. But the two are different and can helpfully be kept distinct. The emotional rewards from giving are the return from being generous, whereas reciprocated gifts are the recipient's return gifts as part of the exchange. Generosity can bring its own rewards irrespective of the recipient's response.

12 Christmas, when mutual giving happens at the same time, may seem to be an exception to delayed giving. Equally, one could say that gifts are exchanged at Christmas but recipients wait till the next Christmas before reciprocating. Pierre Bourdieu argued that the separation of gift and return gift allows actors to deny that there is any obligation to make a return. It also creates a social debt, which in the case of large gifts enables givers to gain control over recipients. For an accessible exposition of this aspect of Bourdieu's thought, see Cheal, 2016, pp. 20–2.

13 The views of Milbank and Tanner may be complementary. Milbank can be read as claiming that *ultimately* humans must make a return gift to God, while Tanner suggests that God keeps loving even when return gifts *in this life* are withheld. When the kingdom comes, however, will eternal life not include obedient giving back to the one who gave life in the first place, a view closer to Milbank? In his exegesis of Paul, John Barclay (2015) pursues a line not dissimilar to Milbank.

## GIVING THE CHURCH

Grace for Paul was not unconditional. It was 'incongruent' (it did not depend on the worth of the recipient) and superabundant (it expects and enables giving to God and to others, which are return gifts to God).

14 This spectrum may appear to have an affinity with the one suggested by Sahlins (2017, pp. 174–8). But it avoids the tendency of the 'generalized' end of his spectrum to downplay the rewards to the giver of being generous. It foregrounds more strongly than the 'pure gift' what the giver communicates by giving. It also includes the category of 'harmful' giving, which differs to Sahlins' 'negative reciprocity' (the attempt to get something for nothing).

# PART I

# The Church's Identity

# I

# Called to Give? The Church's Vocation

As the church stands before the sliding doors of perhaps a new theological era, *Giving the Church* is a thought experiment. Alongside Dulles's six models of the church, I am asking whether there might be a seventh – the church as a gift. Out of thanks for grace, God's people are called to a life of generosity towards humanity and nature. As one aspect of this vocation they are to join the Holy Spirit in offering the church to others, in the form of new Christian communities, for the benefit of the world. What are the grounds for suggesting this, and how might it change the way we think about the church? Chapter 1 lays the foundations of an answer. Despite its limitations and sinfulness, the Christian community is a gift of communal life in Jesus. The gift is given by the Spirit to the world. The gift is to be shared with others in many ways, but is especially generous when it takes the form of the church's self, communion in Christ. This communion can rightly be offered as an invitation to an existing congregation, but often today it will be more appropriately given in the shape of new Christian communities. The gift blesses the wider society and through the process of being offered helps the Christians involved to grow in their discipleship.

## A gift of communion

That the church is a gift of God is rooted, first, in the doctrine of God, which 'puts gift and dispossession at the foundation of everything' (Williams, 2005, p. 169). The Father is the source of generosity, not least in giving his Son (John 3.16). The Son 'who gave himself for us' (Titus 2.14) is the incarnation of generosity. And the life-giving Spirit (Rom. 8.2) is a gift (Acts 2.38) by bringing Godly generosity into creation. God is shaped for giving, which continually overflows the 'boundaries' of the Trinity through divine creation and redemption. In particular, God's generosity breaks cover, as it were, in the gift of the church, which though flawed is both central to the gospel, communion in Christ, and the means through which the gospel is offered.[1]

# GIVING THE CHURCH

## A gift

Though the New Testament does not apply the language of gift to the church as it does 'body' and 'bride' for example, the notion of gift lurks in the shadows. For instance, summarizing the gospels' portrayal of Jesus' teaching about his people, Kevin Giles writes that Jesus makes those who repent

> members of his family. He calls them a flock, is present with them as their shepherd, sends them into the world on mission, sustains them with spiritual food, and provides them with leaders. (Giles, 1995, p. 45)

In other words, as part of God's gift of 'all things' (Rom, 8.2) Jesus graciously *gives* repentant sinners community (a 'family'). He *gives* them identity (his 'flock'). He *gives* them guidance for life in community ('shepherd'). He *gives* them a purpose ('mission'). He *gives* them 'spiritual food', and he *gives* them 'leaders'. Communal life is a gift from Jesus to his followers and is sustained by his spiritual gifts.[2]

In Acts 20.32 Paul commends the Ephesian elders 'to the word of the Lord's grace, which has the power to establish the house and bequeath the inheritance to all who have been made holy.'[3] The church ('the house') is established by 'the power' of grace – that is, by God's gift of mercy and salvation. As an *object*, the church is part of this all-encompassing gift; it is not earned, but graciously given. As an *activity*, the church remains a gift; 'the inheritance', the gift of sharing in God's kingdom, is bequeathed through the church as people gather with Jesus. The church is given by grace and channels grace.

Changing tack, if we combine the description of the Son as a gift of the Father with the description of the church as Christ's body (Col. 1.18), again we can deduce that the church is a gift because it is joined to Christ, head of the body. Thereby the church shares the gift character of the Son; as the Son is a gift to humanity so the church also is a gift to women and men. Moreover, just as Christ does not change in his nature (Heb. 13.8) and hence never ceases to be a gift, so the church does not change in its character; it too is always a gift.

From a human standpoint, gift better describes God's people than possession. The church does not originate in the people themselves; it arrives from God as a gift when they gather round the risen Lord. Nor is the church some kind of contract in which mutual obligations are defined with a lawyer's precision; the human response to God, the creative return gift of the church's life, varies enormously. Nor, again, is the church a loan that recipients must repay; given the infinite generosity that births the church, how could God's people ever pay enough! However, from God's perspective the church *is* a possession, in the sense that a parent might say to a child, 'You're mine!' It is 'a people belonging to God' (1 Peter 2.9). It is a belonging that God does not hold on to but shares with others. It is a gift like a sculpture on permanent loan to a gallery, or a talented young soccer player loaned free to another club. God generously cedes the rights of use while retaining the rights of possession.

The notion of church as a gift brings to the fore the generosity that is fundamental to mission but is not always made explicit. Similarly, it fills out sacramental, communal and other understandings of the church, which contain the idea of gift without necessarily placing it at the centre. It also begins to flesh out descriptions of the church in terms of love. Speech about love today is not always clear about what love involves. By contrast, the church as a gift from God puts generosity at the centre of divine love. Not least, giving is often combined with celebration – think of birthdays and Christmas. The church has a festive dimension. It is received with gladsome thanks and shared with others in the same spirit. The church gives with explosions of joy.

## Of communion

Can we say more about what sort of gift the church is? The 'convergent' ecumenical understanding is rooted in God's great design for creation. Humanity's creation in God's image gave men and women an inherent capacity for communion with God and with one another. But this capacity has been limited by human disobedience. In response to sin, God embarked on 'the dynamic history' of restoring communion, and this history found its irreversible achievement in the life, death and resurrection of Jesus. By means of the Spirit, the church continues Christ's work of restoration. Communion is 'the gift by which the Church lives', rooted in the very life of the Trinity (WCC, 2013b, p. 5). As such, the church is to witness to the gift of communal conviviality in God's kingdom.

At its heart, in Dietrich Bonhoeffer's phrase, the church is 'Christ existing as community'. Michael Mawson notes that while Bonhoeffer held that Christ 'even "exists as" the empirical community, he does so in a way that avoids collapsing Christ into the community' (Mawson, 2018, p. 27). Christ exists as community rather like I exist as a Moynagh. I am completely identified with my family but am still a distinct person. In the church Christians are sealed together and with Christ. They are joined to Christ, as body to a head, but they remain distinct from Christ. They become a communion in Jesus, a communion that shares in Christ's

# GIVING THE CHURCH

generosity. So when God gives the church, what is offered is communal life in Jesus characterized by giving. Communion in Christ is the church's fundamental reality. It is the church's self (which is described more fully in the next chapter).[4] Tiptoeing carefully through theological language, communal life and communion are better terms than community because they imply greater intimacy. 'In Christ' implies 'in the Trinity'. For it is by being joined to Christ that the church participates in the life of the triune God while remaining distinct. Communion in Christ must always be understood in this fullest sense of participation in God. The church is the gift of a community that participates in the trinitarian life.

Some might prefer to emphasize the gift of Christ rather than the gift of the church. But because Jesus has made his followers his family he cannot be separated from them. 'My mother and my brothers are those who hear the word of God and do it' (Luke 8.21). As Paul says, believers are 'one in Christ' (Gal. 3.28). In other words, the risen Lord would not be who he is without his human community. Just as you cannot have Christ without his heavenly communion, the Trinity, you cannot have Christ without his earthly communion, the church.

Of course, someone might wish to befriend Christ but not his family, just as they might wish to befriend me but not my family. However, if my hospitality always included members of my family ('Come to supper' involves eating with the family), they would join me in hanging out with my relatives. To accept my hospitality would be to accept my family. Likewise, to receive Christ as a gift is not to receive him as a solitary divine person. Nor is it first to accept Jesus in your heart and then, later, to receive the church. It is to receive simultaneously with Christ all others who are in him. This in no way diminishes the supremacy of Christ. It simply describes his identity. This is who Jesus is – the head of the church. To receive the gift of Christ is to receive the gift of being with him – in communion.

It follows that being baptized and confirmed are not sufficient to express the Christian faith, as is sometimes thought especially in European countries with national churches (mainly Lutheran and Anglican). The fruits of baptism cannot be grown without the Eucharist, teaching and other means of grace embedded in the church's communal life. Moreover, because Christ is one with his body, to ignore his body by failing to participate in the church is to ignore Christ. And to ignore Jesus is to diminish him. The baptized may retort that the church is inaccessible to them culturally, and perhaps because of when and where it meets. If so, God's people should repent for placing baptized persons in an impossible position: initiating them into a community without visible means for them to participate. The answer is not to refuse the initiation but to make

## CALLED TO GIVE? THE CHURCH'S VOCATION

the community available. God's people should join with those who don't attend church to create new forms of communal life within which the baptized can flourish. A gift is not a gift if it is inaccessible.

### Through grace

Communion in Christ is the heart of the gift of salvation, which comes through the gracious death and resurrection of Jesus. Though salvation encompasses a multitude of gifts, God's people as a gift are intrinsic to it. The church is a vehicle for growing in life with Christ, for coming into the Father's presence in prayer and worship, for receiving the Spirit and the Spirit's gifts, and for joining the Spirit in taking forward Christ's mission to the world. As a manifestation of grace the church is a reflection of God's initiative in giving: God's giving without regard to recipients' worth, the extravagance of God's generosity, the benevolent goodness (the purity) of divine giving, the gift's ability to enable an appropriate response and yet, equally, divine giving without any guarantee of that response.[5] The church is a gift in multiple overlapping ways.

Salvation, of course, is intrinsic to God's reign. So we can say that communion in Christ is also central to the gift of the kingdom. The church arises from God's reign, which comes as a gift to the created order. When this reign totally arrives, all creatures will be brought to perfection within communal life in Jesus. Meanwhile, foretastes of this reign are given in the world. Clearly, as one of these appetizers, the church is far from an *exclusive gift* of the kingdom. Healthy families, restorative communities and life-giving experiences of nature, for example, can also be rustlings of God's reign. Nor is the church a *flawless gift* of the kingdom, as if by receiving the church you receive the kingdom. Because God's people are too sinful to actualize the kingdom, they cannot be wholly equated with God's reign (Pannenberg, 2004, pp. 27–48).

Even so, the church is not an *insignificant gift*. By gathering round Jesus, the centre of the kingdom, through the Spirit the church is a sign, instrument and preview of God's reign. The church points to the unrestricted fellowship between Christ and humans when the kingdom totally arrives; it draws people into this fellowship and enables people to experience a flavour of it. However, to witness thus to the kingdom is not as outward moving as to be a gift. You can witness while standing still, whereas the essence of gifts is that they move; they are passed on to their recipients. The church is therefore a *dynamic gift* of God's reign. To be welcomed as such requires God's people to stand under the judgement of the kingdom, repent of what makes them an unattractive gift and be cleansed for their testifying role. Dare we believe that when this repentance happens the church is the *foremost gift* of the kingdom? The kingdom does not depend on the church. On the other hand, God's supreme gift to the world, life explicitly in Christ, is offered through no other human group or organization.

## A gift of the Spirit

In the first instance communion in Christ, the church, is not a gift from human beings. Of course, church members have a role: to participate in the Spirit's offering of the church. By grace, God's people are enabled to *give in* to the Spirit so as to join the third person in *giving out* to others. The church's self-giving, therefore, is to the Spirit, who offers the church to the world. Shorthands, such as the church is a gift to the world or the church is given to others, are legitimate only if the Spirit's central role is kept in mind.

The church is a gift of the Spirit because it is given by means of the Spirit. In another tiptoe, gift *of* the Spirit is better than *from* the Spirit. The latter might sound as if the Spirit puts the church in the post and has no more to do with it. 'Of' can imply that the Spirit releases the gift but remains invested in it. In discussions of the *missio Dei*, the mission of God, the Spirit is seen as being sent by the Father and the Son to be the divine agent of mission. In the outpouring at Pentecost the Spirit is revealed as the milieu in which 'all people' exist (Acts 2.17). In particular, the Spirit works to conform humanity to the incarnate Son. In the world implicitly and through the church explicitly, the Spirit teaches men and women to imitate Christ. The church is offered to human beings and through them to other creatures as part of the Spirit's planet-wide activity.

### A purified gift?

Why does the Spirit give the church? Is it because God wants fellowship with women and men, a fundamental purpose of creation? And given human sinfulness, is not this relationship now graciously achieved mainly through the church, the sphere in which people explicitly relate to Christ? Certainly God delights in drawing close to humanity and the church is the supreme context for this. But we must understand the Spirit's offering of the church for this purpose carefully, recognizing our limited capacity to probe God's inner thoughts.[6] The Spirit's gift of the church is pure liberality – generosity through and through.

## CALLED TO GIVE? THE CHURCH'S VOCATION

So we must not imagine that the Spirit gives the church as an assertion of power, that God seeks to gain the support of creatures by creating relationships of obligation and dependence. That would be true if the Spirit's giving was coercive. But the Spirit is characterized by forbearance. Even when believers ignore or disobey the Spirit, the Spirit remains with and open to them. 'The Holy Spirit is present in self-emptying and in patience – in self-forgetting – by being there alongside our fallibility, not taking it over, not overcoming it, not ironing it out' (Williams, 2008b, p. 29). Far from enchaining people, the Spirit offers the church in ways that respect their freedom, an example the church would do well to follow. Once the gift has been received, however, there are return obligations as in any relationship. But these obligations are freely chosen and not forcibly policed.

If the gift is not an instrument of control, does the Spirit give the church so that God can enjoy a relationship with human beings that would otherwise be absent? And might this lack leave God dissatisfied? If so, the Spirit's giving would satisfy a need that was missing in trinitarian life. Yet in divine perfection God is not dissatisfied and God lacks or needs nothing. In fact, it is this perfection that guarantees the Spirit's unlimited generosity. Because God has all that God needs (and is therefore completely satisfied), the Spirit gives from a never-ending store of riches – from God's total power, complete love and so on. And this guarantees that, unlike human generosity, divine giving can never run out. God's riches are so ample, so satisfying in themselves, that God has no need for a relationship with humans.

If the Spirit does not give the church to meet a need, is the gift a form of self-indulgence? Does not the Spirit hope that through the church God's relationships with human beings will be transformed into intimacy and mutual giving? And are not philosophers such as Derrida and Marion[7] correct in believing that intentions by definition are selfish – 'this is what *I* want'? However, not all intentions need be self-serving, as we saw in the Introduction. You can have a virtuous intention, such as painting a picture to give a friend. Personal satisfaction would come from harnessing your creativity to benefit another. The Spirit can be said to offer the church in that sense. Rather than restricting giving to within the Trinity (which might be thought selfish), generosity overflows the Godhead to bring other creatures into existence and pours through the church to enrich human lives. 'God creates in order to give Godself in love' (Edwards, 1999, p. 71). The joy from such giving lies in expressing the divine self and sharing in the recipients' delighted response. Divine joy accompanies divine love.

## GIVING THE CHURCH

If the Spirit's giving has an outward focus, is it something that the Spirit *has* to do? Is giving so much part of God's nature that the Spirit cannot do anything else – a divine compulsive disorder? Might the Spirit be free to choose which gift to offer but not whether to give in the first place? If this was true, God's giving might seem less generous. For it is part of generosity that giving is freely undertaken. If each child said to the birthday girl, 'I've *got* to give you this present,' the party would not be quite the same! Certainly, the Spirit offers the church because it is the divine nature to give. Indeed, as a gift the Spirit encapsulates that nature. But God's nature also contains, as part of God's sovereignty, the attribute of freedom. God's freedom and generosity combine so that giving the church becomes the Spirit's freely chosen decision.

Divine giving may be a choice, but is it not designed to secure a worthwhile end, God's relationship with redeemed humanity? And does that not make the Spirit's gift of the church a means to an end, praiseworthy only because it achieves a valuable purpose? Yet the value of divine giving does not lie in the goal it attains. God's generosity has worth in itself. When the Spirit offers the church, the Spirit does so not for some ulterior purpose but because generosity is its own purpose. The giving has no need to achieve something. It has value in its own right. The Spirit gives because generosity is good. Moreover, the end, a relationship with humans, is not distinct from the means, offering the church. End and means combine in the one gift – of the opportunity and capacity for humans to return God's gifts in worship, in giving to one another, and in giving to people outside the church. Giving the church enables further giving, which – if it occurs – proliferates divine generosity. Means and end are part of one continuing process, God's multiplying largesse. Might the church see its generosity in similar terms?

Does this mean that the gift's value depends on it being accepted? If people were to refuse the church, the giving process would come to an end and, like an ignored birthday present, the gift would have no value ('What a waste of money!' thinks the giver). Yet in the case of the church, were everyone to decline the gift it would still have inherent worth. People would have had an option (to respond to the gift) not previously open to them. Giving people this opportunity, we can imagine, is God's first cup of joy. God's second cup is the human acceptance of the gift. God's enjoyment of the first drink does not depend on the second. The Spirit pours the first as reward enough in itself. The church too will be more like God if its generosity, offered appropriately, does not require the gift's acceptance.

## CALLED TO GIVE? THE CHURCH'S VOCATION

### *A gift through and through*

Thus, in its origins, nothing compromises the church's status as a gift. The Spirit offers the church not as an instrument of control, nor from an unmet need, nor from selfishness, nor from a compulsion within God, nor as a means to a separate end. Nor does the gift's value depend on its acceptance. Because God is infinitely purer than men and women, the Spirit's giving has a more perfect character than human generosity can ever attain. The Spirit gives the church out of an uncontaminated generosity, not to benefit the Godhead but to multiply generosity for the sake of generosity. The church is given because giving is in the trinitarian nature. God's generosity is a truth that 'thought can neither go behind nor exhaust' (von Balthasar, 1982, p. 137).[8] You cannot discover reasons behind divine giving. Keep digging and all you find is generosity.[9]

It is significant, therefore, that in the first instance the church is given by the Spirit rather than by sinful human beings. It means that in the Spirit's hands the church is a gift not just at the purified end of the spectrum discussed in the Introduction, but off the scale! That is why the church is called to offer communion in Christ not in its own strength but by joining the Spirit. For if the Spirit's giving is totally pure, might not some of that perfection rub off on the church?[10]

## A gift to others

Who is the church given to? Is it a gift mainly to its members, rather like giving someone a club membership? Belonging to the club is a gift. Now the church *is* a gift to its members in that sense. Their belonging, and hence the church, is a gift of grace. But the gift is offered for a purpose. It is to be enjoyed not as an end in itself but by being shared. 'Communion ... [is] the gift that God calls the Church to offer to a wounded and divided humanity in hope of reconciliation and healing' (WCC, 2013b, p. 5). God's people are to be most fulfilled when, in gratitude for grace, they give the church to the world so that both can flourish. This giving can take a variety of forms. Just as I might share a monetary gift by taking a friend out for a meal or buying them a present or showing photos of the experience the gift made possible, the church can be passed on by sharing its resources, serving other people or sharing its interior life.

The church is a gift to the world because, first, it is in the nature of gifts to be passed on. An object whose owner has no plan to share it with another is not a gift. It may have arrived as a gift but it is now a possession. The object only remains a gift when the owner decides to

hand it to someone else. By definition gifts are passed on. If the church
– like its head – never ceases to be a gift, it too must be handed on in
some way, just as Christ continually gives himself to others. Otherwise
the church would stop being a gift and become its members' possession.

## A gift for others

Second, the church is a gift to others because through the Spirit it is
indwelt by God. Just as the Son is a gift and the Spirit is a gift, the church
is also a gift because it shares in God's nature. Equally, just as the Son is
active in giving (he gave himself – Gal. 2.20) and the Spirit actively gives
(John 6.63), the church too is to be active in giving. Without blurring the
gulf between God and humanity, the church shares the trinitarian life
by joining the Son and Spirit in being a gift that gives. And again, as the
Son and the Spirit give outwardly to the world, the church also must give
beyond itself.

In his doctrine of election, Karl Barth maintained that from all eternity
God has been for humanity. In obedience to his Father, the Son eternally
chose to become a human so as to have fellowship with every woman and
man. If the church is God's community, then it must take its character
from this divine decision. It too must be for the world. Were that not
the case, the church's life would be inconsistent with its founder and
sustainer (Barth, 2004, pp. 788–9). Just as Christ's being (who he is)
cannot be separated from his calling (to give himself to the world), so the
church's identity cannot be separated from the church's task (to share
what it has been given with others). Barth pointed out that the church is
the only human community that Scripture describes as Christ's body. In
the light of its basis in Christ, 'It is sent in the same direction as He is,
i.e., into the world, in order that it may exist, not for itself, but for the
world as He did' (p. 791). Just as Christ is a gift that gives to the world,
so must his body be.

The church cannot be a gift primarily to its members. It originated by
being given to people who were not at the time a community with God.
And it continues to flourish only by remaining a gift to non-members.
Baptism, even of churchgoers' children, is the culmination of a movement
from non-membership to membership. Without this often gradual movement, the church's earthly life would die as members pass away. The
church's very survival therefore depends on being given to others. But
more than that, the church's *fulfilment* also depends on being born constantly among people outside its walls. Only then can the church achieve
its purpose of drawing humanity into communion with God.

## CALLED TO GIVE? THE CHURCH'S VOCATION

Indeed, if the church were an end in itself, a gift to its members, it would become a cul-de-sac for divine grace. As part of God's giving to the world, divine generosity would pour into the church and then stop. Church members would consume God's blessings as gifts for themselves. No longer would the Son be given through the church *to the world* (see John 3.16). And no longer would the church play a role in Christ's reconciliation of 'all things' to himself (Col. 1.20). The idea that the body should keep God's gifts chiefly for itself is impossible to reconcile with its head. Jesus did not grasp what he had from the Father, but emptied himself so that at his name 'every knee should bow' (Phil. 2.10).

### Not a second step

But should giving to others be a priority? In his exposition of Barth, John Flett shows that the church's self-giving cannot be a second step for the Christian community because it is not a second step for God. Because mission, which takes the form of self-giving, is fundamental to God's character, there can never have been a 'time' when God's heart did not beat with a missionary rhythm. Otherwise God would be inconsistent. God would change from not being missional to being missional. And God's essential character never changes. God's generous plans for humanity have 'always' been in God's mind (Eph. 1.4). Thus mission cannot be a second step for God. It cannot be that first God is, and *then* God gives to others.

If the church is to reflect God, therefore, self-giving mission cannot be a second step for the church. Mission cannot be like make-up, applied only when, having worshipped, enjoyed fellowship and organized its life, the church wants to go out. To be faithful to the church's identity, rather than being painted on the face of the Christian community, self-giving must be the face itself, always there, central to who the church is and as much a priority in the ecclesial life as it is in the divine life (Flett, 2010, pp. 204–8, 287–95). This means that sharing the church's self – communion in Christ that constantly gives to others – is more than one item on the shopping list of God's people. It belongs to their fundamental vocation.

Barth went so far as to say that 'In every respect, even in what seems to be purely inner activity like prayer and the liturgy and the cure of souls and biblical exegesis and theology, [the church's] activity is always *ad extra*' – towards people outside (Barth, 2004, p. 780). Everything the church does is directed towards others. This is not something that church members can achieve themselves. They are given the freedom to exist for others by God. As they exercise this freedom, they enjoy the gift of being liberated to serve others, which includes passing on what God has given to them. Thus the church is a gift, not like a box of chocolates that you could enjoy on your own, but more like a traditional board game. The gift can be enjoyed only by being played with others. The church is true to its identity when it is 'played' with the world. If members enjoy the church as an end in itself, they are not playing church. They are playing another game.

## A one-dimensional church?

Does this reduce worship, fellowship, pastoral care, spiritual gifts and other aspects of the church's internal life to mere instruments of the church's self-giving? Are they valuable only if they directly contribute to the Spirit's giving of the church? Or are they valuable ends in themselves? Perhaps we can say that, like omnipotence, love and other divine attributes that comprise the gift of God's self to the world, the internal life of the Christian community is the content of the church's gift to others. It follows that just as there is more to the divine attributes than self-giving, there is more to the church's internal life than being opportunities for the church's giving to the world. A Christmas party can be fun in itself rather than merely an opportunity to invite friends from outside the church. Worship has an inherent value over and above its contribution to mission. Healing and pastoral care of church members are good in themselves. It is the intrinsic value of its internal life that makes the church a gift to others. The church would have nothing to offer if it did not have a joyful interior life.

However, without being reduced to mission, this inner life is most aligned to God when it is saturated with the vocation to be a gift to the world. When set in the context of the church's outward movement, this life is flavoured with giving to others, just as the divine attributes are seasoned with God's giving to creation. The church is like a car on a missional journey. Conversations within the car may have nothing to do with the trip and be enjoyed for their own sake, but they happen as the car travels towards its destination. Or, to use the Pauline analogy, the church is like a body. Walking gives the body an orientation but that does not mean the body only has legs. The eyes may be enjoying the view even as the body hastens to a meeting. The church is a gift that gives to the world when all aspects of its interior life, with their intrinsic motivations and rewards, are steered in an outward direction.

In short, the church is called not to be a gift of communal life mainly for its members, but a gift that in thanks for grace keeps on giving to others. Does this make too sharp a distinction between the church and the world? The church is a giving gift on one side and the world is the recipient on the other. These two sides certainly exist but, as with gift exchanges in a family, givers and recipients need not be unrelated. Church and 'world' share a common humanity. The Spirit is active in both and so can enable the recipients of God's generosity in the church to step into God's generosity in the world. And as we saw in the Introduction, gifts are typically reciprocated, which gives life to and deepens relationships. Thus the potential exists for *mutual* giving to draw the church and the world together in a deepening connection.

## The gift of self

The church is a gift – a gift of Communion in Christ, a pure gift offered by the Spirit, a gift to the world. But in what sense is the church a gift to others? Is it a communion that passes on the blessings it has received from God, like a food bank that receives gifts of food and distributes them to people without food? Or is the church a gift by sharing its very self, communion in Christ, with others – more like a communal supper in which the meal is shared with outsiders? Now, the church *is* often a gift in the first way. The church shares its resources by serving other people, offering its spiritual gifts and joining campaigns for social and environmental justice. The church gives to others by putting itself on display through music, literature and architecture, and sometimes through the quality of its life. Members may describe their experiences of church as someone might share her holiday experience to enrich a conversation. When the church acts in these ways, as it frequently does and frequently does very well, it behaves appropriately like many other organizations. They too can become gifts by sharing their resources, putting themselves on display and describing their experiences.

### *More meal than food parcels*

However, were this all the church gives, its love would be limited. God's people would fail to follow Jesus, who goes beyond dispersing gifts through the Spirit to give his very self. As a statement of love, it is one thing to share your resources, such as giving a theatre ticket to a friend, but quite another to share the heart of your life. When the Christian community offers to others the essence of its existence, communion in Christ, it corresponds to its Lord. By offering what is most precious to it – the church's self – it declares how much the world means to it.

GIVING THE CHURCH

Indeed, the church is the only community that can offer fellowship with Jesus. No other organization can do this. The church is therefore unique. Of course, uniqueness need not be worth much – something can be uniquely bad! But as with the only surviving work of a special talent, rarity may generate value. The church has unparalleled value because it is the work of the supreme craftsman through whom all things were made (Col. 1.16). It is also one of a kind; it is the sole human community that is Christ's body. So to offer the church's self, communal life in Jesus, is to offer a priceless gift, a gift beyond compare.

Moreover, the gift offers a sampling of ultimate reality, the eternal banquet when Christ returns. This foretaste is not a gift that will one day wear out and disappear. The church's care of people in distress will pass away, so will its activities to combat structural evil, so too may its artistic contributions (its music may be forgotten and its buildings perish), but when God's reign completely arrives, communion in Christ will never cease. Divine dwelling with people in Christ will last for ever (Rev. 21. 3). Thus by offering communion in Jesus, the essence of the church's life, the Christian community offers an anticipation of what endures in the kingdom. The gift is the people's fullest witness to the fellowship in Christ that lasts through all eternity. Were communion in Jesus not to be offered, how could people beyond the church savour the never-ending heart of God's reign? They might taste it in healthy communities outside the church, but these are not communities explicitly in Jesus. For people to have some experience of communal life *in Christ*, the church must be given to them.

It follows that sharing this communal life is to offer the gospel, which is captured by so much more than a verbal proclamation. The gospel is about encountering Jesus, who draws the person into encounters with all others who have encountered him and into healthy encounters with the world. It is about communal life in Christ that flowers in the trans-formation of creation. To proclaim the good news, therefore, is to share this communal life in word and deed. If the church is to witness to the gospel, God's people cannot fail to offer communion in Christ as a normal part of their vocation.

All of which means that the church is like more than a food bank. It is closer to a bring-and-share community supper in which people with-out food are fed, share fellowship with each other and work together to share what they have with others – a giving *with* as much as a giving *to*.[11] The fullness of the gift lies in the richness of the church's internal life, which bubbles out in generosity to people beyond. This includes 'dis-tributing food' as an overflow of the church's life, but this overflow is as nothing compared to the banquet that defines the church and to which all are invited. By giving the church's inside to others on the outside, God's people testify most powerfully to the abundant life of God's reign (see John 10.10). More than ringing loudly in their outreach programmes, they give the bell itself.

Such giving echoes the self-giving of Jesus, which includes his earthly preaching, miracles, attentiveness to people and so on, but is revealed most fully on the cross. The church's self-giving, too, is expressed in the panorama of mission, but is most profoundly manifest in the offer of the church's heart, communal life in Jesus. Just as Christ's self-donation is not limited to, but is supremely disclosed in, his self-giving at Calvary, the church's self-donation is not restricted to, but is most clearly conveyed in, the giving of communion in Christ. Communion in Jesus is not the only expression of the church's self-giving, but it is the jewel in the church's missional crown.

## *An imperfect self*

When the church offers to others the throbbing heart of its existence, what is given is not the entirety of the church's self. For mortals, total self-giving is impossible. 'In giving myself totally, I lose myself totally as well' (Holm, 2009, p. 94). The church can offer itself merely in portions. Only a few in the congregation may bring to others an experience of communion in Christ, for example. In particular, the church's self may be too damaged, too lacking in worth to be given – perhaps a struggling congregation close to extinction, or one that is disillusioned or uncertain, or maybe one whose members are crushed by life. In such cases, like someone who is too shamed or emotionally bruised to imagine they have anything to give, church members may need to feel graciously restored and valued before their generosity can be released.

Nor, by contrast, is the self that is given a satisfied, 'We've got it together' self. Rather, it is a self that laments its sinfulness, repents and is grateful when recipients help the church put things right. And this matters. We often assume that gifts must be as perfect as possible – new rather than secondhand, perhaps. But with goodness all too often intermingling with wickedness, clearly the Christian community is far from flawless. Maybe we should compare the church to a healthy marriage: the partners give themselves to each other with all their imperfections, these reciprocal gifts of self are non-coercively offered and freely received, and the partners help one another to overcome their shortcomings and flourish. Similarly, the church is a defective gift. No one is obliged to accept it, but those who do can help God's people surmount their frailties.

As in marriage the giving is two-way. The church's imperfect self is given to others in love and recipients give themselves in return. Their return gift includes wisdom and experience (in the form of 'good practice' for example), which can help the church purge its shortcomings. The church welcomes the world as a mate who enables it to become a better self. The church *does* have something to offer despite its deformities, but it is also blessed by what the world can bring to the marriage. The church may humbly hope to be a source of healing for the world, but the world can be a means of healing for the church.

## In the form of new communities

If communion in Christ is the church's most precious gift, how is it to be offered? The answer is that the gift must be given appropriately. It is in the nature of generosity that we seek out gifts that suit the recipient. You would not give a bottle of wine to a friend who was teetotal. So when the Spirit offers communion in Jesus, as part of divine generosity the gift will take an appropriate form. For some people, the gift will be suitable if it comprises an invitation to an existing congregation. This bears fruit where the congregation is well connected to networks beyond it and gives generously to them, and where members are willing to invite others in their networks to church events. Even in a context of church decline, there are plenty of examples where this still happens.

In 2013, a report commissioned by the Church of England found that

> The Church's reach extends well beyond itself by several orders of magnitude with those it directly helps, those it works with and those it simply lets use its buildings. Many in the Church will be surprised by the range of things that the Church itself does, even more outside the Church will be a little astonished by its reach, range and depth.[12]

Arising from this loving generosity, many congregations today still fruitfully offer communion in Christ through a warm welcome to their services on Sunday.

However, for numerous people such an invitation will be inappropriate. That is because *every* congregation is exclusive by nature (a point often forgotten). Once Christians have decided to meet at a particular time and place with a certain style and agenda, they will attract some people but they are bound to exclude many others. They will exclude those who cannot come at that time (because of shift work or family commitments perhaps), who cannot come to that place (because they live too far away, are too elderly to travel or cannot access the facilities because they are disabled), who are put off by the congregation's style (the type of music for instance), and who do not share its agenda (to worship Christ). In such cases, to offer communion in Jesus only in the form of an existing congregation would be to offer a gift that is too inaccessible to be received, which would be self-defeating; a gift you cannot receive is not a gift. The Spirit would be narrowing God's generosity to the minority who can receive the gift, whereas divine generosity embraces the whole world.

To make the gift available more widely, the church will join the Spirit in offering communion in Christ in a manner that *is* accessible. It will offer new communities, joined to the whole body, at times and places and with styles and agendas that connect with people for whom the existing church is out of reach.[13] As described in Chapter 10, members will gather in small Christian groups among people beyond the church, share their lives with them around an activity or theme that the people relate to, and welcome those who want it into communal life in Christ. These will be communities of service that witness to the gospel through deed first and then by word. Depending on the tradition, they may become congregations of the parish church, or worshipping communities linked to the congregation, or new local churches in their own right (but integrated into the structures of their ecclesiastical tradition).

For example, between 2010 and 2014, Christ Church Bayston Hill, on the edge of Shrewsbury, England, doubled the number of people it was in touch with to over 500. It did this by serving its neighbourhood through a variety of communities that were intended to become congregations for people currently outside the church. They included:

- *Coffee in the Living Room*, a weekly cafe for patients of the local medical practice.
- *Messy Church*, a monthly all-age event combining craft, Bible story, prayer and food.
- *Outlook* for the over-55s, with a monthly guest speaker and refreshments.
- *Senior citizens lunch*, followed by a few hymns, prayers and a short talk.
- *Stepping Out*, a group formed around walking.
- *Tiddlywinks*, a mini Messy Church for families with children under five years old.
- *Zone*, a weekly gathering for teenagers.

Starting new Christian communities became a normal part of the church's life, even though only a minority of church members were involved, there was no obsessive pressure to begin something new, and other missional objectives were simultaneously pursued.

GIVING THE CHURCH

Christ Church's approach addresses a danger with holistic (or integrated) definitions of mission, such as the five marks of mission now widely used in Anglican and some other circles: *tell* others about Christ, *teach* them how to be disciples, *tend* those in need, work to *transform* society and *treasure* creation. The pitfall is that these goals are pursued while neglecting the one focus, growing new Christian communities, that can actually expand the church's missional capacity. In contexts where the church is becoming strange to the culture, inviting people to an established congregation as part of 'tell' is proving ever less fruitful.

This is a real threat to all forms of mission. For failure to offer the church at a time and place and with a style and agenda that connect with people outside the church risks chopping off the missional branch on which the Christian community sits. If today's ageing congregations wither to a husk, as is starting to happen in many places, and if they are not supplemented by new ones with new people, ecclesiastical entropy will leave fewer resources for any type of mission. Lack of a church-multiplying focus for mission, therefore, may gnaw at other forms of outreach. While the church's self-donation is not limited to offering new Christian communities, in the long term mission on a broad front vitally depends on giving these communities away. Understandings of mission that fail to make new Christian communities explicit hole mission below the water line.

## Communities that bless the world

It follows that these communities should be offered for the benefit of people beyond the church as well as the recipients. When this happens, the church fulfils its vocation to bless all people though multiplication (as well as being blessed by them). In Genesis 22.15–18 God promised Abraham that his descendants would be as numerous as the sand on the seashore so that all the nations would be blessed. Blessing in the Old Testament has the idea of well-being and is a gift (for example, Job 42.10–17). By multiplying, God's people were to bring to the world the gift of fullness of life.

### Multiplying blessings

Ancient Israel by and large came to understand this calling in attractional terms. The emphasis of the Jewish Scriptures – for example, Zechariah 8.20–23 – was on God summoning the nations to Israel 'in the great

## CALLED TO GIVE? THE CHURCH'S VOCATION

pilgrimage to Zion' at the end times (Wright, 2006, pp. 502–3). The nations were to *come* to God's people. However, Jesus reinterpreted this. Recognizing that Mark 16.9–20 is most likely a later addition, the concluding chapters of all four gospels as we now have them contain strong notes of *sending*: Matthew 28.18–20, Mark 16.15–18, Luke 24.47 and John 20.21–23. The world is not to come to the disciples, they are sent to the world.[14] At the end of Matthew 28, for example, Jesus declares: 'Therefore go and make disciples of all nations, baptizing them ... teaching them.' As entry to God's people, baptism assumes the presence of the church; otherwise there would be no community for new believers to join. The disciples were to baptize because they were to take the church with them. The galactic scope of the kingdom, from pastoral care to struggles for justice, is subsumed in the instruction to pass on Jesus' teachings.

Matthew's original audience would have seen the church's multiplication, as described in Acts, as obedience to this command. New churches descended from Jerusalem became known for their generosity to people in need. Nearly 200 years after Christ Tertullian believed that 'It is our good works that make us to be the lights of the world' (Kreider, 2016, p. 91). Down the centuries since, multiplying these lights so that the church is now global has been a recurring theme. Founded on the 12 apostles in continuity with Israel, God's people fulfil the Abrahamic covenant by proliferating through history. God has chosen the church to carpet the world in love by giving new Christian communities away.

Through the Spirit the church is to multiply not as a form of ecclesial imperialism ('let's grow because big is good') but because the expanding suburbs of the church bring gifts to the world. Time and again in the church's history more congregations mean that God's people have had more resources to share for the fullness of life – more volunteers, more charitable activities and organizations, more capacity to campaign and support movements for social reform, more people who can contribute to the creative arts, and more funds to invest in pastoral care, reconciliation and ecological transformation. Multiplication stuffs gifts into an ecclesial Christmas stocking. That is why my claim will repeatedly be that the church is called, as a normal part of its wider generosity, to join the Spirit in giving its self to others, in the form of new Christian communities, *for the benefit of the world.*

This is the logic of the conclusion to David Bosch's classic *Transforming Mission.* Bosch is at pains to emphasize that God is active outside as well as inside the church. He repeatedly stresses the breadth of mission, from personal conversion to social, economic and political activity. Yet when he reduces mission to two sentences, he writes that mission is, quite simply, the participation of Christians in the liberating mission of Jesus, wagering on a future that verifiable experience seems to belie. It is the good news of God's love, incarnated in the witness of a community, for the sake of the world. (Bosch, 1991, p. 519)

If the gospel is incarnated in the witness of the Christian community 'for the sake of the world', magnifying mission requires cascading the community. Proceeding on a narrow front (starting new congregations) can amplify mission on a broad front (social justice and more). As one bonanza of gifts then another and another, the church's self-donation is to enrich the entire creation.

Just as in charitable giving the donor gives to the charity for the benefit of those the charity serves, so with the church. God's people offer the church to others for the benefit of third parties. As with certain forms of charitable giving (to support dying with dignity, for example), some of these benefits may be controversial. Not all the church's gifts will be welcome. Even so, if the gifts genuinely promote a fuller life (see John 10.10 ) they will probably find an audience. The more this abundant life bears fruit (and the more the church is given ethically, which is discussed in Part 2), the more attractive to outsiders the gift of the church will be.

## Enhancing any missional manifesto

In particular, giving the church enables the Christian community to contribute distinctively to the world's preoccupations – climate change, poverty, human rights, mental health and much more. As Vatican II proclaimed, for Christ's followers 'nothing genuinely human fails to raise an echo in their hearts' (*Gaudium et Spes*, 1965, §1). There is *no* echo, *no* Spirit-inspired agenda that new Christian communities cannot potentially serve – a big claim! If the focus is the environment, social justice or global poverty, Christians can listen to people outside the church who share their concern, find ways of working together, form community as they do so, learn from one another, and be nourished – if people want – by relevant tastes of Christian spirituality. If the priority is a specific demographic – people who are homeless, women who have been abused, asylum seekers, teenagers in a run-down neighbourhood or people with learning difficulties – a small team can listen to them, love them, receive *their* love, build community with them, introduce those interested to Jesus and encourage a safe and supportive Christian community to emerge.

If the challenge is to be a kingdom presence in the workplace, examples exist of new Christian communities serving an office, a school, gang leaders wanting to become legitimate entrepreneurs, and patients of a medical practice. If the intention is to practise 'whole-life' discipleship, new Christian communities have emerged among people who enjoy singing, art and crafts, playing sport, walking their dog or going for a run. Whether in a village or urban centre, in an inner-city apartment block or on a new housing estate, in a neighbourhood with multi-deprivation or in a wealthy suburb, new Christian communities can be painted on to *any* missional landscape as an enhancement of the picture.

Adding 'Dinner Church' to a food pantry, for instance, can transform one-way giving (distributing free food) into mutual generosity as community forms. Or as well as witnessing as individuals in a grief group, two or three Christians can jointly offer a short time of reflection after the session with a lighted candle, a Scripture reading, silent and spoken prayers, and some Christian music – a first step, perhaps, towards an optional Christian community alongside the original group. Without imposing it on people, who can stay or leave as they like, the group will be enriched by an extra spiritual dimension. Thus, new Christian communities can embellish the breadth of mission, while importantly mission on a broad front can happen *in the process* of birthing a new congregation, not just as a result of it being born.

Offering communion in Christ is unique among the church's missional gifts. All the church's other gifts have limited, though sometimes large, audiences. There would be no sense, for example, in the church giving food to people who are well fed, sharing its financial resources with people oozing with money, or extending pastoral care to people with no need of it. Communal life in Jesus, on the other hand, has the potential to include everyone. For if Christ reigns over all (Matt. 28.18) and will fill, or complete, all things on his return (Eph. 1.23; 4.10), there can be no place where his body is unable to anticipate this future (Newbigin, 1977, pp. 118–23). Communion in Christ is a ubiquitous gift.

The 1967 World Council of Churches report, *The Church for Others*, recognized these multiple and disparate opportunities for witness. The report called for 'little congregations ... fashioned in very diverse shapes to enable Christians to be present in all spheres of life, in order that they may participate in mission, not as an occasional activity but as their very *raison d'être*' (p. 29). However, the report was keen to avoid self-aggrandizing mission that benefited the church more than the world. So it downplayed the role of evangelism. To some, it appeared to reduce mission to social action. That was unfortunate. Giving away communion in Christ can encompass the entire latitude of the kingdom. The Great Commandment to love others and the Great Commission to make disciples can flow together, like blood and oxygen, in the arteries of everyday life.

## GIVING THE CHURCH

For example, in north Bradford, England, *Sorted* emerged among working-class teenagers beyond the church, who are now young adults. A small group of Christians *listened* to young people in the local school. They *loved* the teenagers by helping them to organize fun activities on a Friday night, with five or ten minutes of Christian input. *Community* formed as the teenagers came regularly. The teenagers were enabled to *explore Jesus* at a separate time of the week; skateboarding or computer games were followed by 'chat time', such as discussion about God, life issues or a Bible story. A worship service, the beginnings of *church*, was started with teenagers who were responding to Christ. Later, some of these new Christians *repeated* the process; they helped to start another *Sorted* among the next generation. Though messy and hugely varied, as described in Chapter 10 we have seen this process of listening, loving, community, exploring Jesus, church taking shape, and – at its best – repeat of the process recurring over the past 20 years in an expanding range of settings in Europe, North America and other countries. To claim that there is no missional activity that spiritual lungs cannot animate is based on a growing number of observed examples.[15]

## Communities that grow disciples

Offering others the church's communal self, in the form of new Christian communities, for the benefit of the world deepens personal discipleship. Jenny Leith (2023) has described the dominant account of Christian ethical formation: formation is thought to happen almost exclusively through participation in the liturgy, structures and processes of the church. This leads to an over-reliance on the internal life of God's people, an under-estimation of sin's contamination of this life and a sidelining of the Spirit's activity beyond the church. She argues that formation 'requires openness to surprising encounters with the Spirit out in the world' (p. 9). These encounters may challenge ecclesial practices that are exclusive, manipulative or abusive, while enabling believers to grow in their personal likeness to Christ.

Her argument gains strength, first, if we move beyond a binary distinction between the gathered and scattered church. Typically today, congregations gather for worship and scatter for the rest of the week. Of course the congregation's worship, prayers and ongoing fellowship sustain its members 'in life'. So communion in Christ remains, but it is largely implicit. Christians witness as individuals rather than as an explicit community. However, when the church prioritizes its call to join the Spirit in giving away new Christian communities, this 'lone ranger' form of

## CALLED TO GIVE? THE CHURCH'S VOCATION

discipleship is redefined. Christians come together to offer the church. Their generosity combines practical kindness with sensitive opportunities (no pressure!) to explore Christian spirituality as part of a fuller life. This collective action expands the possibilities for self-giving love, which ingrains generosity more deeply into believers' lives.

Second, love is far more than spontaneous good turns within a one-to-one relationship. Often it has to be organized. Think of a family – getting the children to school, marshalling the evening meal, arranging a family treat, preparing a birthday party, or fixing a holiday. This love needs organizing. It is possible to do it on your own, and many single parents succeed brilliantly. But how many would prefer to have a partner? As part of discipleship, it is easier and more fun to practise love with someone – to form a small community for this purpose. It then becomes feasible to love on a more ambitious scale. Rather than feeding one person who has no food, for example, generosity can be expanded to feeding a group. Discipleship has a greater impact.

Third, organizing pockets of generosity 'in life' gives Christian witness a focus. For many churchgoers, following Jesus is like playing basketball without a hoop or soccer without goal posts. Their witness lacks a focal point, which can be demotivating. This changes when believers are on mission, in ordinary life, with fellow Christians. Faith is stretched and prayer intensified as these Christians organize love without being sure of the outcome. Patience and other fruits of the Spirit are displayed as they surmount obstacles and face setbacks. Believers learn to articulate their Christian experience and connect it to others' lives. Within a small group, they share more in leading (simple) worship than they could in a larger congregation. They are like Christian young adults who return from a short-term mission placement in an unfamiliar setting and describe how their faith has been transformed. But in the case of new Christian communities, the 'placement' is longer term and it is where life takes place nearby. Offering these communities becomes a crucible for spiritual formation.[16]

Fourth, we can support Leith's concern about church-centric formation by noting how sometimes the church can actually undermine Christian witness. Barth lamented that

> it may be that the community finds so great joy and satisfaction in what is proper to it, yet also so many problems, e.g., of worship, pastoral care, social life and theology, so many tasks, so many claims in what has to be experienced, considered and done in its own inner circle, that it simply neither has time nor energy for those who are without, and therefore thinks it better either to proceed without them or to maintain only that loose relationship which can easily be broken. (Barth, 2004, p. 825)

Internal preoccupations become kryptonite, diverting supernatural energy into sideshows that dodge the main event.

As a contemporary example, Alison Milbank has complained that to keep the Church of England afloat while clergy numbers fall, lay people are being conscripted into church leadership at the expense of their vocations in the world (Milbank, 2023, pp. 100–1). It is not uncommon for lay people to feel trapped in an either-or. Either a demanding church pulls them away from their lay vocations, or the latter pulls them away from church. Might new Christian communities help reduce this tension? If these communities can potentially support any missional agenda, they can be present in any lay vocation. So instead of volunteering in the church conflicting with work, family, friendships, hobbies or voluntary opportunities outside the church, lay callings in the church have the possibility of marrying up with lay vocations in the world. In other words, might new Christian communities give some callings in society an ecclesial hue? Lay vocations would include taking the church to others where life occurs.

Fifth, when this happens church, discipleship and mission would no longer be kept apart (church on Sunday, discipleship during the week and mission as an after-thought). They would be clasped together. Congregations would assume a new role – to enable their members to offer Christian community to others as part of their vocations in the world. Congregations would become launch pads for missional satellites each connected to base and to one another, each led by Christians as a centre of their discipleship, and each dispatching further communities when they were ready. The church's interior would blend with its exterior life to form missional disciples.[17] For instance, *Coffee in the Living Room*, mentioned earlier, a weekly drop-in for patients of a medical practice, was led by a recently-retired teacher and her friend who had been praying about starting a cafe. For the two of them, as well as for other Christians who helped, spirituality was not a mainly inward experience as it is for many people today, nor was it an individualistic faith without communal support, nor was it food for the soul without the church. Discipleship, mission and church were woven together so that spirituality had an outward thrust towards others, faith grew through organized love around which community formed, and the resulting possibility of a new congregation gave mission an ecclesial edge.[18]

This comes close to Barth's plea for 'special working fellowships' based on the Spirit's gifts to the church. These gifts can build up not just the church's internal life, but also its witness to people beyond. Through these working fellowships, groups of Christians would render service to people outside the church in a particular way. Thereby believers would 'achieve in closer fellowship the ministry and witness of [the congregation] in the world' and enable the living Christ to 'be more powerful and visible' (Barth, 2004, p. 856). New Christian communities go an important step further: they gather people from outside the church to savour Jesus within these 'working fellowships'; and these fellowships become congregations in their own right, connected to their parent church. For the Christian core of the fellowship, church and lay vocations are no longer in tension with each other. Church, mission and discipleship blend into one. Christian formation happens in a church community, on mission, in life. It becomes even more holistic than Leith imagines.

## Implications

My claim is that, despite its sinfulness, the church is a gift. It is the gift of communal life in Jesus, offered to the world by means of the Spirit. This gift must be shared with others and this can be done in many ways – care, creative arts, cultivating a just society and more. However, the church's most precious gift is the offer of its self, communion in Christ. This can properly take the form of an invitation to an existing congregation, but often the invitation will be inappropriate because many people find today's church inaccessible. In such cases, communion in Christ will be offered in the shape of new Christian communities, embedded within the institutional arrangements of the church. Giving away these communities benefits people beyond them and helps the Christians involved to grow in their discipleship.

This chapter brings gift to the fore in our understanding of the church. In doing so, it challenges the typical neglect of church multiplication in doctrines of the Christian community. Church planting is seen as a fitting topic for writers about mission, but not worthy of attention by theologians of the church. An example is Mike Higton's chapter on Rowan Williams' ecclesiology in *The Oxford Handbook of Ecclesiology* (Higton, 2018). Not once does Higton mention how Williams championed contextualized forms of church planting, 'fresh expressions of church', when he was Archbishop of Canterbury. Yet arguably this was one of Williams' most distinctive contributions in that role.[19] By contrast, this chapter argues that cultivating new congregations should have a more pronounced place in church doctrine. As part of its life of generosity, the Christian community is to participate in the Spirit's offering of the church to others, in the form of new Christian communities around which burgeon multiple forms of giving. If offering these communities is a most precious aspect of the church's vocation, how can it be ignored in theologies of the Christian community?

## GIVING THE CHURCH

Second and relatedly, this chapter brings church multiplication to the fore of mission. Among the many concerns of mission (reconciliation, climate change and much else), giving away new Christian communities should be seen as a normal dimension of the church's life – not always, not for everyone, not at the expense of other elements of mission, but commonplace, to be expected and intrinsic to the church's call to generosity. Today's talk about integrated mission, therefore, must go beyond expecting that the various giants of mission – evangelism, making disciples, pastoral care, social justice, care for creation and more – will be entrenched in the church's life. These missional clothes should hang increasingly from church-multiplication. For without new Christian communities, if congregations wither in size even as they engage in mission, eventually mission on a wide canvas will also atrophy. Equally, because new Christian communities can contribute to any missional agenda, their procreation will potentially expand all forms of outreach. It follows that mission is the purpose of church multiplication, multiplication is not the purpose of mission; even if the church included the whole world, other missional tasks would remain – protecting the climate, eliminating poverty and generally promoting a fuller life. Offering new Christian communities should be a vital dimension of mission, but not the sum of it.

Given its importance, a diocese, denomination or network of churches should make multiplication a strategic focus. Instead of youth, social concern, training and other departments digging their own silos, each in their distinctive way should contribute to the shared goal of offering the church to others for the benefit of society. The youth department should foster the multiplication of teenage congregations. Social concern should promote the formation of justice communities with a Christian spiritual dimension. The discipleship team should encourage new Christian communities as a means not just of making new disciples, but of spiritual growth for the Christians involved. Training should be offered to those leading these initiatives. The Christian community would go beyond being 'missional church' to become a multiplying church.

Third, and looking forward, this chapter begins to offer a distinctive response to the radical critique of mission – that mission is a Trojan horse to advance the church's interests. Mission, it is said, starts from the church's agenda rather than the world's; the church 'sends' initiatives it has predetermined and the world 'receives' them. Various attempts have been made to provide a more mutual account, such as 'intercultural missiology' in which both 'sides' send and receive from each other (Paas, 2019, pp. 10–11). This chapter lays foundations to reframe that response. If the church is called to a life of generosity, with a particular role for new Christian communities, this creates a platform for seeing

50

## CALLED TO GIVE? THE CHURCH'S VOCATION

mission as the relational exchange of gifts. As Part 2 will describe, the exchange involves receiving first, giving appropriately, releasing the gift, accepting the gift (which forms community), giving back and transformation. Crucially, the church and the world come together as partners through their exchanges. If their relationship can bear the weight, they jointly create a new community in Christ for the sake of people beyond. Intercultural missiology becomes defined by reciprocal generosity.

## Notes

1 For Hans Urs von Balthasar, the Godhead is three persons who eternally give themselves to one another in love. The 'self-donating Father' (von Balthasar, 2004, p. 155) gives all that he is to the Son. In thankfulness and obedience, the Son gives all that he is back to the Father. And, without their divinity running out, both give their entire selves to the Spirit, who returns their wholehearted gift of self. (These mutual givings, of course, are not sequential but simultaneous beyond time.) Thus the three persons are united through the origins of Son and Spirit in the giving of the Father, in their shared nature of self-giving, and by indwelling each other through generosity. Reflecting rather crudely this 'social' model of the Trinity, the actress Judi Dench recounts being in a show with Ian McKellen early in their careers. Nervous on the first night, she said to him, 'I am going to concentrate on the three seats at the centre of the front row and imagine that the Father, Son and Holy Ghost are sitting there.' McKellen (echoing a second 'psychological' model of the Trinity) replied, 'They'd be sitting on the one seat, surely?' Keith Ward (2015, pp. 219ff.) helpfully suggests that these 'seating arrangements' need not be as different as they seem.

2 This need not mean that Jesus intentionally founded the church as an ongoing institution, even though he himself is the foundation of the church. See, for example, Avis, 2021.

3 Translation by David Bentley Hart, 2018, *The New Testament: A Translation*, New Haven, CT: Yale University Press, p. 268.

4 I am using 'self' somewhat colloquially. Space prevents a discussion of the differences between the self of a person, the self of a group or organization, and the self of the church. Suffice to say that the idea that the church is a self (a corporate self rather than a person's self) is not far from the New Testament's description of the church as a body with a head.

5 Barclay (2015, pp. 66–78) describes these characteristics of Paul's understanding of grace.

6 Though we must not take this reservation too far. If we unhook the economic from the immanent Trinity by too much, we risk unhooking God from God's self-revelation in Christ.

7 For an accessible exposition of their views, see Malo, 2012, especially pp. 167–78.

8 For Balthasar, the 'why-less' of God's love preserves the mystery, the incomprehensibility, of God. We can never plumb the depth of God's groundless love (see McInerny, 2020, pp. 125–56). This view helps to protect the reflections here from being over-presumptuous about knowledge of the immanent Trinity.

9 Does such generosity impose a burden on humans because we cannot repay it? Or are we like children who are thrilled to return their parents' love with a present, even though their gift may have little material worth? Despite being unequal, which grace enables humans to accept as a consequence of God's transcendence, the unequal exchange is not a burden because it has symbolic value as an expression of mutual love.

10 Part 2 describes some of what this should look like.

11 As one person working with poor people commented, 'When we hold bring-and-share meals, our hope is that everyone, however poor, will bring something. It gives them dignity.' This something might be time, such as helping to set up and clear the tables.

12 James Noyce and Philip Blond, 2013, *Holistic Mission*, London: ResPublica, p. 6, quoted by Milbank, 2023, p. 51.

13 This is not the same as giving people only what they want. As argued in Part 2, giving must be appropriate to the giver as well as the recipient.

14 For a fuller treatment of this shift from a gathered to a dispersed view of mission, see Moynagh, 2017, pp. 165–8.

15 Case and other empirical studies include Cole, 2005; Glasson, 2006; Moore, 2006; Male, 2008; Potter, 2009; Volland, 2009; Howson, 2011; Moynagh, 2012; Paas, 2012; Dutton, 2014; Keith, 2014; Walker, 2014; Watkins and Shepherd, 2014; Lings, 2016; Milne, 2016; Moynagh, 2017; James, 2017; Dunlop, 2018; Taylor, 2019; Moynagh and Beck, 2020; Aldous and Moynagh, 2021; the *Encounters on the Edge* series by the Church Army Research Unit, Sheffield, UK.

16 These benefits to Christian formation are illustrated in a 2022 study of 19 actual or potential (on the way to becoming) new Christian communities, involving 218 participants (mainly the core team), 71% of whom were regular churchgoers. The proportion reporting that they prayed regularly increased from 45% when they joined the community to 65% at the time of the survey. 86% agreed that their community had improved their relationship with God. 88% agreed that their community had improved their personal life, such as feeling more worthy, being more authentic, behaving in line with their values and dealing with difficult issues. The proportion who almost always felt like helping others nearly doubled from 28% to 54%. Those who frequently felt a sense of purpose increased from 44% to 79%. Eido Research, *Fresh Expressions of Church: Fruitfulness Framework Report*, London: The Church of England/Eido Research, 2022. A caveat is that there were no comparisons with other forms of Christian service.

17 Might this help address an ongoing tension in Roman Catholic theology since Vatican II 'between the interrelated centripetal and centrifugal forces of communio and missio' (Rush, 2018, p. 284)?

18 For case studies of Christ Church Bayston Hill and *Coffee in the Living Room*, see Moynagh, 2017, pp. 80–98 and 357–66.

19 In particular, Williams coined the widely-used phrase 'mixed economy', which referred to new and older forms of church existing side-by-side in mutual respect and support, and wrote the Foreword to the *Mission-shaped Church* report (Cray, 2004) that put 'fresh expressions of church' on the global map.

# 2

# What is the Gift? The Church's Nature

If the church is called to a life of generosity, receivers of the church's gifts – like the recipients of any gift – will want to know about the gift and also a bit about the giver. The two of course are bound together. Writers on giving frequently note that something of the giver accompanies the gift.[1] Indeed, the more you put yourself into the gift – thought, time, effort or wealth – the more generous you are. This personal involvement has been taken further in recent Roman Catholic reflection on marriage. Sharing in the total giving of the trinitarian persons as revealed in Jesus, spouses are understood to give their whole selves to each other (Ouellet, 2006, p. 61ff.). In a giving that opens up the possibility of a further gift, that of a child, each spouse gives not a *thing* but a complete self.

Something like this is involved in the church's giving to others. The church gives itself to the world through its whole life of generosity, such as pastoral care, alleviating poverty, solidarity for justice, and contributions to the creative arts. But it goes further when, as a special part of this giving, it gratefully joins the Spirit in offering its very self, communion in Christ, to others in the form of new Christian communities. This self is given as a partner. Potential recipients are invited to join the Christian community in creating a new entity, not Christ-centred conjugal life but Christ-centred communal life. As in many theologies of marriage, integral to this new life is the potential for offspring. When the church's self is given to the world and the world's self to the church, a Christian community emerges with the possibility of birthing further communities. Thus the gift of the church's self is a radical form of generosity. Rather than a small portion of the church's self being offered, the core of the church's self, communion in Christ, becomes the gift.

And just as partners want to know more about the other before committing to marriage, so potential recipients will want to know more about the church before entrusting themselves to it. So what is the nature of the gift that is offered to them? Recent theologians have commonly rooted the church in the Trinity. As mentioned in the Introduction, the Trinity has been seen as a communion and so the church, originating in the Godhead and drawn into its life, is said fundamentally to share God's communal nature. But communion is not the only defining feature of the Trinity. Another is self-giving love (which is expressed in communion). As starting points for understanding the church's nature the two are inseparable. The gift offered to others is a communion of mutual generosity, grounded in God and enabling recipients to participate in God.

But what does this mean – tangibly? Against an ecumenical background with multiple understandings of the church, this chapter offers an ecclesiastical skeleton that can be enfleshed in different ways. It suggests that in essence the Christian community is a communion of four interlocking sets of relationships in which Christians give to, and receive from others in love. The church is what happens when, in mutual generosity, people encounter the risen Lord, gather round him with others, connect through him to the communion of saints, and join with him in God's mission to the world. The church would not be the church if it lacked any of these four overlapping sets of relationships – with God directly, within the Christian community, with the wider church and with the world.

Second, the chapter nuances the traditional view of the church's *esse* (essence) to suggest in effect two *esses*: the four ecclesial relations (the essence of the church) and four essentials – word, sacraments, ministry and disciplines (such as spiritual rhythms, rules, habits and confessional statements). Given by God, the essentials are necessary types of practice that enable the ecclesial relations to participate in the self-giving of Christ. The essentials look different in different contexts, which raises the question – addressed in the third section – of how to discern their shape for the church's good (the church's *bene esse*, adapted from the term's traditional usage). When giving the church to others, the Spirit offers a combination of the four sets of relationships, the four types of essentials and the process of discernment. These provide structural bones that help us recognize and describe the church.

## Relationships or practices?

Gifts can of course take many forms – purchased objects, a meal out, contributions to a conversation and much else. What distinguishes the gift of self is that it goes beyond these types of giving, while including them. It fundamentally comprises all the relationships out of which the giver's identity has emerged. As Rowan Williams remarked, 'Who we are becomes clear to those around when we put ourselves in a map of relationships.'[2] Identity, in fact, is a sum of relationships. True, many of these relationships may be forgotten or appear insignificant, but all will have had some impact, however tiny, on the person whose self is given.

## WHAT IS THE GIFT? THE CHURCH'S NATURE

In contemporary marriage, for example, partners give themselves along with their family, friendships and other networks. Whether the persons involved are liked or disliked, these relationships are typically accepted by the other as intrinsic to their partner, and to varying degrees they enrich the couple's life together. Much the same applies to the gift of the Christian community. The gift that is offered, the church's self, is immersed in the relationships that define it. These relationships, we pray, will be drawn into Christ and filled with his generous character.

For much of its history, the church was understood by reference not to its relationships but to certain practices, such as the sacraments, proclaiming the word, authorized ministry and confessional statements. These were thought to define the nature of the church. Debate centred on which practices were fundamental to the church and the form they should take. Since the 1960s, however, in ecumenical discussions the church has come to be seen as more than its practices. It is described as a divinely established communion. The church is a fellowship headed by Jesus, whose members share certain customs and habits. This ecumenical 'convergence' is reflected in the landmark text, *The Church. Towards a common vision* (WCC, 2013a).

The report describes the church as 'fundamentally a communion in the Triune God' whose members share in God's life and mission (§23). In this common life specified practices play a key role. The Eucharist, for instance, is 'a dynamic paradigm' of communion. God's people 'gather with their president, proclaim the Good News, confess their faith, pray, teach and learn, offer praise and thanksgiving, receive the Body and Blood of the Lord, and are sent out in mission' (§67). This encapsulates many of the practices broadly seen as being vital to the church, however they are expressed. Full union, the report suggests, will be possible only when Christians agree what fundamental practices should be recognized (§37).

This description of the church leaves unclear which takes precedence: practices or people-in-their-relationships (shorthanded here to 'relationships')? Who curtsies to whom? Now of course the distinction between relationships and practices is far from absolute. The church's practices, perhaps like most practices, are relational by nature. Holy Communion, studying Scripture or leadership bring people together and into relationship with God. Equally, relationships involve practices. Christians do things together. But this does not mean that the church's relationships can be collapsed into its practices. Imagine, by analogy, a friendship formed around bike riding. If for some reason the two people stop cycling, the friendship may wither and die. Or else it may continue in a different way; the friends' mutual commitment sustains the relationship beyond the initial practice of cycling. The church's relationships are closer to this

55

second kind. They emerge from and are sustained by four types of practice (studying the word, sacraments, ministry and disciplines), but they do not depend on specific practices within these categories.

Thus the church's relationships will outlast at least some practices, such as Holy Communion, which is given till the Lord returns (1 Cor. 11.26). The sacrament will end, but relationships in the communion of saints will persist. Moreover, though churches share particular practices, they disagree about their importance. For example, in some Pentecostal churches weeks can go by without the Lord's Supper; other practices sustain relationships such as sung worship, a congregational 'discipline'. Furthermore, churches differ considerably in how they perform shared practices. Think of an informal Lord's Supper over a meal versus a High Mass, a 45-minute Bible exposition or a discussion-based sermon, and debates over infant baptism.

If relationships can endure beyond certain practices, be sustained by different practices, and if common practices are understood variously and inconsistently, there must be some distinction between practices and relationships. Unlike a friendship so entwined with cycling that it could not exist without it, ecclesial relationships are not totally dependent on *specific* practices. The church's relationships are bound up with certain *types* of practice (word, sacraments and so on), but they have a degree of independence from them. This means we can ask how relationships and practices relate – not least, which side calls the shots?

For example, what happens if practices cherished by a tradition – certain liturgies perhaps – stifle a congregation? Maybe a congregation is full of life, but sinks like a soufflé during an authorized liturgy, which feels awkward and inauthentic to the community. Worship fails to feed the congregation's relationship with God and the world, while relations are strained with the wider church, which is resented for imposing the formality. New believers find their ecclesial shoes too tight and sometimes vote with their feet. From one angle, this is a matter of how the congregation relates to the larger church. But it is also about how practices of the church are understood. How fixed are they, and how far can they be tailored to people in their 'map of relationships'?

If the answer is unclear, harmful ambiguities may emerge around not only authorized liturgies, but the exercise of leadership, how the word is taught (dogmatically or with space for disagreement), and the sort of disciplines expected of church members. If the health of the church's relationships are thought to depend on these practices being performed in a certain preconceived way, ministers – confident in their authority – may feel more comfortable riding roughshod over others. They may more readily impose their interpretations of Scripture without appro-

# WHAT IS THE GIFT? THE CHURCH'S NATURE

priate checks and balances. Their expectations of church members may more often be quietly self-serving. Without firm *relational* boundaries, abuse can more easily flourish, which is a serious problem for a church tarnished by scandal.

Put differently, if the word, sacraments and ministry for instance are the defining features of the church, it is not so difficult to think of them as ends in themselves. 'If we celebrate the sacraments, preach the word and exercise priestly ministry, the job's done.' Spiritual fruitfulness becomes secondary. But this does not square with Jesus' constant search for fruit in people's lives. Once you enquire about fruitfulness, however, you have to ask what fruit the sacraments, word and ministry are called to bear. What is the purpose of these types of practice? Many would say it is to gather followers of Jesus and build them up in Christ.

In which case, are not sacraments, word and ministry means to an end, the spiritual health of believers? And is not the spiritual health of believers ultimately about their relationships – with God directly, with people outside the church, and with people inside (both within the congregation and more widely)? If so, does not this end put helpful relational boundaries round how practices are performed? Yet equally, might this not imply that practices are less important than relationships, that believers (in their relationships) are the fundamental reality of the church and these means are secondary? That would make some feel queasy. It would challenge their deeply-held conviction that the word, sacraments or ministry, or some combination, are not secondary but foundational to the church. So again, how should we describe the connection between Christians-in-their-relations and the practices deemed necessary for their corporate life?

In addition, the ecumenical convergence fails to say enough. If the church's identity becomes clear when the Christian community is put into a map of relationships, to understand the communion in Christ offered to others as part of the church's generosity, these relationships must be sketched out. After all, other communities and organizations are also defined by their relationships. A business, for example, is differentiated by which groups of shareholders, customers, suppliers, employees and other 'stakeholders' it relates to. So what makes the church different to a business? As a distinctive gift, the Christian community will remain an empty package unless its defining relationships are described.

## Four sets of relationships

Building on the Church of England's report, *Mission-shaped Church* (Cray, 2004), which speaks of four dimensions of the church, I would like to suggest that the church comprises four overlapping sets of relationships in which mutual giving should occur: with God directly in prayer, worship and study, with the world, with the wider church and within each ecclesial community, all grounded on Christ. No other community or organization has a combination of these particular sets of relationships. They mark the church out. They are the essence of the church.

These four interlocking sets of relationships integrate three influential starting points for contemporary understandings of the church – the Trinity (for example, Volf, 1998), the kingdom (for example, Pannenberg, 2004) and experience (for example, Healy, 2000). In the case of the Trinity, the Father's giving to the Son (Matt. 28.18) and the Son's obedience to the Father (John 8.28–9) have their counterpart, within the Godward relationship, in divine giving to the church and the church's return gift of obedience. The church's mutually generous relationships with the world happen by participating in God's mission through the Holy Spirit. Relationships inside each church community correspond to loving interactions within the Trinity. Relations with the whole body, which enable each gathering to generously influence and be influenced by the wider church, are the ecclesial counterpart to the *perichoretic* nature of the trinitarian relationships – one affects all. Through their *perichoretic* relations Father, Son and Spirit permeate each other without ceasing to be distinct persons. Likewise, all parts of the church are present to each other while remaining distinct (Volf, 1998, p. 209).

The relational Trinity gives birth to the relational kingdom, whose relationships too are shared by the church. As pictured in Revelation 21 for instance, God dwells among his peoples, which is the Godward relationship (v. 3). The city consists of 'peoples' (plural) – a variety of people groups; each group is related to the others by being part of the whole city, just as each Christian community is connected to the whole church. Relations within each group are mirrored by relationships within each ecclesial community. The city's openness to the kings and the nations outside (vv. 24, 26) is reflected in the church's mission to the world.

The relational kingdom gives birth to the relational church, which is experienced through its four interlocking sets of relationships. Nicholas Healy's warning (2000) against 'blueprint ecclesiologies' – reflections on the church using abstract models – has helped spawn ethnographic approaches to ecclesiology, which start from the lived experience of congregations (Ward, 2012). These approaches eschew ideal versions of the

## WHAT IS THE GIFT? THE CHURCH'S NATURE

church that are too remote from ecclesial messiness to challenge the latter's shortcomings. Earthing the church's essence in the day-to-day relationships of the Christian community likewise bows to reality, bringing the described and experienced church closer together. Just as our faith begins concretely with the recorded experiences of Jesus, so our understanding of his body must start tangibly with connections to God directly, the wider church, the world and to others within each ecclesial community. Can we see God's generosity pouring into these relationships?

### Equally important

The ecclesial relationships can be demarcated for analytical purposes, but in everyday life they are all deeply entwined and enrich each other. For instance, the relationship with God is experienced within the gathering, in encounters with the wider church and in going out to the world. The relationship with the whole body is experienced when members of a congregation pray for the wider family, share in the larger church's mission, and discuss the tradition together.

One set of relations must not take precedence over the others, not even direct relations with the Trinity. Prioritizing the latter would risk devaluing God's involvement in the other ecclesial relationships; God is thought to be more pleased by being encountered in worship than in mission, for example. Equally, if missional relationships were given priority the church would risk being reduced to outreach; the other sets of relations might become means to that end. Yet creating a community of love, involving all the relationships, is one of the purposes of mission. In being such a community, the church commends the purpose for which mission exists. 'It is precisely because she is not merely instrumental that she can be instrumental' (Newbigin, 1953, pp. 147–8).

In a similar vein, prioritizing fellowship would risk reducing mission to a second step, whereas mission is fundamental to the church, as we saw in Chapter 1. Likewise, if relationships with the wider church were to take centre stage, once more mission would be downgraded or the interests of the particular community might be trampled upon. Elevating any of the relationships with the world, the wider church or within the community itself would demote relations with God through Scripture, prayer and worship. The four sets of relationships not only interpenetrate each other, they are equally important and correct one another.

Their equality is secured by all four ultimately dwelling in Christ, the church's head (Eph. 4.15–16). In his earthly life Jesus had no other relationships beyond those with God directly (with the Father and the Spirit),

GIVING THE CHURCH

with the Jewish people (the 'wider church' of his day), with religious outsiders like the lepers he healed (the world), and with his immediate community of followers. Subtract any of these relationships and Jesus would not have been who he was. Equally, subtract Jesus from any of the ecclesial relationships and they would not be what together *they* are – the essence of the church.

## Some advantages

This definition of the church's essence has several advantages. First, by grounding the church's relationships on Jesus, self-donation is brought to the fore because Jesus is the incarnation of self-giving. To be in communion in him, the ecclesial relationships must be infused with his generosity. The instinctive giving in all human relationships, such as the giving of time necessary for any relationship, can then come to full bloom. Thus mapping the church's relations depicts a setting, the Christian community, in which humanity's mutual giving can rise to crescendo. The gift of the church, therefore, is the gift of four interlocking sets of *generous* relationships.

Second, this relational view is faithful to the New Testament. The Corinthian church, for instance, experienced God directly (1 Cor. 12.7–11). Members also connected to other Christian communities by reading Paul's letters, for example, and following leaders in the church at large (1 Cor. 1.12). They engaged with the outside world (1 Cor. 14.23–25). And they interacted relationally in worship (1 Cor. 14.26–31). The New Testament imagery of the church is strongly relational, such as the vine and the branches. In his classic *Images of Church in the New Testament* (1960), Paul Minear described four controlling images – the people of God, the new creation (which includes the restoration of fractured relationships), the fellowship of faith and the body of Christ. All are relational pictures.

Third, this relational perspective fits with the idea of the church as the people of God, currently taken for granted in ecumenical circles. Now, if humans exist in and through their relationships (a truism for theologians and social scientists alike), 'people' must include the relationships that make them a people. 'People of God' recognizes that the church is more than a collection of individuals; it is persons in relationships. Identifying the nature of these relations – with God directly, with the world, with the wider church and within each ecclesial community, all centred on Christ – makes this recognition explicit. It clarifies what is involved in seeing the church as people belonging to God.

60

## WHAT IS THE GIFT? THE CHURCH'S NATURE

Fourth, demarcating the four sets of relationships avoids too thin or thick a description of the church. The account goes beyond language like 'people of God' and 'mystical communion' to outline the relational frame that determines what sort of communion the church is. But it does not go so far as to detail the fabric around the frame – how the relationships are expressed in particular contexts. The latter varies, just as covenant stipulations in the Old Testament differed according to circumstances. In the covenant the law taught Israel how to respond contextually to Yahweh's generosity. The covenant relationship was the ultimate reality and the law showed how it was to be made concrete in the nation's life (Brueggemann, 1997, pp. 419–20). The stipulations could alter according to historical circumstances so long as they still served the covenant – worship shifted from the tabernacle to the temple, for example. In like manner, the church's relationships are of ultimate importance, and practices that give them life can differ from context to context.

Fifth, being explicit about the four sets of relationships and their equal importance can avoid certain relationships being put on a pedestal and others ignored. For example, influenced by Robert Warren (1995, p. 89), many British evangelicals have come to understand the church as three circles, representing three sets of relationships: worship (relationships with God), community (within the church) and mission (with the world). This has been echoed by the American church-planting theologian Christopher James, who has described the church as 'a community defined by its unique relationships to God, one another, and the world' (James, 2018, p. 16). But this conflates relationships with the wider church and those within the immediate community, enabling relations with the whole church to fade from view. Believers may fail to see the church for looking at the congregation. This is especially a danger in everyday Christian life, where the congregation typically looms larger than the wider church. Language shapes thought.

Sixth, this relational view resonates with complexity thinkers who assume that contemporary organizations are little more than strings of conversation (Shaw, 2002; Griffin and Stacey, 2005; Stacey, 2010). Organizations talk themselves into existence through relationships. Imagine an organization without any conversations, whether online or in person. What would be left? Understanding the church mainly in terms of practices like gathering round the word and the altar fails to do justice to how practices originate in conversation, are constantly changed through conversation, and have a meaning that varies between conversations. The Last Supper, for example, was instituted in the context of a Jewish community that had been on the road with Jesus for three years. It has taken multiple forms since, in multiple cultures, as the church has discussed how best it should be celebrated. Just as defining marriage in terms of a legal document and having sex fails to capture the fullness of the relationships involved, so describing the church in terms of practices omits too much of what it means to be the church. Of course practices are important. They give substance to the ecclesial relationships. But the latter provide a richer account of the church's fundamental nature than practices per se.

Finally, and of particular importance, this relational approach affirms the priority of healthy relationships in the church's life. If the heart of the church lies in relationships of mutual generosity, the latter must never be jeopardized. How the word is proclaimed, the sacraments celebrated, ministry exercised and disciplines defined and enforced must always build up the ecclesial relations. 'Let all things be done for edification' (1 Cor. 14.26). This provides a theological touchstone against which to evaluate the exercise of power and other behaviours within the church. Are they cultivating generosity in the church's relations with God, the world, the wider body, and within each ecclesial community? And can these relational fruits be seen and tasted?

## Word, sacraments, ministry and disciplines

What then is the place of the word, sacraments (at least baptism and holy communion), ministry and disciplines such as spiritual habits, confessional statements and customs and rules? Are not some or all of these fundamental to the church, as theologians have typically believed? Again, this can be approached through the notion of gift. When you offer yourself to another in a marriage-type relationship, the identity of the self you give not only arises from the relationships in which you have been and are embedded, it is supported by certain behaviours and beliefs. You draw on various forms of learning, engage in certain 'rituals' like regular exercise, are guided by the views of your favourite celebrities and structure your life around a host of beliefs and routines. All these are influenced by the marriage and shape your contributions to it.

The church's gift of its self is not dissimilar. The gift comprises the four overlapping sets of ecclesial relations, and also four essential types of practice that grow out of these relationships and contribute to them. Theologians have long talked about the *esse* of the church, the church's essence. But could there be as it were two *esses* – the essence of the gift and what is essential for the gift to flourish? Perhaps we should say that the church's *esse* comprises both the four interlocking sets of relationships that are the *essence* of the church, and four necessary types of practice –

the word, sacraments, ministry and disciplines, which are the *essentials* of the church.

Given the common linguistic grounding of the two words, the distinction between essence and essential may seem strained. Yet being essential to something need not be the same as being the essence of it. A referee is essential to a soccer match but is not the essence of the game. A marriage contract is essential to be legally married but is not the essence of union. An annual general meeting is legally necessary for a charity but is not the essence of the charity's work. A chalice is essential for the wine to be distributed but is not the essence of what is shared. So claiming that the word, sacraments, ministry and disciplines are not the essence of the church does not mean they are inessential. They are as necessary as the chalice for the distribution.

## *The essentials*

That is because they are gifts through the Spirit to enable the church's essence, the four sets of ecclesial relationships, to share in Christ's generosity. The essentials are channels through which the Holy Spirit brings Jesus into the ecclesial relations and draws the latter, through Christ, into the trinitarian life. By means of the essentials, Christ is received in individual hearts: 'The sermon spoke to me'; 'Jesus came to me in my devotions.' However, recipients' inner lives are not plucked from the web of relationships in which they dwell. Even when people are on their own, they still think about these relationships and how they play out in specific situations. Thus when people experience Christ, they do so in mental landscapes criss-crossed by their church connections. The essentials mediate Christ not to solo individuals, but to relational persons.

When this happens, the essentials become *instruments* for flavouring the ecclesial relationships with divine generosity. The word, sacraments, ministry and disciplines empower Christians to receive Jesus and walk with him day by day. In the process believers are fashioned in Christ's likeness, transforming their competitive egos into generous selves. Members of the congregation are equipped to give to God directly, the world, the wider church and to one another while striding through life. Just as the chalice is a channel for the wine, the essentials – the church's relational ties – are channels for God's generosity.

More than that, the essentials are *sites* where generosity in the four sets of ecclesial relations can be directly experienced. Most obviously, God is encountered in the word and the sacraments, through Spirit-filled leaders who mediate Christ to others, and through spiritual disciplines.

Second, believers are brought into the presence of all the saints when they are drawn to Christ, and this presence is made tangible in the witness of the tradition through the sacraments, the exposition of Scripture, the godly leadership of ministers who pass on the church's heritage, and in spiritual rhythms tested and adapted down the centuries. Third, the faithful encounter the world through the generous eyes of the Spirit when they are led by Christly ministers, lay their lives before God in the sacraments, hear the word and in their personal devotions. Gathering around the word, sacraments, divinely called leaders and shared spiritual habits can bring the congregation together in mutual generosity.

Indeed, might it be said that the essentials are not just instruments and sites, they are *prerequisites* for the church? A feature of many 'essentials' is that they precede 'essences'. A chalice is on the altar before being filled with wine; the match does not start till the referee blows the whistle. They are *pre*requisites: they have to be present before the activity can start. Likewise, just as the chalice makes the distribution possible, the word, sacraments, godly ministers and spiritual disciplines, such as meeting regularly, make the church possible. They gather people around Christ. As this happens, people encounter Christ directly in prayer, study and worship, they are drawn through him into the whole communion of saints, they join God's mission to the world and they form relationships within the congregation. If the church is a creature of the word, made present by the Eucharist, enabled by its ministry and sustained by its disciplines, clearly it would not exist without these essentials. Might we say that it is not just the Eucharist that makes the church (in de Lubac's famous phrase)? The word, leadership and disciplines, they too make the church by bringing the ecclesial relations into existence and imbuing them with Christ's beneficence.

Few theologians would challenge the central role of sacraments, word, ministry and disciplines. But Christians have debated whether particular practices belong to the very essence of the church (the church would not be the church without them). For example, the Reformers were not always clear or agreed whether discipline to maintain the church's order was part of the fundamental being of the church or existed for the health of the church. Anglicans have a similar debate over the place of bishops. Roman Catholics see the Eucharist as indispensable to the church's being, while the Salvation Army is thought to take a different view.

Might the concept of essentials help bridge these divides? Just as the wine cannot be shared without the chalice nor is its nature defined by the chalice, the four essentials are necessary for the church but in themselves do not define it. The church could not exist without certain disciplines such as maintaining order, or without some form of leadership such as bishops or elders, or without sacraments such as baptism and Eucharist,

## WHAT IS THE GIFT? THE CHURCH'S NATURE

or without the word, but these practices do not describe the essence of the church. Might 'essentials' provide common ground between Christians who see certain practices as intrinsic to the church's being and those who see them as good for the church but not part of its defining nature? Could both sides meet in an essential middle?

From an ecumenical perspective, it may be more helpful to stress the interdependence of the four types of essentials rather than to argue for the supremacy of any one. The word is heard during the Eucharist, through guidance, teaching and encouragement by church leaders and during the disciplines of personal study and devotions. The sacraments are animated by the word, their celebration is overseen by ministers and they flow into people's lives through such disciplines as gathering regularly, eucharistic adoration, and adherence to core Christian beliefs. Leaders minister the word, celebrate the sacraments and nurture spiritual disciplines. Disciplines are inspired by the word, fed by the sacraments and supported by ministers. When the essentials are so deeply entwined with each other, does it make sense to elevate any category above the rest?

### Faithful to the tradition?

Distinguishing essence from essentials is not how theologians have usually described the church. Yet it is true to the instincts of the tradition. Taking our cue from the New Testament, the essentials can be seen as gifts from God to edify the church. 1 Corinthians 11.30 warns that the Lord's Supper (a gift from the Lord – v. 23) must not be celebrated unworthily lest it damage the church (the opposite of building it up). Ephesians 4.11–12 describes apostles, prophets, evangelists, pastors and teachers, all leaders in different ways, as gifts from Christ for building up the body. Timothy 3.16 declares that Scripture (which is given by God – 'God-breathed') is useful for the church. Hebrews 10.25 urges believers to be disciplined in meeting together for their encouragement, which again has the idea of building up the congregation. Seeing the essentials as necessary for growing the ecclesial relationships flows naturally from Scripture.

Recent ecumenical statements have viewed the essentials in similar terms. *The Church: Towards a common vision* describes baptism, Eucharist and other rites as means by which the Holy Spirit 'equips those who receive the sacraments with a variety of gifts for the edification of the Church and its mission in and for the world' (WCC, 2013a, §44). Soon after, it quotes the ecumenical text, *Baptism, Eucharist and Ministry*: ordained ministers 'may appropriately be called priests because they fulfil a particular priestly service by strengthening and building up the royal and prophetic priesthood

## GIVING THE CHURCH

of the faithful through word and sacraments, through their prayers of intercession, and through their pastoral guidance of the community' (§45).

Earlier, it refers to the substantial agreement of Christians concerning the Nicene Creed. A confessional statement publicly professed as a liturgical discipline, the Creed helps churches recognize fidelity to the gospel in themselves and others (§39). A previous report concluded that the Bible 'is a critical court of appeal to which the church must constantly defer'.[3] Though not the only source of authority, Scripture is to guide the church in following Christ. Eucharist (sacraments), Ministers (leadership), Creed (disciplines) and Scripture (the word) are the bricks that build the church's relationships on the foundations of Jesus. Just as a building needs walls, the ecclesial relationships cannot stand tall without the ecclesial essentials. Both are required for the church to be the church.

More generally, the essentials belong to the broad stream of reflection on ecclesial mediation. Though Christ is the sole mediator between God and humanity (1 Tim. 2.5), as his body the church shares in the outworking of his mediating role. In his sermon on the means of grace, John Wesley (1988, II.2) claimed that God works supremely through the sacraments, searching the Scriptures and prayer (which, in the form of private prayer for example, is a discipline). To this can be added other disciplines, such as rules and customs ordering the church, and the priestly role of leadership, which includes representing God to the people. The essentials are channels of grace that build up the four sets of ecclesial relationships by mediating the generous God to them. They fulfil this role by being instruments, sites and prerequisites that bring divine generosity into the church's essence. In this they do not add anything to grace. They are the manner in which the church receives grace. Just as you might hold out your hands to accept a present, so the church opens its hands to God in the sacraments, in prayerful study of the word, in sharing Christ's leadership, and in its rules, rhythms and credal statements.

### Both ... and

As means that breathe divine life into the ecclesial relations, the essentials are special. They are vital to Christ's body with its unique role in God's purposes. So they do not sit on the same level as the Spirit's means outside the church. On the other hand, they are not so special as to rule out means of grace in the world; God's presence and work are not limited to the church. Likewise, the essentials are not to be seen as a junior partner to the church's essence, lacking authority to challenge the church's relationships. If that was so, they would not be enablers of the relation-

## WHAT IS THE GIFT? THE CHURCH'S NATURE

ships. Equally, they are not to stand on a podium, lording it over the church's essence. That would release the relational handcuffs on bad practice and open the door to abuse.

Rather than competing for supremacy, the essence and the essentials need each other. Sacraments, word, ministry and disciplines furnish the ecclesial relationships with *content* (relationships form when people do things together), while the relationships supply the essentials with *context* (people do things together when relationships form). Both comprise the ontology – the being – of the church; when we see the four sets of ecclesial relationships *and* the four types of essential practice, we see the church. Might this help elucidate the connection between relationships and practices? The church is a 'mystical communion' whose four over-lapping sets of relationships share in Christ's generosity by means of four essential types of practice.

In making this claim, we must hold Christ and the Spirit together. The Spirit joins the body to the head by means of the essentials, seasoning the church's essence with the self-giving of Jesus. The church is the body of Christ, but its life is the breath of the Spirit. The church's lasting identity depends on Christ, but its daily existence relies on the Spirit. By infusing Christ's self-giving into the ecclesial relationships via the essentials, the Spirit creates a communion in which, at its best, giving is so abundant that it borders on the superfluous – 'I'll give you more than you can ever expect.' So when the church is given to the world, what is offered is a gift whose fundamental character is generosity – a giving gift.

Yet we should never forget that the church is contaminated by sin, which represents the refusal of God's people to receive and 'use' the essentials. Despite this refusal, word, sacraments, ministry and disciplines never lose their capacity to mediate the divine. Their potential as means of grace does not depend on human goodness. The Spirit can break through sin to create an environment in which the Christian community feels brokenhearted for its failures, recognizes its limited generosity and allows its relationships to be remade in Christ's self-giving image. The ongoing struggle between this sanctifying work and human sinfulness means that the church is forever a mixed blessing to the world – a ruin compared to what God intends, but a glorious ruin because traces of divine generosity remain.

## Discernment

Within a church, denomination or network, rules and customs determine which disciplines are prioritized, how leaders are authorized, how the sacraments are celebrated and which authorities govern the interpreta-

## GIVING THE CHURCH

tion of Scripture (from the Roman Catholic Dicastery for the Doctrine of the Faith to evangelicals' favourite Christian writers). Even when these formal and informal boundaries are tightly drawn, practices may vary considerably. Differences are even greater in an ecumenical context, where a much wider range of possibilities exist (and are in dispute). If the church's essence is the four overlapping sets of relationships with God directly, the world, the wider church and within each ecclesial community and if the church's essentials are the word, sacraments, ministry and disciplines, might we describe variations in the essentials as the *bene esse* of the church?

This term has traditionally referred to practices that are for the good of the church, as against those that comprise the essence – the *esse* – of the church. But given my distinction between the church's essence and essentials, might *bene esse* be repurposed to describe the form the essentials take? When we survey the myriad practices of God's people, whether desirable or not, there is clearly a discretionary element in what practices count as essential (especially in the case of disciplines), the weight attached to each and how the practice is performed. Confessional statements, for example, are a discipline, but might which one (the Nicene Creed or otherwise), the degree of importance attached to it, and how it is acknowledged belong to the church's *bene esse*? *Bene esse* would keep its traditional concern for the church's welfare, but be redefined as the composition, place and nature of the essentials – how the essentials are practised for the health of church. The essentials are necessary, but their form is discretionary.

Some Christians will complain that this pays insufficient attention to tradition, leaving too much up for grabs. However, this objection has less force if we think about the ecumenical boulevard on which the different traditions promenade their views. Obviously Christians differ about which practices they value, the significance attached to each and how the practice is performed. Disagreements over such issues (debates about the church's *bene esse*) need not mean that the practice *should* be discretionary. That is what's in dispute. *Bene esse* simply recognizes that Christians approach these matters differently, which should encourage believers to be humble about their claims.

### Balanced discernment

How, then, should the church discern essentials that are good for the Christian community? This is about what is known as 'reception'.[4] In this context, it is about a gathering receiving the essentials from the wider

## WHAT IS THE GIFT? THE CHURCH'S NATURE

church and prayerfully discovering how the latter can best serve the ecclesial relationships in that setting. The essentials are given by the church at large and the community receives them in its own way. This giving and receiving, the heart of reception, necessarily involves the direct relationship with God, whose Spirit gives insight, knowledge and prophecy for this purpose; so too with the wider church, which passes on the essentials and wisdom about how they should be performed; so also relations with the world, since the essentials should be expressed in ways that support the community's mission; so, further, relationships within the community as members prayerfully discuss what the essentials should look like.

We can see these four sets of relationships at work in the Acts 15 Council of Jerusalem, which met to discuss the admission of Gentiles to the church. The gathering listened directly to God in Scripture (vv. 15–18) and through promptings of the Spirit (v. 28). They paid attention to the Jewish believers, who comprised the wider church, by involving the whole Jerusalem church in the final decision (v. 22). They listened to the world through the experiences of Peter and of Barnabas and Paul, who represented the precipitating missional context (vv. 7–12). And through 'much discussion' they listened to each other (v. 7). There is no evidence that the apostles and elders gave more weight to one set of relationships than the others, which may come as a surprise. We might have expected them to prioritize Scripture, for example. But when James 'spoke up' (v. 13), he interpreted the prophets (vv. 15–18) in the light of the missional situation (vv. 12, 14, 19), with an eye to the concerns of Jewish believers (vv. 20–21), and as part of a collective process of discernment – 'it seems good ... to *us*' (v. 28; see v. 22).

In general, giving precedence to one set of ecclesial relations risks discernment being foreclosed too quickly. By defaulting rapidly to a conclusion based on the view of the wider church or 'our' congregation or the needs of the context, the discussion rejects a solution acceptable in *all* the relationships. It threads a needle with one strand rather than four, yet the latter produces a stronger result. Discernment is an *ecclesial* activity because it should be shared with others in the Christian community and be undertaken in dialogue with the wider church, the missional context and God directly. The process looks different in different situations, but it invariably requires much patience, a spiritual fruit (Gal. 5.22).

Rather than expecting a perfect equilibrium, balanced discernment is an ideal that can correct lopsided approaches. A parent congregation, for instance, might hope to broaden its tent by birthing a new community that inherits its practices. But ecclesial discernment might challenge that assumption. In the context of listening to God in prayer, worship and study, the expectations of the congregation would be balanced by the demands of the missional setting, the views of the new community and the experience of the wider church. The outcome might be a new community in a different style of tent. Equally, the community could not strike out on its own, ignoring 2,000 years of wisdom. The church at large would provide another voice.[5]

Here then is a framework for missional discernment, whose importance has been recognized in a number of ecumenical statements. 'Discernment is the core practice of the missional church' (Niemandt, 2012, p. 6). Missional discernment, which starts by asking how the church can be a generous presence in the world and then explores what form that presence should take, needs theological bones to avoid being too abstract. That structure is the church's four overlapping sets of relationships, each jockeying for an equal voice.

## Disagreement – relationships first?

This framework does not of course guarantee agreement. Indeed, the church can be described as 2,000 years of argument! And often very useful argument. As in the early centuries, disagreement can play a positive role in clarifying what God's people believe. Disagreement, often acrimonious, can also be the price of the Spirit's guidance into new terrains – new types of ministry among new people, for example. Yet, as Ephraim Radner emphasizes (2012), even the most robust procedural framework cannot guarantee that debate brings unity and truth as part of God's own giving. Processes and structures can provide a context in which unity and truth sometimes prevail, but human limitations mean that all too often error and division scorch the ecclesial earth.

Radner points out that church divisions are often couched in terms of unity versus truth. Which must be sacrificed: unity (either agreeing or going along with the other's opinion) or truth (standing firm on a principle)? However, Radner argues that this is a false polarity. 'What is the truth of the gospel?' he asks. At heart, it is that while we were still enemies Christ died for us (Rom. 5.10). The gospel truth that transcends all other truths is that Jesus has crossed over to the side of his opponents. Radner suggests that this should be the habit of Christians when they disagree with each other. They should stand their ground, which integrity demands, while finding ways to stand also on the other's ground. This is not foreign to our everyday experience. When we disagree, it is common to acquiesce in the other's view for the sake of the relationship; we decide not to make the difference an issue. Standing with your 'enemy' in the midst of a bitter dispute takes this practice much further.[6]

## WHAT IS THE GIFT? THE CHURCH'S NATURE

Solidarity may involve acknowledging the worst the person has said or done, but also (with their permission) standing by the better side of that person where God is present too. Radner quotes a Rowan Williams story from the Desert Fathers about a monk, Makarios the Great, who,

> at the monastic gathering where another monk is being quite properly disciplined, rises up and leaves with him. Makarios, with the others, condemns rightly – the monk in question has truly sinned; but Makarios must also follow, for who accompanies the condemned and expelled sinner? 'That too is a challenge of unity,' Williams notes. For that is 'where Jesus is and has gone' and thus where also the Church is being borne, that is, to the godless, even the godless within the Church's own nominal membership. (Radner, 2012, pp. 444–5)

By attaching such importance to relationships, Radner is breathing the same air as my emphasis on the four overlapping sets of ecclesial relations. In the midst of disagreement about practices these relationships must be preserved, especially if they are the church's essence. To destroy any of these relationships would be to destroy one corner of the church. We may disagree about how the essentials can best nourish the relationships and our disagreement may well impair the edifying work of the essentials, but so long as our dispute does not actually sever the ecclesial relations it will not threaten Christ's body itself. When practices or doctrines are contested, the ecclesial relationships together provide a yardstick of what is ultimately important to the Christian community. In wearing its debates lightly (as far as possible), the church wears its relational heart on its sleeve.

Think of Paul's advice on eating meat offered to idols. Love was to be the guiding principle (1 Cor. 8.9–13). On the same basis, emphasizing relationships will encourage differences to be discussed with kindness and generosity. Disagreement will be framed by the need to maintain health not just in one set of ecclesial relations but in all four. And as these relationships are defended, as some sort of fellowship within them is maintained, people in dispute will be kept within the Christian family. However wayward their views, they will still be connected to God directly, to the wider church, to others within the particular community, and to the world.

Of course, relations with the wider church can be preserved as *ecclesial* relationships only if the whole church views those involved as part of the Christian community. If the rest of the people judge the disputants' beliefs or behaviour to be beyond the pale of church, the wider-church relationship will inevitably be ruptured. However, Radner's argument encourages Christians to be generously slow to reach that conclusion, and then to stand alongside the other as one who is outside the church but still much loved by God. In that way they can demonstrate to observers the relational truth of the gospel. At the same time, through the ecclesial relationships and the practices embedded in them, we may pray that the Spirit will draw battling partners together and enable a common mind perhaps eventually to emerge.

## Implications

This chapter has X-rayed the skeleton that gives communal shape to Christ's body. The essence (*esse*) of the Christian community given to others, as part of the church's entire life of generosity, is four overlapping sets of relationships: with God directly in prayer, study and worship, with the world, with the wider church, and within each ecclesial community. The Spirit brings the self-giving Christ into these relationships by means of the essentials of word, sacrament, ministry and disciplines (the *essentialia*). These are indispensable because they feed the relationships with Christ's generosity. What the essentials comprise and how they are expressed belong to the well-being – the *bene esse* – of the church. To discern the latter, as far as possible all four sets of relationships should have equal weight. Thus when the church is offered to others in thanks for grace, what should be given is a combination of ecclesial relationships, the essentials and the ecclesial process of discernment. Together, they are the earthly shape of communion in Christ, a communion that brings recipients into the life of the Trinity.

This has implications, first, for a tension in mission theology: how can the church be God's instrument of mission – a vehicle for social justice, making disciples and so forth – without being reduced to a means to an end? If the church as means is elevated, the church as the goal of mission – communion in Christ to which all are invited – risks receding from view. This is a particular danger in the church-growth model of church planting, where preaching, the rest of worship and other aspects of the new congregation's life are often seen as mere paths to an evangelistic goal.

In contrast, this chapter emphasizes that all the ecclesial relations are equally important. People are invited into relationships with God directly, with the wider church and within the particular community not because these relationships serve the church's relations with the world, but as ends in themselves. All four relationships together are the gift. It follows that the Christian community is both the means and the goal of mission. As one aspect of the church's generosity, the relationships are

## WHAT IS THE GIFT? THE CHURCH'S NATURE

offered in the form of new Christian communities (means), but within these communities they are enjoyed for themselves (the goal). Mission has an ecclesial destination.

Second, this account of the church helps address a very live issue in mission circles: how to contextualize the Christian faith. In relation to the church, for example, what can change to fit the culture and what must stay the same? Now, when church plants replicate an existing congregation, the question scarcely arises. But in post-Christian contexts, where inherited forms of church seem increasingly irrelevant and more contextually diverse shapes of church are now emerging, the question is more acute. My bare bones answer is that what must stay the same is the presence of the four sets of ecclesial relationships, the quintessence of church. No community can be a fully *Christian* community without them. What must also always be present are the four essentials – word, sacraments, ministry and disciplines. Through the Spirit, these are necessary for the essence to flower with generosity. Within a tradition's understanding of the essentials, however, what can change are the practices that are included, the significance attached to them and how they are expressed. These belong to the well-being rather than the intrinsic nature of the church. One hand can fit a multitude of gloves.

How far these gloves can differ will remain contested. But could a benchmark be lurking that contributes to the debate? Might leaders and congregations ask for evidence that the essentials really are building up the ecclesial relations? When they look for testimonies of this, are they satisfied with what they hear? If not, what might be the reasons? Ample ways exist, including ethnographic studies, to seek answers by consulting the congregation and people outside. Against fears that this could be a slippery road to 'theology-lite' pragmatism, shorn of wisdom from previous generations, one can ask: if Christ has given word, sacraments, ministry and disciplines to deepen the ecclesial relationships in godly generosity, should not the results be capable of empirical validation? And if the results are fewer or smaller than the Christian community might reasonably expect, might this not suggest – at least as a possibility – that practices comprising these essentials need more thorough contextualization?

Third, this chapter helps to recognize when an ecclesial sapling has grown into church, either a new congregation attached to an existing one or a new church in its own right connected to the whole. This was not a problem when church planting reproduced an existing form of church. The public launch of the new congregation could coincide with its recognition. But the issue has become more complicated today in situations where people outside the church have been listened to, have gathered around a shared interest or common concern and – at least for some –

73

have begun intentionally to journey towards Christ. This could be an intergenerational church based on craft, a cafe church for patients of a medical practice, or a dinner church arising from a food parlour. In such cases, the journey to 'being church' is more ill-defined. Often there is no clear-cut launch of the congregation. The new Christian community emerges imperceptibly, perhaps recognized only when participants surprise the leaders by calling it 'my church'.

But is this church as understood by the wider Christian community? Drawing on this chapter, might we say that new ecclesial communities lacking any of the church's four defining sets of relationships are 'on their way to being church'? Communities that have begun to grow in these four sets of relations but have yet to embrace all four essentials might be described as 'beginning to be church'. They are paddling in the shallow end of the church, where ecclesial grace extends to those involved.[7] As communities wade further into the deeper end and embrace all the essentials, they will be 'fully church' (though perhaps not mature church). They will receive more abundant ecclesial grace, be empowered to express the church more completely, and be drawn more strongly towards the coming kingdom. Progressive recognition – more and more rather than either/or – would affirm the community on its journey and encourage members to keep pressing on.

## Notes

1 See the discussion of this in Chapter 6.

2 Rowan Williams, 'Christian Identity and Religious Pluralism', Address to World Council of Churches Assembly, Porto Alegre, 17 February 2006.

3 'The Authority of the Bible' in *Faith and Order, Louvain 1971. Study Reports and Documents*, Geneva: WCC Faith and Order Paper No. 59, 1971, p. 21.

4 For an accessible introduction to notions of reception, see Rusch, 2007.

5 Indeed, if balanced weight is given to the church's tradition, describing the content and nature of the essentials as the church's *bene esse* may not leave practices as open as some may fear.

6 This bald summary of Radner needs obvious qualification. For example, failing to make an issue of disagreement is not desirable if it cements unhealthy power dynamics and allows a dominant person to keep getting their own way, perhaps reinforcing an abusive relationship. Clearly, there are some difficult conceptual and practical issues here which cannot be treated in the space available. How unhealthy, for instance, can power dynamics be and these relationships remain legitimately part of the church?

7 For use of this metaphor, based on a case study, see Watkins and Shepherd, 2014.

# 3

# An Attractive Gift? The Four Marks

The Christian community is called to a life of generosity in thankfulness to God. As a particular aspect of this vocation, it is to join the Spirit in offering the church to others, in the form of new Christian communities, for the benefit of the world. Giving the church in this way expands the generosity of the Christian community by multiplying *all* the church's missional gifts. The last chapter began to describe the church that is given. God's people are a fourfold web of relationships, centred on the self-giving Christ; the Spirit builds up these relationships through four types of essential practice; and the content of these essentials is discerned through receiving and giving within the ecclesial relations.

But what might make the church as a gift attractive? This chapter suggests an answer based on the four historic and widely accepted marks of the church – one, holy, catholic and apostolic. Hans Küng (1967) and Jürgen Moltmann (1977) are among those in the last half century who have written most extensively on the marks. Both stress their missional dimension. Moltmann notably interprets the marks from his distinctive understanding of the church's mission, which is to side with the poor. This chapter adopts a similar methodology. It approaches the marks from a specific view of mission – mission as generosity, with a particular focus on giving away new Christian communities.

After discussing the purpose of the marks, the chapter describes the nature of each mark, the human resonance that can make the mark attractive to others, how the mark is present in the first instance when the church's generosity takes the form of new Christian communities, and how this presence can renew the church's internal life so that the Christian community becomes more lovable. The church need not first reform its internal life to become fit for mission, as some think. Rather, the process of giving can itself be a spur to reform, making the church a more welcome gift.

## The purpose of the marks

The offer of communion in Jesus should be a wonderful gift. As envisaged by God, the church's depth of unity should set it apart from other human groups. So should its likeness to God (its holiness). And too its diversity; no other community seeks to include the whole of humanity. So also should its cherished traditions, which are distinctive in their historical ties to Jesus. These are the four marks of the church – one, holy, catholic and apostolic. They emerged in the Nicene creed in the year AD 325, and after further discussion were ratified at Chalcedon in 451. Encrusted in the church's credal history, they cannot be lightly set aside. But they have been understood variously – as defining the church (but how, when their nature is disputed?); as criteria distinguishing the true from the false church (but doesn't this allow one church to use the criteria against another, which undermines the mark of unity?); and as identifiers of God's reign in the world – wherever we see the kingdom, we see the church (but if Jesus is not explicitly acknowledged, is not the church construed too widely?).

Building on the last chapter, my suggestion is that the marks are signposts for God's people to steer by. They do not define the church; the four overlapping sets of ecclesial relationships do that. Nor are they means by which these relationships flourish; the four essential types of practice bear that responsibility. The marks serve as a health check. Is the gift being made attractive? Perhaps better, they are a diagnostic tool. Where is the church going wrong? Possibly better still, they are a summons, a call to the church to be made an appealing gift. The marks give direction to the essentials. As such, they guide the church away from much that makes it unattractive – its factionalism, the abuse and other impurities scratched across its surface, its exclusiveness (like barring certain types of people from leadership), and all too often its inward rather than outward focus.

One, holy, catholic and apostolic propel the church in a heathy direction because, as with the entirety of the church's life, they derive from Christ. It is Christ who draws people to himself in unity, who is the embodiment of holiness, who is catholic because he is the representative of all humanity, and who is apostolic because he was sent by the Father and sends us. Being equally rooted in Christ, the marks should have equal status in the church. One is not to be applauded more than another. As is often pointed out, the marks feed in and out of, and strengthen, each other.

Rowan Williams once said that to see the origins of the marks in Christ liberates us from any idea that they 'are either characteristics that we possess in our own right, or even goals that we can plan for.' They are gifts to be received.[1] But equally they are a task. They must be made a

## AN ATTRACTIVE GIFT? THE FOUR MARKS

reality in the church's life. Gift and task should be held together. As Küng points out, the marks

> May exist in such a way that they are no longer seen to be convincing from outside, perhaps not even from inside ... Unity, holiness, catholicity, and apostolicity are therefore not only gifts, granted to the Church by God's grace, but at the same time tasks which it is vital for the Church to fulfil in a responsible way. (Küng, 1967, p. 268)[2]

Indeed, it is in the nature of gifts that they give rise to tasks. Recipients must do something to activate the gift, whether unwrapping it, following the instructions on how to use it, or driving to a class to enjoy the gift, say, of woodwork lessons. These tasks do not create the gift, nor would they be performed if the gift did not exist. They are the process of receiving the gift. Think of a gift of Lego, where the gift lies in building the model. If you like, the relational essence of the church is the model and the four types of essentials are the bricks, without which the model cannot be built. A third element also helps, a picture on the box that moves you to make the model and shows you what it might be like. The marks are that third ingredient. They inspire and guide the essentials in deepening the relationships that comprise the church.

Yet can the model ever match the picture on the box? Given the church's sinfulness, are we not talking about battered, second-hand pieces of Lego, some of which are missing? On this side of eternity, are not the marks ideals to be striven for rather than pristine realities today? Moltmann suggests that the marks are fully received at the end of time but seep into the present. The church receives the marks 'in the workings of the Spirit for the coming kingdom' (Moltmann, 1977, p. 338). In the murkiness of life, they are billboards of faith and hope in God's promise of a new communal existence. They are a living tableau, however sketchy, of God's future.[3]

## One

Through the Spirit, Christ brings into the church something of the Godhead's unity. In Moltmann's language, 'Christ gathers his church. Consequently the unity of the church lies in his uniting activity' (Moltmann, 1977, p. 338). Central to this activity is Christ's giving of himself. His reconciliation of all things to himself through the cross (Col. 1.20) speaks of connection. Christians are connected to each other as part of the connectedness that Christ brings to all creation. The mark, therefore, appeals to humanity's deep-seated need for attachment – to feel close to others and through this closeness to feel loved, cared for and valued. It summons the church to be a family whose members feel secure in their relations with one another and with their heavenly Father. Without stifling the individual, the church's unity resonates with a baby's longing for intimacy with its mother, marriage partners to be one and friends for companionship. The mark's attractiveness lies in echoing this instinct to avoid separation.

However, Christians have struggled to reconcile this mark with the brutal knots of hostility within and sometimes between denominations. Some Roman Catholics have responded by declaring that theirs is the only observable church entitled to be known as the true church – an institutional oneness. By contrast, a Platonic approach sharply distinguishes between the visible divided church and the church invisibly united, as if there were two churches (which would hardly meet the challenge of unity!). A more common eschatological view suggests that present divisions in the church will be abolished when Christ returns. For Moltmann and others, instances of unity in today's church are pointers to God's reconciling reign.

Küng emphasizes that self-giving is the pathway to solidarity within the church (Küng, 1967, pp. 289, 293). Just as Christ gave himself so that he could become one with humanity, members of the church must give themselves to one another to become united. This self-giving will be the offering not of unhealed broken selves who collude with an abusive situation, but of secure selves experiencing God's restorative grace within and through the Christian community. This self-giving is itself a gift – the gift of a pure heart. 'What does "pure in heart" mean if it is not the heart concerned about others? What does it mean if it is not the heart that motivates the personalities of all of us to dance together?' (Koyama, 1979, p. 27). Though the desire to tango and the moves are given by the Spirit, to receive these gifts the church must get on the dance floor.

## Unity in the church's external life

It would be natural to think that we should first look for this unity in the church's internal life. But Moltmann points out that the church's call to stand with people who suffer can and perhaps should cause internal friction. Siding with the oppressed against the powerful may be played out in conflicts within the church (Moltmann, 1977, pp. 345–7). In a classic example, when some Christians gave themselves to abolish slavery, a price was paid in the church's harmony; Christians took different sides.

Yet no one today would deny the price was worth paying. The logic is that mission can trump internal unity.

If we follow this logic and prioritize the church's outside rather than inside life, could the church's generosity to others be a sphere in which to see evidence of unity? In a sense, of course, in whatever way they give to others all parts of the Christian community share in a common manner of life that derives from Christ. The church is one in its giving, despite the variety of forms this giving takes. However, when – as a particular aspect of this generosity – the church gives in the shape of new Christian communities, the church's unity is displayed in a fuller way. Despite all the examples of competitive and divisive church planting, at root the church is one because every congregation and every denomination was originally a piece of the one body 'broken for you'. As Christianity snowballed across Europe and later across the world, new churches and monasteries were 'broken off' from the existing church and offered to non-believers. The process reflected the church as it is meant to be – a communion that is given to others for the benefit of the world.

True, new congregations have not always been gifts to people beyond. Many have been breakaways from the existing church to express their faith more purely. 'Each [new denomination or Church] is now a grown-up and self-sufficient daughter, who thinks there were very good reasons why she could no longer put up with living at home with mother' (Küng, 1967, pp. 307–8). Despite leaving home, these churches are still within the Christian family.[4] And they remain united by their common origin in the self-donating history of the Christian community. This history has a spatial element: the church has spread out to new areas and new people. It also has a temporal dimension; through a sequence of self-giving, all parts of the body have an unbroken lineage stretching back to the first community around Jesus. Thus, however it came into existence, no congregation, denomination or Church can deny that it is an offshoot of the one tree planted in Israel's soil at Jerusalem. No Christian community can escape the reality that in some way, at some stage, it has its origins in the church being given to others, starting at Pentecost.

Of course, other organizations can claim a similar unity. Starbucks cafes around the world can trace their descent from the original in Seattle. What differentiates the church is that its oneness is founded not on millions of commercial contracts, as between Starbucks and its customers, but on gift – on the self-donation of Christ. Through the gift of himself, motivated not by profit, power or prestige but by sacrificial love, Jesus brought to birth a communion whose self-giving to the world includes drawing others into his life. The church is an explosion not of shards but of fractals, each bearing the image of Christ.

Here then is a tangible sign of Christian unity. Beyond all the church's divisions, the spatial and temporal self-giving of new Christian communities offers a glimpse of the church's unity in Christ. Multiplication is the single trunk on which the whole church grows. So we should not relegate this mark to the unseen church. We should recognize its presence, however dimly, in the church's two millennia of mission. Moreover, by drawing people from diverse backgrounds into a single body, the mark's presence in the church's outreach creates opportunities to weld motley people into a harmony, to match a union of origin in the church with a union of life inside the church. Valuing this first mark in the church's mission will encourage believers to make it a reality within the Christian community. Thereby the gospel's hope of reconciliation will be displayed to a fragmented world.

## Internal unity

A first step towards internal unity is to recognize that while churches have their origins in common, commonality is not the deepest form of union. Plenty of families with shared genes feel emotionally divided. So to produce a stronger unity, just as self-giving can create solidarity with people outside the church, self-giving must entrench solidarity within the Christian community. This will not happen top down or bottom up, but side-by-side. It will be a unity of mutual indwelling, as top and bottom and groups in the middle reach out to each other, enter into one another's lives and identify with the other through reciprocal generosity. For this to occur, connections must be strengthened between different parts of the body, so that ties of mutual giving can bind people together.

Just as the Son gave himself utterly to become one with humanity, so God's people individually and in groups will donate themselves healthily to one another. They will put themselves in each other's shoes, see things from the other's standpoint and identify with the other person's thoughts and actions. Mutual indwelling is about getting inside people's heads, giving your thoughts, imagination and feelings over to the other person so that you can think, imagine and feel from that person's vantage point. This requires structures that do not impede relationships but lay a path for the Spirit to foster behaviours (especially towards Christians you disagree with) such as careful listening, the confession of guilt, the offer of forgiveness and the exchange of appropriate gifts.

As with each of the marks, all four sets of ecclesial relations should be involved. Every relationship must be notable for the oneness that is achieved through turn-and-turn-again generosity.[5] When this happens, the unity discernible in the church's giving of new Christian communities will have its deeper counterpart in the internal life of the church. And this will help to make the body of Christ more attractive. As is frequently pointed out, bitter quarrels damage the church's reputation and drain energy from serving people outside. Conversely, being at one with each other can help church members feel secure, cared for and appreciated. The gift becomes more credible to others and so it can be more easily offered and accepted. This first mark pencils unity on the outside of the church. Then, as an inspiration for unity within, it erases divisiveness inside the Christian community.

## Holy

At its most basic, holiness is about separation. Küng notes that the Old Testament word implies 'a distinguishing and dividing of what is profane and impure from what is pure. It implies a separation for God's service; pure things become holy by being removed from their profane usage and dedicated to God' (Küng, 1967, p. 324). Christ makes the church holy by setting it apart, marking it out as his own and justifying and sanctifying its members. This is a separation in character rather than space. Holiness lies in the church's godly life within, rather than apart from ordinary existence. It makes the church a diamond out-dazzling the glass around.

Holiness, therefore, is about distinctiveness – 'We are this community, not that.' And distinctiveness is the basis of human identity. From one evolutionary perspective, people form groups with those whom they instinctively believe will return favours. If others look and behave like us we assume they can be relied upon to reciprocate. So we do our best to fit in with them (Wright, 1996, pp. 189–209). Holiness thus resonates with a profound need to distinguish between people who are like us and those who are not, to feel safe with people we associate with, to feel comfortable with 'our kind of people'.[6] But this distinctiveness is developed in an explicitly Godward direction. The church's distinct identity lies in being aligned with God's unique identity. Holiness answers the question, 'Who are we?'

### Divine holiness

Although the four marks together make the church distinctive, holiness is the sun that lights up the other marks. This is because holiness refers to God's self-giving character, which lies behind all the marks. Of course God has other 'holy' attributes such as omniscience, wisdom and omnipotence. But knowledge, power and so on need not in themselves be expressions of holiness. Were fallen humans to write the script, these attributes would frequently be used selfishly. Yet in divine hands they combine to give God's self to others in love. *This* generosity is at the root of holiness. Love speaks of moving out towards the other person and giving them our attention, abilities, possessions and so forth. God's capacity for such love derives from the willingness of the trinitarian persons to go to inexhaustible lengths in offering themselves within and beyond the Godhead. And it derives also from the unlimited character of the power, knowledge, wisdom and other divine attributes that expand immeasurably God's ability to give. This boundless capacity to offer God's self makes divine generosity holy in the sense of being infinitely distinct from women and men, while also being shared with them.

The crown of divine holiness lies in the self-giving of Jesus, who gave himself in a manner totally different to our expectations of a human being. Despite the infinite power available to him, Jesus renounced power to achieve his objectives. Rather than using compulsion to rise above his circumstances, he deliberately allowed others to determine his fate, his death by crucifixion. This surrender ran counter to the entire trajectory of human experience, in which women and men seek the power to control their destinies. From scientific discovery to artistic exploration, human culture is largely driven by the desire to beat mortality or produce works that outlast death. Yet Jesus took a different course.

It might be objected that his resurrection was the triumphant assertion of divine control. Williams counters that, although it was an expression of power, it was not the *assertion* of power. Rather, it demonstrated the utter impossibility of reducing the creator of life to a permanent corpse (Williams, 2018, p. 242).[7] Moreover, Jesus died not for his friends but his enemies – 'While we were enemies we were reconciled to God' (Rom. 5.10). As St Paul points out, though it is conceivable that someone will die for a good person, it defies our human expectations that in Christ God would die for a sinner (vv. 7–8). Would victims sacrifice their lives to save their oppressor? Yet Jesus died for all his opponents. Uniquely, rather than asserting his authority he handed control to those against him.

What inspired Jesus' self-giving was not motives that would have bolstered his ego, such as to be liked or recognized. Instead of the anxiety-compelled giving of a fragile self, seeking esteem by pleasing others, Jesus acted out of a secure, undefended self. Thus his giving was altogether different to ours because behind our generosity is always a need we are protecting. A mother risks her life in saving her child to avoid the pain of

## The church's holiness

Now, if Jesus' self-giving exemplifies holiness on a different plane to the rest of humanity, in what sense can we speak of his body as holy? How can the church be a holy gift to the world when God's people are so manifestly full of sin? An obvious response is that the church is a defective gift, a blend of sinfulness and holiness. Yet if that is so, how are we to understand this combination? Is the church's holiness invisible, for example, so much a 'depth reality' (Koyama, 1979, p. 23) that it is hidden from view? Do we hold on to it by faith rather than seeing it in the church's earthly life?

Some have taken this view, claiming that the church itself cannot sin because it is the body of the sinless Christ. When the church is given to others, recipients receive the sinless church spiritually. They become members of the invisible pure church, which will be revealed in the last days. This could make the church a more acceptable gift because it remains intrinsically good, despite its packaging being as it were pockmarked and damaged by the church's custodians. But this draws too sharp a distinction between the true church, which we can't see, and the church we can. We may be less motivated to combat institutional sin because it is not occurring in the 'real' church. Moreover, because sin can be systemically ingrained, it *is* appropriate to speak of the church sinning. It accurately describes the reality we experience. This, however, leaves the challenge: in what sense are the sinless head and the sinful body connected? How can we hold them together?

Rewind to our Lego model. A gift from his parents, the child plans to display the completed model in his sister's bedroom as a gift to her. (The church is a gift from God for the benefit of the world.) But the boy works on the model intermittently, carelessly damages some of the pieces, scatters them over his sister's desk and leaves them there, turning what might have been a welcome gift into a nightmare. The Lego was given by a generous father, who helps the boy when asked. Inspired by his father, the boy himself from time to time has good intentions. But his lackadaisical approach prevents the model from being a vehicle of generosity. Perhaps later, prodded by his father, the boy completes the model and his sister (with relief!) receives the gift in her room. With his father's

GIVING THE CHURCH

help, the gift has become a means of generosity but in a limited manner; making the gift caused tension and some of the bits remain damaged. In the whole saga, goodness and imperfection existed side by side. Yet the boy's mistakes can be reflected upon and learnt from.

Somewhat similarly, divine holiness and human sinfulness co-mingle within the church. Sin contaminates the essential types of practice described in the last chapter, restricting their ability to build up the four overlapping sets of ecclesial relationships. Yet without being touched by sin, the Holy Spirit, who connects Christ to his body, restrains the sinful inclinations of the Christian community, inspires the church to reflect on its failures and calls the church to continuous repentance and reform. Despite manifold shortcomings in how the essentials are practised, the Spirit works through the word, sacraments, ministry and disciplines to sanctify the Christian community and through it the world beyond.[8] Holiness, the gift of self-giving, begins in this life but is fully present only when Christ returns.

### Where is the church's holiness?

If God's holy generosity thereby trickles through the church, where is it to be seen? Though it may be visible in splashes of self-giving within each of the ecclesial relationships, in the first instance we can glimpse it in the church's mission. After all, divine holiness is revealed in God's self-giving *to the world* – in God's dealings with Israel and in the life and death of the incarnate Son. As with unity, therefore, should we not expect the church's holiness to have a corresponding outward thrust, to be revealed in the church's whole range of generosity? Whenever the church shares its life and resources with people beyond its walls, it gives something of itself and thereby participates in the holiness of God.

This participation occurs especially when the church offers its very self, communion in Christ, in the form of new Christian communities. True, this giving may be deformed by impure motives, self-aggrandizing strategies and harmful outcomes. Yet amid this sinfulness is a self-donating activity that expresses fundamentally the self-giving nature of holiness. When the church gives its self to the world it may do so badly, but it is still giving its self. The impurities that accompany the church's self-donation, however extensive they may be, can never destroy the reality that the church is giving its self – communal life in Jesus – to others.

Put differently, however much it is corrupted by sin, offering new Christian communities has an orientation that will always correspond to the self-giving of Christ. By contrast, when Christians listen to the

# AN ATTRACTIVE GIFT? THE FOUR MARKS

word in an apathetic manner or receive the Eucharist in a perfunctory way, their indifference may limit their self-giving response to God and to others; without word or sacrament depending on worshippers' response, human self-absorption may block any meaningful giving of self to Christ and the world. But when Christians give themselves to people outside the church, however sinful their hopes and behaviour, they still enact a self-donating response to God. Whereas sin can prevent any self-giving to God or others in the Eucharist or in gathering round the word, once the movement of self-giving that is integral to mission has begun sin can never totally erase it. You can receive the bread and wine mechanically or hear the word unresponsively without offering yourself to Christ, but the church cannot be given away, however selfishly, without actually being passed on. Whereas the Eucharist and word are practices in which human self-giving can be relatively absent, fundamentally the church's self-donation is a practice that will always involve giving the church's self. Offering new Christian communities cannot be so sinful that it totally fails to echo Christ.

The self-donation that brings newcomers into the Christian community creates opportunities for them to share in the church's internal life of self-giving. They have access to the essentials – word, sacraments, ministry and disciplines – through which they are drawn into the self-giving of Christ. Rather like working back from God's missional holiness to infer the holiness of the Trinity's internal life, the church's self-giving to people outside the body 'works back' to converts' formation in self-giving within the church. This requires the Christian community to be under the essentials and the essentials under the Spirit; otherwise the transfusion of divine generosity is hindered and the joy of mutual giving becomes an ordeal. The more the Spirit dips every morsel of the church's life into Christ's generosity, the more the church becomes distinct from the world – separate not in its aloofness but in its lovingness. Holiness bathes the church in vibrant hues, making it a gift that others may be more likely to desire. Giving the church's self becomes a more attractive proposition.

## Catholic

This third mark has been understood in various ways. One is universality. The church is universal geographically (throughout the world), anthropologically (no one is rejected) and chronologically (it will continue for eternity). However, the oldest meaning, which has come to the fore in recent ecumenical discussions, is totality. Each congregation is an expression of the whole church. For Küng, catholicity is about 'The fact that

GIVING THE CHURCH

despite all the constant and necessary changes of the times and of varying forms, and despite its blemishes and weaknesses, the Church in every place and in every age remains unchanged in its essence, whatever form it takes' (Küng, 1967, pp. 300–1). However different it looks, each congregation still represents the whole church.

## Each piece is a whole

Congregations and denominations are not pieces of the church – incomplete on their own, but add them together and you get the one, universal church. That would mean the church could not be fully church everywhere. A new Christian community would be a mere toenail on the universal body. By contrast, the New Testament is clear that each household gathering is as much church as the city-wide assembly, just as the latter is as much church as the entire community of believers. 'Church' is used to describe them all, without any hint of different degrees of church. Every congregation that acknowledges Jesus as Lord is completely church because in Christ it is united with all other members of the body, past, present and future. Thus when the Christian community gathers around Christ through word and sacrament the whole church, unseen, shows up. However, this sense of totality cannot be divorced from the church's universality. To say that the whole church folds into each congregation assumes that a whole, a more universal church, exists in the first place.

Even though it represents the whole, a congregation cannot be fully church if it exists in isolation from other parts of the body. Just as a brother and sister express being family not only in their genetic code but in communicating with one another and in the manner in which they relate, so the fullness of the church lies in more than a congregation's ecclesial genes. It also exists in its visible relationships with other congregations and in the institutional forms these relationships take. Catholicity lies in the whole church's concentration in the particular congregation and in its visible extension across the congregations.

Catholicity, therefore, includes demographic breadth and diversity. It describes a church that welcomes a multitude of different people. If oneness speaks to emotional connectedness and holiness to having a distinct identity, catholicity has the idea of inclusion, of your particular group being made at home. As a generality, being included has all sorts of benefits, such as enabling the person to feel they belong, to participate and play a valued role in the community, to access economic and other resources, to develop relationships and friendships and to pursue an interest of their choice. It is a prerequisite for being one with others and finding your identity through them. Catholicity is therefore bound up with the first two marks and like them resonates with what it means to be human.

## Catholicity through multiplication

William Cavanaugh argues that though the normal condition of catholicity is diaspora, spreading out, the concentration of the whole body in the *local* church should be uppermost in the Christian community's imagination. This will counteract the wider church's homogenizing tendencies, which often dominate the congregation. In saying this, Cavanaugh claims that 'Catholicity is not dependent on extension through space' (Cavanaugh, 2003, pp. 114–16), which in one sense is true. The Jerusalem church was catholic – it was invisibly joined to all God's people – before it had begun to multiply. However, mission brought it into being. When the apostles burst on to the streets at Pentecost proclaiming the risen Christ, the variety of language speakers who responded anticipated the church's outward spread to a multiplicity of cultural groups.

While not wholly dependent upon it, catholicity nevertheless *arises from* 'extension through space'. In Moltmann's words, catholicity begins with 'the limitless lordship of Christ', from which the church derives its mission to the entire world (Moltmann, 1977, p. 338). Catholicity is possible only because the church represents an ever unfolding quilt of diversity, a patchwork of congregations in multiple places. In the first instance, therefore, as with the other marks, we should expect to see catholicity in mission. 'Catholic' is 'not an adjective describing the church's state; it is an attribute describing its movement, its mission and its hope' (Moltmann, 1977, p. 349). In moving out, the church exhibits none other than the openness of God's future society to every human group. This openness is demonstrated whenever the church reaches out to others in generosity. Whenever it shares its gifts with people outside its doors, the church displays to some degree a catholicity of spirit. Every gift is a statement of welcome to others. And the more varied the gifts, the more catholic, the more diverse, the church becomes in its generosity.

However, catholicity is expressed more fully when the church offers new Christian communities. These communities raise an ensign, visible to all, for God's all-inclusive reign. The whole becomes more universal – God's people are present in more places among more varied populations – when the church gives itself to others in the form of communion in Christ. Indeed, the more the church gives its self to others, the more catholic it will be. There will be a bigger 'whole', if you like, for each congregation to represent. This is especially the case when the church offers its self contextually. The church is most likely to be welcomed in new settings when the gift is given appropriately and so makes sense to its recipients.

The gift, therefore, must be indigenized. It must be received in the recipients' own way. Beatrice Bruteau suggests that God's self-giving love includes divine self-restraint, which opens up space for creation to be fully itself. Part of the divine gift is to let 'you be you' as each species contributes to sustaining the others. Every bit of creation enables another to flourish (Bruteau, 2018, p. 33). The church's self-donation joins this pattern of love when, as churches multiply, each too says to the others, 'Let you be you.' Without neglecting the dress sense of the wider church, recipients are invited to attire their communal life not in second-hand clothes passed on from the rest of God's people, but in customs, music, words and structures that authentically reflect who they are in their contexts. The more a group has unique blessings, the more it can offer distinctive gifts to others, the more varied the whole then becomes and the more the church can hum with the richness of diversity.[9] You cannot write a symphony with one note.

Such variety requires a balance between local congregations, which may be tempted to turn in on themselves and ignore the church at large, and the universal church, which can swamp the congregation with its standardizing rules and expectations. Too much weight on the local veils catholicity; the greater church retreats from view. Equally, too much emphasis on the universal cloaks catholicity as well; the congregation's uniqueness is put at risk. When the church strikes a balance between the two, it relativizes both. Local and universal cannot dictate to the other. They have to dialogue on equal terms. This can produce – in Komonchak's phrase – 'redemptive integration', which is the non-coercive reconciliation of unity and diversity through Christ (Komonchak, 1997, pp. 611–12).

## Internal catholicity

This redemptive approach enables the church's interior catholicity to support its missional catholicity. It helps the complete church, while remaining one, to better represent humanity in the diversity of its membership and in the variety of its forms. For catholicity assumes unity. Each congregation represents a single whole. Alongside 'you be you', therefore, every part of Christ's body will also say, 'In our imaginations, let *us* be you. Let us see reality from your perspective.' Empathy fertilizes unity, as we have seen. As God's people become more varied, affinity with one another glues them together.

# AN ATTRACTIVE GIFT? THE FOUR MARKS

This requires a high view not only of the congregation, but of the institutional church, whether traditional connections or new networks. We must value mediating structures and processes as enablers and expressions of unity, while asking whether the particular arrangements are best for hosting diverse groups and sewing them together. If not, what changes would allow the church to entertain all types of people from all types of background, all treated with equal respect, and all equally comfortable in the larger whole? Unless the church's structures and behaviours welcome the people whom new Christian communities introduce, unless they bring catholicity to life, the call to self-donation will be undercut from within. People with disadvantages, for example, will hardly feel accepted if the unjust circumstances they daily experience are mimicked by the church. To avoid the church's sweet crust on the outside being betrayed by a bitter taste within, catholicity through reaching out must be matched by catholicity when drawing in.

## Apostolic

As with the other marks, this fourth one can also point in different directions. Some have associated it with leadership in continuity with the apostles. Others have noted that this continuity is not an end in itself but is for the purpose of staying faithful to the apostles' teaching – steering theological wagons along ancient ecclesiastical routes. This has opened an even wider perspective. The church's tradition extends beyond teaching to the church's life as a whole. Apostolicity comes to mean the continuity not just of leadership and teaching, but of the church: what forms of ecclesial continuity are faithful to the church's origins?

The apostolic mark in this broadest sense is about vertical relationships through time. It speaks to the human inclination for rootedness, which has the idea of being connected to previous generations. The strength of this longing is reflected in the origin stories societies typically tell about themselves, in the preservation of ethnic and local traditions, in the tracing of family histories, in displaced peoples' longing to be grounded, and more. Rootedness enables people to understand where they have come from, what their lives are based upon, which forest of trees they belong to. Even if someone is not impressed by their pedigree, knowing their past can help the person forge a different future. Rootedness strengthens identity. Like the other marks, therefore, apostolicity resonates with a fundamental human desire.[10]

## Apostolic in mission

The church's continuity should not be sought exclusively in the internal life of the Christian community. To do so would be to ignore the tradition itself. Küng says that 'It is the teaching of our own traditions and confessions that we should not listen to those traditions and confessions, but to Christ and his message' (Küng, 1967, p. 292). What we know about Christ is primarily through his missional vocation. Indeed, Christ is revealed mainly as a missionary. He is the one who is sent (John 20.21). If that is the identity he shows to the world, why should we look for his body's identity anywhere except in the church's mission?

The apostles were drawn into Jesus' mission and God's people must follow suit by being drawn into the apostles' mission.

> The apostolic Church least of all can be an end in itself. Everything the Church does must be directed towards fulfilling its apostolic mission to the outside world ... To be itself, the Church must follow the apostles in continually recognizing and demonstrating that it has been sent out to the world. In this sense apostolic succession not only means following the faith and confession of the apostles, it means, in consequence of that faith, following in the footsteps of the apostolic ministry. (Küng, 1967, p. 358)

To look first for continuity in the church's interior life would be to overlook the missional tradition of the Christian community. Within the canon of Scripture, these origins can be traced from Israel's missionary vocation, through Jesus' gathering of a community for mission to Israel, his sending of this community 'to the ends of the earth', his empowering of this community to proclaim the gospel at Pentecost, and on to the expansion of this community thereafter. Later centuries saw the church span Europe and eventually the world. That the original Christians seem to have been the first religious group to seek the conversion of other peoples,[11] together with this global reach, makes the church's practice of mission highly distinctive. Mission is the backbone of the church's history.

In John Flett's words, theorists of world Christianity argue that the church 'has been historically continuous *only* because it has moved across cultural borders' (Flett, 2016, p. 243). Andrew Walls, for example, has described how the church has grown in a 'serial' fashion, first expanding and then withering in its heartlands. Places that were once major centres of Christianity – Jerusalem, Egypt, Syria, or cities once stirred by the preaching of Knox and Wesley but now full of unwanted churches

– have become ecclesial deserts, only to be replaced by new Christian wellsprings (Walls, 2002, p. 29). The church has survived largely because it took root in another culture. Thus *mission* 'is the nature of the church's continuity' (Flett, 2016, p. 248).

## Apostolic in self-multiplication

What form does this continuity take? Most broadly, generosity: whenever the church gives to others, recipients of the church's gifts are the beneficiaries of a tradition that, however inadequate, goes back to the perfect giving of the church's founder. More specifically, Flett quotes Barth's description of Christ's life as a '*self-multiplying* history', evoking 'its own reflection in the world' (Flett, 2016, p. 321; italics original). As the church has spread terrestrially through the centuries, Christ's body has been given to ever more demographic groups. By being the self-donation of Christ through geography, the church is also the self-multiplication of Christ in history. This self-multiplication is the most obvious form of the church's apostolicity. In Henry Swete's words, 'Gentile Christendom was ultimately of Apostolic planting' (Swete, 1919, p. 44).[12] Leonardo Boff notes that the apostles were sent out not individually but as the community of the twelve. It was the small gathering around Jesus that was sent (Boff, 2011, p. 123). To be in continuity with the apostles, the church must go out like the apostles – in communal form. It does this when it offers to others its self, communal life with Jesus, in the shape of new Christian communities.

This must include a willingness to offer new manifestations of the Christian community. For the church's genetic authority is founded upon the apostles' witness to an innovative event, the risen Christ; his Easter appearances 'substantiate the promise of coming glory and eschatological hope' for the entire creation (Moltmann, 1977, p. 359). This orientation towards the future means that the church should not slavishly repeat the apostolic age but 'leap forward to what is new and surprising' (p. 360). The Spirit is always bringing the unexpected. Therefore, writing of new churches in the global South but surely with application also to the North, Moltmann says:

> the missionary church will not aim to spread its own form and found 'daughter churches' everywhere. A 'young church' is not the subsidiary branch of an old church ... It is 'a new church' of the same apostolate. It preserves its unity when it fulfils Christ's apostolic mission in its own historical situation. (p. 360)

# GIVING THE CHURCH

Picking up Walls' point, when these new Christian communities in their turn take the tradition to new settings and new people, the missional continuity of the church will become more resilient. A sending congregation may one day dwindle and die but its life will continue in its offspring. The more numerous the offspring, the more robust will be the church's continuity. And the more opportunities the church will have to contribute to Jesus' mission of love through campaigning for justice, sharing resources and caring for people in need. Thus self-donation is not just one means of expressing the church's apostolic origins. It is vital to the apostolic mission in its entirety.

Fidelity to Christ's self-multiplying history draws people into the church's internal life, where faithfulness to Christ is learnt through the church's traditions. As they are drawn by grace into the heritage of the Christian community, recipients of the gift are formed in the ways of Jesus, which includes being schooled in self-giving beyond the church. Just as living with Jesus trained the twelve for his mission of self-donation, so the church's worship, teaching, organization and fellowship, honed down the generations, will shape believers for the same mission. This does not mean every detail of church life will be geared to self-donation, just as every action of a top athlete (such as going to a film) need not be dictated by training for the Olympics. Like the athlete's orientation towards the Olympics, the church's interior life will take its bearings from the call to self-donation, without every jot and tittle being fashioned by it. Being sculpted for this vocation, by an inheritance stretching back to Jesus, will strengthen the church's attachment to its origins, reinforcing the appeal of the Christian community to those who value having roots.

## Implications

This chapter enters one of the debates about mission, which is how the church dares show its face to the world when it is so corrupted by evil. How far can mission be about the church when the church has such a soiled reputation? One response is to emphasize the church's call to generosity, and in particular its gift of communion in Christ for the world's sake. It is through the very process of offering the gift that the church can scrape down its barnacles of sin. For whenever the church is given to others, the four marks are put on display. Believers are shown to be one because through the church's self-donation they can trace themselves to the one church in Jerusalem. This lineage echoes the self-giving of the Godhead, which lies at the heart of holiness. Receipt of the church by more and more people increases catholicity. And when recipients in

## AN ATTRACTIVE GIFT? THE FOUR MARKS

turn gratefully pass the gift on, they are faithful to the apostolic tradition of the church.

This relocates the four marks from the church's interior life in the first instance to its missional topography. Historically, the marks have often been employed for the purpose of internal church politics. The Fathers used them to distinguish the true church from heretical or false churches. But when the marks are weaponized to exclude a large chunk of God's people, as happens when one Church refuses to recognize another, the marks themselves are undermined. Christians are less united. The self-assertion involved (us against you) travels away from the self-giving central to holiness. Catholicity is reduced – the 'true' church is less diverse – when other churches are viewed as false. The apostolicity of all God's people is put in doubt if, on a narrow definition of the term, some churches are judged to be outside the tradition. Used in a divisive way, the marks make the church less attractive.

But if the marks are intrinsic to the church's mission, they have the potential to make the Christian community more healthy. They become a vehicle for the kingdom to challenge the institution, an important theme in studies of the church. How can the Christian community be an agent of the kingdom? Part of the answer is that when these external marks peer over the church's shoulder, Christians are encouraged to make them urgently present inside the church. For the institution will lack integrity if its face betrays what is in its heart. If believers are one in their origins, how can they claim fidelity to their roots when they are bitterly divided? If their self-giving in mission echoes the holiness of the Godhead, how can they claim to be children *of God* when self-giving is absent from their interior relationships? If they become more catholic through giving the church to others, how can they celebrate their diversity when they smother differences within the church? How can believers be faithful to the apostolic practice of giving the church to others if the church they offer is no longer church because it strays from the apostles' teachings? By living out the four marks in the church's generosity to others, the Christian community is challenged to lament the dearth of these characteristics in its internal life, to pray that the marks be made more visible and to seek the grace with which to receive them in full.

As these prayers are answered, the church will be made more attractive. This is because each of the four marks speaks to a human need. Oneness resonates with the longing for connection, holiness with the desire to distinguish between 'my people' and others (the basis of identity), catholicity with the hope that 'my group' will be included, and apostolicity with the yearning to be grounded through time. The more the historic marks are present in the church's life, the more the Christian community will

# GIVING THE CHURCH

be a society of intimacy, of specialness based on generosity, of welcome (to everyone) and of rootedness. And the more, therefore, that cultures of antipathy, self-aggrandisement, exclusion and ephemeral shallowness will be resisted within the church.

The four marks find echoes in the contemporary appeal of franchise entertainment such as the Marvel, Harry Potter and Lord of the Rings series of films. Devotees of a series are united to others who love the same series (one); they buy into the values of the series (holy); they join millions of other devotees across the world (catholic); they belong to a tradition with recurring themes (apostolic). The four marks thus resonate with a profound cultural hunger. So if they are present in the church, maybe the world won't need to pinch its nose quite so firmly when entering what at times can feel like an ecclesial sty.

Sometimes, how the kingdom keeps the church on its spiritual toes is left studiously vague. But here we have a very practical starting point. The marks suggest four arguments that can encourage congregations, as part of their generosity, to birth further Christian communities and thereby magnify the church's giving to the world:

- *One:* if a local church starts a new congregation, it will do what the Christian community has repeatedly done. Every congregation was once a church plant. Forming a new Christian community will join that long history of church multiplication.
- *Holy:* congregations participate in divine holiness whenever they give to others in some way. However, they particularly share in God's holiness, revealed in the self-giving of Christ, when the church's very self – communal life in Jesus – becomes a gift to the world.
- *Catholic:* when a congregation gives its self to another group, the totality of the church mirrors a tiny bit more the wholeness of the human race. The church's catholicity comes closer to the world's 'catholicity', which makes the Christian community more socially inclusive.
- *Apostolic:* beginning a new Christian community helps demonstrate a congregation's theological orthodoxy. Doctrine and ministry with roots in the apostles are not on their own a sufficient sign of apostolic faithfulness. To be apostolic in a full sense, a congregation must actively intend to birth an offspring.

In the Christian race (Heb. 12.1–3), the marks are spurs to giving away the church for society's good. By driving internal reforms to make the gift attractive, they should breed an ecclesial thoroughbred worthy of the crowd's applause.

94

## AN ATTRACTIVE GIFT? THE FOUR MARKS

## Notes

1 Rowan Williams, 'One Holy Catholic and Apostolic Church', Archbishop's Address to the Third Global South to South Encounter, Ain al Sukhna, Egypt, 28 October 2005.

2 In an ecumenical spirit, Küng also suggests that the four marks, if they are genuine, must depend on the two Protestant signs: the preaching of the gospel and the proper administration of the sacraments (p. 268).

3 As a promise of what life will be like in God's coming reign, the marks are a double gift. They are both the pledge – the gift of the promissory note, if you like – and then the provisional giving of what is promised (the redemption of the note), which extends into eternity. See Walter, 2013.

4 Of course, there have been deviant offshoots – certain cults for example – that are disowned by the wider church, which raises the question (discussed in the previous chapter) of what counts as church.

5 The Church of England's *Mission-shaped Church* report, which has been highly influential in spreading 'fresh expressions of church', identified the four marks with particular dimensions of the church – the Godward dimension (holy), the inward unity of each gathering (one), the outward movement in mission (apostolic), and the participation of all church members in the communion of saints (catholic) (Cray, 2004, pp. 98–9). But this is not how the tradition has generally understood the marks. Rather, each mark belongs to the entirety of church. Thus each of the four sets of ecclesial relationships should display the four marks. Unity, for example, should be evident in a gathering's direct relationship with God (in worship for instance), in its relations to the wider church, in working with other gatherings in mission, and within each Christian community. Likewise holiness and the other marks.

6 How this distinctiveness can be expressed inclusively is discussed in Chapter 5.

7 The resurrection does not vindicate Christ by God's omnipotence overcoming (and so ending) Jesus' self-emptying powerlessness. Rather, the resurrection guarantees the *continuation* of Christ's self-emptying. It is proof that giving away power is not self-destructive, but that Christ can remain a giving self through the ultimate adversity. Through the Spirit, the ascended Jesus continues to give himself, not least in Scripture and the Eucharist.

8 Moltmann claims that just as the non-Christian marriage partner is sanctified by the Christian partner and so are the children of the marriage (1 Cor. 7.14), sanctified members of the church sanctify the world through their call to service, suffering and poverty (Moltmann, 1977, pp. 354–5).

9 As with other forms of exchange, gifts are often subject to the law of diminishing returns. 'Not another bunch of flowers!' sighs the hostess. Love of course is an exception. It can be offered time and again without being diminished, though the form in which it is expressed may lose its lustre if it is constantly repeated.

10 The emotional power of this mark was illustrated in a 2012 report that Chinese Christian tourists refer to Barnsley, England as their spiritual home. They trace their Christian heritage through the Chinese Overseas Mission Fellowship, which was founded by the nineteenth-century missionary Hudson Taylor who was born in the town. One tourist, overwhelmed with emotion, kissed the ground in Barnsley (Choy, 2021, p. 3).

## GIVING THE CHURCH

11 Martin Goodman and others have shown that Judaism did not contain a proselytizing tendency before Christian mission began. The later emergence in Judaism of Christian-type proselytizing owed less to impulses within Judaism than to what the *Christians* were doing (Goodman, 1994, pp. 60–91; Riesner, 2000, pp. 211–50). For Matthew 23.15's reference to scribes and Pharisees proselytizing, see Chapter 5, note 6 on page 143.

12 Swete claimed that 'The Catholic Church is Apostolic in three respects: as planted in the world by the Apostles; as adhering to the teaching of the Apostles; as carrying on the succession of Apostolic ministry' (p. 44).

# 4

# An Available Gift?
# The Hidden and Visible Church

The church must be born again. As one aspect of its grateful life of generosity, through the Spirit the church must offer others communion in Christ in the form of new Christian communities for the sake of the world. The church must be *made available* to those who do not yet belong. After all, the Christian community would not be much of a gift if it was inaccessible. One way to understand this availability is to revisit the distinction, which has been drawn in several ways, between the visible and hidden church. Sometimes the church we can see is contrasted with God's unseen activity in the church, such as the Spirit's work in human hearts. On other occasions, this first distinction shades into a second: the sinful visible church is differentiated from the hidden holy church; the church's perfection is largely beyond sight and will be fully revealed only when Christ returns. At still other times, the distinction is made between church members as a whole, the visible church, and members who have been saved by Christ, the hidden church: we cannot be sure who the saved are. Here 'hidden' has the sense of 'unknown'.[1]

To discuss the church's availability, I shall describe these perspectives from a gift standpoint and add a fourth. I shall start at the divine centre of the Christian community and offer a gift-based understanding of God's unseen work in gathering a communion in Christ. Next I consider how this hidden story, which brings the church to perfection, relates to the visible, sullied life of the church. Striding further out towards the boundaries of the Christian community, I shall discuss the distinction between those who welcome the church in their hearts (who are hidden because they are not known with certainty by others) and the church's visible membership, which includes those who only appear to value the gift. Finally, scaling the church's boundaries I shall suggest a further distinction, based on the church's communal presence in the world. 'Hidden' in this fourth sense means 'unavailable'. The church as a visible community certainly exists but frequently it is out of sight, the gift is not within reach, where much of life takes place. This chapter thus broadens the visible/hidden discussion to encompass the gift's accessibility to others.[2]

## The hidden church

Starting with the church's divine hub, there is common ground that in gathering people around Jesus and sending them in mission, part of God's activity is hidden from human view. During worship, for example, we cannot see what God is doing inside people's hearts and minds, though later the results may be visible. Robin Horner's description of the Trinity as giver, gift and giving (Horner, 2001, p. ix) and similar language within the Presbyterian Church (USA) suggests a way of thinking about this divine activity in relation to the world.[3] Giver, Gift and Giving are not replacement terms for Father, Son and Holy Spirit. Rather, more adjectives than nouns, they amplify what is meant by the traditional language.[4]

### *Giver, Gift and Giving*

As revealed in Scripture, the Father is the ultimate Giver, the source of every good gift (James 1.17), including the church. Discussion often focuses on the roles of Christ and the Spirit in the church's life, yet if the Father is the Giver who initiates the church, the importance of the Father should not be glossed over. The supreme Giver takes the initiative in offering the world his divine Gift, Jesus Christ, around whom the church gathers (Matt. 18.20). Though it is the Spirit who is normally described as a gift, the New Testament is clear that the Son is also a Gift (John 3.16). 'The Son and the Spirit are in different ways the gift' (Jenson, 2002, p. 289). The Son is a Gift to the world because in the midst of human history he is the presence of God in human form. He is human life fulfilled as God intends. When human beings are enabled to receive and be united to the Gift, the Gift's perfection rubs off on them. They become like the Gift itself (2 Cor. 3.18).

Anticipating Part 2's discussion of appropriate gifts, the Son is a suitable Gift. First, he is appropriate to the Giver (the Father) because the Giver is heavily invested in the Gift. As Chapter 2 pointed out, it is in the nature of giving that the giver puts something of his or her self into the gift. The ultimate example is the perfect expression of the Giver in the Gift because the Father is infinitely present in his Son. 'Anyone who has seen me has seen the Father' (John 14.9). Second, the Gift is appropriate to the recipients because the Gift takes human form in Jesus. Women

AN AVAILABLE GIFT? THE HIDDEN AND VISIBLE CHURCH

and men can relate to the Son as 'one of us'. Third, the Gift is proper to the relationship between the Giver and humanity because the Son is the Father's beloved (Mark 1.11). By giving the one he adores, the Father trumpets how much he values the human recipients. They are so precious that from all eternity he willed his only Son to become one of them.

As the bond of self-giving love between the Father and the Son, the Spirit can be said to come eternally into being through the mutual giving of Father and Son. As Father and Son give to each other they also give out, and that giving outward is the Spirit. The Spirit is the Trinity giving beyond itself. Thus while the Gift is the *saving* gift to the world of the incarnate Son, Giving is the *bestowing* gift to the world of the Holy Spirit (Acts 2.38). The Giving Spirit unites the Giver and the Gift, Father and Son, by being the One who lavishes God's treasures on creation.[5]

The Giver sent the Gift to the world by means of Giving. The Giving Spirit enabled the Christ Gift to assume his incarnate identity (Luke 1.35), to be a gift in his life and ministry (Mark 1.12) and, by raising him from the dead (Rom. 8.11), to be a return gift to the Father. Subsequently, Giving makes the Gift available to humanity (John 16.15). 'The Spirit is the *beyond* history, and when he [sic] acts in history he does so in order to bring into history the last days, the *eschaton*' (Zizioulas, 1985, p. 130; italics original). The Giving Spirit offers Christ as a Gift from the future to the present, and enables people to receive this Gift in their own way. In accepting the Gift they are united to it. The church as it were fills out the Gift. The Gift is expanded from being a human *person* to being a human *community*.

By receiving and being joined to the Gift, recipients are liberated from the causal chains of sin originating in the past. They are formed into a new community of mutual generosity, which the Giving Spirit enables (1 Cor. 12). By means of the Giving Spirit, this transformed community is given to others in the form of Christian communities that bless their wider contexts (Acts 1.8). Importantly, the Giving Spirit also attaches these communities to the Christ Gift's eternal self-giving back to the Father (see 1 Cor. 15.24). They become a return gift to the Giver who initiates the church. So in a sense the Father receives back more than he originally gave – not just his Son, but all who are united to Christ; not just a single human, but a community of humans.[6] With thankful hearts, recipients of the church are drawn into the joyful life of Giver, Gift and Giving.

### *Totus Christus*

In distinguishing between Giver, Gift and Giving, we must remember of course that the three persons are also one. Though one person may take the lead as it were, what each does in the economy of salvation is undertaken by all three persons. Together, their activity gives rise to what is known as the Totus Christus – the whole Christ. The Gift (Christ) and the gift (church) are united in one spiritual entity while remaining distinct. They are rather like an aunt who is a gift to the family because of her generosity. Her presents are distinct from the aunt, while being intrinsic to the aunt as a gift herself. The church as a gift is distinguishable from Christ, while being essential to his Gift identity.

Arising from the unified activity of Giver, Gift and Giving, the church has an unseen *past*. This includes the Trinity's eternal conversations that give birth to the Christian community and comprise the community's invisible back story. The church also has an unseen *present*. The Father Giver makes the Christ Gift present to God's people here and now by means of the Giving Spirit, who also enables the Gift to be received in individuals' hearts. This giving and receiving occur unseen (though the effects may be visible) through the teaching, institutions and other visible aspects of the church, which in turn represent a return gift to the Giver; they share in the Gift's offer of total obedience to the Father. And the church has an unseen *future* – the perfecting of the relationship between the Giver and the church, the fruits of this relationship in eternity, and the fullness of life yet to come; the Christian community semaphores this future to the world through its visible existence. The hidden past, present and future activity of Giver, Gift and Giving is the first and fundamental way that God makes the church available to the world.

## The visible and hidden church

Stepping out from the church's centre is the 'downward' connection between the Trinity's hidden activity in making God's people holy and the partial results of this activity in the people's visible lives. As we shall see, stressing God's unseen work in purifying the church on the one hand or emphasizing the observable effects of this work on the other produce an unbalanced view of the church. And this creates opportunities for sin to discolour God's people. Allowing the equation to balance, however, helps to keep sin in check. Viewing the church as a gift throws light on this. For gifts too have hidden and visible dimensions. There is the intangible 'thought that counts' and the tangible gift expressing the thought (Belk, 1996, pp. 59–61). Heirlooms are an example. As Mark Osteen notes, they cannot exist without the stories behind them (Osteen, 2002b). Intangible associations always accompany the object itself and these may be valued differently. One family member may cherish the article because of its unique memories while another wants to sell it (Komter, 2001, p. 72). The first appreciates the gift's hidden story, the second its monetary worth as a visible object – and, of course, the two may be linked through the article's provenance.

The New Testament uses various images to describe the Christian community, such as the body of Christ. Might we add heirloom to the list? Though not used explicitly, heirloom is close to Paul's description of God's children as inheritors and 'heirs with Christ' (Acts 20.32; Rom. 8.17). If our inheritance is God's blessings in the kingdom (1 Peter 1.3–4), if through God's unseen work the visible church is to be a foretaste of that inheritance (a theological orthodoxy), and if the church is handed down the generations, does not the church have something of an heirloom's character? The church is a visible bequest from God with a hidden story behind it. This heirloom, worn and torn, is to be passed down the family, including adopted members (see Eph. 1.5), until it is restored to its pristine glory when Christ returns. Like an inherited masterpiece of art, the heirloom is of such potential interest to others that the family should put it on public display without yielding ownership.

## Out of balance

However, churchgoers may value the heirloom's hidden and visible dimensions differently. Some Christians emphasize God's hidden work in sanctifying the church, downplaying the gift's visible dimension. They are a bit like an heir to a damaged painting who is more interested in the family story linked to the picture than restoring the work. Rachel Hurdley notes that heirlooms used to be displayed whether families liked them or not (Hurdley, 2007, p. 130). What mattered was the story they represented. Similarly, the visible church – the quality of its practices and organization – may be minimized in favour of its invisible narrative, God's unseen work in bringing the church to perfection. Emphasis is placed on imputed unity, holiness and other forms of sanctification, while moral scratchings that deface the visible church's reputation are ignored. Just as lack of attention to the physical properties of an inherited painting may lead to a lack of care, so with the church. The hidden church becomes the opium of God's people, lulling them into a false complacency. The

# GIVING THE CHURCH

behaviours and structures of the church are neglected, which corrodes the gift's value to others.

Or the church may be like a painting valued by the heir for what it means to him rather than to the rest of the family. The story *he* has constructed, happy childhood memories perhaps, overlays the family story behind the picture.[7] Members prioritize their individual biographies with God over the visible life of God's people. What God says to me privately weighs more heavily than what he says to *us* when we meet publicly. The church is reduced to personal stories with God that downgrade the common story embodied in a shared, visible life. Communal checks to individuals' faulty thinking and behaviour melt away. The physical church recedes from view.

By contrast, others emphasize God's presence and work in the visible church. They are rather like heirs who value the picture for its beauty and artistic merit but forget its family history. The painting is divested of its invisible story and treasured for its aesthetic qualities. This is not uncommon with heirlooms. Hurdley describes family bequests that have no sentimental value and are seen purely as aesthetic objects (Hurdley, 2007, p. 137–8). In like manner, the visible church has been cherished for its tangible life, its buildings, musical traditions and contributions to the common good, while the intangible story about the church's spiritual significance is largely ignored. Cultural refinement comes at the expense of spiritual philistinism. This pride in their achievements closes God's people to correction through the Spirit's unseen work of sanctification.

Or Christians become like heirs who play up the history of the picture to increase the painting's value on the market. Mark Osteen refers to owners who 'fabricate histories of association with the object in order to manufacture prestige' (Osteen, 2002b, p. 234). Just as heirs exaggerate the family's closeness to the artist to improve the painting's alleged provenance, instead of neglecting the hidden church Christians may exaggerate its closeness to the visible church. They display an excessive confidence in the goodness of the church's structures and processes, bordering on arrogance and perhaps even leading to coercion: 'We know God's mind and will enforce it.' The institutions of the church acquire an authority they do not warrant, the membership is blinded to their shortcomings, criticism of them is discouraged and conformity imposed, making the church an unattractive gift to others. The visible church colonizes the hidden church. But far from burnishing, this tarnishes the church's reputation.

Thus the Christian community walks a perilous tightrope. Lean too far towards the hidden church and it may neglect the church's visible life. Or it may elevate the personal at the expense of the communal, reducing checks to the visible church's sinfulness. Lean too far the other way and Christians may neglect the spiritual health of the church. Or they may associate the visible church too closely with God's unseen sanctifying activity, blind to how the latter could challenge and repair their corporate life. By sitting too heavily on the hidden or visible end of the ecclesial seesaw, believers fail to make the church available to others in a balanced way.

### Even-handed

A self-correcting balance will enable the hidden work of the Giver, Gift and Giving to perpetually challenge the visible church. This will not prevent the Christian community from sinking rather than rising to the ethical occasion, from being offered as a defective gift, but it may limit the descent. In God's grace the hidden church keeps sin in check by enabling 'moral licence' to operate differently to other organizations. Psychologists have found that when people do good in one arena they often assume moral licence to behave badly in another. For example, two Chicago economists reported that working for a socially responsible company increased the tendency for employees to act unethically within the firm (List and Momeni, 2021). By contrast, God's hidden activity highlights the misdeeds of God's people, removes their excuses and calls them to repent and reform. Far from licensing sin, God proscribes it.

So what might balancing the hidden and visible church involve? First, it means valuing the church's visible life alongside and because of its unseen dimension. The Giver who lovingly initiates the church, the Gift who is received by and embraces the church, and the Giving Spirit's perfecting of the church (to be completed when Christ returns) all bestow immense worth on the visible Christian community, despite its shortcomings. The church's visible life matters just as an heirloom, though damaged, might still matter to the family because of its rich history. Careful attention must therefore be paid to the structures and behaviours of the Christian community. The visible church must be worthy of the unseen story behind it.

Second, the hidden church must be valued for bringing the visible church to repentance. William Cavanaugh asks: What does the world see that reveals the unity of the church's divine and human natures? In the case of Christ, the Gift disclosed this union by becoming sin without sinning. But that is impossible for the church because, unlike Christ, God's people cannot consistently resist sin. Their only alternative is to adopt the stance of continuous repentance. This, evident in the church's life and attitudes, will confirm to the world that the perfect hidden Gift is united

GIVING THE CHURCH

to the Gift's imperfect visible recipients. What reveals the union is the believers' acknowledgement that they have damaged the Giver's bequest, their resulting prayers of repentance, their gratitude for being undeservedly forgiven, and their ongoing sanctification, however stuttering and incomplete. The church must be known for burning its failures on a pyre of lament.[8]

Third, the Christian community must pray that its visible life is joined to the hidden Gift and refined with the Gift's generosity. It must beseech God for the sanctifying work of the Spirit, who refashions the church in Christ's image. It must beg God to work unseen *in* the visible church, turning it into high-speed broadband for divine beneficence. When this happens, the Giving Spirit will offer communion in Jesus to others as part of Christ's self-giving to the world and as a particular aspect of the church's generosity. Like heirs who recognize that the public would be short-changed if their inherited masterpiece was kept to themselves, the church will be made available to others.

## Icon and sacrament

If this rhythm of attentiveness, repentance and prayer is the Spirit's means of keeping the visible and hidden church in balance, what is the *connection* between the two? Again, think of an heirloom. It functions like an icon by drawing the viewer into the story behind the object.[9] In my analogy, the painting represents a story about the artist's intentions, how the painting came to be in the family and the meaning of the picture to its heirs. The narrative behind the picture is hidden – you cannot touch, see or hear it in the painting itself – but the picture makes the story tangible.

The visible church does something similar.[10] It is the painting through which the Spirit conveys to the world the story of the gift of God's reign. The coming kingdom remains largely unseen, but its character breaks into history within and beyond the church, not least in the person of Jesus. As an icon of purity, the church's visible life – despite its defects – can reveal some of the spiritual pearls on a mostly hidden necklace. As a result, observing the church takes onlookers to a different realm, to God's yet-to-be disclosed future that leaves an image on the canvas today. Because of this special capacity to open up God's hidden milieu, for all its faults the visible church can still be a gift to others.

More than an icon, the seeable church has a sacramental quality. Its observable life and structures are not only an image, a sign, of God's hidden grace in recipients' lives, they make God's saving action effective in the Christian community. Like heirlooms that forge and strengthen

104

## AN AVAILABLE GIFT? THE HIDDEN AND VISIBLE CHURCH

family relationships across time, the visible church more than *represents* the connection between the divine Giver and the Gift's recipients. Through the Spirit, it actually *establishes and sustains* the bond. Recipients encounter God through the visible essentials of the church (word, sacraments, ministry and disciplines), however blemished these may be. This spiritual rendezvous brings the eternal to bear on the transient, thereby restraining the sinfulness of the church, opening it to divine generosity and making it more attractive. This is the second way the gift becomes available to others.

## Who has received the gift?

To say the least, God's hidden finger draws Christ unevenly on the church's visible life. Divine love breaks through more plainly in some corners than others. So marching towards the boundary of the church, we come to a third perspective: an understanding of the hidden and visible church in terms of membership. The visible church contains all the official members, while the hidden church comprises the true believers ('the elect') who have received the gospel in their hearts. The latter belong to the visible church but, as a faithful remnant within it, do not represent the entire membership. Essentially, therefore, this is a boundary question. Who in the visible membership is the true, hidden church and who is not?

This way of thinking dates back to St Augustine. He argued that the visible church includes people who hear the gospel and receive the sacraments, not all of whom may be saved. The hidden church consists of those who *are* saved, who take the gospel and sacraments to heart. Who they are will be revealed at the end of history. The Reformers picked this up to distinguish between the Roman Catholic Church, which in their view included many who only appeared to follow Christ, and those within that Church (as well as in their own churches) who truly believed. This distinction made sense in the context of national churches with widespread infant baptism. Not all the baptized accepted Christ intentionally as adults. They might nominally belong to the church but not sing God's song. Perhaps they are like a family who inherits an artistic masterpiece but stuff the heirloom in the attic and forget it.[11] One of the children, however, is mesmerized by the painting. Periodically she creeps into the loft, uncovers the picture and ponders it in rapt delight. She is resonant of the hidden church. Some members welcome what they have received, while others don't.

There is an obvious minefield in making this distinction. What could make sense theoretically risks becoming a weapon of judgement in practice. So-called true believers may try to identify the sheep who have properly accepted community in Christ as against the goats who haven't. They look for markers that distinguish the true church. Going beyond criteria such as preaching the word and celebrating the sacraments, they seek evidence of people's faithful response. Then they may act as border control, set requirements for true belonging so high that the faint-hearted give up, and exclude those with the wrong spiritual passports. In so doing, they hijack God's role (Matt. 13.24ff.). God alone knows whether apparent gratitude for the gift masks an indifference, for example, or whether seeming indifference hides a growing appreciation of Christ. Rather than being highways for divine grace to spread through the church, the presumptuous faithful become roadblocks.

Even so, *conceptually* distinguishing between the visible and hidden church helpfully reminds us that the divine Gift must be received with genuine thanks if communion in Christ is to properly form. Consequently, the distinction recognizes, as all the Reformers wanted to assert, that

> No ecclesial structure is able to guarantee the church remains faithful to the gospel and thus remains the – One, Holy, Catholic, and Apostolic – church. Rather the visible church may turn into the false church against which the faithful cannot but resist ... Resistance in the name of the gospel then aims at embodying the true church again institutionally. (Wendebourg, 2018, p. 236)

From a 'giving the church' perspective, might the visible/hidden distinction lie less in who have received the gift, and more in who welcome the invitation to share the gift? On this view, the hidden church is those within the visible church who take seriously the call to a life of generosity towards people outside the church, expressed in a multitude of ways. Since only God can judge the adequacy of their response, the spiritual worth of their commitment remains hidden from view. It is as such that they are the hidden church. As one aspect of this vocation, some church members may offer new Christian communities or support other Christians in doing so. They are hidden in an additional sense: until this particular dimension of generosity is articulated and enabled, no one can be sure who will respond. Of course, as with the conventional distinction, this is a snapshot. Church members may move from a reluctance to heed the summons to give to a willingness to do so. Attitudes are not set in stone.

This perspective shifts attention away from crude 'Are you in or out?' discussions to 'Have you fully understood God's call on the church and the implications for you?' Notably, as claimed in Chapter 1, offering

AN AVAILABLE GIFT? THE HIDDEN AND VISIBLE CHURCH

new Christian communities can draw believers closer to Christ in prayer and action as they lean on his grace. In such cases, renewal can become less about ensuring members are 'proper Christians' – Have they had a personal conversion experience? Have they been baptized in the Spirit? – and can centre more on God's call to generosity, especially to give communion in Christ away. As Christians respond, we can prayerfully expect that other dimensions of their spiritual life will be renewed.[12]

Extending the visible/hidden distinction to new Christian communities invites the question: why might some church members hesitate to offer these communities? Are they embarrassed by the gift? Is the church too unattractive to be shared? For example, in the eyes of potential recipients has the church become:

- A thoughtless gift, such as the bequest of a piece of furniture too big for the recipient's room. Is the church 'the right fit' for members' lives and the lives of their friends? Is it relevant?
- A moralizing gift, such as handing down a Bible to an agnostic son? Have church leaders (or members) alienated potential recipients of the church by preaching at them 'from on high'?
- A demeaning gift, such as an item fit for a young child bequeathed to a teenager? Does the church make the recipients of its generosity feel inadequate?
- A dark gift, designed to put the inheritor in debt to the family? Recipients are subtly reminded of how much they owe the church and feel trapped, perhaps within abusive relationships.
- An ostentatious gift, designed to show off? The congregation parades its generosity to enhance its reputation, but this leaves some members embarrassed and therefore reluctant to share the church.
- A redundant gift? Recipients have no use for the gift. God is sufficiently active outside the church, it is thought, and so there is no need to give the church to others.

Might the Spirit use such questions to help the church respond gratefully to God with a life of 'purified' generosity?

## Visible in life

God works unseen behind the visible life of the church; this activity flows from God into the church as a whole and there it is concentrated in the lives of members who truly believe. But the flow of grace does stop with them. It is transmitted to people outside the church. The family is not to

# GIVING THE CHURCH

enjoy the heirloom for themselves, they are to put it on public display. This turns our attention from the boundary of the 'true' church to people beyond the membership. How does God's hidden activity make the gift available to them? Does God work through the church as a hidden or visible community in everyday life?

Here the distinction lies between the visibly gathered and the hidden dispersed church. Believers typically gather for worship, which makes the church visible as a community. Then they are sent into the world to witness as individuals, at which point the communal visibility of the church disappears. Now of course this distinction needs qualifying. Some members join together during the week to serve the world and proclaim the gospel. The worship and prayers of the congregation sustain individuals in their missional settings. So does the ongoing fellowship of believing friends and relatives. To an extent, church members take the congregation with them into the week. Even so, the felt experience of most Christians is that having met for worship, they go into the rest of life as individuals. Most of their connections with friends, at work, or in their networks are among people outside the church. When relationships are with fellow Christians, believers typically meet as companions rather than as an explicit Christian community.

Whereas worshipping congregations are central to the church's visibility, the dispersal of the congregation leaves the *community* of the church largely unseen in daily life. Scattered as individuals, believers do not live as noticeable communities where much of life happens. When others look at believers, by and large they do not see them meeting together for prayer or working together to share gifts of mercy and justice. What they observe are persons acting on their own. God works intangibly through a disorganized collection of individuals rather than tangibly through an expanding network of organized Christian communities. The community of God's people is hidden in plain sight. Thus through the week there is a triple weighting towards the unseen church – the hiddenness of God's activity behind the scenes of the church in general, the hiddenness of believers whose willingness to share the church is as yet unknown and, in much of everyday life, the hiddenness of the Christian community itself.

## The disappearance of the church

Reflecting on God's people, Gerhard Lohfink attributes the lack of Christian faith in contemporary Europe largely to the church's disappearance as the setting in which God is revealed.

## AN AVAILABLE GIFT? THE HIDDEN AND VISIBLE CHURCH

> The fundamental movement of salvation history is precisely this, that God becomes accessible to the world, that God finds a place in the world where the divine will can be known and the divine name can be called upon. (Lohfink, 1999, pp. 318–19)

God does this by binding himself irrevocably to the world in his people and in Christ. The church must be recognizable as 'the place of God's physical presence' (p. 319), as the community in which God is at work.

The feeding of the 5,000 in Mark 6.34–44 illustrates what being such a community means. God's people are not to be like the disciples, who knew it was growing late and proposed that the crowd be sent away to find food themselves. The church is not to proclaim the gospel and then return people to their everyday lives, creating a wedge between ministry to the congregation and the rest of life. Nor is the church to be like the disciples when Jesus rejected this option. In Lohfink's account, they plan to get organized. They would ask the crowd for 200 denarii (roughly enough for 5,000 half-day poverty rations of food), buy bread themselves and distribute it. This would have met the immediate practical need, but left social injustices unchanged. The people would have heard Jesus' teaching, but seen no concrete evidence of the reign he proclaimed.

Instead, Jesus performs a miracle. He orders the crowd to self-organize into groups of 50 and 100 (a sign of the messianic banquet at the end times), multiplies a handful of loaves and fish, and feeds the crowd – not with poverty rations, but with such generosity that the leftovers fill 12 baskets (Lohfink, 1999, pp. 145–8). This is what it means for the church to be a visible community. It is to be present with a generosity that disrupts day-to-day life and points to the even greater disruption when Christ returns. As Lohfink points out, the signs of the Messiah 'are not restricted to Jesus; they continue in the Church, repeatedly coming to the fore – *in order to be looked upon*' (p. 321; italics added). The church as a living community with Jesus must be visible to people, able to be looked upon, which means it must be present where they lead their lives. Otherwise they will have no opportunity to see communal life in God and make a decision about it. If communion in Christ is not unwrapped in front of people, how can they see the gift, experience it and decide whether it is worth receiving?

Unless you are given a present, you cannot receive it. And a gift is only given when it is made available to its recipient. 'A gift is made present, it is brought before its intended recipient, it enters into the presence of the one who is to receive' (Horner, 2001, p. 3). These verbal connections are important. If the church is to *present* Christ (the divine Gift), it must itself be *a present*, a generous gift joined to the ultimate Gift. And it can

## GIVING THE CHURCH

only be such if it is *present* to people, including where life takes place. Equally, presents make the church present in a presentable – a present-enabled – way. Gifts of care, charity and more witness to the divine Gift and prepare the ground for the church itself to be offered as a gift in the form of new Christian communities, as a climax to this wider generosity. For the church, therefore, being a present and being acceptably present in life are inextricably linked. If the church is to be like an heirloom on public display, it cannot be tucked away in someone's home, viewed only by special appointment. It must be made available to people in an accessible way, like an inherited work of art permanently loaned to a gallery. The church has to be seen (as generous) to be believed.

### Present and absent in history

Now there was a time when the church *was* present to people in their everyday lives. In pre-industrial Europe, the parish ideally was a territorial unit that would allow the priest to offer wide-ranging pastoral care to the whole population; he should be able to walk to the parish boundaries in an hour or two. The village church was at the centre of family, work and festivals. In England in the later Middle Ages, the church porch was where business was transacted, oaths sworn, disputes settled, marriages solemnized, and part of the baptismal rite conducted. The building hosted mystery plays and feasts, until church ales were suppressed by the Puritans. Holidays celebrating exotic saints thronged the medieval calendar.

This changed especially with the Industrial Revolution. As work split off from home, leisure expanded and the consumer economy thrived, society became steadily more fragmented. 'The larger segments of society like family, neighborhood, and church ... have come to function more independently from each other due to processes of differentiation and increasing scale.' As sports, volunteering, theatre, film, music and other pastimes have multiplied, 'they no longer form an "organic" whole from which solidarity arises automatically as it were, but have become independent, autonomously functioning segments' (Komter, 2005, p. 211). Faced with these fissures, the visibly gathered church has been cloistered mainly in residential areas, where it can no longer connect with the totality of life. Despite chaplaincies and the witness of individual Christians, as a community the church is largely hidden in the non-domestic arenas of society. It can no longer 'be looked upon' as a generous site of God's presence. Theologically, this is untenable. To be a present, the church as an observable community must be present in all life's rhythms and spaces.

## AN AVAILABLE GIFT? THE HIDDEN AND VISIBLE CHURCH

Doing so follows the logic of God's generosity. The church is joined to the Christ Gift by means of the Giving Spirit. It therefore receives its identity from the Gift, just as the bequest of a work of art changes the identity of the heir – 'I am now the owner of a masterpiece!' Even more does the Gift forge the identity of the church, whose attachment to Christ is as close as a body to its head. It follows that to be true to itself the church will seek – through the Spirit – to participate in the Gift's character. It will prayerfully seek to be a gift in the manner of Christ. Just as Christ took flesh and became visibly human, so the church will seize opportunities to be visible in the flesh-and-blood life of humanity. Just as in his incarnation Christ identified with the whole of humanity, so also will his community. Barth recognized this in his discussion of the hidden and invisible church: 'We start off with the general observation that it is not improper but proper to the Christian community to be visible, and indeed basically and virtually to be so *to every eye in every possible aspect of human affairs*' (Barth, 2004, p. 722; italics added). No slice of life can be out of bounds to the church's communal life.

Nor can any part of human existence be too ordinary for this life. As Hans Urs von Balthasar said, for God to explain God to humans by means of their own being and life, God must 'be a man like everyone because he will be a man for everyone, and he will exhibit his uniqueness precisely through his ordinariness ... The insignificant must be the appearance of what is most significant' (von Balthasar, 1982, pp. 457–8). If the Gift was originally displayed through and amid the ordinary things of life, and if the Christian community has received the Gift and is joined to it, it too must be visible in the mundane – in shops and schools, in hospitals and homes, in factories and food banks. When this happens, the church testifies to the boundless sovereignty of its lord. It declares that there is no square inch on the landscape of life where Christ cannot be, and with him his church. It signposts the future: when Christ returns he will fill – or complete – all things (Eph. 1.23; see also 4.10). The church signals the time when Christ, finishing his movement from Giver to recipients, will have fulfilled his nature as the ultimate Gift – Emmanuel, God with us, totally and without geographical limit.

### Making the church visible

Today, when identities are constantly on display, when how you're seen in terms of personal appearance or on social media is a cultural obsession, it would be remarkably perverse for the church *not* to make itself visible. Being visible as community with Christ in the finger tips of life is an

# GIVING THE CHURCH

entirely appropriate way for the church to be a present *to* people by being present *with* them, to live out its identity as a generous people gathered round the divine Gift. Not least, when the church is present as an attractive community, fragments of divine love are given a larger foothold in the world. To underline a point made in Chapter 1, effective love must often be organized. A group supporting colleagues made redundant, free canoeing for families, cleaning up the neighbourhood's environment, a community supper with people who are poor, campaigning against racial injustice: these and many other pockets of love need more than the presence in life of scattered individuals. They require individuals to become organized communities. This then expands the church's capacity to be generous on a broad front. How can the church kiss the world in love if its communal lips remain distant from life?

To speak of the church being made visible in this way is consistent with Barth's advocacy, mentioned in Chapter 1, of 'special working fellowships' that witness to Christ. It resonates with the 1967 World Council of Churches report, also referred to, that called for small congregations to percolate through life. It realizes the dreams, ignored in their times, of two well-regarded British missiologists: John Taylor, who wrote enthusiastically about 'little congregations' scattered through life (Taylor, 2004, pp. 147–52), and Lesslie Newbigin, who expanded the notion of the 'local church' to include all the 'places' where life occurs (Newbigin, 1977). It echoes the best-selling Church of England report, *Mission-shaped Church* (2004), which advocates 'fresh expressions of church'.

And it is reflected in the current wave of new types of Christian community.[13] These communities typically emerge as teams listen to God and their context, discern practical ways to love the people near them, build community with those who gather round their activities of love, share the gospel as part of these deepening relationships, encourage people coming to faith to form a Christian community where they are and connect to the wider church, and – at their best – encourage members of the community to repeat the process in their own manner (Moynagh, 2017, pp. 44–57). These new communities are challenging the hiddenness of the church in much of life. Of course, before Christ returns the church will never be communally available to everyone in every human reality. Even so, new Christian communities are beginning to roll back areas of society where the church has no visibility. They are challenging the church's scattered existence in life. Ecclesial atoms are assembling in Spirit-filled, organized molecules of visible love through which fuller life emerges. The family heirloom is being unveiled to the world.

The punch line? As the church becomes a communal presence in daily life, the Christians involved can grow in their discipleship through the

AN AVAILABLE GIFT? THE HIDDEN AND VISIBLE CHURCH

Spirit's activity in the world. Christian formation occurs within the church (through its liturgy and communal practices) on the one hand, but also – as Chapter 1 argued – by the Spirit outside the church. As Christians work out their calling in civic life, they are schooled in Christ-likeness by engaging with the Spirit's movement in their social context. Besides encountering the Spirit as the scattered church (as individual care workers, individual consumers and the like), as communities in life believers experience the blending of the gathered church and the world. By joining the Spirit's social 'disruptions of grace' (Leith, 2023, p. 11), these communities allow Christian formation to occur *in community, in the world*. Communal mission becomes a venue for making disciples alongside Christian formation within the church.

## Implications

It is commonplace for theologians to say that the church does not have a mission. *God* has a mission and the church is called to join in. This chapter offers one description of how that happens. When the Father Giver offers the Christ Gift to the world by means of the Giving Spirit, those who respond are joined to the Gift. They become the visible church, and through the Spirit this visible church is passed down the generations, a bit like a family heirloom, and offered to others. The visible church's divine provenance gives it immense worth, which means that the church's embodied life should not be neglected or spoilt. Enabled by God's hidden activity, it should be treated with a care reflecting its value and be continuously reformed. This will help the church to be a gift worth receiving.

However, not all church members have equal regard for the heirloom. Some ignore it, others take it for granted, while others actively damage it. Those who value the heirloom should ask 'How are our attitudes towards the gift encouraging these reactions?' Among members who do value the heirloom will be those who, through the Spirit, are eager for it to be made available outside the family. Recognizing its potential worth to others, they want communion in Christ to be publicly displayed. God's unseen activity flows into the church's visible life via these faithful disciples and is expressed through generosity in general to others outside the church and through offering new Christian communities in particular. Yet – and often this is not stressed enough – the heirloom can only be a present *to* people outside the family if it is present *with* them. It must be put on display where people lead their lives. What is displayed will be the entire edifice of the church's mission – solidarity with the weak, care for

# GIVING THE CHURCH

creation and much else, all enabled by the Spirit's gifts. Included as a vital dimension will be the offer of the church's self to others.

This, however, is where the heirloom metaphor runs out of rope, as eventually do all images of the church (and indeed any metaphor). The visible church differs to an heirloom in that it is not the possession of a family, it *is* the family. The church is not handed down the generations as an entity separate from Christian kith and kin. Unique among heirlooms, the family itself is passed down the generations and then offered to others; those who accept the gift are adopted as members. This qualification points to the church's ultimate vocation, which is to give its *self* to the world. Is the metaphor most eloquent, perhaps, in its limitation?

## An alternative society?

This story about the church corrects an omission in the 'new ecclesiology' of Stanley Hauerwas and others, who portray the church as an alternative community to the world. They argue that rather than striving for a Christianized social and political order, the church's quality of life should witness to the politics and economics of God's reign. It should remind the secular powers that they are under divine judgement and offer an earthly vision of God's alternative. However, this view pays insufficient attention to the church being present, in the form of new Christian communities, where life actually happens. How can the church narrate to the world the ongoing story of Jesus, who lives not on his own but in his community, if God's people are not communally present amid life's sunshine and thunderstorms?

Indeed, if Christians spend more time through the week in secular rather than in church communities and if, as new ecclesiologists claim, communities shape individuals' thoughts and behaviour, how can church members avoid being discipled by the world? And is this not a big risk when, in our highly organized society, the powers arrayed against the kingdom work through social systems and structures? Doesn't God's kingdom – a term that implies organization – need human organization to respond? And will the church not best resist secular influences and serve the kingdom by forming simple but structured communities in work, entertainment and other parts of society where the powers have their strongholds?

Further, new ecclesiologists fail to explain how the world can be enabled to recognize and welcome the gospel. If the secular powers are in opposition to the kingdom, what can prevent them blinding the world to God's reign in the church? Part of the answer, surely, is that the church must be present in arenas of life that people value if it is to witness effectively to them. But especially it must be present in a way that benefits life. The church must be presentable to others because its generosity brings kindness into the context. As Christian communities give to and receive from their neighbours through the whole spectrum of mission, the Spirit will enable observers to recognize the kingdom and prepare their hearts to receive Christ's communal life. This is not inconsistent with the new ecclesiology, but the focus shifts from a counter-cultural model of mission ('We are an alternative society') to a transformational one ('We seek to change society'). The world is prepared for the gospel as Christian generosity joins the Spirit in disrupting life for the purpose of love.

## Evaluating success

To discern and evaluate their contribution to this disturbance, the Christian community should embrace a theology of iconography to balance the one of fruitfulness. The latter asks whether a church planting initiative is bearing fruit, especially numerical fruit. How large is the new congregation? How many people have come to faith? Are they being fruitful in bringing others to faith? Advocates appeal for example to the parables of the sower and the vine and branches. But this is not the only yardstick of success. At least as valid is whether the church has been made lovingly visible in the setting. Has the founding team been an icon, a sacrament, of the lordship of Christ, a window into another world?

As Stefan Paas points out, 'Time and again, Jesus and the apostles speak about the church as "salt," "light," a "pilgrim people," a "colony of heaven," the "first fruits," a "little flock," "resident aliens," and so forth' (Paas, 2016, p. 116). This is not the language of size, but of a minority witnessing faithfully. And that is the first call of the church – to provide others with a glimpse of the unseen work of the Giver, Gift and Giving in bringing about the new creation. The church does that by drawing alongside people wherever life happens and making available to them whatever gifts it has, gifts that change – if only a fraction – the surrounding culture. Even if their most precious gift, their communal self, is ignored, God's people can still be a present to others by being present with them.

## Notes

1 Sometimes the same writer understands the hidden and visible church in all three senses. So when the mature Barth describes the church as a divine event, intended by God from all eternity and brought into existence by the Spirit, his focus is on God's unseen activity in creating and guiding the church. When he explores the relationship between God's secret activity and the visible human church, he comes closer to the second sense. By the power of the Spirit, the church's visible life of preaching, worship and so on witnesses to the church's hidden life in Christ, is not to be confused with it and depends on it. When he contrasts the 'true' church that remains faithful to God with the 'nominal' or 'apparent' church, which is no longer addressed by Christ or renewed by the Spirit, he is in the tradition of the third sense – of the Reformers who distinguished between the saved and the unsaved within the church (though the latter is not Barth's language). For an introduction to Barth's ecclesiology, see Bender, 2013.

2 There is a further view that widens the horizon still more. The church includes people who are well disposed to God's reign, even though they are not aware of the reign and have never received the church. They belong to the visible church because they cooperate with the kingdom, but they belong invisibly. This view is not expanded on here because if we allow the possibility that visible members of the church, who acknowledge Christ as Lord, may be outnumbered by invisible ones who don't, the church's Christ-centredness is compromised.

3 A General Assembly Report for the Presbyterian Church (USA), 'The Trinity: God's Love Overflowing', 17 March 2010, on p. 9 explores metaphors for the Godhead. As one of these, it says 'the triune God is Giver, Gift, and Giving (Jas 1: 17; Jn 3: 16; 2 Cor 9: 15; 1 Jn 3: 24).'

4 Because of God's transcendence, all our language about God is of course an approximation. Though the primary metaphors of Father, Son and Holy Spirit and secondary metaphors like Giver, Gift and Giving can take us towards God, they can never pin God down.

5 Yves Congar says that Spirit must be understood to proceed from both Father and Son, 'but in the first place from the Father, since the Son derives his being from the Father, although he is also, with the Father, the origin of the Spirit' (Congar, 1983, p. 79). The Giving Spirit proceeds from the Giver in the first place because there cannot be any giving without the initial Giver. Equally, there cannot be any Giving towards the world without the Gift. Thus the divine Giving must 'proceed' also from the Gift.

6 The qualification 'in a sense' recognizes that if all creation originates with the Father, no return gift from creation can add to what the Father eternally has. However, once creation has happened, we can in a limited way speak of a return gift adding to the Father. As creatures distinct from God who are free to give or not to give, when humans give themselves to the Father, the Father by grace receives a gift he did not have before. Of course, this human capacity to give is from God in the first place, a gift in creation and salvation.

7 Hurdley describes a clock given as a retirement present. Though the clock was displayed where the whole family could see it, only its original recipient was allowed to wind it up (Hurdley, 2007, p. 132). The clock had a special relationship to a particular family member, just as believers sometimes act as if the Gift of Christ is special to them as individuals rather than shared by the whole church.

# AN AVAILABLE GIFT? THE HIDDEN AND VISIBLE CHURCH

8 Without following him exactly, I am drawing heavily in this paragraph on Cavanaugh, 2011, pp. 161–9. See also McBride's account of 'responsible repentance', in which the church takes responsibility for its own sin and the sin of others in which it is always enmeshed, confesses that sin on behalf of itself and others, and engages in repentant activity as a sign and result of that confession (McBride, 2012, pp. 119–52).

9 Malo quotes Marion as saying that a gift-object works as an icon. For Marion, 'the gift-object simply serves as support to the "real" gift that is not an object; the gift object is a symbol of that gift, always inadequate to the fullness of what the "real" gift signifies (the gift-object works as an icon that does not avoid seeing beyond). In Marion's view, the gift is the presence of otherness, of the infinite ... Marion believes that a phenomenological experience beyond an intentional horizon is possible. This experience is donation or givenness' (Malo, 2012, p. 161). I am using icon in the sense of a sign that represents something beyond by virtue of being an analogy to it.

10 In the eighth century John of Damascus thought about the church in iconic terms when he wrote, almost as an aside, 'that our worship is an image [icon] of the good things to come' (2003, *Three Treatises on the Divine Images*, trans. Andrew Louth, Crestwood NY: St Vladimir's Seminary Press, II. 23).

11 Hurdley notes the growing phenomenon of unwanted heirlooms (Hurdley, 2007, pp. 130–1).

12 See pages 46–9 above.

13 Case and other empirical studies include Cole, 2005; Glasson, 2006; Moore, 2006; Male, 2008; Potter, 2009; Volland, 2009; Howson, 2011; Moynagh, 2012; Pass, 2012; Dutton, 2014; Keith, 2014; Walker, 2014; Watkins and Shepherd, 2014; Lings, 2016; Milne, 2016; Moynagh, 2017; Dunlop, 2018; James, 2018; Taylor, 2019; Moynagh and Beck, 2021; Aldous and Moynagh, 2021; the *Encounters on the Edge* series by the Church Army Research Unit, Sheffield, UK.

# 5

# A Gift for Everyone?
# The Socially Inclusive Church

Gifts are exclusive by nature. They are offered to some people but not others. Aafke Komter writes that 'reciprocal gift exchange function[s] as a principle of exclusion by – consciously or unconsciously – affirming ties between the members of one's own group, and excluding others from participation within networks of mutual gift giving' (Komter, 2005, p. 78). She notes that in their gift relationships people seem to choose partners who are attractive because they can be expected to give in return at some stage (p. 138). A friendship formed over cooking, for example, will deepen as the friends give each other lifts to the class. These gift exchanges will draw them together while omitting others. As Komter puts it, solidarity and exclusion are two sides of the same coin (p. 136).[1]

This is true of the church's gifts. Inevitably, each is given to some people but not everyone. If the Christian community is to be a blessing to all people (Gen. 12.3), the Spirit must swell the number of recipients who can receive the church's gifts and enable the church to include new people in its generosity. By expanding the circle of recipients, the inclusiveness of the church's overall generosity will counter the exclusiveness of each gift. This expansion of giving occurs crucially when new Christian communities are offered to more people in the settings of their everyday lives.

But when this happens the church again faces the problem of exclusion. Chapter 1 pointed out that, as a gift, every Christian community is exclusive by necessity. Once a community has decided to meet at a certain time, in a specific place, with a particular style and with an agreed agenda, although it will attract some people it is bound to exclude many others. It will leave out all those who for family, work and other reasons cannot come at the prescribed time, those who cannot access the facilities because of their disabilities or where they live, those who are put off by the style of the meeting (such as its formality or informality) or who don't identify with the agenda (the community's theological stance, or even to worship Christ).

# A GIFT FOR EVERYONE? THE SOCIALLY INCLUSIVE CHURCH

Of course, these Great Walls of China are not normally intended. Communities are trapped by what it means to be a group. The homophily principle – birds of a feather flock together – is chiselled deep into our humanity. Sociologists McPherson, Smith-Lovin and Cook cite study after study showing that similarity 'structures network ties of every type, including marriage, friendship, work, advice, support, information transfer, exchange, comembership, and other types of relationship' (McPherson et al., 2001, p. 415). They found that 'The literature is remarkably consistent across many different relationships and many different dimensions of similarity' (p. 429). Like attracts like. People are drawn together by what they have in common and giving reinforces their solidarity.

This is a problem for the church. Christians worship a God whose Son died on the cross with his arms outstretched in a welcome to all. The exclusiveness of congregations is at odds with such a God. So how can the circle be squared? This chapter suggests an answer. A gift stops being exclusive when it is shared. If a recipient refuses to treat a gift as a possession, sees it now as a gift for others and passes it on, and if the next recipient does the same and the next and the next, like retweeting a humorous birthday message, the gift will steadily include more people. The church is called to act likewise – never to be its members' possession but always a permanent gift.

Congregations are to offer new Christian communities as gifts to the people they currently leave out. These communities will be a source of further giving, including – we hope and pray – further new Christian communities. As the latter roll through society, more people will become recipients of the church's total generosity. These new communities will often be niche, tailored to the interests and circumstances of the gift's intended recipients. Rather than being lonely atolls, however, niche communities will be connected in a giant archipelago of mutual giving, each part enriching and being enriched by the others. Expressing the one all-embracing society that Jesus has founded, they will be beachheads to a greater whole.

## What is a homogenous unit?

The idea that the gift of the church should be tailored to specific people, fitting their context, is known as the homogenous unit principle. It is highly controversial. The notion was made famous by Donald McGavran, founder of the church growth movement, who declared that 'People like to become Christians without crossing racial, linguistic, or class barriers' (McGavran, 1980, p. 223); new converts should not be extracted from their social groupings. But McGavran didn't do himself any favours. By describing homogenous congregations in ethnic, class and linguistic terms, he seemed to legitimize racially segregated congregations and class divisions, which many Christians have found offensive.

However, other writers have defined the principle more broadly. For example, in his 'anthropological apologetic' for homogenous units, Charles Kraft listed 'common language, culture, kinship, history, ritual, territory, time, and the like' as the overt focus of groups' homogeneity. 'From an anthropological perspective, if there is no homogeneity, there is no groupness' (Kraft, 1978, p. 121). Any group based on a commonality such as a shared interest or background is a homogenous unit. This definition may seem sweepingly broad, but it avoids being arbitrary. If homogenous units are equated with groups sharing only certain characteristics such as ethnicity, where do you draw the definitional line? If an ethnically-based group is homogenous, why not one with people from a similar social background such as a neighbourhood? Or an age-based one? Or one based on a shared interest? Kraft's definition refers not specifically to racial or class segregation but groups in general.

## What is the issue?

If every group is a homogenous unit, does this reduce the concept to a truism? And where then is the debate? Peter Wagner defended homogenous congregations as expressions of Christian love. Love accepts converts as they are; it does not ask them to leave their cultures outside the church. Love respects others' identities; it does not cut off their cultural roots when they worship. Love eradicates barriers to grace; it does not erect moral preconditions for coming to faith; mixing with people who are very different may happen later, but should not be a hurdle at the start (Wagner, 1978, p. 12–19). Yet for many Christians this appeal to love has failed to carry the day. The same criterion can be used to argue *against* culturally specific congregations. Instead of demonstrating Christian love, homogenous congregations have been blamed for cementing social divisions, being inherently exclusive and allowing wealthy congregations to turn in on themselves and leave poor congregations behind (Hull, 2006). Homogenous congregations violate the gospel of reconciliation; instead of witnessing to the glorious inclusivity of God's people, they are more likely to erect defensive barriers to outsiders.[2] They sell out to a consumerist, choose-what-I-want mindset (Metzger, 2007).[3]

Here, then, is the crux of the debate. If the church is unavoidably comprised of homogenous congregations, where and how are social barriers knocked down? How does the gospel bring all social groups together so that in Christ there is visibly neither Jew nor Greek, slave nor free, male nor female (Gal. 3.28)? My answer unfolds in three stages. The first is that God uses homogenous congregations to offer the church as a gift. I argue that the doctrine of election mandates niche congregations as the means by which the church is given to others. God's gift of the church circulates in expanding circles through election. Second, I describe how the New Testament church broke down the barriers between communities. Believers could have their cake in groups reflecting neighbourhood ties and eat it in larger gatherings that bridged social divides. Third, I suggest that bridging structures such as denominations help to realize this New Testament vision today. My conclusion is that beachhead congregations should be the basis of a *geographical* (as well as network) approach to mission. Thus, if the last chapter was about making the church available, this one is about making it available to *everyone*.[4]

## A specific gift

Beachhead congregations are underpinned by the doctrine of election. Through election, God chooses the particular to reach the universal. God selects one group to bring God's plenitude of salvation gifts to another. Applied to the Christian family, election is the means by which the church with its life of generosity is given away, group by group. If 'no man is an island', the church can be offered appropriately to individuals via their social group. However, many Christians find the idea of election difficult. It appears to suggest that a capricious God chooses some people but not others, putting exclusion at the heart of God's purposes.

### Election and mission

Karl Barth transformed this understanding. He saw election as referring first to Christ rather than to human individuals. To simplify, God did not create men and women and next decide that Christ would become a human being among them. God eternally chose that Christ would become a human, and created women and men (and the rest of the universe) to make this choice a reality. Christ did not, in the first instance, become a human for us; we were created for Christ. Ephesians 1.4 states that the Father of our Lord Jesus Christ 'chose us in him before the creation of the world'. As Ross Hastings puts it, when conceiving creation 'God put us and Christ together in his mind' (Hastings, 2012, p. 109). Thus election is the best news of the gospel. Election declares that God is for humanity in Christ – not for a mere section of humanity but for humanity as a whole. Christ became a human being in order to have a human-to-human relationship, to exchange gifts, with *all* women and men. Fundamentally, election is a divine strategy to embrace all people, without coercion, in the loving arms of Jesus.

So in the election of Israel, Abraham's descendants are to be the recipients of God's blessing in order that 'all peoples on earth' will be blessed (Gen. 12.2). The purpose 'is repeated six times in Genesis and is clearly a central dimension of Israel's election' (Wright, 2004, pp. 473). Later, Abraham's heirs were brought out of slavery so that, as a nation of priests (Ex. 19.5–6), they could perform the priestly function of making God known to the surrounding peoples. God selects a specific entity, Israel, to be a blessing to other social entities.[5]

Though Israel came to understand election as being for service to the world, strangely the people 'never attempted to contribute to the realization of this purpose through active missionary activity' (Imchen, 2001, p. 26). Despite the exception of Jonah, mission was predominantly seen in attractional terms. The emphasis of the Jewish Scriptures such as Isaiah 61.5–6 and Zechariah 8.20–23 was on God summoning the nations to himself 'in the great pilgrimage to Zion' at the end times (Wright, 2006, pp. 502–3). Outsiders would come to Israel, drawn by the nation's ethical purity, just as many churches today hope an attractive communal life will draw outsiders to them.[6]

Yet welcoming outsiders raised questions about Israel's identity. Would newcomers dilute the nation's uniqueness? This sparked debate within the Jewish Scriptures. Alongside the fling-open-the-doors vision of the future was a desire to close ranks against outsiders, reflected for instance in Ezra and Nehemiah. This second view held that faithfulness to Yahweh could be maintained only by strict separation from other nations; after all, Israel's previous apostasy had sprung from hankering after the religious practices of her neighbours.

> There is a strong universalist tendency in Israelite faith. Israel is called to be the light to the nations. On the other hand, Israel remains bound to her racial origins. She remains a particular people. Here is the tension. If she opens herself outward as bearer of the promise for all, there is the danger of losing her identity. But in closing in upon herself, there is an equally grave danger of loss of identity by failing to bear the promise. (O'Donnell SJ, 1992, p. 15)

# A GIFT FOR EVERYONE? THE SOCIALLY INCLUSIVE CHURCH

An attract-all approach creates a similar headache for congregations today. Congregations may want to invite everybody, but because of when, where, how and for what reason they meet they are unable to welcome all. Either they can be true to themselves, to their social background, interests, preferences and so on, or they can sign up to God's mission to everyone. But, like Israel, can they do both?

It required Jesus to reimagine the course of election. With the incarnation, election was narrowed down to one person, who represented all that Israel was meant to be. Jesus then showed how exclusive gatherings could welcome others without losing their identities. He did not go to everyone, but chose a small group of followers with the same Jewish background to take his salvation to all. These elect were to go to other cultural groups and start further communities, which in turn – with their identities intact – would give birth to still further communities. Thus the church spread to a multiplicity of Gentile settings, forming diverse portraits of Jesus as it did so.[7] The Jesus from Jewish culture was translated into the Christ for all cultures. From a gift perspective, communion in Jesus was not given to everyone at once. Like many gifts, it circulated by being shared.

Gerhard Lohfink argues that election respects people's freedom. Unlike revolutionaries, who are short of time and use violence to move the inert masses to act, God brings radical change without duress. Rather than using persuasion, which can be manipulative, God *shows* people the gift, freeing them to make up their own minds.[8] Writing of Abraham, Lohfink says:

> It can only be that God begins in a small way, at one single place in the world. There must be a place, visible, tangible, where the salvation of the world can begin: that is, where the world becomes what it is supposed to be according to God's plan. Beginning at that place, the new thing can spread abroad, but not through persuasion, not through indoctrination, not through violence. Everyone must have the opportunity to come and see. All must have the chance to behold and test this new thing. Then, if they want to, they can allow themselves to be drawn into the history of salvation that God is creating. (Lohfink, 1999, p. 27)

Like all gifts, the church is transmitted through relationships, in this case between one group and another. Because the church heralds the restoration of relationships, this relational method fits the relational goal of mission (Newbigin, 1989, p. 82).

Election-as-mission has particular salience today, when individuals frequently belong to a variety of networks. 'Bridging ties' take people from

## GIVING THE CHURCH

one network to another, creating opportunities to offer communion in Christ to new settings. The number of such ties are ballooning through improved communications, greater population density, the expansion of professional and managerial occupations (people who are most likely to engage in bridging behaviour), and the spread of market mechanisms (Granovetter, 1983, p. 208, 210). Giving the church to others, group by group, rubs elbows with today's 'network society' in which people have more and more social connections (Castells, 1996).

### The crux of election

The risk, of course, is that congregations turn in on themselves and prove unattractive. They interpret their calling in a self-serving rather than self-giving manner. Concern centres on 'my' or 'our' salvation rather than the salvation of other people. Election becomes a fence that keeps others out. This danger is overcome by what Sigurd Grindheim calls 'the crux of election', which is the reversal of values. 'That which has no outstanding inherent value becomes precious by divine election and that which is not choice in itself becomes the object of God's choice' (Grindheim, 2005, p. 9). Deuteronomy 7.7–8 illustrates the point. The Israelites were chosen out of divine love, not because of any merit in themselves; they were the fewest of all peoples. Far from being earned, God's grace in election was a gift.

Being valued by God creates a giving momentum. Recipients are freed from spiritual arrogance and preoccupation with status. As St Paul repeatedly argued, the gift of Christ without regard for worth levels social distinctions (Barclay, 2014, pp. 11–17). All are on the same grade. This frees believers from defensiveness and self-concern – 'Am I as good as you?' It gives them an identity (being valued by God), confidence in that identity, and a sense of grateful well-being which releases them to give the church away.

> If a Christian community has no sense of its identity in Christ as the center of its life, it will not have a great deal of generosity and compassion to share with others ... Just as persons cannot give themselves away to others if they have no sense of self-worth to share, churches with no sense of identity and worth have little to share also. (Russell, 1993, p. 178)

When undeserved grace empowers congregations to turn outward, identity is expressed not by affirming who *we* are but by affirming who

## A GIFT FOR EVERYONE? THE SOCIALLY INCLUSIVE CHURCH

*you* are. 'Our identity as a community lies in prioritizing you, not us,' members can think. So, for instance, a new skateboarders' Christian community (examples exist) will have several identities, such as followers of Christ, youth, skateboarding and the neighbourhood. If members reach out to teenagers younger than themselves, the community's identity will be enlarged, perhaps to 'We're people who support those excluded from school.' Once identity lies in the church's external rather than internal life, church members can define themselves not *against* other groups but against the *exclusion* of other groups.[9]

### Connecting election to gift

In the context of ecumenism, Letty Russell proposes that election be recast as hospitality, which is one type of giving. To avoid election shrivelling to group defensiveness and so disrupting ecumenical relations, she suggests that 'One possibility would be to speak of hospitality and diversity rather than unity and diversity. In this way we move away from chosenness as a basis for unity in Christ toward the metaphor of compassion and hospitality as a basis for unity' (Russell, 1993, p. 173). Unity would not be built on denominations' shared origins in divine election – 'We are one because we are all elected.' It would be founded on hospitality, which 'is an expression of unity without uniformity, because unity in Christ has as its purpose the sharing of God's hospitality with the stranger, the one who is "other".'

Echoing this last point in relation to migration, the ecumenical 'Affirmation on Mission and Evangelism' asserts that 'in God's hospitality, God is host' and we are all invited to participate in his mission (WCC, 2013b §71). It concludes that 'Mission ... is an invitation to the "feast in the kingdom of God" (Luke 14:15). The mission of the church is to prepare the banquet and to invite all people to the feast of life' (§101). According to some mission writers, cross-cultural missionaries do this best when they 'understand themselves as guests, accepting in humility that they depend on the hospitality of the host community, adapting as far as possible to local customs and expectations as a guest would do' (van den Toren-Lekkerkerker and van den Toren, 2015, p. 229). The church receives hospitality from the world and then offers back God's hospitality, an invitation to the eternal banquet. Election would describe how this invitation is passed from group to group.

But does hospitality adequately capture what is involved? Russell claims that hospitality is not a subtle invitation to adopt the lifestyle of the host. Yet in its everyday usage that is precisely what hospitality entails. Guests

GIVING THE CHURCH

typically conform to the host's expectations. If you are invited to stay in someone's home, the home is not a gift to be received however you want. You can't dictate what food is served nor go about redecorating the rooms. You must fit in. Indeed, as Robyn Horner points out, hospitality works precisely because the gift is limited; by dictating the terms, hosts can keep their hospitality affordable (Horner, 2001, p. 12).

If God's hospitality is like a feast, does this not begin to subvert hospitality's limitations by suggesting an abundance of giving? So why not put the idea of divine giving on the menu rather than hospitality, which is just one aspect of supernatural generosity? Why not see election as an outworking of God's infinite largesse? As we saw in Chapter 1, a common feature of giving is that the gift is passed on. It benefits more and more people by being shared. When this happens with the church, the gift in a sense becomes more generous. As membership grows, God's people have more blessings to offer externally and to exchange internally. This enlargement of generosity is what election points to. The number of guests and the amount of food continually increase. The frontiers of hospitality ('only so many guests', 'we can only provide so much food') constantly expand.

To be passed on, the gift must be released. As Part 2 will stress, a gift is not a gift unless the giver lets go. This again subverts the hospitality model. The gift is offered in a way that indigenizes the church. The 'guests' are allowed to determine the rules of the household – how they worship, practise mission, govern themselves and so on, remembering of course that they must also fit into the neighbourhood (the wider Christian community). Encouraging recipients to indigenize the church is important if discipleship, prayer, Bible study, worship and outreach are to make sense in the context. How can the church witness to God's coming reign if the latter is not earthed in the people's everyday lives? The generosity model recognizes this by taming the controlling aspect of hospitality. Of course, giving too can be overbearing. But this is avoided when the church is joined to Christ. United with him, the church can be offered to others in the manner of Christ, who gave himself to the world by releasing himself into the hands of others.

Obviously, this example must be followed within limits. Like Jesus, the church will give its self to others with its own essential character – communion in Christ – intact. (Otherwise, what would it be offering?) The church takes account of recipients' identities while remaining true to its own. Can a community be authentic without others feeling excluded? Sanctuary, in Birmingham UK, originally described itself as being 'for British Asians, their families and friends'. Later (when the group's identity was more settled), it described itself as 'a safe space for British Asians or anyone interested in exploring eastern and western spiritualities in Christ'.

## Have we misread the New Testament?

The danger is that, having solved one problem, new Christian communities recreate it inside the church. Rather than excluding people outside they become emblems of exclusion within. Given group by group, congregations take on the social characteristics of their recipients. These characteristics then become markers of difference which form barriers to other Christian groups. Congregations stand apart from, become suspicious of, or are even hostile to one another. The church becomes disfigured by division and strife.

This critique can be countered by the tendency of gifts to take recipients into a wider community. The gift of a cinema ticket brings you into an audience who enjoys the same film. The gift of an article of clothing attaches you to a largely invisible collection of people who admire the same item. When gifts are shared they strengthen the relationships of those involved. It is no coincidence that gift giving, at birthdays or Christmas for example, is often associated with festivity, which brings people together. Gifts strengthen community.

We can see something of this in the New Testament church. It is widely assumed – by Bruce Fong (1996) and others – that the only alternative to culturally segregated churches is to have congregational melanges that combine people from as many different backgrounds as possible. 'Isn't this what happened in the New Testament?' they ask. Pauline scholar Eckhard Schnabel argues that it was. St Paul was committed to a church in which all social divisions were overcome. He did not establish separate house churches for Jews and Gentiles, slaves and freemen, rich people and poor people. As Galatians 3.28 puts it, he wanted all to be one in Christ Jesus (Schnabel, 2008, pp. 404–13).

However, Acts and the epistles can be read differently. As Roger Gehring notes, recent scholars tend to agree that the first-century Christians gathered basically in two church forms: the house church and the whole church in any city or town (Gehring, 2004, p. 157). Almost certainly, as

GIVING THE CHURCH

we shall see, house churches reflected the social characteristics of their neighbourhood or network. The town or city-wide gatherings brought these varied congregations together. Recipients of the gift, communion in Jesus, were drawn into the whole Christian community. Niche was combined with breadth. It is surprising how often this synthesis is overlooked. Theologians widely assume that it was in the house churches that people from different backgrounds mingled together. Yet it is more likely that this blending happened in the wider gathering. It was there that the church avoided the danger of cultural segregation. If this was so, it answers the question: how can God's people embody the twin aspects of gift – the gift's narrowing down to the recipient and its widening out to a larger community?

## Jerusalem, Antioch and Rome

René Padilla, a trenchant critic of culturally-specific congregations, maintained that there is nothing in Acts to support the view that the Jerusalem believers met in homogenous gatherings. He claimed that 'All the evidence points in the opposite direction' (Padilla, 1982, p. 25). Luke emphasizes that the believers were 'all together' (2.44). They held 'all things in common' (2.44; 4.32). They were 'of one heart and mind' (4.32). However, these statements do not preclude meetings of socially distinct groups. Acts 2.46 describes believers breaking bread in people's homes. The latter were scattered around the city, and most likely would have included people from local networks. New Testament scholar Reta Finger, for example, suggests that families sharing the same courtyard may have come together (Finger, 2007, p. 238). Believers would have met as homogenous units, based largely on geography.

The first followers of Jesus were almost certainly influenced by the synagogues they were used to. From where else would they have drawn inspiration? Though the Talmudic assertion that there were 390 synagogues in first-century Jerusalem may have been an exaggeration, there do seem to have been a considerable number. Meeting in various parts of the city, they catered for people with a shared social background who were drawn to the neighbourhood. Acts 6.9 may be referring to no less than five synagogues: for freedmen, people from Cyrenaica, Alexandrians, those from Cilicia, and people from Asia (Fiensy, 1995, p. 233). It would have been natural for followers of Jesus likewise to break into gatherings of people from similar backgrounds. Yet, importantly, these groups came together 'every day' in the temple courts (Acts 2.46). This wider gathering expressed visibly the unity of believers emphasized by

## A GIFT FOR EVERYONE? THE SOCIALLY INCLUSIVE CHURCH

Luke, and made strategic decisions such as appointing the seven deacons (Acts 6.2–6). Significantly, the latter recognized the existence of a distinct cultural entity: Hellenistic Jewish deacons were to look after the Hellenistic Jewish widows. City-wide gatherings respected social differences while joining up the various dots.

The church in Antioch appears to have been similar. Gehring believes that Galatians 2.11–14 assumes that a number of house churches existed (Gehring, 2004, p. 112). On his visit to Antioch, Peter was accustomed to eating with the Gentiles in these churches. But when challenged by recent arrivals from Jerusalem, he restricted his table fellowship to the Jews. Though what happened is debated, withdrawal would have been relatively simple if believers mostly met in ethnically different homes. Peter would have declined Gentile invitations. Antioch, the empire's third or fourth largest city, had 18 ethnic quarters (Drane, 2011, p. 160). Jewish synagogues were separated according to ethnic background (Gehring, 2004, p. 113) and it is reasonable to assume that this was true also of the house churches. Ethnic and other social groupings would have lived in different parts of the city, and it would have been natural and convenient for each church to welcome people from its vicinity and from its family and friendship networks, including slaves.

Gehring does not argue this last point. Indeed, he believes that such separation was improbable. It would have created social barriers in a church that, from its beginning, had been anxious to haul barriers down. Yet as he himself points out (p. 113), the confrontation between Paul and Peter took place in front of the whole Antiochian church – 'in front of them all' (Gal. 2.14). This hints that, as in Jerusalem, all the house churches periodically came together. Most likely it was in this setting that people from different backgrounds jumped ethnic and social hurdles to express their oneness in Christ. Blending in a city-wide gathering would have achieved the goal Gehring points to, but without defying geographical logic by combining all types in a local mix.

In Rome there was a similar pattern of scattered neighbourhood churches. Robert Jewett suggests that most Christians lived in the slum districts. They would have met in one of the workshops on a tenement block ground floor, or in a temporarily cleared space on one of the upper levels (Jewett, 2007, pp. 54, 64–5). Typically, attendees would have lived nearby and shared a similar social and ethnic background. Luxury apartments and, for the very rich, entire houses were located elsewhere. Some churches met in these parts of the city (pp. 64–5) and appealed to different networks to the tenement groups, including family members, slaves and the head of the household's clients (reflecting the ubiquitous system of patronage).

There is no evidence that these neighbourhood churches met together, but they were clearly well networked. Paul could address his letter 'to all in Rome' (Rom. 1. 7), which implies that the letter was passed from gathering to gathering. Indeed, though not followed by most scholars, Paul Minear argued that the letter to the Romans, with its theme of Jews and Gentiles being one in Christ, was written in the hope that 'A larger number of segregated house churches would at last be able to worship together – Jews praising God among Gentiles and Gentiles praising God with his people' (Minear, 1971, pp. 16–17).

## Paul's churches

Certainly the churches Paul founded continued the Jerusalem and Antioch practice of meeting both separately and together. The mainstream view is that they met in people's homes: 'The household was much broader than the family in modern Western societies, including not only immediate relatives but also slaves, freemen, hired workers, and sometimes tenants and partners in trade or craft' (Meeks, 2003, pp. 75–6).

Patronage networks were important, too. We should not assume that this mixture of freemen, slaves and so on represented a heterogeneous gathering. House churches were 'inserted into or superimposed upon an existing network of relationships' (p. 76). Despite differences of age, gender and status, each household comprised a homogeneous unit in the sense that it reflected a particular network. Note: every homogeneous unit, whether in the ancient world or today, contains people who are different by age, occupation or whatever but who share a commonality that overrides these differences. This was true of ancient households, which is one reason why on occasion entire homes could convert (for example, 1 Cor. 1.16; 16.15). They were homogeneous units defined not by social stratification (such as freemen versus slaves), but by being drawn from a distinct network.

Some New Testament scholars have recently explored the non-family basis of at least some of the so-called house churches. Richard Ascough (2000), for example, has suggested that occupational ties played a crucial role among a number of the Thessalonian believers. Richard Last has argued that the basic unit of the Corinthian church was the neighbour-hood rather than family. He adds, significantly, 'There is little warrant to imagine the small Jesus movement in Corinth to have included recruits from multiple neighborhoods' (Last, 2016, p. 417). On the basis of such studies, Edward Adams questions whether house churches are as much to write home about as scholars have thought. Future research should explore the street or neighbourhood as a foundation for the early church's expansion (Adams, 2018, pp. 122–3). If gatherings emerged from within occupational and geographical ties as well as family ones, local churches would have been homogeneous units, forerunners of today's culturally-specific congregations. The difference is that today's more complex society has a greater diversity of niches. So giving the church within these segments will probably increase the variation of church forms.

It is clear from 1 Corinthians 14.23, where Paul writes of the 'whole church' coming together, that these separate gatherings periodically met as a single group, probably in a large home such as the one apparently owned by Gaius. In the concluding section of Romans, most probably written in Corinth, Paul sends greetings from Gaius, whose hospitality 'the whole church here' enjoyed (Rom. 16.23). 'In the Greek Old Testament this expression consistently refers to an assembly of all Israel; thus it must be the totality of Christians in Corinth which is in view' (Banks, 1980, p. 38).

In Acts 20 Luke records that 'Paul sent to Ephesus for the elders of the church' (v. 17). The reference is to the church as a single unit. The thought is echoed in verse 28, where Paul urged the elders to keep watch over 'the flock', again singular. Evidently the Ephesian house churches, which presumably emerged from the homes Paul had visited in verse 20, saw themselves as a city-wide entity. This would have been natural if they periodically met together. Indeed, the elders may well have been the house churches' leaders. Paul could summon them because they were used to meeting up, perhaps to plan the larger assemblies.

New Testament believers received communion in Christ within culturally specific churches, but these churches were drawn into the wider Christian community through gatherings that spanned social divides. The structure held together social similarity and diversity, small meetings and bigger ones, the safety of a known group and the challenge of people with different outlooks, and it combined intimacy with looser relationships. This both/and approach was far from easy, as the divisions in Corinth illustrate, but the first Christians seem to have made it a priority.

## Bridging ties

Also apparent in the New Testament are the beginnings of a visible universal church. The latter comprised a 'holy internet' of connections between believers in one urban centre and another (Thompson, 1998), such as the strict Jews from Jerusalem who came to Antioch (Gal. 2.12), people who carried letters from one church to another (like Phoebe who most likely took Paul's letter to Rome – Rom. 16.1–2), believers who arranged and took financial gifts to places where Christians were in need (see 2 Cor. 9), itinerant teachers and prophets who connected Christian communities (Kreider, 2016, p. 77), and merchants travelling on business.

Between the neighbourhood churches on the one hand and this nascent global church on the other were a variety of formal and informal intermediate structures. The most obvious were the city-wide gatherings, with links outward to the larger body and inward to the neighbourhood meetings. In addition there were groups who connected neighbourhood churches to the town-wide gatherings by arranging food for the poor (Acts 6.1; see James 2.15) or by exercising pastoral oversight as elders (Acts 20.17; 21.18; 1 Tim. 4.14). Not least were groupings of churches that linked to the growing international church through their itinerant founder (1 Cor. 1.10–16).

These connections provided pathways from neighbourhood churches to the whole Christian community. Believers' horizons would have expanded as letters from the church's founder circulated round the house churches or were read out in the city-wide assembly, as news was shared by visitors from out of town, and as people from different backgrounds met in the city-wide gathering and perhaps in a service group to organize food distribution or a financial collection. At the same time, each house church would have contributed to the life of the whole by sharing the gifts of its members and its insights into the gospel. Because of integrated gatherings combined with niche groups, the growing diversity of neighbourhood churches could stretch the ecclesial fabric without tearing it apart.

Niche communities opened doors into the household of Christ, while bridging structures provided corridors to the church at large. No doubt this seemed a pragmatic way of getting organized. But these arrangements also witnessed to a time when cultural identities would be preserved while social barriers were completely overcome. In the glimpse of this future revealed in Revelation 5.9–10, the 'kingdom' (singular) is described in terms of people 'from every tribe and language and people and nation'. The word for 'tribe' can describe subgroups in a city such as the tribe of shoemakers in Philadelphia (Koester, 2014, p. 380). Homogeneous units at subgroup, ethnic and national levels will be found within the one kingdom. No social group need be excluded. Social niches will be drawn *into* the whole and drawn *to* one another. A multitude of different notes will harmonize in an extended chord – music to those longing for diversity to be combined with unity.

## Bridging structures

From their beginnings in the New Testament, bridging structures have become increasingly complex. They now include Christian traditions regarded as denominations, networks that function as a denomination, the Roman Catholic and Orthodox Churches who have traditionally seen themselves as the one church of Christ, and a variety of networks within and across the denominations and Churches. Their role in enabling gift exchanges between beachhead congregations and the wider church challenges those who, like giving someone a mobile phone short of a SIM card, want to offer Christian community without the encumbrance of the institutional church. Bridging structures provide connectivity by functioning like homogeneous units. Participants in each Christian tradition comprise a shared spiritual culture, while within a tradition prayer retreats, interest groups, committees and synods are also homogeneous units because they assemble around a common theme or task. Like any homogeneous unit, alongside its commonality each grouping also contains people with varying experiences and backgrounds. These differences multiply as groups increase in size.

Homogeneous units within God's people provide stepping stones from the congregation to the universal church. A congregation introduces its members to the tradition in which it grows. In time, the tradition becomes part of believers' Christian identity, giving them the confidence to walk into the wider church. Perhaps someone in a new young adults community invites another member who is passionate about the environment to one of the denomination's ecology groups. There she meets people of different ages and backgrounds who share her concern. Maybe she recognizes pieces of liturgy or shared assumptions and thinks, 'I am one of them.' Gradually she becomes comfortable enough to start attending other denominational events, and later perhaps steps beyond the tradition to other parts of the church. When she and others cross these homogeneous stepping stones at their own pace, dipping their toes into one event and then another as their confidence grows, the dynamic of election, group by group, is echoed *within* the church.

### An end to denominations?

Some people understandably object to the *competition* between bridging structures, not least between denominations. Paul Avis writes:

> The fact of denominationalism is a standing rebuke to the churches. It is eloquent testimony to the fact that they have failed – failed to heed the

prayer and command of Christ and the apostles in the New Testament
that the church should be visibly one ... To acquiesce in denomin-
ationalism is to confess failure; to glory in it is a sickness. (Avis, 2011,
pp. 26–7)

Avis and others pray that separate traditions will learn to work as one,
while remaining distinct, as a step towards full visible communion (Avis,
2022, p. 124).

However, others see articulated unity, or reconciled diversity, as a
desirable alternative. Unity lies in improving relationships between the
different traditions, not ultimately bringing everyone into a single church.
'The unity to which the church is called is a unity of relationship, and only
secondarily of institutional structures' (Ensign-George, 2018, p. 279).
The argument is similar to the one for homogeneous units. Identity
requires distinction – we know who we are because we are not the other.
Unity that blurs difference undermines identity. So rather than pursuing
this kind of unity, it is better to respect differences of ethos, organization,
worship and more and strive for a solidarity based on generous relationships between the Christian traditions.

Partly reflecting a widespread post-institutional mood, still others
worry about the existence of *any* structures. They fear that bridging
structures will suck the life out of the congregation. Fresh insights from
the Spirit will be stifled as traditions defend their heritages against local
innovation. However, this danger can be reduced if the tradition has a
narrative rather than essentialist identity. Put briefly, an essentialist identity is based on certain practices, structures and beliefs which the tradition
seeks to preserve for future generations. Emphasis is put on preserving
the forms of the tradition's visible life because form is seen to have theological significance; how things are done makes a theological statement.
A narrative identity, on the other hand, is based on the tradition's story,
as part of Jesus' story. What is primarily cherished and passed on is not
the specific forms of the tradition's life, for the Spirit can bring change
as circumstances alter. Rather, the tradition's developing account of its
interactions with God is handed on. The narrative will certainly include
practices, structures and beliefs that embody the tradition's understanding of the gospel, but these will evolve as the narrative unfolds. The form
of episcopacy, for example male bishops, can change to include women.

The closer its identity lies to the narrative end of the spectrum, the
more easily the tradition will welcome the new. It will be less inclined to
defend its inherited structures and practices as if these can never change.
Rather, it will be open to their reform so that they can support a new
chapter in the tradition's memoir. The tradition will be more accepting

of experimentation because this will create opportunities for the Spirit to turn a page in its story. It will feel freer to embrace diversity of practice because identity will lie more in allegiance to the tradition's evolving drama than in everyone doing the same thing.[10]

At their best, bridging structures remind us that when we accept Jesus into our lives we do not receive him as an individual. We welcome him with all those who are in Christ. For, as Barth said, Jesus Christ would not be who he is if he lacked his community (Barth, 1958, p. 275). It would, of course, be unthinkably presumptuous to limit this community to the immediate gathering, as if all other believers did not exist. Bridging structures help each gathering to avoid silencing the rest of God's people. Instead, they enable Christians to live out their membership of the whole body in a concrete and particular way. Rather than this membership being vague and abstract, bridging structures make it visible and practical by providing navigable avenues from the congregation to the wider church. In particular, faced with the variety of Christian beliefs and practices, they allow congregations to traverse the many options without having to choose at every turn. Received as givens ('This is what we do'), doctrines and customs can be treated as gifts rather than as tasks to be constantly and exhaustingly negotiated. Congregations need not flail around without support, like beached fish. They can draw on oceans of wisdom.

Bridging structures enable congregations, as they combine in an institution or network, to become collective gifts to one another. The gift includes joining together to recruit, train, support and oversee leaders, establish and enforce agreed norms and practices, provide resources and organize mission at regional, national and international levels. Especially importantly, bridging structures connect poorer to wealthier congregations, challenging the latter's social complacency. There is clear evidence that networks in general contribute to overcoming poverty (for example, Finney, Kapadia and Peters, 2015), and that faith-based networks in particular do so; well-endowed congregations can share their resources (Furbey et al., 2006). As one congregation shakes hands with another, human and financial riches can be redistributed to those in greatest need. Furthermore, the God who uses all kinds to make a world delights in the multiple expressions of Christian life. True, diversity may narrow when certain customs (like types of Christian music) spread so widely that they become 'good practice'. But equally, as traditions adapt and combine practices from different sources or create something new, and as they give the church away in new cultural settings, diversity will increase. This greater variety, supported by bridging structures, will widen the range of gifts exchanged within and between the traditions.

It follows that bridging structures can free congregations from the parish of their minds. They open congregations to theological, liturgical, missional and organizational insights from other parts of the church. The witness of other congregations reminds each one that it is the church but not the fullness of the church; it has much to learn from the rest of God's people (Ensign-George, 2018, p. 149). Likewise, bridging structures themselves can transcend their limited horizons through ecumenical relationships. As Richard Rohr apparently said, 'It requires the whole church to reveal the whole Christ.' This means that bridging structures can aid discernment. Just as the encounter between the first Jewish believers and the Gentiles helped to clarify the Christian faith, each structure's way of life enriches the whole by bringing into relief – and tension! – existing understandings of the gospel. The church may take centuries, if it ever does, to reach consensus on differing expressions of Christian belief. Meanwhile, what are in effect extended trials can reveal the strengths and weaknesses of a practice or structure, allow corrections to be made and give the church time to discern whether the Spirit is at work.

All this leans against today's tendency to feel embarrassed by the institutional side of the church. 'Let's talk about mission,' some say, 'rather than the church.' However, if bridging structures draw people into the whole communion of saints, if they enable congregations to support, enrich and correct one another, if they channel resources to parts of the church most in need, if they require organizational forms to serve these functions and if, further, the term church includes being organized for these purposes, then talking about 'the church' is unavoidable. Highlighting bridging structures, whether traditional arrangements or new apostolic networks, underlines that what is given is *an institution*.

Mission is the church and the church is mission. Mission is the church because mission is communal. As a stark example, generosity takes the form of new Christian communities from which arise further types of service. The church is mission because its organization has a vocational purpose: bridging structures are to continue this communal mission by drawing new believers into the palpable life of the Christian community. Without these structures, believers would be visibly excluded from the larger church and mission would cease to be about inclusion in the whole Christian family. Mission would cement social division rather than dissolve it. If you love inclusion you must love the institutional church. For the church exists in its synapses as much as its cells.

This means that new Christian communities cannot be solo ventures, independent of the existing church. They must be integrated into the whole through arrangements that are appropriate to the specific Church, denomination or network. For example, maybe a few Christians draw together a justice group of people from outside the church. The group scours the Christian tradition to explore spiritual resources that will support its activities. In time, some members come to worship Christ, perhaps in a 'spiritual extra' after the group's main meeting. This worshipping community becomes the new congregation, whether large or small; as Jesus said, where *two or three* are gathered he is in the midst of them (Matt. 18.20).

Oversight of this congregation's birth should involve:

- Low control/high accountability of the initiative from the very beginning, with proper attention to such issues as health and safety, safeguarding and data protection.
- Recognition of the worshipping community, when it emerges, as a congregation of the local church or an offshoot (language will vary) of its parent congregation. This will include authorizing its leaders to conduct worship however informal, making sure that they are equipped for and supported in their roles, and ensuring that they are fully integrated into the governance of the church.
- Nailing down pathways to the whole church so that gifts can be exchanged between older and newer parts of the body. This will start by connecting the new Christian community to its parent congregation, for example by making members aware of volunteering opportunities in its parent from an early stage,[11] joint social events, study groups and missional action, shared celebrations at Easter and other times of the year, and maybe – as some churches do – having combined worship once a month. In time these connections will be extended to the wider church – an invitation to a denomination's prayer retreat, for example, or to a network's festival. The prayer should be for 'blended church' to emerge eventually, with old and new weaving together in seamless connectivity.
- Christian formation, so that people's journeys into Christ are supported with appropriate spiritual disciplines, theological education and personal mentoring.

## *Thin and dense relationships*

The challenge of connecting to the whole church is that believers' most dense relationships tend to be with people in the immediate gathering. They see others in the congregation most often and feel closest to them. Relationships typically get thinner as they ripple out to the particular Church, denomination or network, and thinner still to the church beyond. Because people are less invested in these thinner relationships, the pull of the congregation is greater than the church at large. Members then underplay the importance of the wider church. Yet in 1 Corinthians 12 Paul is at pains to stress that all parts of the body are to be equally valued. So although some relationships are necessarily thicker than others, we must resist the temptation to assume God most values *our* closest relationships. Relations with the whole church may consume less of our time, but they don't consume less of Christ's time! As head of the body, can we say the brain is more implicated in movements of a limb than of the body as a whole?[12]

Cultivating what should be the densest relationship of all – with Christ – will help avoid elevating the congregation. For Christ draws all people and their church connections together (Eph. 4.15–16). Deepening our life in him, therefore, will also strengthen our ties to the whole communion of saints. Knowing this can give perspective to involvement with the congregation. Through Christ, commitment to the latter will be balanced by an equal commitment to the church's other relationships, many of which we cannot see. In the church's deliberations, the congregational voice will not be allowed to drown out the choir.

## Implications

The church can be a gift to the world by circulating ever more widely group by group; by drawing its recipients, like many gifts, into a wider community, the universal church; and by offering structures that provide access to this larger community. A first implication arises from today's growing awareness of the coloniality of power. This is the basis and justification for the continued exploitation of the world and its resources by European systems of domination (Dexter-Dreis, 2019, pp. 1–2). As Christians begin to recognize the pervasiveness of coloniality, their shame intensifies at the racist attitudes in much of the church and the difficulty of bringing change.

However, rather than starting with attitudes in the congregation, might the key first lie in cultivating new, culturally-specific Christian communities? These black, white and other types of community would reflect the locality's social diversity, develop connections with each other and periodically come together (as in the Wildwood example in Chapter 10). To avoid echoing coloniality-type relationships, these local ecosystems would eschew the mental picture of lesser moons orbiting a parent sun. Instead, all the new Christian communities would have equal status with each other and with their parent. Adopting more an *inter*cultural than a multicultural approach, they would forge with one another criss-crossing ties of mutual generosity that would extend to the wider church.

## A GIFT FOR EVERYONE? THE SOCIALLY INCLUSIVE CHURCH

These deepening relationships have the potential to birth a new ecclesial imagination in which identities are based not on race but on being joined to Israel's God, whose Jewish Son dethrones all other races. Rather than ethnic superiority, this shared identity in Israel arises from God's election of a people who were – as we have seen – the least of all nations. Christians are drawn into a people whose very lack of intrinsic merit relativizes all other ethnic groups. ('How can I think my ethnic group is superior to yours, when our identities ultimately lie in the least of ethnic groups?') When ethnic minority and white communities embrace this 'least' identity and connect with the wider church, feedback loops can challenge racist attitudes in the parent congregation and in God's people beyond. Identifying with the new Israel trumps racial prejudice. Thus giving away new Christian communities can enable the church to become anti-racist and multi-ethnic in small archipelagos of diversity and unity. By multiplying these archipelagos, the church – we pray – can progressively be cleansed of its racist demeanour.[13]

Crucially, this begins to resolve a tension deep within contemporary understandings of the church. On the one hand is the desire that each congregation's style and activities should fit its particular context. On the other is the widespread suspicion of congregations based on the homogeneous unit principle. But is the former consistent with the latter? How can a congregation be contextual without being specific to a particular people? Yet if we champion cultural distinctiveness, how can we also express the ideal of a single all-inclusive church? Can diversity avoid undermining oneness, while oneness avoids smothering diversity? The New Testament suggests an answer. Congregations should both reflect their particular cultures transformed by the Spirit *and* engage with Christians from different backgrounds in wider settings. Catholicity combines with unity, while heresy is treated with the antidote of opposing views.

### A geographical orientation

Second, for all this to happen the church needs a renewed geographical vision, a twenty-first-century version perhaps of the traditional European parish. In defence of the latter, John Milbank has castigated evangelicals who prioritize the production of converts. They ape capitalism, which puts the production of goods and services on a plinth. Appealing to the like-minded is an efficient way to win souls. It is easy 'to get them in' because they are 'like us'. But the cost is not being available to everyone. Rather than being generous to the geographical neighbourhood as a whole, the congregation selects a segment. Loving others is directed not to whoever crosses our path but only to those we choose. This contradicts Jesus' teaching that *anyone* potentially is a neighbour to be loved (Milbank, 2009a, pp. 269–76). The church, which is exclusive like any gift (gifts are given to certain people, not everyone), becomes an even more selective gift.

Milbank wants the parish church to be a gift to the whole locality. Clearly, this can happen when the church draws together people from different ages, streets and backgrounds to join a festival, a community fun day, or a campaign to fight crime. But it is hard to be a close friend to everyone. Friendships are with specific people. The local church will often be a better friend and more generous gift to its neighbours when it draws near to people group by group, engaging each in depth. Around the original congregation will emerge new Christian communities, each representing people from a particular ethnic group, social setting or with a particular interest, but all connected to one another in a single biosphere.

Need these groups go as far as being separate eucharistic communities? Might the like-minded not gather to pursue their particular interests, include simple forms of worship in their activities, and yet – as some would contend (for example, Davison and Milbank, 2010) – celebrate the Lord's Supper all together as an expression of their oneness in Christ? Centralizing the meal has no scriptural warrant, however. The Jerusalem church broke bread in their homes (Acts 2.46); the Supper was scattered. Though it seems also to have been remembered when believers 'came together' in the town-wide assemblies (1 Cor. 11.17ff.), there is no New Testament evidence that the celebration was restricted to these gatherings.

So why should centralized celebrations have precedence today? Just as Jesus – born, ascended and reigning as a Jew – brought his Jewishness into his Father's presence when he returned to heaven, why shouldn't each interest group within a parish bring its particular way of life, transformed by the Spirit, into the Father's presence during its own celebration of an authorized Eucharist? Remember: the unity of believers is secured not by as many groups as possible visibly worshipping as one, though this may be desirable from time to time, but by the Spirit joining the groups together in Christ. No celebration can bring all Christians physically together![14]

By gratefully offering its worshipping self – communion in Christ – to others in a bespoke manner, a congregation can scratch below the surface of its neighbourhood and relate to each group in depth. Otherwise the congregation will remain exclusive because of when, where, how and why it meets. This exclusiveness, I have argued, can be overcome by following the pattern of election. One group of Christians transmits the church to others in an accessible manner; these recipients themselves hand on the church; and the same happens repeatedly to form an ecclesiastical paper chain. Election is theological language for a sociological truism: gifts are given to selected people. You can't offer a gift to everyone at the same time, *but you can pass the gift on*. That is the calling of the Christian community in response to grace. An exclusive gift becomes a universal gift by circulating ever more widely. In the process, following New Testament practice, recipients are drawn into a larger community through the bridging structures of the church. The latter enable members of each new community to circulate as gifts within, as well as beyond, the Christian family.

This warns against an exclusive emphasis on networks. The danger, as Milbank says, is that Christians reach out in mission to their existing networks and forget others. The gift's circulation is restricted. By contrast, if the church has a geographical orientation, it will be prompted to ask: who in the area are we not yet reaching and how can we lovingly connect? This question arises whether the geographical unit is local (a neighbourhood, office block, shopping centre, hospital or some other smallish place of human activity) or whether it is a town, city, region or nation (served by churches working together). The church's mission will include developing tailor-made relationships with one people group and then another until – God willing – the church is visibly present, as a loving community, wherever life happens. Networks bring you to particular demographic groups; geography checks whether you are excluding certain groups. Through networks the Christian community joins the fragments of a locality; through geography they join the fragments up. Geography and networks together are the route to social cohesion.

### Election as method

Third, election suggests a strategy for church multiplication based on one at a time. It follows the example of God, who did not start with a conference or a workshop, but with a single family, Abraham's. Centuries later a descendant of that family, Jesus, started with a small group of 12 who spread Christian communities one at a time, the first in Jerusalem, then in the next town, and then the next. This was multiplication not by policy document, not by impersonal communication, not by mass mobilization, but with the character of Community Organizing – at the grass roots, through relationships, step by step. Relationships are the currency of election.

And they need time. Election reveals that God is not in a hurry (see Koyama, 1979). It will take thousands of years for Abraham's family to bless the entire world. Just as gift exchanges are shaped by the ebb and flow of the relationships concerned, becoming more generous as the relationship deepens, offering God's people group by group can proceed only at the tempo of the relationships involved. So institutions and net-workers wishing to multiply new Christian communities must beware of forcing the pace. If God is replanting parts of the church so that it can flower in post-Christendom soil, human initiatives must reflect the patience of the Spirit, who graciously works at the speed of nature. One at a time, at the beat of the other, more bridleway than motorway – this is the route to ecclesial fruitfulness. Should a movement of multiplication eventually emerge, it will do so organically, in the mode of election to whose unfolding it will belong.

This provides a theological rationale for the experience of founders: starting a new congregation is easier the more specific the demographic they seek to love. A naive founding team may hope to serve an entire neighbourhood immediately. But the team will soon realize it must begin perhaps with young families or with people who have disabilities, and move out from there, group by group. It cannot start with everyone. Having identified the group, rather than wondering how to reach the group in general, founders fare better by asking, 'How can we reach the first few people – indeed, perhaps, the first person?' That initial con-nection is everything.[15]

In due course, on the grounds of unity, founders will be called to echo election within the church by introducing new believers to the wider Christian family, again group by group. These groups will be paving stones from outside the Christian community to the whole church, where ecclesial traditions can tap new believers on the shoulder and invite them to contribute. Whether these stones are within existing arrangements or take new institutional forms, encouraging the faithful along the path is vital. It requires the founding team to be bilingual: familiar with the languages of both the context and the wider church. If founders lack this second skill, might they need alongside them, within suitable structures, 'chaplains' or 'connectors' who link the new community to the church at large?

## Notes

1 In his research into giving David Cheal quotes an interviewee: 'gifts are given to people we know, and who know us, and who we know that we like better than others' (Cheal, 2016, p. 174).

2 'We recognize that in all human groupings there is a latent tendency either to claim from their members too high a loyalty (and so become idolatrous), or to shun outsiders (and so become self-centred)' (Pasadena Consultation 1978 (1987), §6).

3 For three views of homogeneous congregations – as a missional goal, a missional first step and a missional no-go – see Moynagh, 2017, pp. 220–2. For alternative categories, 'Scandalized', 'Skeptical' and 'Supportive', see Plaisted, 1987, p. 217.

4 I am grateful to Bishop Graham Cray for the term 'beachhead congregations'.

5 Not everyone has described Israel's election in such generous terms. Some have blamed election for Israel's genocidal treatment of the Canaanites, for example. Joel Kaminsky counters that the genocide was due more to the Canaanites being enemies of Israel than to election itself. In a great number of biblical texts (though not all), election does not occasion the call for a holy war. Rather, it 'gave rise to some of the most sensitive ideas concerning the treatment of aliens and foreigners found anywhere in the ancient world' (Kaminsky, 2003, p. 408). Deuteronomy 10.14–22, for example, sees love for the alien as an appropriate response to the people's election. Deuteronomy 26 includes the alien among those who are to be fed through the distribution of tithes (vv. 12–13). Again, this is presented as a proper response to being chosen (vv. 16–19).

6 Matthew 23.15's reference to scribes and Pharisees proselytizing, the only ancient source that explicitly ascribes a missionary policy to a Jewish group, can be interpreted in four ways, three of which would not imply Jewish mission to the Gentiles. It may, for instance, refer to the conversion of other Jews to Pharisaism or the attempt to turn Gentile God-fearers in diaspora synagogues into full Jews (Bird, 2010, pp. 66–70). See also Goodman, 1994.

7 New Testament scholars today tend to recognize the diversity of the primitive church. For example, Paula Gooder writes: 'The key point to mention here is variety. The Jewish synagogues from before the Rabbinic era were different from each other, with little set form of what happened when people came together, and the same would have been true of the early Christians. Those Christian communities that were Jewish in origin might have modelled their time together on the synagogue, but those that were Gentile in origin may well have had different patterns … each community would have done things differently,' though with common elements (Gooder, 2018, p. 243). Community with Christ was offered in a form that was appropriate to the context and was received in recipients' own social and cultural way.

8 Presumably showing can include describing the gift, which leaves room for verbal forms of faith sharing. Description and persuasion are importantly different.

9 Of course, in their journeys to Christ the skateboarders may also have to lose certain identities, such as a 'tough guy' image that leads to bullying.

10 See Moynagh, 2017, pp. 250–3.

11 For example, a printed version of the parent church's notice sheet might be put on the tables at a 'dinner church'. As members give it an occasional glance, they will be reminded that the initiative belongs to a larger whole. Maybe a notice

# GIVING THE CHURCH

catches someone's eye. 'I see you are forming a choir for the carol service,' says one person. 'Can I join?' Another asks, 'I see you are advertising for a book-keeper to help the church Treasurer. I used to do that sort of thing. Can I help?' Members of the dinner church might become volunteers in their local church long before they think of themselves as churchgoers.

12 In his study of the New Testament church, Kevin Giles notes that Paul and Luke use the word 'church' to describe all Christians, Christians in one location and Christians who assemble together. Paul can also speak of 'the churches of the Gentiles' (Rom. 16.4; see also 16.16). 'It is true that he uses the plural, but if the apostle can allow this wider usage then surely it is permissible to speak of Christians united together by common heritage and confession ... as a church' (Giles, 1995, p. 206). If 'church' refers to the whole Christian community in all its groupings, it must embrace *all* the people's relationships with each other.

13 I am grateful to Michael Beck for encouraging me to make this point.

14 Even Roman Catholic parishes, where the central Mass is highly prized, may have several congregations with their own eucharistic lives.

15 I have watched a team plan and advertise an all-age initiative without the involvement of local families, making assumptions about what would attract families. But hardly anyone came and the team disbanded in disappointment. Another team took a coffee urn to the school gate and offered parents dropping off their children free mugs of coffee once a week for a term. They got to know some parents, became friends with them, and co-created an all-age initiative that flourished. This illustrates the difference between starting with the group in general and starting with particular relationships.

# PART 2

# The Church's Self-donation

# 6

# A Sociological Framework

The church is like a hall of mirrors. Change the direction of your gaze and the church takes a different shape – institution, community, sacrament, herald, servant and school of disciples. Each is a distorted view if not balanced by the others. As the church transitions to a new theological era, *Giving the Church* asks whether we might see the Christian community reflected in a further mirror. Might a doctrine of the church centre on the church's call to a life of generosity in gratitude for divine love? This vocation can be unpacked in several ways, but as one vitally important aspect the church is to join the Spirit in offering others new Christian communities for the benefit of the world. Such a gift will be an offer of the church's very self, communion in Christ, which exists for the world and draws recipients into the life of the Trinity.

Part 1 argued that for some people this gift will be suitable when it comes as an invitation to join an existing congregation. But for many, such a gift will be inappropriate because the time, place, style and agenda of the congregation puts it out of reach. In these cases, the gift should comprise a new Christian community that *is* accessible. This gift is the fulcrum around which numerous other missional gifts can be multiplied. It is a well that can potentially nourish any of the Spirit's missional agendas. And it fosters spiritual growth among the Christians involved by bringing church, mission and discipleship together. In other words, new Christian communities are to be ecclesiastical Catherine wheels shooting off creation care, social concern, artistic creativity, reconciliation, evangelism, Christian formation and other missional sparks to light up the human and natural skies.

I went on to describe the nature of the gift – in essence, four overlapping sets of relationships with God directly, with the world, with the wider church and within each ecclesial community. These relationships are to be infused with the self-giving character of Christ through four essentials – word, sacraments, ministry and disciplines. When this happens, the church's four marks – one, holy, catholic and apostolic – will be expressed in the church's generosity to others, particularly in the form of new Christian communities. Offering these will encourage the marks to be present also in the church's internal life, making the Christian community a more attractive gift. To be such a gift, the church must be available. Accordingly, I extended the discussion of the visible/hidden church to the church's visibility (or otherwise) in all arenas of life. As a visible community, the church must take up tenancy where it can be seen. It must be present *with* people wherever they are if it is to be a present of fuller life *to* them. But can the church be available to everyone when gifts by their nature are exclusive? I used the doctrine of election to argue that the church can become generous to an expanding circle of people if communion in Christ is given to others relationally, group by group. Following the New Testament pattern, recipients of the church are to gather in culturally-specific communities that draw them into a mixture of backgrounds in the greater ecclesial whole. The particular is to be joined to the universal.

If generosity (in the widest sense) is fundamental to the church's vocation, how this happens must be a priority for church doctrine. The manner in which the church gives cannot be theologically insignificant. It is as important as reflecting on ministry, the sacraments and other indispensable practices of the Christian community. Accordingly, and aware of the ambivalent nature of giving, Part 2 lays down an ethical pathway for the church's giving. This framework, I believe, applies to the church's generosity in general. But I illustrate it with the gift of new Christian communities because, as mentioned in the Introduction, they are receiving growing attention today, church planting has been largely neglected in doctrinal treatments of the church, and these new communities are theologically important in themselves. A longer study would be needed to develop the framework in relation to other dimensions of the church's giving.

New Christian communities are not to be given in a one-way paternalistic movement but through a mutual exchange of gifts that forms and deepens the church's relations with the world. For these relationships to be morally healthy, offering these communities must be at the purified end of the spectrum described in the Introduction. It must involve an outward movement of receiving first, giving appropriately and letting go, a hinge process of accepting the gift (which forms community) and a return movement of giving back and bringing transformation. This fills out Marcel Mauss's structure of gift exchange as giving, receiving and returning (Mauss, 1990, p. 4).

This chapter describes this framework theologically, but adds depth by drawing on some of the social science and other literature on giving. As a whole, this literature is extensive and points in a number of directions; generosity has been understood differently down the centuries. My selec-

# A SOCIOLOGICAL FRAMEWORK

tion is driven by the pattern we see in the giving and receiving of Christ and is designed to flesh out that pattern as it applies to the church's own self-giving. Chapter 7 then draws on liberation theology to describe the ethical goal that drives this framework of gift exchange. Reinterpreting the herald model to see the church as God's conversationalist, Chapter 8 suggests a conversational methodology to deliver the goal, while Chapter 9 proposes a eucharistic spirituality to support this methodology. By bringing these liberationist, proclamation and eucharistic models into dialogue with the gift of new Christian communities, the models – I pray – can be reimagined to elaborate the church's entire vocation of generosity. Chapter 10 concludes that offering its self to others can help the church become a more attractive gift.

## The church must first receive

Oscar Wilde has probably best described how awful giving can be. In a scorching 1891 attack he argued that charity degrades and demoralizes its objects. It reinforces the status quo by reconciling the poor to their poverty. Charity is a means of control since it is normally offered with strings attached. And it elevates the material over other forms of well-being (Wilde, 2004). Generosity can be degrading, defensive, dictatorial and dehumanizing. But need the church's giving be quite so dark? Might we free the church's generosity from ethical gloom by framing it with the life and witness of Jesus?

### Brings out the best

Christ is a gift from God to the world (John 3.16). As such, Jesus encapsulates what being a gift should involve. Not least, he shows that being a gift starts with receiving. Jesus received his humanity before he gave his life; he received his surrounding culture before he gave anything back to it (Luke 2.41–52); and at his baptism he received the Holy Spirit before being led into his public ministry of self-giving. To be a gift to the world in the slipstream of Jesus, the church too must be a recipient before it is a giver – for three reasons.

First, receiving before giving increases the church's capacity to give. To offer a gift the person must have the necessary resources. The gift must be in the giver's possession, or the giver must have the materials and the skills to make the gift, or the money with which to buy it. 'We can give because we have first received from others. Without the giving of others

149

(nourishment, physical and spiritual care, love) we cannot develop ourselves as humans: walk, speak, love' (Malo, 2012, p. 165). What is true of humanity is true of the church. The church must receive from others if it is to be in a position to give to them.

By receiving the fruits of God's activity in the world, God's people are enabled to give back to the world the fruits of God's activity in the church. Indeed, the more the church receives from the world, whether it is resources for daily life or practical help in its mission, the more the church will possess to give away. This includes being able to give even when the church is poor; by receiving from others, the Christian community receives gifts that increase the ability to give out of its poverty. In particular, as the next chapter explores, the world's gifts may include painful criticisms of the church, criticisms that bring the church to repentance. One of the gifts God's people can request from the world is help in addressing those criticisms and in learning how they themselves can be a better gift.

Second, receiving before giving brings out the best in others. So often the church equates love with doing things *for* other people. Yet one of the greatest acts of love is to allow people to do things for *us,* because when people give they are enabled to flourish. A person who gives a meal can express their cooking abilities. A friend who drives you to hospital expresses their concern. Any act of giving can be an opportunity to show love. And when people show love they reveal themselves at their best. That is why inviting others to give to the church, without reducing this to fundraising, can be an act of love by the church.[1] In the act of giving, the other person puts their better side on display. Time and again in the Gospels Jesus allowed other people to give to him, such as the woman who anointed him with oil and all those who extended hospitality. 'Give me some water to drink,' Jesus said to the Samaritan woman (John 4.7). Likewise, when he encountered Zacchaeus, Jesus did not shame him for his misdeeds. He healed and saved him by asking for a kindness; shame was countered with acceptance (Vanstone, 1997, pp. 60–3). Thus, paradoxically, the church becomes a giver through the very process of receiving.

### Giving freedom

Third and most importantly, receiving first addresses some of the difficult power dynamics of generosity. Giving is ambiguous and fraught with difficulty. Givers and recipients may interpret giving differently, as with unwanted gifts; the recipient may refuse the gift or fail to reciprocate, offending the giver. Giving can create dependency, such as charitable giving that denies recipients an opportunity to give in return and leaves them vulnerable to the gift's withdrawal. Worse, gifts can be weaponized. They can be a means of manipulating or controlling others. Power is intrinsic to giving (Komter, 2005, p. 77).

The church resists malignant giving by declining to be the initial giver.[2] Being the first to give can be a threat to potential recipients. Giving invites a return gift, an obligation that may feel like an imposition. Not least it invites a relationship. 'The recipient gains a relationship with the donor through the medium of the gift' (Walter, 2013, p. 17). The recipient may not be ready for that. Receiving before giving, on the other hand, transforms the direction of obligation. Instead of the church's generosity putting the world under a duty to respond, the world's giving places a duty on the church. By changing the balance of obligation the church gives the world the freedom to initiate the giving cycle. The church makes one or more requests of the world. Those to whom a request is made can make excuses for declining the request, and if the excuses are convincing the refusal need not seem rude.

Perhaps, for example, a local church sends a team to offer communal life in Christ to residents of an apartment block. Some of the team move in and on the first evening find they are out of coffee. Rather than popping out to buy some, they ask the people next door. 'Let's be neighbours' is their implicit request. But despite having plenty of coffee, the occupants reply that they have run out too. Suspicious of newcomers, they keep their distance till they know the new arrivals better. Their excuse is plausible, so they can decline the request without appearing impolite.

By reducing the uncertainty in giving, the request for coffee makes it easier for the next-door occupants to initiate neighbourliness if they wish. They needn't worry that a welcome gift out of the blue would seem too forward, nor what sort of gift would be appropriate. They can provide a jar of coffee knowing it will be gratefully received. However, having asked for help and given their neighbours freedom to start the gift exchange, the churchgoers will not have the same freedom in whether to respond. To avoid appearing ungrateful they must return the gift at some stage. To an extent, their hands are tied. They must give maybe a jar of coffee in return, plus a box of biscuits as a 'thank you'.

Summarizing Georg Simmel, Rebecca Colesworthy comments that 'whereas the initial gift may be voluntary, the counter-gift can only ever be given out of obligation' (Colesworthy, 2018, p. 183). In freeing others to enter or not into a giving relationship with the Christian community, the church surrenders some of its own freedom. If the world chooses to give to the church, good manners require the church to give in response; the church is placed under an obligation. However, once they have received the church's return gift, the original givers can view the exchange as complete. They were asked for coffee, they responded, the new arrivals have expressed their gratitude, and the seesaw in giving and receiving is now level. The initial givers need not offer another gift unless they wish to maintain and develop the relationship. Once more, the initiative is in their hands.

The church thereby tilts the power balance towards the world. It places itself in the world's debt. Because being grateful 'involves an admission of our vulnerability and our dependence on other people' (Solomon, 2004, pp. v–vi), the church rather than the world feels the slight discomfort that can accompany gratitude. The Christian community trades its autonomy for a relationship on equal terms. This helps to avoid a Christendom paradigm of mission 'in which Christians benevolently sacrifice their time and resources for the material and spiritual benefit of others, whose identities are constructed on the basis of their material and spiritual need' (James, 2017, pp. 194–5). Instead of being treated as objects of mission, people outside the church are treated as subjects, as people in whom God is already at work, as persons who already have gifts from God to bring – without obligation. Receiving before giving is the first step in offering new Christian communities, as it typically is when offering all the church's gifts.

## An appropriate gift

God gave his Son appropriately. As a human, Christ revealed God in a form that women and men can understand. As God, he retained his divine identity, which includes infinite generosity. The combination of these two natures, distinct but one, bridges the gulf between God and humanity and makes possible an appropriate relationship between the two. Christ therefore modelled what is typical of healthy gifts. Gifts are appropriate to the recipient, to the giver, and to the relationship between them.

To fit the relationship, a gift must be appropriate to both sides' investment in the relationship, to how much it means to them. 'You do not expect the same from close friends and slight acquaintances, from lovers and your godmother' (Berking, 1999, pp. 4–5). So when the church seeks to be a gift of the Spirit to others, as with all its acts of generosity it will ask: 'What would be an appropriate thing to say about our relationship at this stage?' It follows that God's people will pause before offering communion in Christ until the relationship can carry the weight (see Matt.

7. 6). They will hold back until the patient trudge of repeated conversations creates the right moment. As suggested in Chapter 1, communion in Christ is an especially valuable gift because it comprises the church's self. It says how much the church esteems the recipients because precious gifts are reserved for people who are precious.[3] A gift that assumes its recipients are cherished will be an honest form of communication only if the recipients have been treated as such.

So time may be needed to establish relationships of trust through which the church's affection can be demonstrated. Acts of kindness, such as providing a soup kitchen for people without homes while mobilizing against the housing shortage, will show how much the church values the recipients. These kindnesses will occur within relationships of mutual generosity. Guests of the soup kitchen, for instance, will be encouraged to share their gifts of time and talent so that the kitchen becomes a giving *with* as much as a giving to. Evangelism will follow once people know from previous gift exchanges that they are loved for who they are (and when they have shown potential interest in the gospel). Thus a new Christian community will be offered within an *ongoing* gift exchange and when the relationship has reached an appropriate stage.

### Appropriate to recipients and givers

A gift is only a gift if it is received as such, and it will be received with pleasure if it is the 'right fit' for the recipient. An appropriate gift is not one that is deserved by, or due to, the person. Otherwise it would be a repayment. Rather, the gift is 'an unexpected surplus that comes without prior conditions set by the recipient' (Schmitz, 1982, p. 33). As an expression of concern for the other, 'purified' giving is more for the recipient than the giver. It is designed to surprise and gratify the recipient. So when the church offers communion in Christ, the form of the gift will chime with the best interests of the recipients. The community will be accessible; it will be where recipients lead their lives so that they can take hold of it. Its style and agenda will resonate with them. It will help them enjoy a fuller life and realize their potential. And when recipients unwrap the gift they will delight in it. As such, this will be a far cry from manipulative giving controlled by the giver's desires. It will be giving that puts the recipient first.[4]

To give in this way, the church must attend to recipients so that their longings, needs and character come to dominate its thoughts. This is a form of contemplation that enables the church to learn about recipients. The church allows recipients to impress themselves on its mind and steer

# GIVING THE CHURCH

its thinking, just as an emerging story impresses itself on the novelist and gives direction to what the writer seeks to create. Through contemplation, undertaken in the light of Christ, a picture will form of those to whom the church wishes to give, and – as with all gifts (Schwartz, 1967, pp. 1–2) – this picture will be conveyed in the gift that is given.

If gifts must be 'consonant with the character of the recipient' (p. 2), the church's gift of communion in Christ will correspond to the cultural expectations of those who receive it. New Christian communities, therefore, will be given away contextually. God's people will tread mentally in the footsteps of those who receive the gift. This does not require believers to lose their spiritual distinctiveness. Gifts add something to the lives of their recipients. And a new Christian community will be an addition to people's lives only if it is different in character to what recipients already have. In Jürgen Moltmann's provocative phrase, the new community will be 'alienated from its environment in Christ's way' (Moltmann, 2000, p. 68). The church will not be stuck on the same note as recipients. It will be distinct in the manner of Christ, which encompasses the way of inclusion. Jesus died on the cross for everyone. So, like Jesus, the church will differ from its recipients not least in the degree of its welcome. It will be distinctive in a fashion that warmly embraces people in their setting and adds to their lives.[5]

Just as a gift requires a receiver, it also needs a giver. Writers on giving have long said that gifts reveal something about the one who gives. As Ralph Waldo Emerson famously put it, 'a man's biography is conveyed in a gift' (Emerson, 1907). Gifts reflect the thought (or lack of it) that went into choosing or making the gift, and this thought accompanies the gift when it is handed over. The more thought and care put into the gift, the more the giver's self will be in what is bestowed.[6] 'Why did they bring such a cheap wine?' the hosts privately complain after the guests leave. 'I guess they don't think much of us.' A giver isn't just proving her magnanimity. She is making a statement about herself, her view of the recipient and how she sees the relationship (Osteen, 2002a, p. 23).

When Jesus turned water into wine at a wedding, the wine was admired for its quality (John 2.10). By holding nothing back, Jesus revealed something of his character. In like manner, the church's gift of new Christian communities must accurately convey who the church is. Through the Spirit, the gift must faithfully reflect the church's nature as communion in Christ. This must also be true of particular traditions within the church. Each will offer new Christian communities with the fingerprints of its history in Jesus. The gift must be signed by the giver.

## A SOCIOLOGICAL FRAMEWORK

### *A negotiated gift*

How do the different perspectives of giver, recipient and their relationship merge into one gift? In most cases, some sort of negotiation occurs. This is not normally a negotiation between the parties, as in a contractual relationship. It occurs inside the giver's head. Givers have an internal conversation. They create an imaginary present list from which they select a gift for its symbolic value. Lee Fennell describes these conversations as 'empathetic dialogue':

> To choose a gift, the donor imaginatively puts herself in the position of the recipient, seeking to discern preferences of which the recipient may not even be fully aware. The donor's task ... is to divine what the recipient would most wish to receive within the specific framework of the relationship. People wish to receive gifts that appropriately reflect the relationship as well as the individual identities of the donor and recipient. (Fennell, 2002, p. 94)

This requires insight into the other person. Fennell gives the example of a friend who has little current appreciation of jazz but who might wish to become someone who enjoys that type of music. 'Such a person would view a jazz collection as a particularly insightful gift, because it would demonstrate the donor's recognition of the recipient's interest in a specific form of self-transformation' (p. 94).

> A good gift is something like an act of recognition, in which the donor makes her knowledge of the recipient known to the recipient, who in turn may come to recognize something new about herself, or the donor, or the relationship. The desire to surprise and be surprised arises out of this deeper desire to know and be known by another. (p. 95)

The dialogue is complete when the recipient enters imaginatively and empathetically into the giver's thinking and appreciates the result. If the gift succeeds, it comes to represent the giver's imaginary empathetic dialogue that gave rise to it and which the recipient values. By triggering these associations the gift gains sentimental value, which may cause the gift to be assessed at far more than its monetary worth. 'Such empathetic dialogue is intrinsically valuable as a form of communication between parties, and is also instrumental in developing significant relationships' (p. 94).

To give away communal life in Jesus appropriately, the church will link arms with recipients through a similar alchemy. Via empathetic conversation, the Christians involved will seek prayerfully to understand at depth the potential recipients. They will imaginatively discuss how best the church can be offered, taking into account their own identities, the identities of the recipients, and the giver–receiver relationship. And as the gift exchange starts, develops and deepens the relationship, hopefully receivers will come to welcome the new Christian community, appreciating the thought behind it.

## Handing over the gift

David Cheal quotes Mauss as saying that gift transactions are 'first and foremost a means of controlling others' (Cheal, 2016, p. 3). This may be true of many gifts, but it is not true of a generous one. A 'purified gift' is not a gift unless it is released. The giver lets the gift go and allows the other to receive it in their own fashion. If I give a toy aeroplane to my grandson but spend the whole afternoon holding his hand, showing him exactly how to play with it, the present stops being a gift to him. It becomes in effect a gift to me – to relive my childhood! But if I allow my grandson to play with the gift as he likes, I may be surprised by what he does with it. The aeroplane may become a car, a boat or a rocket.

God's gift of his Son modelled letting go. Jesus did not arrive in Nazareth fully formed. He was implanted in Mary's womb, nurtured by her, raised by his parents, shaped by the synagogue he attended, influenced by his surroundings and, at the end of his life, subject to events. As a gift to Jews in the first instance, the Father released his Son into their hands and allowed the people to receive the gift in their own way, even to the extent of putting the gift to death.

### Passing on an heirloom

Gifts slip their moorings in different ways. Chains of ownership may be placed in new hands – 'This is now yours.' Or the gift may be shared, as when a guest's box of chocolates is passed round after a meal. Or the gift may be more like a family heirloom. The family values the object's accompanying story so much that the gift never leaves the family's possession. 'This necklace was given to me by my mother, who received it from her mother. I would love you to have it and then to pass it on to the next generation.' The gift is enjoyed, while held in trust till handed on. As Chapter 4 described, offering new Christian communities is a bit

A SOCIOLOGICAL FRAMEWORK

like giving an heirloom. Its members reap the benefits while guarding it for others.

When the church joins the Spirit in giving these communities away, the process will probably entail a progressive sharing of the gift. Some aspects of this communal life will be offered first, such as practical love and the experience of community, but other aspects (like worship) will be held back until people wish to receive them.[7] In these initial stages, leadership of the community will also be shared. Otherwise the community will not belong to those who join it. As families told the founder of one new Christian community in the UK, a community is only *their* community if they can help lead it.

After a while, this progressive sharing will culminate in a more complete transmission of the gift. When this happens, the gift will not be released so that the recipients now *own* it, like the toy aeroplane. Rather, as with the necklace, communion in Christ will be *entrusted* to recipients. They will treasure it on behalf of others and pass it on. The gift will be transferred within certain parameters. On the one hand, as with some gifts, recipients will be instructed in how to use it. They will be given Scripture and the Christian tradition and will be guided by the Spirit. As they draw on these resources they will learn how to be communion in Christ in a manner that fits the gift's character. The gift will be kept within God's family.

## *The risk of letting go*

On the other hand, within these limits recipients will be encouraged to accept the community in their own fashion. To do otherwise would be to live a secondhand faith, the faith of those who brought the gospel. The gift would not be properly released and owned by its recipients. Imagine the mother telling her daughter that she can only wear the necklace with her mother's clothes! Just as the daughter will wear the necklace with her own choice of attire, so recipients of communion in Christ will express the church in their particular way. As Rowan Williams said:

> [W]e may often find that we have offered a gift that is welcome, yet it is not received as we should expect it to be; Jesus is recognizable, yet the responses that to us seem orthodox or obvious are not necessarily made. This demands of us both patience and courage to let go of the gift into the hands of those who receive it. (Williams, 1994, p. 20)

Just as the mother may be surprised by how the necklace looks on her daughter and must get used to it, so those who offer new Christian communities may have to accustom themselves to how the community looks in others' hands. Our own reception of life with Jesus reminds us that this gift is not something that we have of our own choice or ingenuity. It is given by divine invitation. It 'cannot be administered by the institution' (p. 21). It comes to us through the Spirit, who shapes our responses. The Spirit is therefore free to offer the gift in whatever form God chooses. This may be different to how we ourselves received it.

Of course, there is a risk that recipients will adopt beliefs and practices unacceptable to the wider church. Those who brought the gift will then suffer because an aspect of their selves is in the gift; to an extent their selves will be abused. A willingness to bear that risk is intrinsic to sacrificial giving. The more completely the gift is handed over – rather than merely lending, the mother relinquishes the necklace – the greater the risk involved and the more magnanimous the letting go. This subverts power-hungry approaches to mission. Communion in Christ is given not in the spirit of control or self-aggrandizement, nor with the effect of keeping recipients in a position of dependency. It is offered as a gift of the Spirit that is progressively released into recipients' hands. By inviting the latter to accept the gift in their own way, while (we pray) keeping it within the Christian family, power is transferred from givers to receivers. The autumn trees can encourage us to apply this principle to all the church's generosity: they remind us of how beautiful letting go can be.

## Accepting the gift

Obviously, gifts must be accepted for the transaction to be complete, and this is the stage at which they particularly strengthen relationships. Because givers offer part of themselves in their gifts, in deciding whether to accept the gift recipients decide whether to accept the giver. If they do, the relationship is established or deepened. At some stage recipients will probably invest part of themselves in a return gift. If this too is accepted they in turn will have been accepted, which further strengthens the relationship. A study of giving within romantic relationships found that 'many informants believe that the best gifts are extensions of the giver. The gift recipient who accepts such a gift is symbolically accepting the giver at the same time' (Belk and Coon, 1993, p. 405). As Jonathan Parry puts it in his exposition of Mauss, 'it is because of this participation of the person in the object that the gift creates an enduring bond between persons'

# A SOCIOLOGICAL FRAMEWORK

(Parry, 1986, p. 457). The mutual acceptance of gifts creates community because it implies the mutual acceptance of the persons behind the gifts.

## Drawn into community

In addition, accepting a gift frequently draws the recipient into a community of people who value the same gift, even though the community may go unnoticed. For example, a gift of swimming lessons connects the child to others who are enjoying the same experience. The gift of a pair of shoes links the recipient to those who appreciate that brand of footwear. True, these fashion aficionados will not all know each other and so they are not a community in a visible sense. But if we understand community as a group of people who have certain attitudes and interests in common, they are an implicit community, a crowd you fall in with but never meet.

Once more, Jesus exemplifies these features of giving. Having been released into the hands of the Jewish people, in his public ministry he invited people to accept him. Whoever accepted him, he said, also accepted the Father who sent him (John 13.20). Accepting the gift of the Father's Son established a relationship with the giver of the Son. Moreover, accepting this gift establishes a relationship with all others who welcome the gift. All who embrace Jesus and receive his teaching become his family (Mark 3.34). As in the shoes example, individuals and congregations do not all know each other and are often not even aware of one another. Nonetheless, strung together in Christ and fastened by the Spirit, they each belong to the communion of saints.

All this is true when the church offers new Christian communities. When the community is accepted, the community is joined to the church and recipients participate in a network of gift exchanges that sustains the church's communal existence. To a degree this extends to the church's other forms of giving; many of the gifts draw recipients into the outer orbit of the Christian community. Obviously this extension of the Christian community can happen by using gifts to dominate others and reinforce a hierarchical model of church. Ministers may offer pastoral care in ways that brook little dissent. However, such giving is at odds with the self-emptying of Christ, whose servant form of giving left *recipients* in control. Christlike reciprocity solidifies bonds within the congregation and between the congregation and the wider church on a more egalitarian basis (see Osteen, 2002a, pp. 17–18). 'No longer do I call you servants ... but I have called you friends' (John 15.15).

### Reciprocal giving

Appropriate gratitude – *not* wagging tails of obsequious thanks – helps glue these social ties. By obliging recipients to return a gift, gratitude reinforces the social expectation that gifts are reciprocated. Recipients feel indebted to givers and want to thank them. 'The continuing balance of debt – now in favor of one member, now in favor of the other – insures that the relationship between the two continues, for gratitude will always constitute a part of the bond linking them' (Schwartz, 1967, p. 8).

In their study of generosity among Americans, Christian Smith and Hilary Davidson note how volunteers identify with the places in which they serve. They become 'a volunteer at the shelter' or 'a volunteer at the museum'. Donors who give regularly to a charity think of it as 'my college' or 'my church' (Smith and Davidson, 2014, p. 69). Recipients of communion in Christ are likely, therefore, to become more committed to the new community as they give thankfully to its life, and to identify more strongly with the whole body as they gratefully give back to the wider church.

This resonates with Paul's call for mutual giving to edify the body of Christ (for example 1 Cor. 12). It is a vision that builds firmer foundations for community than market exchange. Contracts do not impel the parties towards a continuing relationship. Once the drinks are paid for you need never return. Giving, by contrast, does cement relationships. It obliges the recipient to gratefully return the gift. However, there may be subtle pressure to conform. Only certain types of gift may be acceptable, for example, which stifles the individual. For Paul on the other hand, members of the church give to one another in their own distinctive fashions (Rom. 12.4–5; 1 Cor. 12.4–6). Indeed, the source of gifts, the Spirit, can be understood as the one who gives space to the other, who does not coerce believers but enables them to thrive in their uniqueness and give in their own way. Thus givers and receivers are drawn together without either side losing their identity. The reverse in fact: creative forms of reciprocal giving enlarge and enrich the identities of those involved. Givers may surprise themselves in their imaginative gift of a new Christian community; recipients may come to see themselves in a new light.

## Giving back

Gifts, we have begun to see, generate return gifts – at the very least gratitude, but often also an object or action that sustains or deepens the giver–recipient relationship. This feature of giving is central to the mystery of the cross. First, Jesus is a gift to humanity. Next God transforms

## A SOCIOLOGICAL FRAMEWORK

the wilful destruction of this gift into a human return offering to God, the Passover lamb (John 1.29; 1 Cor. 5.7); Christ sacrificially becomes a gift back to the Father on behalf of humanity. Then the Spirit enables women and men to participate in this return gift; they are joined to Christ in giving their lives back to God for the purpose of doing good (see Rom 6.13; 12.1).

An echoing movement of return generosity can be expected whenever the church shares its gifts with others. In particular, when recipients accept communion in Jesus, they receive the gift of having access to the church's tradition. As (hopefully) they grow in their appreciation of the tradition, they will want to express their gratitude for it. Gratitude represents 'an attitude toward the giver, and an attitude toward the gift, a determination to use it well, to employ it imaginatively and inventively in accordance with the giver's intention' (Harned, 1997, p. 175). Schwartz comments,

> It must be noted that gratitude binds not only the living, but connects the living and the dead as well. The [legal] will is an institutionaliza-tion of such a connection. Inherited benefits, insofar as they cannot be reciprocated, generate eternal indebtedness and thereby link together present and past. (Schwartz, 1967, p. 9)

This well describes the position of those who accept new Christian communities. They are in debt to believers who in earlier centuries con-tributed to the tradition, not least by sharing it with others, but they have no practical means of thanking them directly. They are like a pupil who as an adult comes to appreciate a school teacher but has no way of directly thanking the person. Instead, the adult may express her gratitude by diligently passing on her own skill or knowledge to others. 'What you did for me,' she thinks, 'I'll do for other people.' Were she to give some flowers to a stranger in thanks for what her teacher did, her response would be inappropriate and odd. Instead, the adult performs an action that she knows the teacher would value and this becomes her return gift. In like manner, recipients of the church can thank past contributors by passing on to people outside the church their own experience of the trad-ition, the essence of which is gathering around Jesus. 'Just as you gave communion in Christ to others, we too will pass the gift on.'

In the case of new Christian communities, handing on the gift is the most appropriate way for one Christian generation to thank previous ones. This is because the return gift is fitting; it is true to type. To be mature is to express fully your type – think of a flower in full bloom. Passing on communal life in Jesus is a sign of maturity. It expresses the church's type, the sort of community the church is: the church is a type

161

of community whose vocation includes giving its communal self away. What is given, though, will not be exactly the same as what was received. As noted in the Introduction, gifts are returned non-identically. It would seem odd or rude if my birthday present to you was exactly the same as yours to me. So recipients of a new Christian community will hand on the church non-identically. Their gratitude to former generations will be expressed in the spirit of the Reformation. Recipients will pass on the church reformed (they received the gift in their own way) but always reforming: the new recipients receive the church in *their* own way.

Lewis Hyde points out: 'A gift that cannot move loses its gift properties' (Hyde, 2012, p. 8). It becomes a possession to be consumed by its owner. But if what you have received is viewed as something to be passed on, the object retains its gift status. Handing on communion in Christ prevents this particular gift becoming a possession of its members. The church remains a perpetual gift. This is very different to some gifts that cannot be continuously passed on, such as perishable goods which once eaten are no longer available. The church, which lasts till eternity, is more like a tweet or music file that can be forwarded without leaving the hands of the giver. It can be given to others without depleting itself, though of course the file can be deleted just as congregations can die. Being a perpetual gift is the means by which the church becomes the self-multiplication of Christ in history.

## Transformation

Giving brings change to both givers and receivers. The gift of Christ brought change to the experience of the divine giver. The Father faced the new situation of relating to his Son as a human being – and not just to a single divine human, but also to all humans in Christ. This was not new in the sense of a change in God's eternal attributes of love, omnipotence and so on. Nor was it new in bringing a change of mind; there was never a time when the incarnation was not in God's thoughts. What was new was the realization of this intention – the actual presence in the Godhead of a human being with his community. In addition, the gift of Christ changes the human recipients. They have a new identity as God's children, who are also the body of Christ and the temple of the Spirit. Embraced by the Trinity, they are transformed into God's likeness (2 Corinthians 3.18), which includes giving to others.

That giving brings change may seem obvious in today's world, where change is all around. But Dan McAdams and Jack Bauer note that in the past giving and gratitude for a gift supported the status quo:

# A SOCIOLOGICAL FRAMEWORK

> For Thomas Aquinas and the medieval Christian church, debts of gratitude helped to keep order in the great chains of being, wherein humankind owed gratitude to God, peasants to their lords, lords to their kings, wives to their husbands, children to their parents, recipients to their benefactors, and so on. (McAdams and Bauer, 2004, p. 82)

## Givers and recipients

In contemporary society, healthy giving can be understood in a more transformational light. An object is transformed in the giver's mind from being a possession to being a gift. It is no longer something to be held on to but to be offered to others. There is a resulting change in the person who holds the object; he or she becomes a giver. If the gift has yet to be obtained, the giver's flow of life is interrupted to secure the gift. Perhaps the giver walks home by a different route to buy a birthday card. As the giver imagines what the other person would like, she may come to see the recipient, the relationship, or her contribution to the relationship (and hence herself) in a different way.[8] Much the same happens when the church is given to others in the form of a new Christian community. The lives of the founders change course and they come to see themselves through new eyes.[9] At the same time, the parent congregation is changed as the missional task draws certain members away from their previous commitments.

Recipients are altered because the gift is added to what they already have and this may be life-changing, such as when charitable giving transforms the recipient's circumstances. They may also come to view themselves differently, as we have noted, because the donor makes his knowledge of the recipient known to the person, who then sees himself in a new way. In particular, Hyde describes the 'labor of gratitude' that transforms recipients so that they become similar to the gift or to its donor (Hyde, 2012, pp. 48–57). For instance, the apprentice becomes like the master who spotted an ability, drew it to the other's attention and helped to nurture it. As the apprentice labours in gratitude to develop her talent, she is gradually transformed from a stumbling to a proficient carpenter. Then she takes on an apprentice herself. She has become like her master both in his woodwork skills and in his desire to pass those skills on. Similarly, people who receive new Christian communities are changed so that they become more like those who gave them communion in Christ. This involves learning generosity themselves.

People around the recipients are also changed. Like any form of charity, givers of the church should care 'not just for the beneficiary's survival,

## GIVING THE CHURCH

but for their dignity, well-being, network of relationships, ability to earn a living, education, training, health and general flourishing, not least their ability to be a benefactor to others' (Wells, 2019. p. 106). When that happens recipients are enabled to be more generous themselves, which radiates out feelings of gratitude. Robert Roberts argues that being grateful can reduce the anger, resentment, envy and bitterness that tend to undermine satisfying relationships. As white blood cells for the soul, gratitude is an antidote to negative emotions, replacing them with something happier (Roberts, 2004, p. 59). In particular, it trains the brain to seed gratefulness into other connections. Feeling better about life, the person becomes more disposed to give. Gratitude here writes odes of joy there. Thus offering new Christian communities well can generate a tailwind of gratitude that turns receivers into givers and accelerates a wider circulation of gifts. Aromatic waves of kingdom giving, thankfulness and further generosity are released into society.[10]

### Restored relationships

One type of giving is especially transformative. It is giving that mends broken relationships. In these contexts, gifts can be a form of apology – perhaps flowers to say sorry for keeping a girlfriend waiting. Or, as in many cultures, sacrificial gifts may be offered to restore peace with the divine, with people around them and with nature. In both cases, a return gift of forgiveness – of pardon and of accepting the guilty party – completes the transformation. Having received an apology, the offended party forgoes the right of redress and the disrupted relationship is restored. However, in a radical departure, the Christian God makes available forgiveness *before* the apologetic gift is bestowed. Christ first gives himself on the cross and then the return gifts of repentance and sacrificial lives are offered.

This substantially deepens the human practice of forgiveness so that it becomes more than letting go of the right to be recompensed. Forgiveness goes as far as putting yourself in the shoes of the wrongdoer and thinking, 'If I had been that person with those accumulated experiences, I could have done the same.' In a pale echo of, and yet a participation in, the incarnate Son's self-giving, you give yourself to the other by becoming that person in your imagination and surrendering your desire for compensation. Your gift of self initiates the healing of the relationship and clears a path for the other to apologize. Mutual giving – offering forgiveness and offering an apology (in that order) – becomes the key to renewed interpersonal harmony. In this vein, through deep and forgiving relationships of love perhaps developed over a long period, new Christian communities may be offered (alongside other gifts) to people who have despised, opposed or even hurt the church. When this happens, when the church acts out forgiveness before it receives an apology, not just the gift but the manner of giving can profoundly transform recipients' lives. Such a radical form of gift exchange gets to the heart of the human condition – broken relationships in need of repair. Communities in Christ become lodestars of a new relational reality.

## Implications

First, using new Christian communities as an example, this chapter has described an ethical framework for the church's generosity, a framework that can mitigate the moral abyss of giving that so offended Oscar Wilde. Church multiplication should arise from healthy forms of gift exchange that involve receiving first, giving appropriately, letting the gift go, accepting the gift (which creates community), offering a return gift and being transformed. Enabled by the Spirit, this framework follows the pattern of Christ's self-giving described in Philippians 2.6–11. Just as Christ did not grasp at his divinity but entered the world as a servant, the church will not elevate itself through giving but make itself vulnerable by receiving before it gives. Just as Christ gave himself appropriately to the world, 'being made in human likeness', so the church will give its self in a way that is appropriate to the recipients and to the relationship of mutual generosity it seeks with them. Just as Christ let go of his life 'to death, even to death on a cross', the church will let go of its self into the hands of those who wish to receive it, even at the risk of the gift being neglected, damaged, or 'killed' by heresy.

Just as God 'exalted' Jesus, a sign of his enduring fellowship with the other divine persons, so giving the church to others will not rupture relationships within the body but extend them. Furthermore, just as Jesus returned 'to the highest place', the gift to others of communion in Christ will become a return gift to the wider church from which it came. And just as Jesus was transformed from a servant to one at whose name 'every knee should bow', so the new Christian community will be transformed from being a slave to selfishness to becoming a master of generosity. In this 'kenotic', self-emptying manner, the church can be made a purified rather than contaminated gift to the world.

Might this framework help the church navigate the thorny ethics of witnessing to Christ in a pluralist society? For example, how can communion in Christ be offered to people with a different faith while respecting their beliefs? Part of the answer lies in the church receiving from other faiths first, in the best spirit of multi-faith dialogue. Appropriate giving will include offering gifts that suit the relationship at that stage. Initially, these will comprise loving service in its broadest sense. Only if and when the relationship can bear the weight will faith experiences be exchanged and then perhaps, later, communion in Christ be made available. Once offered, of course, this last gift will be released, which will include letting it go in such a way that it can be declined without embarrassment. Recipients will be invited to receive the new Christian community in their own way, which will include bringing insights and practices from their previous faith into their life in Christ. Thus the new community will be offered in a fashion that is restrained, lacks self-aggrandizement and makes it easy for the gift to be refused.

Second, though this ethical framework has been illustrated by new Christian communities, it need not be restricted to them. As pixels to make a kinder world, all the church's generosity should be characterized by a similar pattern of gift exchange. The Christian community should receive the gifts of the natural world, for example, and give back the careful stewardship of these gifts. It should receive the gifts of being blessed by people on society's edge and offer the return gifts of support for justice. It should receive the artistic gifts of people beyond the church and make available the church's own creative gifts. It should give pastoral care to people in the wider community and receive society's wisdom on how to improve care. It should offer the gift of being alongside others (in a mission of presence) and receive the gift of others being alongside the church. It should offer gifts of ethical and spiritual challenge to the world but receive from the world *its* request that the church strive for higher standards. All these exchanges can be shaped ethically by receiving first, giving appropriately, letting go, accepting (which builds community), giving back and transformation.

Alongside other perspectives, therefore, might gift exchange be a helpful framework for thinking about mission in general? It would mean that mission is not about opposing the world, as in the spiritual warfare model and some versions of the transformational one (the world is so full of evil it must be attacked to bring change). Mission would be about seeing where the Spirit is at work and finding social partners with whom gifts can appropriately be swapped. Mission would be reciprocal, not one way – gifts are *exchanged*. God's people would enter these interchanges not with predetermined conditions but by allowing the other to decide the intensity of the exchange and how deep the relationship becomes. Moreover, mission would work not on a deficit model ('you have a need we must meet') but in the spirit of Asset-Based Community Development

# A SOCIOLOGICAL FRAMEWORK

(ABCD): mission would facilitate others to use the resources they already have. These resources are given and harnessed by the Spirit, in whose activity the church is called to participate. Mission would therefore be ecclesial (the church's communal role is central) but not ecclesio-centric; the world would be an equal partner in the exchange.

Third, might adopting a gift-exchange framework replace programmatic mission ('Let's organize another initiative') with relational mission (gifts emerge from and build relationships)? Mission would not be imperialistic ('this is what we think you need') but explore what types of gift are appropriate to the relationship and to the other. Nor would mission be limited to service, which can seem rather joyless and has unfortunate connotations where histories of servitude exist; it would be more celebratory, as when gifts are exchanged at a party. Moreover, missional horizons of generosity would not by definition be constrained, as with the hospitality model (hosts limit the gift and guests fit in); a giving model by nature has no boundaries (there are no caps on generosity and gifts are released). Above all, the heart of mission would best be summarized not by sending (as in *missio Dei*, the sending of God) but by mutual generosity (as in Christ's self giving that evokes a giving response). Mission would be seen as a series of gift exchanges that can gradually bring the church and the world together – less *missio Dei* perhaps and more *liberalitas Dei*.

## Notes

1 Fund-raising becomes problematic if the church always seems to be asking for money. If non-members feel they are being imposed upon or being asked to give more than the value they receive from the church, the relationship begins to feel one-sided and unattractive.

2 Here is one of the contrasts between the sinful church and the holy God. God is always the first giver, whereas one way the church resists its sinful arrogance is to be a recipient first.

3 From his research into the symbolic meaning of consumption, Russell Belk notes, 'A key element of the message of the perfect gift is conveying that the recipient is unique, extraordinary, and special, and the gift itself helps to convey this by displaying these same characteristics' (Belk, 1996, p. 64).

4 The priority of the recipient is reflected in Belk's characterization of the perfect gift – the giver makes an extraordinary sacrifice (which expresses selfless generosity); the giver wishes solely to please the recipient; the gift is a luxury, an extra, rather than a humdrum necessity (demonstrating the extravagance of the giver's love for the recipient); the gift is uniquely appropriate to the recipient; the recipient is surprised by the gift (because it is more than the giver could reasonably have expected); the recipient is delighted by the gift (Belk, 1996, pp. 61–8).

# GIVING THE CHURCH

5 Part of the church's distinctiveness will lie in being a vehicle for the Spirit to convert recipients' consumerist attitudes ('the community must be tailored to my needs') to generosity of heart ('the community exists for others, and so do I').

6 As one giver put it, when describing her selection of Christmas presents, 'I like getting stuff for people that they really like so that they look at it and go, "Oh, wow," and that they remember me... "Anne got me that ... nobody else has been able to buy me something like that"' (Lowrey et al., 1996, p. 50).

7 This assumes the missional journey described in Chapter 10.

8 Gift vouchers or gifts of money can be obvious exceptions. The giver may avoid imaginatively entering the life of the recipient, who is left to choose their own gift, although in some cases giving money may be exactly what the recipient wants.

9 Moynagh, 2017, pp. 297–314 presents a model for understanding the 'vocational voyage' they undertake.

10 Tempering this, however, is that being over-thankful can be a form of gratitude obesity. Too much gratitude may blunt the drive to improve others' welfare and encourage the grateful person to accept their lot. People may be thankful for an unjust status quo instead of resisting it.

# 7

# A Liberating Purpose

The last 50 years have seen the irruption of liberation theologies, which have laid the ground for today's decolonial theology.[1] They include those focusing on a geographical region like Latin America, feminist, Black and other theologies centring on a demographic group, and postcolonial and decolonial theologies that address the experience and continued legacy of colonization. 'Liberation theologies emerge from the underside of history and argue that the oppressed and the marginalized must be the starting point and centre of theological reflection' (González, 2018, p. 574). They challenge ways of doing theology and being church that derive from white, male-dominated churches in Europe and North America. Their agenda is to bring liberation – fullness of life – to people whose voices have been suppressed. Though liberation theology in its Latin American version may not be the force it once was, many of its aims and central tenets have found their way into the bloodstream of the global church. Might allying a liberationist perspective to the church's generosity add a further dimension to this theological tradition?

Drawing on several strands of liberation theology, this chapter argues that when the church gives to others in thanks for grace, receiving, giving appropriately, releasing the gift, forging community, giving back and transformation are all processes that properly understood throb with liberationist potential. This has implications for the church's generosity in general, but is developed here with reference to the offer of new Christian communities, as a vital example of the church's giving. The chapter uses the exodus story to string these giving processes together in a paradigmatic narrative of liberating generosity. It argues that the goal of the last chapter's ethical framework is the liberation of people from every form of injustice in a foretaste of the abundant life to be received when Christ returns. Ecclesial generosity must side with the oppressed.

## Oppressive or liberating?

As we have seen, the church's giving runs up against the corruption of generosity by the power dynamics involved. Christian charity has been criticized for creating dependency, leaving oppressive social structures untouched and promoting the church's agenda more than that of the recipients'.[2] Offering others communion in Christ has repeatedly been warped by similar perversions. Bearers of the gift have frequently been slow to relinquish leadership, leaving recipients dependent upon them. New Christian communities have commonly been given without questioning social injustices in the wider setting. Often the new community's life has reflected givers' expectations more than the recipients' creativity. And the new community's inherited spirituality has regularly been impoverished by neglecting the potential richness of gifts from the context. Along with the church's other failings, this contaminated giving leaves many outside the church too cynical to welcome the Christian community, and some inside too embarrassed to offer the gift.

Liberation theologians challenge the church to use whatever power it has not to bolster its own interests, but under the shadow of God's reign to serve the least powerful in society. Jürgen Moltmann, whose writings share the trajectory of 'global South' liberationists, has distinguished between the future as an extrapolation of the present and the future as radically different (Moltmann, 1999). God's kingdom is not a continuation of what already exists. It is an inbreaking of justice from the end times. It frees recipients from cause-and-effect chains of oppression arising from the past by offering liberating alternatives from the future. Embracing these options fundamentally changes reality. Rather than arriving ready made, these new possibilities are co-created prayerfully by humans and the Spirit working together. What results are placards advertising the flourishing of all creation within God's coming reign.

### *Liberating communities*

The church is to be a gift by being a pocket of the future in the present. Liberation theologies throw light on how this can happen when, as part of the church's giving, the Spirit offers new Christian communities to others. The key is for the church to be restructured around 'base ecclesial communities'. These communities are typically within the Roman Catholic Church, originally in Latin America, and comprise people at the base of society who join struggles for justice in their contexts. A Roman Catholic parish is normally too large for meaningful community at the

## A LIBERATING PURPOSE

parish level. So in Latin America 15–20 families form smaller communities in which they pray, sing, read and reflect on the Bible, eat together and share bread and wine 'both eucharistically and informally'. Members support one another, undertake charitable and community work in their neighbourhood, and critically analyse their social and economic context with a view to political action (Schipani, 1995, p. 291).

Being at ground level makes it easier for base communities to link faith to justice in everyday life. Obedient to the gospel's demands, these communities recognize the need for society to be transformed. 'Thus faith is not locked in the mind and even less within the private, individual horizon. Faith is a dynamic factor of personal conversion and societal transformation' (Azevedo, 1985, pp. 602–3). Through base communities, the church serves the common people without paternalistically ignoring their views (p. 616). Initiatives arise from the people's experience and are informed by theological reflection upon it. Members don't just study their faith. They ask how the Christian tradition can inspire and guide them to act with, or on behalf of, people on the social rim.

Base communities can be seen as gifts. They are liberating gifts to the world by mobilizing people for transformative action.

> An underlying assumption of the base communities is that ... true generosity means empowering people, enabling relationships to change so that the lowly can do things they never imagined would be possible, and so that the mighty divest themselves of the control they have been used to exercising. Then those who have played a passive role, suffering poverty and possibly receiving others' generosity, move to playing an active role, becoming agents of change, and subjects of history. (Hebblethwaite, 1993a, p. 93)

Gustavo Gutiérrez, an early and prominent advocate of liberation theology, declared that base-level, transformative communities are 'the active agents of the evangelization of a whole people'. Evangelization includes proclamation of the word, but it also involves solidarity that gives authenticity to that proclamation (Gutiérrez, 1981, p. 118). Comradeship soothes the wounds of those battered by life.

Base communities originally emerged in poorer countries but need not be confined to them. Margaret Hebblethwaite has championed base communities in wealthier societies. They will normally have a geographical focus, but as in the case of industrial and student chaplaincies they can also serve a specific network. Often minority groups can express their culture better when they have a chaplaincy for themselves, 'and recognition of culture is very important in a base community' (Hebblethwaite,

1993b, p. 55). The community can be of any size, as small as four or five people (p. 57).

When extended to richer societies, Hebblethwaite suggests, base communities will be liberating if the church prioritizes the formation of these communities among people who are poor. In a community co-created with the poor, affluent persons would directly serve others less well off. Alternatively, a middle-class base community might not be formed among poor people, but the members can put their gifts at the service of the poor nearby or further away (p. 87). Supported by her community, a photographer might share her photographic skills with teenagers in a poor neighbourhood, or professionals might work to reshape their disciplines around the concerns of the oppressed (Petrella, 2008, pp. 148–50). Hebblethwaite misses a third and critical condition. When a community is formed in a middle-class setting, people on the social edge of the context – those who don't fit in, who are bullied and mistreated or are absent from decision-making about them – should loom largest in the new community's eyes. An affluent neighbourhood group, for instance, might form community with people who have disabilities, putting them at the centre.

## Liberating the church's vocation

Might we repaint the church's call to generosity in the light of liberation theology? In particular, when Christians offer new Christian communities they cannot view the context from a standpoint of neutrality. Neutrality, liberationists stress, equals the status quo. Rather, bearers of the gift must ask: who within this demographic is the new community for? Who is in mind when leaders of these new communities decide how, when, where and what to do? Influential gatekeepers who can open the crucial doors? The founding team who seeks 'an easy win' perhaps? Or the lost, the last and the lonely in the setting? Givers must attend to the social biases in their generosity and ensure that their new community gives pride of place to people on the social edge of *that particular context*. As the Brazilian liberationist Leonardo Boff says, the church is directed towards all in the setting, but it must begin from the desires and struggles of the marginalized (Boff, 2011, p. 10).

Christians offering a new Christian community in their workplace, for instance, might initially serve people who are ignored or mistreated, form community with them and ensure that 'the "absent ones" make their presence felt' (Gutiérrez, 1981, p. 108). 'The biggest act of charity disciples do isn't the way they give away their money, it's with whom they choose to be in relationship' (Wells, 2019, p. 98). Others can be drawn into the community, but this must be around its focus on those who have been sidelined the most. If in time recipients of the community grow towards Jesus, they can be encouraged to offer their gifts to less fortunate people in different settings and perhaps – in some cases – to go out and form community with them. Affluent people would find their identities in the self-giving of Christ, live these identities by becoming givers themselves, and turn the acquisitive elements of consumer behaviour into generosity towards others in need.

In addition, Chapter 1 claimed that there is no item on the missional menu that cannot be supported by new Christian communities. This is particularly true of justice. If Christians wish to campaign for human rights or for a better environment, they can meet with people outside the church who share their concern and from a Christian perspective explore spiritual resources to support their campaign. Writing letters to the immigration authorities on behalf of asylum seekers can become enacted prayers as a step towards a campaign-and-worship community. A community supper among people who are marginalized can become a much fuller experience when worship is added (Aldous and Moynagh, 2021). Struggles for liberation are enriched when community, justice and worship are clamped together.

In the spirit of base communities, therefore, the 'missional church' will be most fruitful when it offers new Christian communities for the sake of social and ecological justice. These insurgent expressions of church will bring together people from within and outside the church to conduct guerrilla raids on in-situ forms of oppression and environmental harm, or to campaign for liberation further afield. Simultaneously, they will mine spiritual quarries to help construct their initiatives. When the gift of new Christian communities acquires this radical hue, the church will be given to others in the form of social action. It will become a gift that expands into the holes of unfairness and frees people for fulfilment in God's subversive future.

## Receiving before giving

Liberationists tend to view God's release of the Israelites from Egypt as a paradigm of political liberation. However, the exodus story as we now have it can also be seen as a model of divine generosity. God offers the ancient Israelites the gift of being freed from oppression so that they can live in community with him. In today's language, God gives the Israelites 'church'. This gift involves the same gift-exchange processes described in the last chapter. Accordingly, God first becomes receptive to the Israelites. Yahweh sees the misery of the people, crushed on the social margins, and hears their cry of suffering (Ex. 3.7). Though not addressed to Yahweh, the cry rises up to God anyway (Ex. 2.23), because Yahweh is like a magnet for the cries of the abused (Brueggemann, 2021, p. 4). Likewise, the church must be especially attuned to people who suffer. In empathy the church must allow itself first to receive people's cries of anguish before giving in response.

## Receiving means listening

When God became human in Jesus, and especially when Jesus became the Passover lamb at the crucifixion, God again became receptive to those on the social edge. Orlando Costas points out that Jesus died outside the city gate (Heb. 13.11–12). In contrast to the temple, which was the centre of Judaism and inside the Holy City, outside the gate was where the remains of the people's sin offerings were burnt. It was beyond the edge of Israel's institutional faith. Thus Jesus died on the religious periphery, in solidarity with those beyond the edge of organized religion (Costas, 2005, p. 189). Dying the death of a criminal, he died in solidarity with those who are punished by society. And by dying on a cross, a symbol of shame, he died in solidarity with all who feel ashamed.

The church is summoned to meet Christ where he died. 'bearing the disgrace he bore' (Heb. 13.13). It is to meet him among the people who are outside the gate of religion, beyond the gate of mainstream society and outside the gate of social acceptance. Liberationists stress that the church meets Jesus by identifying with people on the edge (see Matt. 25.31–46). As the church draws alongside these people, it encounters the risen Lord. As it pays careful attention to their disappointments and hopes, their hurts and joys, and their disillusionment and plans for a better life, it discerns the voice of Christ, who is already there waiting to be heard.

Listening is therefore the first act of solidarity when the church gives to others. Black holes of experience are noticed and heard. From a liberationist perspective, this 'receiving first' includes bringing the Christian tradition to bear on what is heeded to make sense of it, and then acting upon this reflection. Action will give rise to further experience, which again will be listened to, reflected on and acted into. In a mixture of metaphors, listening is intrinsic to the 'see–judge–act' approach that comprises the church's 'praxis', its action for liberation. 'See' means to see reality as it is, just as God saw the reality of the Israelites' suffering in Egypt.

## A LIBERATING PURPOSE

'Judge' is to read what you see in the light of the gospel. 'Act' asks, 'What can we do?'

### Listening with a view to repentance

When new Christian communities are offered to others, watchful listening will include a willingness to receive uncomfortable criticisms of the church. This is especially important where the church has been present for many years but has lost touch with swathes of the population. A common refrain in these societies is that people object not to Christianity but to the church. By listening attentively to people outside the city gate the church may find much to repent of, whether it is scandals of sexual abuse, other misuses of power, the pastoral neglect of people, insensitive evangelism, an arrogant superiority, forms of ecclesial life that fail to connect with others, or simply the refusal to reach out.

Writing in effect from a decolonial perspective, Robert Heaney draws attention to the church's need to seek forgiveness for past mistakes. Repentance addresses power imbalances that have allowed the church to dominate and harm others. Repentance remembers, renews and rewrites historical narratives by refashioning the church's testimony in the light of the experiences of people who have been hurt. It initiates actions that seek to prevent past sin from being repeated (Heaney, 2019, pp. 145–6). Heaney quotes Jeremy Bergen's study of ecclesial repentance. Repentance must ring true to the experience of people who have been let down by the church and include appropriate acts of reparation. To help flush power abuses out of the church's system, for instance, Christians may have to recognize that the new Christian communities they offer on behalf of the church are not at first seen as a gift, and discover why.[3] They may have to go out to people hurt by the church, ask for their help in refashioning the gift, and include them from the start in the initiative's leadership. Absolution must involve people sinned against, or their representatives, who can acknowledge the sincerity of the church's repentance and the appropriateness of its redress (Heaney, 2019, pp. 147–58).

These insights expand receiving first into receiving criticism. Listening goes beyond hearing voices that are often silent to being stirred to repentance by them. It may include seeking out sacrificial forms of service that recipients recognize as restitution. Rather than beneficiaries depending on the givers, bearers of the gift come to depend on the 'absolution' of the people they serve. This completely disrupts the client–provider model of many statutory and voluntary organizations: the organization provides a service, which members of the local community receive as clients. Instead, the emphasis is on relationships in which wrongs the 'clients' identify are put right. As the church restores damaged relationships, healthy and more equal exchanges take centre stage.

## Giving appropriately

In the exodus story the gift of communion in God is offered in a form that addresses the circumstances of the potential recipients – 'Let my people go' (Ex. 5.1). The gift does not involve, for example, releasing the people from hunger, which is how the slaves came to be in Egypt. The people are freed from Pharaoh's abusive labour policies, which is the immediate crisis. Those whom Pharaoh 'holds' (9.2) are to be 'let go' from Egypt's coercive system of production. Moreover, they are to be released so as to celebrate a festival to Yahweh in the desert (Ex. 5.1). 'It is a resolve to depart the zone of Pharaoh's control' to enter the zone of Yahweh (Brueggemann, 2021, p. 17). Freeing the slaves to worship the Lord is appropriate to the recipients.

It is also appropriate to Yahweh, from whom the gift comes. As Walter Brueggemann points out, the people cannot serve two masters (Brueggemann, 1995, p. 46). If they are to become God's 'treasured possession' (Ex. 19.5), they must recognize only one God and not allow Pharaoh to compete with that God (see Ex. 20.2–3). 'The core point of the drama is theological, god versus god, with no compromises offered' (Brueggemann, 1995, p. 47). The signs and wonders, which are intrinsic to how the gift is given, demonstrate the Lord's superiority over Pharaoh and persuade the Israelites to transfer their allegiance from Pharaoh to Yahweh. 'Yahweh is engaged against Pharaoh ... because Pharaoh's management of social relations is incompatible with Yahweh's character and intention,' which is to emancipate the oppressed (p. 47). The exodus is a gift that fits *both* the enslaved recipients *and* the liberating giver.

### Appropriate to recipients and givers

Using new Christian communities as pointers to how the church can be generous, liberationist perspectives add three insights. First, if recipients of these communities are to include people who are belittled or ignored, the community must be given in a manner *they* (and not just the powerful) can understand. 'The gospel is not something that comes from outside, culturally. It is a seed which sprouts from the ground of suffering and oppressed lives and which breaks the hardness of that ground precisely

# A LIBERATING PURPOSE

because it is rooted therein' (Barreiro, 2010, p. 30). This emphasis on inculturation is shared by all liberationists. Their starting point is the church's presence in a *particular* oppressed community, whether it is poor people in São Paulo, rural women in South Africa, LGBTQ+ communities in San Francisco or people with learning difficulties in South London.

Liberationists have done much to make inculturation a self-conscious process. As the Latin American José Comblin points out, for almost the entire history of the church (with a handful of exceptions) inculturation has been intuitive and hardly noticed. It was unrecognized because, especially in Roman Catholic circles, there was little awareness of how the church is shaped by historical forces (Comblin, 2004, p. 154). People were blind to the contextual nature of the church they inherited. So when they offered the church to others, they typically did so without reflecting on the setting. The gift was a hand-me-down from an older sibling rather than freshly imagined for the new context.

However, when 'diversity' is on everyone's lips, today's new Christian communities are less likely to wear identical uniforms. Founders are more ready to assume that if the church they have come from has been patterned by its historical context, there is no reason why new congregations should not be forged by *their* contexts. It follows that when the church is offered to people who are least visible, it must be given in a form that makes sense to them. If the church is held out, for instance, not to teenagers from a school in general but to teenagers with educational needs, community with Jesus must resonate with those particular recipients. Inculturation must be keenly attuned to each disadvantaged group.

Liberationists know well that inculturation is a mixed blessing. It enables the church to connect, but without discernment this connection may transmit nasty germs. Holy war, the Inquisition and clerical dominance are some of the ways that the Western church and its offshoots have been brutally infected by the surrounding society. 'The church has often let itself be guided more by history than by the gospel' (Comblin, 2004, p. 147). The notion of inculturation should therefore not be accepted uncritically. It should be constantly questioned and reflected upon. Rather than pursued blindly, theological discrimination and prayerful discernment should unsettle the notion and leave it in a state of flux.

Second, if the church is to be offered in a manner true to itself, liberationists invite God's people to reflect *critically* on who they are. Givers of the church must do more than ensure their gift accurately reflects the church's identity. The church has too many identities for that! They must ask *which* identity? In particular, is the gift faithful to the status quo church – the church that represents the interests of the powerful, the comfortably off and those who suffer least? Or is the gift an expression of the prophetic church, which critiques ecclesial practices, destabilizes the tradition from the standpoint of those who have been elbowed aside, and encourages silent voices to speak? A church of the oppressed is closest to the biblical teaching and to the nature of the early church (Comblin, 2004, p. 47). So when the gift fits people on the social edge, it also best fits those who make the gift available.

## Hybridization

Third, post-colonial and decolonial theologies add in the notion of hybridization, which helps describe how givers of the church arrive at a gift that fits both them and the recipients. Hybridization subverts binary views of the world, such as developed versus undeveloped countries, colonizer versus colonized, nonbelievers versus believers, and self versus the other, which is 'that most fundamental of all binaries' (Heaney, 2019, p. 6). Binary thinking keeps people apart. Hybridization brings them together. Hybridization is not the same as syncretism. Syncretism mixes different things up, whereas hybridization brings differences together by shaking up both sides. Syncretism tends to be an unreflective process. Differences are combined without much thought, whereas hybridization is intentional. Thought is given to how both sides can be untied from their moorings.

The death of Jesus was an example of hybridization on several levels. He died as a rebel, while unsettling the notion of rebel; Pilate could find no fault in him. Equally, he died as an authority figure (with the sign 'King of the Jews' above his head), while disrupting the idea of authority; crucifixion was the punishment for insurgents. The *man* Jesus was killed, though his experience was that of countless women; he passively accepted the physical abuse of men. He was resurrected through the assertion of 'masculine' power by his Father (Gal. 1.1), and this vindicated his 'female' path of salvation, based on submission. Jesus who was without sin died accused of blasphemy; yet through his death sinners have been made sinless. The death and resurrection of Jesus dissolved opposites by pricking the balloons on both sides.

As the body of Christ, new Christian communities should be given to others in like manner. The notion of giver is punctured because those who offer the community do so having first received from the potential recipients. The concept of recipient is correspondingly disrupted because recipients of the community are the initial givers. This unsettling of roles brings the two sides together. Givers of the community establish a rela-

## A LIBERATING PURPOSE

tionship with potential recipients by being willing to receive from them. Recipients open themselves to this relationship by accepting the invitation to offer bearers of the church a gift.

As the two sides connect with each other, 'empathetic dialogue' may well disturb the assumptions of both sides. Those offering the church may have to revise how they expect the gift to fit the recipients, the givers and the relationship between them, while recipients may find the gift upsets their values and behaviours, which are reoriented towards Christ (see Shaw, 2018, pp. 17–18). Recipients in their turn dislocate the givers' assumptions by offering back new insights into what it means to be community in Christ. Through reciprocal giving that subverts both sides, givers and receivers of the church are fused into an ever-tightening bond while birthing something new.

## Releasing the gift

In the exodus story the gift of becoming community with Yahweh is released into the people's hands. Yahweh will still guide the community, but the people are given a greater share in Yahweh's leadership. Instead of relying on Moses to bring their enquiries to Yahweh (Ex. 18.15), on the advice of his father-in-law Jethro Moses appoints judges from among the people to share the task (vv. 25–26). As George Pixley points out, 'The Israelites had rebelled against a society in which the tyrant pharaoh could decide the fate of the people arbitrarily' (Pixley, 1987, p. 114). By centring political power on Moses, they risked creating the circumstances for another tyranny. Delegating his responsibilities created the conditions for popular expressions of power to emerge.[4]

The following chapters describe the formal constitution of Israel as a community under the law. Along with the system of judges approved by God (Ex. 18.23), Yahweh establishes the legislative basis of a community that would be capable of governing and sustaining itself under Yahweh's direction. Though Yahweh intends to lead the community through Moses and those appointed to share Moses' role, the structures of nationhood are not so tied to Yahweh that the people cannot wrench them free. Indeed, in the centuries ahead the people often did tear the constitution away from God, thereby hurting their relationship with Yahweh. In allowing them this freedom, Yahweh demonstrated that a gift is not a gift until the giver lets go. At the same time Yahweh clearly warned that damaging this relationship would have consequences, as with any relationship (see, for example, Ex. 32.33–35).

For liberationists, fundamental to the church is that it belongs to the

179

GIVING THE CHURCH

people. 'Thus, we are no longer speaking of the Church for the poor but rather a Church *of* and *with* the poor' (Boff, 2011, p. 10; italics original). This means that when the church gives to others in the form of new Christian communities the gift must be handed over to those who receive it. Especially for Roman Catholic liberationists, this requires the emancipation of the laity from clergy dominance. There can be no true liberation without the clergy placing the church in the hands of its lay recipients and letting go.

## Liberation of the mind

Post-colonial theologians have contributed to this theme by highlighting the colonization of the mind. This is the process by which a dominant group imposes its habit of thinking on others. Less powerful people come to assume that the cultural values of the prevailing group are superior to their own. The Nigerian Elochukwu Uzukwu is one of many to criticize the 'European church' for imposing its values on people who were colonized in the 'global South'. The former married its theology so well with the laws, politics and philosophy of Greco-Roman society that it virtually excluded other possible versions of this same world. The local expression of the one faith became fixed, intolerant of alternatives and resistant to the Spirit's action among races elsewhere (Uzukwu, 2006, p. 51).

From a European perspective, the Introduction suggested that there has been a double decentring of the European church. It has lost its planet-wide dominance as voices from the global South have come to the fore. And it has lost, or is losing, its dominant position *within* Western society. The church is now on the social fringe, with the challenge of serving people whose cultures diverge from those that have moulded the church. To be welcomed into the body, contemporary people must be allowed to draw their communal life in Christ in shapes that have meaning for them but may differ from the past.

Thus for the church to be more than yesterday's church, to be the church of today, minds must be liberated in the 'global North', just as they must be set free in the 'global South'. The post-Christendom and post-colonial agendas come together. Both address the need for the mind-set as well as leadership of the church, in the shape of new Christian communities, to be handed over so that recipients are freed to imagine being communion in Christ in their own ways. As the Cameroon Archbishop, Jean Zoa, joked: 'Allow us to err. You yourselves have had 2,000 years to err' (Uzukwu, 2006, p. 62).

## A LIBERATING PURPOSE

### Large ears and small mouths

This comprehensive release of the gift calls for a particular type of leadership. Drawing an image from the Manja of the Central African Republic, Uzukwu has described leadership that has 'large ears'. This is a listening form of leadership. 'Because it implies consultation or deliberation at all levels of community, it becomes an imagery which testifies ... that the will of God may triumph in the church-community over human presumption or error' (p. 137). God's will prevails because members of the community listen with humility to the Spirit in prayer and study and in the speech of one another.

In a second image, Uzukwu refers to

> The Bambara (Malian) philosophy of the *immensity of the Word*. The Word embraces the whole of humanity. When uttered, it heals and provides humane living. Such a sacred Word is 'too large' for the mouth ... No speaker ever totally masters or appropriates it; rather it belongs to the human community. (pp. 127–8; italics original)

God's truths are too big to be communicated by a single leader, or even by a group of leaders. It is when the community as a whole deliberates that enough mouths can express God's word adequately to the context.

Leaders are called to a participative form of leadership that facilitates the community to discern God's will through patient discussion and mutual listening. 'This is what is generally referred to as African "palaver": the liberation of speech at all levels of community in order to come close to that Word which is too large for an individual mouth, the Word which saves and heals' (p. 128). Uzukwu gives an example of how Western advisers gave up on a political palaver in South Africa, thinking that one of the parties was not willing to cooperate. However, other participants kept talking, and four days after the Westerners left the dangerous impasse was broken.

A leadership of 'large ears' and 'little mouths' prepares the ground for liberating the mind. Communal discernment gives confidence to the recipients of new Christian communities that their views are valued by God as well as by those who brought them the gospel. It creates opportunities to discern who has the gifts to take over from the original leaders. It models a pattern of leadership for subsequent leaders to follow. And it enables receivers of the church to share in sculpting their community from an early stage. Thus through a letting-go type of authority leaders take the first steps in releasing the gift into the divine wind of the future.

## Local theologies

The fruit of this process is seen when the oppressed express themselves freely, directly and creatively both in society and in the heart of God's people – when as an 'authentic theology of liberation' (Gutiérrez, 1973, p. 307) they create their own symbols and rites. Carlos Mesters has described how in Brazilian base communities people gather round the Bible and ask how it can make a difference to their lives. This is not Bible study based on cognitive questions such as 'What does the servant stand for?' Rather, 'their struggle as a people enters the picture' (Mesters, 1981, pp. 198–9). Instead of trying to interpret the Bible, the community seeks to interpret *life* with the aid of the Bible. The Bible 'has shifted its place and moved to the side of the poor. One could almost say it has changed its class status' (p. 207). Subjectivist interpretations can be countered 'by more objective grounding in the literal sense of the Bible and by reading the Bible in community' (p. 210). This should include the community of the whole church, so that the particular community can be challenged by understandings from the church at large. Mesters warns:

> The expert may arrive with his or her more learned and sophisticated approach and once again expropriate the gains won by the people. Once again they grow silent and dependent in the presence of the teacher or expert. Our method is logical ... We say it is scientific. When the people get together to interpret the Bible, they do not proceed by logical reasoning but by the association of ideas. One person says one thing; somebody else says another thing. We tend to think this approach has little value, but ... What approach do psychoanalysts use when they settle their patients into a chair or couch? They use the free association of ideas. And this method is actually better than our 'logical' method. Our method is one for teaching information; the other is one for helping people to discover things themselves. (p. 203)

For Grant Shockley, Black Theology arises from the need to articulate the significance of Black presence in a hostile white world. Black people reflect religiously on their experience, attempting to redefine the relevance of the Christian Gospel for the Black context (Shockley, 1995, pp. 317–18). It is an example of what should happen when, as part of giving away new Christian communities, the gift is relinquished into the hands of the people. Communities should be freed to carefully rewrite the Christian tradition (but without betraying it) against the backdrop of their members' everyday lives. Local theologies of multi hues will then emerge and embroider the wider church (see Schreiter, 1985).

A LIBERATING PURPOSE

## Accepting the gift

The previous chapter suggested that accepting the gift establishes or re-inforces community. When the gift of communion in Christ is welcomed, for example, recipients are formed into a particular community that is part of the larger Christian family. This link between accepting the gift and creating community can be seen in the exodus story. Although God legislated for a new type of community, the community could not emerge unless the people accepted what God offered. They did this by ratifying the covenant at Sinai (Ex. 19.7–8; 24.3, 7). Yet acceptance did not come without a struggle. Exodus records a counter-revolutionary movement, a desire to return to Egypt, 'that springs up again and again, provoked by real or imaginary dangers in the passage through the wasteland' (Pixley, 1987, p. 82). This rebellious streak, evident from the very beginning (Ex. 15.22ff), escalated into an attempt to establish an alternative religion to Yahweh in chapter 32. The golden calf revolt was not the abandon-ment of Moses' project. Rather, scared by Moses' prolonged absence, the people seek alternative gods to 'go before us' (Ex. 32.1).

If we follow the Exodus sequence, the people murmur against the gift of being community with God, they then accept the gift by ratifying the covenant, but almost immediately they rebel against the covenant, and then they repent of their rebellion (Ex. 33.4–6). This is true to the ambiva-lence with which some gifts are received. Gifts invite relationship and recipients may be uncertain whether they want that. When the church offers new Christian communities, for instance, the gift may be received with a degree of equivocation.

The hesitation may include suspicion about participating in the greater church. For, as we have seen, gifts frequently draw recipients into a larger community of people who enjoy the same thing. In the case of Israel, the people's covenant relationship with Yahweh was intended to make them a 'kingdom of priests' (Ex. 19.6). They were to be a community that mediated God to others. Israel was called out from the nations so that it could take Yahweh back to the nations. Connecting to the whole was part of its destiny. Yahweh makes the point that 'the whole earth is mine' (v. 5). Israel was to mediate Yahweh to peoples who in some sense already belonged to God. As the chosen people of God, Israel was to serve nations who were also in some way God's people. Something similar happens when the gift of new Christian communities is accepted. Recipients are to share their experience of Jesus with others in the wider church, who may seem like foreign nations but nevertheless belong to him too. And just as Israel frequently struggled to reach out to other parts of humanity, even though – created by God – they also were God's

183

possessions, so likewise new Christian communities can struggle to grow fruitful connections with the church at large.

Equally, the rest of God's people may be suspicious of their new offspring, rather like the nations were often hostile to Israel. From a Roman Catholic perspective, in 1984 the then Congregation for the Doctrine of the Faith warned that base ecclesial communities risked creating a popular church outside the official church.[5] From the Protestant side, José Miguez Bonino points to the hazard of sectarianism. Congregations or denominations become so inculturated that they insulate themselves from other perspectives, refuse to be challenged by different contexts and become shattered shards because of tensions in their social environment (1981, p. 149). New Christian communities end up smashing rather than enlarging the ecclesial picture of Christ.

Liberationists are alert to this danger of fragmentation. But they are also aware that the inevitable tensions between new and older Christian communities only cause pain if some kind of unity already exists. *Painful* friction is the sign of an underlying oneness. And it need not tug the body apart. Roman Catholic clergy in Brazil, for instance, have countered the risk by themselves helping to form and sustain base communities, connecting them to the parish. The older church enables the new. Equally, the new base communities 'see themselves as a vital part of the Church, without which they would have no meaning' (Azevedo, 1985, p. 606). Going further, second-generation liberation theologian Ivan Petrella has sought to recapture the internationalist approach of some of the first generation such as James Cone. Petrella challenges the excessive emphasis on liberating black, women, LGBTQ+ and other identity groups. This can divert attention from the material deprivation that transcends these identities and is the most important form of oppression. Liberationists should unite around the poor who are the kernel of liberation theology and the nucleus of the church's cohesion (Petrella, 2008, pp. 122–47). As people in poverty are helped to realize their potential and bring their particular riches into the whole, the entire church will be blessed.

In identifying with the whole church, therefore, new Christian communities will focus not on groups that share their particular ethnic or cultural identity (important though these identities are) but on people who are marginalized within the church and on those who prioritize the oppressed outside. Base communities will join with such people to form ecclesial bellows that pump support for the weak across the church. The solidarity these communities prize will renew the Christian community by pushing beyond the functional to *communal* life within church structures (González, 2018, p. 584). At the same time, institutional structures will be refocused to support the proliferation of new communities among the oppressed. The two approaches, communitarian and institutional, will coexist and enrich each other, but on behalf of and with people who are poor.

## Giving back

We have seen that after accepting a gift, typically one is returned. For Israel, having received God's gift of freedom to be community with Yahweh, the covenant stipulated that inventive obedience to Yahweh would be an acceptable offering back. In particular, the people were to form and maintain an economy of neighbourliness towards strangers, widows and orphans, who were especially vulnerable in a patriarchal society because they lacked a male advocate. This 'neighborliness is more important than self-aggrandizing productivity that marks the now-doomed regime of Pharaoh' (Brueggemann, 2021, p. 21). Applied to giving away the 'new Israel' today, a new Christian community's return gift will go beyond passing its self on to others in thanks to previous generations who enabled the original gift. Drawing from its particular context, the community will offer back to the wider church a palette of fresh insights into how 'an economy of neighbourliness' can be expressed.

Liberationists elaborate this prophetic giving back. They urge base communities to evangelize the church by challenging its alliance with dominant social, political and economic structures. These communities represent 'a case of grassroots protest against institutional fossilization as well as a creative alternative to it' (Schipani, 1995, p. 291). Christians who bring the gospel need conversion too, a major theme in post-colonial theology. For example, Heaney quotes the complaint of the Kenyan, John Mbiti, that Lutheran missionaries made African converts more Lutheran than the Germans, the Anglican missionaries made them more Anglican than the English, and the Roman Catholics made them more Roman than the Italians (Heaney, 2019, p. 49). Mbiti argued that the missionaries should have been converted. Had they been more critical of their own cultures and heritage, in dialogue with both African and Christian traditions they might have turned away from their colonial mindset to a greater appreciation of indigenous experience (pp. 68–9).

This conversion must include emancipation from solidified expressions of the church. Instead of being trapped by the church's history, the Spirit brings new kingdom alternatives from the church's future. Those who offer communion in Christ are freed from fixed ideas of what the new Christian community will be like and become open to other possibilities. As a community emerges in the blended colours of both the Christian tradition and the host demographic, it graces the household of faith. It can enlarge the mental peripheries of longstanding believers and enable them to see fresh opportunities for Christian hope. Thus while recipients are offered the gift of behaving differently by reflecting theologically on their *existing* reality, givers receive back the gift of behaving differently by reflecting on a *new* reality, the community that has come to birth. This return gift is an appropriate response to the gift that was originally received.

Hebblethwaite claims that base communities are constantly finding new applications for traditional concepts that might otherwise gather dust, neglected and outdated. Far from being ignored as a thing of the past, the church's tradition

> swims into new and vivid pastures. This constant exploration of new interpretations and new applications is probably what Cardinal Ratzinger had in mind when he criticised liberation theologians for continuing 'to use a great deal of the Church's classical, ascetical and dogmatic language while changing its significance.' However, *changing* its significance is not the same thing as *rediscovering* its significance through new, contemporary applications. (Hebblethwaite, 1993a, pp. 69–70; italics original)

She quotes Cardinal Archbishop Aloisio Lorscheider, whose encounter with base communities in north-east Brazil changed his episcopal style: 'I no longer saw myself as someone leading my flock, but as someone walking in the middle of the flock, together with the flock, without for a moment hiding the figure of the one true shepherd, Jesus Christ' (p. 129). As Boff said, the bishop evangelizes the people and the people evangelize the bishop. Otherwise who sees to the bishop's salvation? (Boff, 1986, p. 40) Mission challenges the *church's* present experience.

## Transformation

The gift of the exodus transformed the Israelites from being slaves to being free, from eking an existence to pursuing life, from a community to a nation, from being under Pharaoh's authority to being under Yahweh's. Transformation is fundamental to liberation theology, which shines a transformational light into every corner of the church's generosity. As exemplified in the gift of new Christian communities, receiving first is translated into attentive listening to people outside the city gate, into receiving the unwelcome gift of being criticized and into making amends for the church's mistakes. Giving appropriately means going beyond offering the church in a form that is intelligible to the generality of people. New Christian communities must be given in a way that makes sense to a specific people who have been rubbed raw by life. This means being faithful to the church's prophetic traditions in particular. It involves shaking up the status quo of both givers and receivers so that communion in Christ can be offered in a way that dissolves opposites and brings them together.

Handing over the gift must be much more than letting go. It should actively encourage recipients to remove the gift from the cultural wrapping paper of those who brought them the church. Leaders must have large ears, respect the immensity of the Word that exceeds any one mouth and foster local theology and liturgy. Rather than multiplying division, expanding the number of Christian communities will grow both the resources that can be shared between communities and the opportunities for one community to benefit from another. Diversity can become a source of cohesion. New Christian communities on the social edge will offer back to the church not just gifts that reinforce the status quo but contributions with power to transform the church's allegiance, so that people on the rim are drawn into the centre of ecclesial life and thought.

Boff describes this as 'ecclesiogenesis'. The church is born – it has a genesis – among people who are poor. A popular church of the grassroots is created which can transform the institutional church, challenge existing social and economic elites and remake society in the image of the loving and liberating Trinity (Boff, 1986). These hopes, often repeated over the past half century, have borne mixed fruit. One case study, for instance, found that base communities were quite effective in some villages in the Philippines but there was less evidence of personal and social transformation among the urban poor (Nadeau, 1999). Given human frailty and sinfulness, mixed outcomes like this should be no surprise. Though we shall always hope for more, we should not allow the desire for complete success to become the enemy of a more limited achievement.

## Implications

At root, liberationist perspectives radicalize the power dynamics threatening the church's generosity. Giving away new Christian communities for the sake of the world throws light on the principles involved in the church's giving. When the Spirit gives to others communion in Christ through a liberating pattern of receiving, giving appropriately, letting go, acceptance (which strengthens community), giving back and transformation, power is used not to control people already under-loved by society but to set them free; this includes sparing them from domination by the institutional church. The Christian community spotlights those who are least noticed in society, offers them Christian community for their fulfilment and joyfully welcomes their return gifts. The last chapter's framework of gift exchange acquires an ethical goal: liberation so that humans and nature can begin to flourish in anticipation of their complete fulfilment when Christ returns.

## Liberating church planting

This changes the church planting narrative from conquering ('winning' more and more souls) to liberating – freeing people from all kinds of bondage. In thankfulness to God, planters should aim not simply to grow the church (which is often their prime motivation) but to offer Christian communities engraved with heavenly justice. When this happens, people are released to pursue wider possibilities. A new congregation based on alleviating hunger will free members from being preoccupied with survival so they have more time and energy for their deepest ambitions. A new Christian community among addicts will support them in discovering life beyond the tyranny of addiction. A new congregation built on challenging social stereotypes will help to unbox people from traditional norms of behaviour. The heart of liberationist church planting becomes the creation of new alternatives for people.

This builds on what is intrinsic to church planting. Because people are offered a God who frees them to embrace new opportunities, church planting is liberating in its instincts. As with bestowing any gift, the very process of offering life in this God gives potential recipients a choice they did not have before: they can accept the gift by exploring Christian community or ignore it. Straight away their options are widened. For those who offer the church, therefore, 'success' can be redefined. It lies in making available not a new congregation but a new *alternative*, communion in Christ, and leaving that possibility on the table. Unlike much giving, the gift will remain available even when it has been refused. This liberates church founders from slavery to targets such as 'We seek to plant a new community of this size by this date.' They can have a different goal: to be the gift of a loving opportunity. Whether an option is accepted or not, it stays a gift by remaining at hand. Thus, as an important dimension of liberation, offering a new Christian community is freed from the anxious need for the gift to be received.

Going further, a liberationist perspective can address many planters' suspicion of the organized church (whether inherited structures or new networks). Aware of the church's legion of shortcomings, planters are often tempted to found a purer version of the Christian community without the albatross of the existing institution. However, a liberationist agenda offers a prophetic alternative. New Christian communities can be offered to others in the hope that recipients' return gifts will challenge middle-class abuses of power within the church. Especially when these communities are given to affluent, well-educated and socially confident women and men, our prayer must be that recipients will develop a passion for liberation from the theology they imbibe. They will draw on their social, human and financial capital to side with disadvantaged people in their own and other contexts, join those who brought them the church in advocating on behalf of people the rest of the church forgets, and draw these neglected people into the councils of the church. By this means, ignored voices will be listened to by the remainder of the Christian community, thereby expanding the church's emancipatory bandwidth. Rather than complaints about the church going largely unheeded because they come from outside, founders and their new communities will become megaphones of justice from within. Might a liberationist perspective, therefore, bring an ecclesial glint to church planters' eyes?

## Rethinking the liberationist agenda

How might *Giving the Church* help to re-imagine and re-energize liberationist forms of mission? One answer is the integrated path to mission described in Chapter 1, which argued that discipleship, mission and church combine in a single process when churchgoers offer new Christian communities. This addresses the complaint that liberationists are 'tempted to put evangelization into parenthesis, as it were, and postpone it until tomorrow' while pursuing the 'earthly gospel' of political and economic justice.[6] By offering new Christian communities to people the church leaves out, evangelism can blend with social struggle to shine the brightest possible hope into corners of misery.

Second, as we have seen, offering communion in Christ helps liberationists achieve their mission of evangelizing the church. Many base communities are comprised largely, if not almost entirely, of Christians who partner with people beyond the church in a variety of kingdom initiatives. However, often the partners are not drawn into these communities and so their voices remain 'outside the city gate'. For sure, middle-class activists can speak to the wider body on behalf of these outsiders. But how much more effective is it when recent converts bring their disadvantaged backgrounds into the church, join the church's deliberations, share their own perhaps bitter-sweet experiences of the church and speak from their first-hand knowledge of life beyond the institution! When liturgical and other innovations at the church's base are resisted by others in the institution, who best to advocate these changes than the recently baptized, speaking on behalf not just of themselves but of their relatives and friends yet to be welcomed into the family? Stones rejected by society can become cornerstones of God's new society.

Third, despite the pleas of Hebblethwaite and others, the gift of new Christian communities risks bifurcating between liberationist communities in contexts shredded with pain and new communities detached from the liberationist vision in contented societies. However, by seeing *all* these communities as agents of liberation, be they 'church plants', 'fresh expressions of church', 'missional communities', 'emerging churches', 'organic churches' or whatever, liberationist ethics can infuse *every* new Christian community. Comfortably-off converts, increasingly shaped by the values of liberation rather than consumerism, will be able to make their volunteering, financial and other resources available for mission among vulnerable groups. The entirety of the church's life – liturgy, mission, organization and more – can have a preference for the poor.[7] Self-donation can ramp up resources for the liberationist cause.

## Notes

1 Decolonial theology challenges the colonial power relationships still dominating our world. Some theologians have built on decolonial critiques, which in their origins tended to refer back to South America and adopt a socio-economic perspective. Others draw on postcolonial critiques, which share much of the decolonial agenda but have arisen largely from within cultural discourses such as literary criticism and referred back to South Asia. This chapter is written from the standpoint of liberation rather than decolonial or postcolonial theology to reflect the tradition's broad trajectory of thought.

2 For a critique aimed at a popular audience, see Lupton, 2011.

3 Stefan Paas asks, with reference to post-Christian Europe, 'Does the gospel return to us in a special, indirect way via its advised rejection by others, and could this lead to a new cultural expression of Christianity?' (Paas, 2019, p. 18).

4 Brueggemann contrasts Egypt's 'pyramidic top-down *theory of social power* that has eventuated in a monopoly of power and control exercised with coercive authority over others, and [Israel's] alternative way of social power *grounded in emancipation* and expressed in covenantal solidarity' (Brueggemann, 2021, p. 24; italics original).

5 Congregation for the Doctrine of the Faith, *Instruction on Certain Aspects of the Theology of Liberation*, 1984, IX, 11–13; X, 16.

6 Congregation for the Doctrine of the Faith, *Instruction*, VI, 3–4.

7 Members of Just Church in Bradford, England, for example, wrote letters on behalf of Amnesty International, including them in their intercessions as expressions of prayer (Howson, 2011, p. 131).

# 8

# A Conversational Manner

In my thought experiment, I am proposing that the church is called to be a gift of the Spirit to the world. As it gratefully responds to God in a life of generosity, an important aspect of its giving is to join the Spirit in offering the church's self – communion in Christ – to others for the common good. What might this look like from a Reformation, herald perspective, which sees the church as the proclaimer of God's word? This chapter explores an answer based on understanding the church as a conversationalist and on seeing conversations as an exchange of gifts. The church, assembled around the divine Word, mediates a continuous conversation between God and the world through which both sides offer conversational gifts to the other.

On the one hand, the Holy Spirit gathers the church as people listen to God speaking through Scripture and respond to God in speech through prayer, worship and discernment. On the other, the Spirit sends the church to listen and speak to the world. As this gathering and sending are drawn seamlessly together, the church provides a conversational bridge between God and humanity; the church converses with God on the world's behalf and with the world on God's behalf. The Christian community fundamentally has a conversational nature; in terms of Chapter 2, the relational church is a conversational church. The church is therefore true to its character when new Christian communities, along with the church's other gifts, are offered to the world in a way that reflects healthy conversation. This will involve an exchange of gifts and have a passing-on dynamic because these are features of conversation at its best. Framing the herald model in this fashion resonates with a world that spins on a conversational axis – think of the ubiquitous mobile phone.

Seeing the church as a conversationalist takes us potentially to numerous strands of literature. They include disciplines such as linguistics, psychology, biology, computer science, philosophy, sociology and anthropology. All of these conceptualize language in different ways – as a biological attribute, for example, a cultural trait, a set of communication skills, or a rules-driven system of signs. Studies of conversation in particular range from interactive approaches to a focus on the mental processes of the people involved. Without being a specialist study of conversation, as the first shot at an argument this chapter sews together patches from various disciplines to establish the connection between proclamation, conversation and giving. Proclamation has the character of conversation, while conversation has the character of gift exchange.

The chapter goes on to use new Christian communities as pointers to the good conversational practice that should shape all the church's generosity. It revisits the processes involved in the church's giving by following the structure of the previous two chapters to claim that these processes are akin to conversation. My contention is that to give away new Christian communities ethically is to offer communion in Christ not only for the goal of liberation but also in the manner of healthy conversation. In making this case, the chapter suggests some overlapping conversational practices that will support a principled approach to offering Christian communities. The result is that giving is brought into the heart of the herald model, while good conversational habits are brought into the centre of the church's generosity.

## The church as a conversationalist

For my purposes, 'conversation' is a more helpful word than 'dialogue'. Dialogue can imply an exchange between two sides (Jews and Christians, for example). A conversation may comprise this but it can also cover a lot more, such as a group chatting in the pub. Dialogue often implies talking for an explicit purpose (such as to gain better understanding of a topic), whereas conversations can also be spontaneous and lack any overt goal. Conversation is broader than dialogue.

In the same vein, in pioneering his Conversation Theory of human-machine interactions in the 1960s and 1970s, Gordon Pask distinguished between communication and conversation. For *conversation* to have occurred, 'something must have changed for one or more of the participants – understandings, concepts, intent, values. That is, something has evolved. Otherwise, it is merely the exchange of messages' (Pangaro, 2017, p. 1581). So an exchange of greetings is not a conversation. But discussing the weather and why you are on the bus would be. Something has changed. You know more about each other. Pask defined a conversation as an active linguistic interaction in which personal concepts are exchanged. 'Concepts are shared by means of requests, commands, persuasions, etc. ... This activity ... is a conversation' (Pask, 1980, p. 1002).[1]

Conversations include physical 'props' that support or are referred to in the verbal exchange, and bodily movements such as gestures. Smiles,

## A CONVERSATIONAL MANNER

for example, can be a language of pleasure without words. Indeed, some people's conversations rely entirely on non-verbal supports. This is important because privileging verbal communication makes it more difficult to account for how the church can fruitfully engage with non-verbal people. Also and by implication, including the non-verbal brings activities of mission to the fore. As a conversationalist, the church not only preaches the word (which in some circles is seen as the sum total of mission), it also speaks through physical action.

### The church as a conversationalist

This chapter stands on three legs. The first is that the church can be seen as God's conversationalist. This is a skylight through which shines the Reformation idea of the church as a gathering around the incarnate Word, called to bear witness to the Word. Church happens when the Spirit enables people to hear Christ speaking through Scripture, to respond to him, and thereby – through conversation with him – to have fellowship with God and with each other. As 'a creature of the Word', the church proclaims Christ by serving the world and offering a verbal account of what it has received. This evokes questioning and other responses and so becomes a conversation between the church and other people. The church's conversation with God spills over into the church's conversation with the world, so that the church ends up hosting exchanges between God, people beyond its walls, and the ecclesial tradition.

In his discussion of 'God as Conversation', Christoph Schwöbel develops Karl Barth's view that the church's nature corresponds to the two natures of Christ. Schwöbel describes Jesus as being the Word in two ways. He is the divine Word, speaking God's word with the authority of God. He is also the human Word, speaking the obedient creature's response to God. The divine nature of Christ is God's word revealed in Jesus. The human nature of Christ is his human response (Schwöbel, 2003, pp. 47–8):

> Jesus' story is the story of the uninterrupted conversation of God with humanity and of humanity with God. Jesus therefore is the *interlocutor* between God and humanity. His word mediates God's address to humanity so that God's word becomes audible in a human voice, and his word mediates the response of humanity to God. (pp. 56–7).

Hans Urs von Balthasar made the point by using a German pun. Jesus is both *Wort* (word) and *Antwort* (response) in total unity (O'Donnell,

GIVING THE CHURCH

1992, p. 50). 'The incarnation is God's dialogue with humanity' (Samartha, 1982, p. 11). Or as Ignatius put it, 'Divine love is revealed as communication from both sides.'[2]

Jesus is the divine conversationalist. He speaks for his Father to humanity and he speaks for humanity to the Father. He then expands the conversation to include the church. Via the teaching and preaching of Scripture, Jesus speaks to the Christian community on his Father's behalf (John 12.49). In prayer, worship, discussion and debate the people reply and through Jesus their words reach the Father (1 Tim. 2.5). Jesus in turn responds to them on the Father's behalf, and the conversation continues.[3] Jesus the conversationalist becomes a corporate conversationalist, the church, which shares in Jesus' exchanges within the Godhead.

The church expands this conversation further to include people outside. The message to them is that others, too, can join Jesus in conversing with the Father. People respond by engaging in conversation with the church. The church thus becomes a conversationalist in two directions – with the Father and with the world. To give away communion in Christ, therefore, is to offer a corporate conversationalist engaged in an endless series of conversations between God and the church and between the church and others. These conversations should so overlap that we can think of the church listening and talking to God on the world's behalf and listening and talking to the world on God's behalf. We might say that the church is a *conversatio Divina* (sacred conversation). Its priestly function is to be a conversationalist who brings God and the world together.

Of course, the church is not the only means by which God talks with the world. The Spirit can prompt people outside the church. But when this happens they are not usually aware that the Holy Trinity is at work. So these are not conversations in the normal sense, when people can identify who they are conversing with. They are perhaps implicit conversations. The church by contrast is God's vehicle to include the rest of humanity in God's explicit conversations. Through the church's witness, the Spirit transforms people's tacit involvement in the exchanges of the Trinity into a fuller and more intentional inclusion.

### Conversations as an exchange of gifts

Second, as God's conversationalist the church is involved in exchanges of gifts. This is because conversations have the character of gift exchange. We have seen that giving is a form of empathetic dialogue, a type of conversation. Givers make a statement about themselves, the recipients, and relations between the two. Recipients reply by offering a return gift.

# A CONVERSATIONAL MANNER

The giving continues back and forth like exchanges in a conversation. Equally, if gifts are a form of conversation, conversations are a form of mutual giving. In a conversation, contributors offer their thoughts and feelings to other participants, who receive these gifts by paying attention to them. Connection occurs between speaker and hearer – community forms – when contributions are accepted. Hearers then offer their utterances as non-identical return gifts. Thus Mauss's three components of gift exchange – giving, receiving, returning – have their equivalents in conversation, while giver, gift and recipient, which are necessary for a gift exchange, are echoed in the requirement that a conversation should contain a sender, a message and a receiver.

Like gifts, conversations are very different to contractual exchanges, in which the timing and nature of the response is dictated by a legal agreement. Typically, in a conversation hearers are not bound in how they reply. Even when contributions expect a particular response – such as 'I agree' – the timing is in the hands of the person(s) who receives the contribution. Just as gifts take multitudinous forms, the reply may be expressed in a variety of ways, from a simple nod to a long explanation. And (again like many gifts) the response may be a surprise. Giving and conversations are also similar in that both have a physical dimension. Gifts typically have a material basis. The gift, for example, of an experience such as a theme park ride or a surprise birthday party is rooted in the physical world. The same applies to conversations. Behind the words is the physical body who speaks and the actions, place and time that accompany the speech (Milbank, 2009b, p. 892).

This overlap between giving as a form of conversation and conversation as a form of giving is reflected in the role of Scripture. God speaks through Scripture and this word comes as a gift to those who hear it. If recipients accept God's word, their relationship with God is formed and deepened. They then reply through prayer, discussion and action, all of which are return gifts to God. Likewise in the Eucharist, Christ is given through speech in the ministry of the word, the remembrance of salvation history and the words of institution. The people respond in words with their gifts of praise, thanksgiving and intercession. When these conversations are extended to include the world, the exchange of gifts is also broadened out. By conversing with the world on God's behalf and with God on the world's behalf, through the Spirit the church hosts gift exchanges between God and humanity.

Because conversations are a form of gift exchange, we should expect to see in them, at their best, the dynamics of giving described previously – receiving, giving appropriately, letting go, accepting, giving back and bringing transformation. However, the association between conversation and gift has not always been a happy one. Just as giving is ambiguous – gifts can be a blessing or a poison – so too are conversations. They are not always at their best. Participants can use their interactions to enrich one another or to manipulate and damage each other (as often on social media). And the same of course is true of the church. As a corporate conversationalist with God and with humanity, sadly it too has been a mixed blessing.[4]

## A multiplying gift

Third, if the church is God's conversationalist and if conversations are a form of gift exchange, we should not be surprised if the church's generosity has similarities to conversation. In particular, one of the features conversations share with gifts is the propensity to be handed on. As we have seen, once I have received a gift it remains a gift if I share it. A similar passing on happens with conversations. Once uttered, a concept is reproduced non-identically in the minds of the hearer. Hearers put the concept into their own words, relate it to their previous knowledge, merge it with other concepts and frequently carry it over into future conversations. Indeed, in one respect conversationalists are more generous than recipients of other gifts. Gifts can lose their gift nature when beneficiaries turn them into a possession for their sole use. By contrast, conversations typically drop into the hearer's conscious or unconscious memory and re-emerge later, at least in part, sometimes unnoticed and in disguise. Their elusiveness ensures that, whatever the person's intentions, elements of a previous exchange may be carried forward almost inexorably. Just as conversations are passed on, the same – as Chapter 1 argued – should be true of the church.

Handing on the church (in the form of new Christian communities) is especially resonant of intimate conversations, in which participants give themselves most fully. In these exchanges you share ingredients of former conversations that most matter to you – a comment that hurt or warmed your heart perhaps. The church behaves similarly when it shares its self, communion in Christ, with others. It shares conversations from its past, from the tradition, that are revelatory of its inner life; they disclose its inner heart. These may include continuing and painful disputes about Scripture, beautiful words within the liturgy and truths that are expressed in the church's creeds and rhythms of life. They become part and parcel of the gift of communal life in Jesus, just as earlier conversations are intrinsic to the self that a person reveals to another.[5]

In intimate conversations participants give more of themselves than in conversations that float across the surface. Something similar happens in mission. In many situations the church gives away a bit of itself – money, care and so on. But when it offers new Christian communities, it shares much more of itself. Its conversations with others have a richness that goes beyond its other missional exchanges. Through talk the church gives its very self to the world, and by joining the Christian family the world gives *its* self to the church. The conversation partners are progressively drawn together in a meeting of minds. Like lovers who are not content with superficial conversations, the church in its love for the world will not be satisfied with limited generosity. The church will pray for greater intimacy, culminating in the deepest expression of love, giving its *self* to others in the shape of a new Christian community. The church professes Christ first in general acts of giving and then, if these are welcomed, in the crowning generosity, the gift of communion in Jesus. Here again, the church's giving has the character of conversation. Different degrees of generosity correspond to differences in conversational intimacy.

## Receiving before giving

In its calling to be God's conversationalist, the church witnesses to God, the supreme conversationalist, by sharing its gifts in the manner of healthy conversations. Offering new Christian communities as a normal part of the church's life illustrates something of what is involved. As in the last two chapters, the offer starts with 'receiving first'. Participants must receive before contributing to a conversation. Not least (and unlike God), ironed into them will be language, which 'is never something we create out of nothing. No one invents language on their own. In the first instance language is received as a gift, even if, once the gift is received, human persons can modify their language with an almost infinite creativity' (O'Donnell, 1992, p. 141). Not only language but all that we contribute to a conversation – information, ideas and much else – are first received. In particular, as part of 'recipient design' the person who starts the conversation receives information from or about the hearer so as to design an opening that attracts his or her attention (Clift, 2016, p. 170ff). Receiving first initiates a conversation just as it initiates the gift exchange, as explained in Chapter 6.

## Drawing in others

Not least (and this is more Godlike), participants in the conversation must be received. Organization theorists who emphasize conversations frequently stress the importance of having the right people in the room, including those on the social edge (see for example Shaw, 2002, pp. 74–5). Often elites either ignore people who do not fit in or they use cultural references, technical language and other cultural codes to baffle outsiders and leave them excluded. Exchanges become private. By contrast, as the opposite of a secret society, the Trinity has opened its conversations to everyone. Rather than conversing on their own, Father, Son and Holy Spirit invite women and men into their exchanges as sisters and brothers of Christ. The New Testament depicts God's Word in Jesus as God's universal address to humanity; Israel's conversation with God is expanded to all nations, who are summoned to address Israel's God as Father.

Yet like the rest of humanity, the man Jesus could not converse face-to-face with everyone at once. Just as he had to send his disciples to the villages and towns where he was not physically present (Luke 10.1ff.), he sends his followers today into new situations across the globe. As they join the world's conversations by speaking on his behalf, through them Christ welcomes people beyond the church into his trinitarian exchanges. As with any conversation, for the church to be this divine invitation its exchanges with the world must be rooted in a context that participants share. Going further the Christian community must not only *have* common ground with others, it must *establish* common ground. This is because speakers seek recognition, invite affirmations of their identity, work together to achieve an objective, modify their perceptions as they hear different ones and co-create ideas. Doing all this produces a shared reality. Conversation generates a world in common. It follows that the more the church builds a shared world with other people, the fuller its conversations with them will be.

This means that if the church is to contribute to the world's conversations on Christ's behalf, it will be alongside people wherever they lead their lives – not just near their homes, but where they work, socialize and pursue their interests. Only then, with the consent of others involved, can it help to create common realities around work, friendships, hobbies and much else that people talk about. In time, these realities will become platforms, if people wish, for jointly creating new Christian communities in which these conversations are deepened, transformed by the Spirit and drawn into the exchanges of the Trinity.

## Listening

Once they have been included, participants continue to receive each other during their conversation. They do this by means of listening, 'one of the great arts of conversation' according to Cicero. Or, as the Cambridge University research psychologist Sarah Savage puts it, 'The experience of being listened to is so close to the experience of being loved as to be indistinguishable.'[6] Listening demands turn-taking. In her introduction to 'conversation analysis', which is one approach to the study of social interaction, Rebecca Clift discusses turn-taking's central role. Conversationalists take it in turns to receive others' contributions and give back their own. This requires each participant, when it is their turn, to show that they have understood the other's contribution (Clift, 2016, p. 139). Elaborate procedures, known as 'repair', correct misunderstandings. Good listening may have to be learnt intentionally so as to minimize the need for repair.

In his earthly life, Jesus made listening the basis of the conversation between God and humanity that he came to reveal. He first listened to the Father before speaking on his Father's behalf (John 12.49) and he listened to the Spirit for guidance (for example, Luke 4.1). He also listened to the people he came to serve. His first recorded act was to listen to the authorities in the Temple (Luke 2.41–52). In his public ministry, he was 40 times more likely to ask a question than to give an answer! He gave straight answers to only eight of the 183 questions he was asked in the Gospels, but asked 307 questions himself (Copenhaver, 2014, p. xviii).[7] He wanted to draw out his listeners' thinking, about which they could then have a conversation.

The church is to converse in a similar way when it offers communion in Christ. Echoing Jesus, the church will ask people questions so as to understand them better. It will make itself vulnerable by exposing its lack of knowledge or insight and inviting others to fill in the gaps.[8] In particular, building on the last chapter, the church will listen to voices that have been silenced – to voices that are unheard by people with influence, and to voices within individuals that are silent because they ache. Listening can soothe bruises that hurt. So the better the church listens, the more it can be drawn into painful experiences on the social edge and relieve distress by co-creating a shared world of attentive solidarity. While listening to others, the church will also listen to the Spirit who speaks for Christ (John 14.26). 'The church's speech is a second, not a first, move, a responsive act whose aim is achieved when it draws attention, not to what it says itself, but to what it has heard' (Webster, 2004, p. 33).

### Conversational practice

To welcome and listen to others, members of the church must above all listen to themselves. In particular, they must attend to how they use language either to exert power over other people or to release the power of others. Critical Discourse Analysis 'deliberately dons a pair of critical spectacles and looks for evidence of the covert exercise of power in supposedly "equal" interactions, or for indications of hidden ideological assumptions about "normal" ways of doing things that disadvantage minority groups' (Holmes and Wilson, 2022, p. 543).

As they engage with people outside the church, leaders of new Christian communities should ask themselves: are they unwittingly manipulating the rules of conversation to gain an advantage? Are they determining, for example, what issues get discussed and what don't? Are their contributions so confident that people with less confidence feel intimidated? Do their claims include facts and use language that their audience would regard as fair?[9] If givers of the church are in a position of power, are they limiting their space in the conversation to create room for others to participate? Self-awareness – critical self-listening – is the foundational practice for receiving first.

## Conversing appropriately

As a pointer to how the church can be generous in the way of healthy conversation, when offering new Christian communities the church's contributions to the exchange must be appropriate. By describing how words are turned into melodies of meaning, Ludwig Wittgenstein helped us to understand how this can happen. Prior to his later work, it was assumed that the use of language was governed by rules. Utterances make sense if they comply with agreed syntactic and semantic rules. To say 'The ham sandwich left without paying' appears not to make sense because the sentence violates our agreed rule of what a ham sandwich is and can do. However, Wittgenstein showed that context, not rules, largely determines how sentences are understood. In a busy cafe whose staff refer to customers by what they ordered, 'The ham sandwich left without paying' makes perfect sense (Dobler, 2013, p. 247). The specific context in which words are used necessarily contributes to our understanding of what was said.

This means, first, that contributions to a conversation must be appropriate to the nature of the relationship, which is an essential part of the context. In particular, whether or not self-disclosure is seen as over-familiar depends on the relationship's degree of closeness. As conversation partners get to know each other, like an onion they can peel back layers of defensiveness, sometimes with tears, offering contributions at an ever-greater depth. This is how God has conversed with the world. Following centuries of conversation with Israel, God spoke through the incarnate Word in a historical context that was now ready for this self-revelation, despite the lack of recognition by many at the time (see Gal. 4.4). Church members must continue Jesus' ministry in a similar vein. Their conversations should fit the level of self-divulgence that they have reached with their conversation partners. Just as they would not share intimate family details with a stranger, Christians normally will not share details about their life in Christ till the relationship is thick enough to bear the weight. In the context of new Christian communities, this warns against premature evangelism but also against unnecessary reticence. If Christ refuses to hold back in sharing the divine self with the world, why should his followers when the other is open to a deeper exchange?

## Appropriate to recipients

Second, contributions to a conversation must fit the circumstances of the hearers. Only then will the contribution make sense. Thus when God talks to the world in the incarnate Word and through the written word, in a truism of communication God speaks in ways that are intelligible to people. The Bible, for example, 'belonged in the ancient worlds that produced it. It was not an abstract, other-worldly book, dropped out of heaven. It was *connected to* and therefore *spoke to* those ancient cultures' (Enns, 2005, p. 17). By means of the Spirit, individual books arose from the lives of men and women, addressed their circumstances and through this historical concreteness are made relevant today. 'When God reveals himself, he always does so to people, which means that he must speak and act in ways that they will understand' (p. 20).

If, therefore, new Christian communities are to be given to others in a fashion that corresponds to good conversation, it will not be enough for church members to be present within a context. In the process of giving, their conversational contributions must be appropriate to their hearers, in particular hearers' 'figured worlds'. A figured world 'is a picture of a simplified world that captures what is taken to be typical or normal' (Gee, 2014, p. 89). A group of photographers who know they are all amateurs and plan an exhibition will assume that 'the exhibition' will be for fun rather than to drum up commercial business.

Sharing a figured world happens in part through the mechanism of 'adjacency pairs'. Within a conversation, adjacency pairs ensure that contributions are appropriate to what the previous person said. A greeting elicits a reciprocal greeting. A question is followed by an answer. A statement evokes a reply that builds on what was said. If the response is not relevant to a previous contribution, the first speaker will assume their utterance was misunderstood and will correct the mistake (a 'repair'). Once the confusion has been removed, the next person adds to the previous speaker's contribution and the understanding of one another grows (Clift, 2016, pp. 64–94).

For the gift to be intelligible, the Spirit will offer the church to the world in the manner of adjacency pairs. The offer will travel along the rail tracks of what others in the context are saying – the themes they are discussing and the type of language they use. The church will be seen as an interesting conversation partner and as such will be invited into others' exchanges. As an input into these conversations the offer of communion in Christ will take a form that others wish to build upon. Only by offering its self contextually will the church be able to converse insightfully with God on behalf of the world and with the world on behalf of God.

## Appropriate to the givers

Third, as emphasized in the previous two chapters, the church will also remain true to its own identity. We 'indicate aspects of our social identity through the way we talk. Our speech provides clues to others about who we are, where we come from and perhaps what sort of social experiences we have had' (Holmes and Wilson, 2022, p. 2). To make decisions about meaning, hearers refer to how the word or phrase has been used previously. For one family 'the wedding' will reference an event the next Saturday, for another the previous year. Likewise, professional and technical groups use language in ways specific to the group. This shared use of language by 'our' group helps to give members their sense of belonging. It follows that when talking to people outside the group speakers may need to translate some of their inherited language to make themselves understood. Lawyers put technical jargon into lay terms for their clients. But they also seek to be faithful to their language's meaning and to their identity; they continue to behave and speak as lawyers.

As a conspicuous branch on a tree of understandings, Jesus belonged to the Jewish tradition of language use. He announced the kingdom using categories of thought and speech that had evolved in Israel over centuries. When his message was taken to people outside the nation, St Paul in particular translated the kingdom into terms his Gentile audience could understand but without jeopardizing the gospel's original Jewish identity.

## A CONVERSATIONAL MANNER

Christians who offer communion in Christ likewise belong to a tradition of language use. They are tied to a community of conversationalists that has existed since Jesus (and even before) but within which are numerous smaller communities, one of which they represent.

As they offer new Christian communities, they will bring their tradition of language use into their conversations with other people, but in a way that others can understand. Their ways of speaking about their experience and understanding of being church will shape the identities they project. The more they are aware of their Christian inheritance the more they will intentionally project an identity they have received that is tethered to the church, while also being themselves in terms others can understand. This helps to answer a question sometimes asked by devotees of the herald model: don't contextualized forms of ecclesial multiplication put the truths of the gospel at risk? Is there not a danger that faithful proclamation will be compromised by being adapted to the receiving culture? Part of the answer is that truth – however understood – is protected when the church talks honestly about itself. Just as an utterance says something about the speaker in a conversation, so the offer of new Christian communities, presented in a form intelligible to recipients, must be an accurate expression of the church's identity.

### Conversational practice

As the church gives away Christian community it will become a conversation partner with people outside. To converse honestly in ways appropriate to its own identity, to outsiders and to the relationship between the two, the church must negotiate a common understanding of the situation participants face. When the consensual elastic stretches no more, this will be an understanding of where views differ as well as of where they coincide. Drawing on Jürgen Habermas's concept of *communicative action*, negotiation will be based on open argument. It will avoid coercion, whether concealed or otherwise. Building on Habermas, Eriksen and Weigard (2004, pp. 207–8) argue that these open conversations involve:

- equal access to discussions
- no limitations on the discussion – that is, anyone can introduce any assertion into the discussion
- equal opportunities to oppose an assertion
- equal opportunities to put forward arguments
- arguments are heard and taken into consideration.

These rules of engagement guarantee *understanding* – shared internal pictures – rather than agreement. They are the calling cards of kingdom exchanges that expand the imagination and allow new things to emerge.

Beyond self-awareness, meeting the criteria of *communicative action* requires self-surrender. Each person will have equal opportunity to contribute to the conversation and probe others' claims only if hearers relinquish their eagerness to speak. To allow one person to share, others must surrender their urge to be heard. Then the speaker must surrender his or her desire to talk so that others have room to reply. Each surrenders the platform to the others. (Otherwise everyone would talk, but there would be no conversation.) Surrendering to one another is the prerequisite for reaching an understanding. It is the conversational practice that allows a *fitting* gift of communion in Christ – appropriate to recipients and givers – to be freely negotiated. It is fundamental, therefore, to 'empathetic dialogue' through which the eloquent gift of God's people is given away.

## Letting go

To give their contributions to others, conversationalists must let their utterances go. Letting go is fundamental to giving, as I have stressed. A gift is not a gift unless it is released. In a conversation contributions are released when speakers stop talking and permit hearers time to digest the utterance and make sense of it. As with any gift, this letting go is a risky process. Once blown, each bubble of words can never be taken back. Hearers can ignore the bubble, prick it, merge it with another bubble from their memory, or combine it with bubbles blown later. It is in the essence of conversations that speakers cannot control what is done with the sentences they write in the air. That is one reason why free-flowing conversations are so interesting. Because you can never be sure what response each utterance will provoke, you can never predict what will emerge by the end.

Yet often conversationalists work against this letting go. In workplaces, for example, meetings may be carefully choreographed, with outcomes specified in advance. This reduces the scope for creativity and for participants to be surprised. By restricting people to what is familiar or predetermined, meetings feel dead and drain energy. In contrast, open-ended exchanges (with open questions) increase the variety of contributions, disturb routine responses, create more potential for novelty and allow participants to develop the possibilities that conversations contain (Shaw, 2002, p. 32). This 'does not mean acting randomly without intention' because patterns of stability, such as language, what partici-

# A CONVERSATIONAL MANNER

pants have in common, their expectations, and any previous history of talking together, exist alongside freedom and spontaneity (p. 70).

Conversational letting go was modelled by the incarnate Word who spoke in parables, asked questions, and then became silent as hearers drew conclusions from what he said. Jesus refused to control the outcome of the exchanges in which he participated. His parables created pictures that people could largely interpret in their own way. Likewise, when he told those without sin to throw the first stone at the woman caught in adultery, his silence while he wrote on the ground left space for his hearers to work out the meaning for them (John 8.1–11). When he returned to heaven, he released the entirety of his teachings into the hands of his followers, some of whom still doubted (Matt. 28.17). He took the risk that his words would be misunderstood, misrepresented and misused.

So, as an example of the church's giving, when new Christian communities are offered in the form of healthy conversation, the church must behave like any contributor to a free-flowing exchange: it must let others receive its 'utterance' in their own way, curating it as they see fit. Faithful to the pattern of the Word's non-controlling conversations, the church will refuse to bulldoze its exchanges with the world. It will become a gift by giving others the freedom to contribute as they wish. This can happen from the very start of the giving process. When the church discusses with people it seeks to serve the nature of communion in Christ, whether this gift should be offered, if so in what form and how it should subsequently evolve, those who offer the new Christian community begin to release decision-making into the hands of the community's recipients.

Later, when founders hand their leadership over to others in the new community, the original leaders can connect with the community at a deeper level. They may find that the Spirit guides the community in directions they did not expect. In which case, this will be an opportunity for the founders to discover that fruitful relationships do not depend on sameness. Like an enriching conversation with someone you disagree with, the founders and the community can come to value, learn from and be challenged by what is unique in each other. Letting go can be a gift through which differences are affirmed and everyone is blessed.

Self-restraint is the conversational practice that is fundamental to releasing the gift. Alongside recognizing the power dynamics you are using and surrendering your role as speaker to allow the other to talk, in this conversational practice you hold back to the point of discomfort. You *remain* judiciously silent. Having spoken the gospel in word and deed and embodied it in the offer of communion in Christ, the church must then be quiet. This allows the other not so much to talk as to evaluate the 'words' the church has offered. A prolonged reticence, enabled by self-control, will give the church's conversation partners time to work through the implications of what has been shared and decide how to respond. Patient self-restraint – giving recipients space, recognizing that a reply may be a while in coming and accepting that the reply may not be what is hoped for – is at the heart of releasing the gift. Paradoxically, this silence is itself an utterance – a wordless communication of love. 'What is it that stands higher than words? Action. What is it that stands higher than action? Silence' (St Francis of Assisi). This applies as much to the church's practice of generosity as to contemplating the divine.

## Accepting the contribution

Just as community is strengthened when gifts in general are accepted, so too is it when people receive contributions in a conversation. Receiving the other, speaking appropriately and releasing your contributions all prepare the ground for conversationalists to draw together. But unless a contribution is accepted the bonding will not occur. The latter begins to happen when listeners signal that they recognize what is being said by little interjections such as 'mm-hmm', 'uh-huh' and by nodding. These answer 'Yes' to an implicit question that marches alongside every utterance: 'Do you understand me and accept what I am saying up to this point?' (Enfield, 2017, p. 109). At the end comes the definitive answer. Good listeners say something that shows they grasp the *emotional* significance of what has been shared. Accepting the contribution is to accept the speaker in some way, and this is vital if a conversation is to have the flavour of community.

One of the earliest to pay close attention to face-to-face interactions, Erving Goffman, described conversations as a 'reciprocally sustained communion of involvement' (quoted by Sidnell, 2010, p. 7).

> This 'interaction order' as he called it, is itself a moral ordering: a complex web of standards, expectations, rules and proscriptions to which people orient in their attempts to show deference, adopt a demeanor appropriate to a given situation, avoid embarrassing themselves and others and so on. (p. 7)

He argued that these interactions are the basis for all other social institutions, be they hospitals, law courts or households. Like generosity in general, healthy conversations create and strengthen community. 'Language is an infrastructure for social coordination' (Enfield, 2022, p. 3).

## A CONVERSATIONAL MANNER

It is not that conversations happen and then something separate, a wider community, appears. Rather, complex responsive process theorists such as Douglas Griffin (2001), Patricia Shaw (2002) and Ralph Stacey (2001, 2010) argue that the macro community (like a company or neighbourhood) exists *in* the multitude of micro conversations. Think of an organization. Take away its conversations and what is left? A building maybe, some equipment, legal documents, a case-load of records perhaps, but that is all. There is no community or life. No conversations, no community.

> Organizations are not things at all, let alone living things, but rather they are processes of communication and joint action. Communication and joint action as such are not alive. It is the human bodies communicating and interacting that are alive. This immediately focuses attention on the communicating interaction between the living human bodies that are an organization. (Griffin, 2001, p. 212)

When the church's gifts are received in the way of good conversation, they too form community. In the case of new Christian communities, community is built on smaller and larger scales. The church will birth a micro communion, equivalent to a face-to-face group of conversationalists, when it gathers people together, loves them and shares the gospel in an accessible way. This new community, where the church's river and the world's tide meet in a conversational estuary, joins other Christian gatherings to become the coastline of the greater church, the macro communion. By conversing together in Christ to benefit others, Christian communities become entrepôts of generosity to the world.

Conversations build community among their participants partly through contributions that seek to elicit agreement rather than disagreement. Contributions are phrased in a way that make it easy for hearers to accept them. Tanya Stivers and her co-authors found that question–answer sequences across ten languages were constructed so that they evoked substantially more confirmations than disconfirmations – 70% or more depending on the language (Stivers et al., 2009, p. 10588). Questions were asked in a way that expected the answer 'Yes' ('You do want to come, don't you?') or anticipated the answer 'No' ('I don't suppose you want to come, do you?'). This is an example of 'speech accommodation'. Each person's speech converges towards the speech of the other. 'It tends to happen when the speakers like one another, or where one speaker has a vested interest in pleasing the other or putting them at ease' (Holmes and Wilson, 2022, p. 346). Conversations are typically structured to promote solidarity.

# GIVING THE CHURCH

A rough equivalent to speech accommodation exists in the variety of stories, personalities and types of literature God uses to converse with humanity through the Bible. Different people can see themselves and their circumstances in different parts of Scripture. God's word is thereby structured to accommodate an immense variety of audiences. The extensive use of paradox takes this further. For example, wisdom literature asserts both the futility and the purposefulness of work (for example, Eccles. 2.18–26; Prov. 12.14; 14.23; 22.29). This creates space for the Bible to converge with people's different work situations as individuals gravitate towards one end of the spectrum or somewhere in the middle – 'the Bible is describing *my* feelings about work!'[10] Through the diversity of Scripture, God goes out to myriad persons in solidarity with their particular experiences while at the same time shaping them into a single people.

Speech accommodation suggests a conversational practice through which givers of new Christian communities can encourage the gift to be received. For example, when the Christian tradition is translated into the recipients' voice using illustrations drawn from their worlds, or when church members simplify their vocabulary and grammar to accommodate the linguistic proficiency of children or migrants, the self the church offers is expressed in a form that can be more readily embraced. When the pace of the church's self-disclosure matches the responsiveness of its conversation partners, givers of the new community will more easily forge bonds with those who receive it. When they talk about topics of interest to people outside the church, again they make it easier for the community to be accepted. In short, to form communion in Christ at both micro and macro levels, not only the gift but the manner of its offering must accommodate the recipients. Givers must speak the receivers' language if they want their gift to be accepted.

## Giving back

Return gifts are intrinsic to this community-creating process. Just as one gift is followed by a reciprocal gift, giving new Christian communities to others will evoke a return gift to those who offered the church. This echoes the turn-taking that is fundamental to conversations. One person offers the gift of a thought, an idea, a question and so forth, and another replies with her own contribution. The reply, as we have noticed, is gift-like in that the contribution is almost always different. If you received a present from a friend it would be surprising if the return gift was exactly the same. Likewise, in conversations someone's contribution may occasionally be repeated ('Say after me'), but typically the reply differs from what was said before. Unlike the 'copy cat' game that digs conversations into a rut, difference moves the conversation on.

Non-identical replies are fundamental to conversations. People converse only because they expect the other to say something dissimilar. If everyone saw reality in the same way there would be no need to ask questions, convey information, discuss ideas or even tell jokes (because hearers would know how the joke ends). Participants expect conversations to alter their mental maps (Pask, 1980, p. 1006), and this happens through contributions that vary. Participants may combine different ideas to create a novel thought – indeed, this is how innovation occurs. Conversations either between people or in your head generate new ideas. Conversations may be structured to promote agreement, but they are premised on difference.

We can see something similar in the life and teaching of the conversational Word. Jesus engaged in conversation with Israel's tradition. He received the tradition and lived consistently with it, but he also refreshed his Jewish faith to enrich the people he encountered. In Matthew 5, for example, he repeated the refrain, 'You have heard it said, but I say to you,' six times. He was not correcting the Old Testament law, but correcting what the people had been taught about the law. By speaking back to the tradition and injecting new insights into the conversation, he offered his contemporaries the gift of renewing their inheritance.

Recipients of new Christian communities gratefully offer their return gifts in a similar manner. Having been drawn into the body of Christ, they become partners in a conversation with the universal church. They receive from the wider body a contribution in the form of the Christian heritage and they make a return contribution by saying something different about the tradition. This may include statements explaining why they are practising the tradition distinctively. They remodel the story so that it connects with their circumstances and insert it as a spiritual transfusion into the church's veins. By receiving the tradition and giving it back in a new form, they affirm the value of both continuity and of diversity-creating innovation. Indeed, variety is what enables conversations and the church to be communities of gift exchange. (Picture a 'secret Santa' in which everyone gives the same present!) Thus 'the church reformed is always reforming' – in a conversational way.

Those who offer the church, therefore, should invite and welcome innovation by adopting the antithesis of speech accommodation, 'speech divergence'. The latter happens when people intentionally refuse to mirror the other's speaking style, such as when minority ethnic groups display their cultural distinctiveness by using their own linguistic variety (Holmes and Wilson, 2022, pp. 348–50). On the same lines, givers of the church should invite recipients to use their own linguistic preferences, accent, idioms and the like in worship and other aspects of the church's life, even if this differs from those who brought the gospel. Importantly, they will extend this principle to the theology expressed by spiritual explorers and new Christians. A heavy-handed approach ('The parable doesn't mean that, it means this') may undermine the person's confidence and promote conformity to the views of those who offer the church. A lighter touch, on the other hand, may embolden the church's recipients to explore, even if their baby steps head in the 'wrong' direction.

Error, however, need not have the last word. As recipients read more of Scripture, are exposed to more of the tradition and learn the practice of discernment described in Chapter 2, the Spirit – we trust and pray – will guide them into 'all the truth' nurtured by the church down the centuries, while also leading them into new insights (John 16.13). Though the extent will be debated, 'all truth' will include accommodating some of the language used by the wider church (certain trinitarian terms, for example). Speech accommodation and speech divergence, therefore, go hand in hand. The former is essential for the communion of saints to exist. The latter is necessary for rich diversity within the communion. Thus speech accommodation to form community will be accompanied by the opposite conversational practice – speech divergence – which prepares the way for return gifts of fruitful innovation.


## Transformation

When conversationalists offer their contributions and are given contributions in return, a degree of transformation is the inevitable result. Indeed, change is rooted in the very fundamentals of speech. In conversations the perceived world is transformed into 'the unlikely medium of noises made by human mouths and larynxes' (Williams, 2014, p. 63). 'My tooth hurts' is not literally the same as the pain I feel. The pain has been transferred into the words that represent it. The realm of feeling is converted into the completely different realm of speech. By connecting language to what is not language, conversations are transformational exchanges by their very nature.

Moreover, as Wittgenstein pointed out, there are countless different kinds of use of what we call 'symbols', 'words' and 'sentences'. This stockpile is not fixed. Rather, new types of language come into existence and others become obsolete and forgotten (Wittgenstein, 2009, §23). Through conversations, the language we use to describe perceived reality constantly evolves. And conversations themselves are continuously on the move. 'Speech-act' theory (Austin, 1962) understands utterances to be comprised largely of actions, known as illocutionary acts. Contributions to conversations do things. They make a promise, ask a question, issue a command, state a fact and much else. As actions they disturb the status quo. Conversations become continuous activity, never at rest in one place.

In healthy conversations, one contribution prompts another, ideas are developed and different ideas are combined to produce new ones. Repetitive ways of thinking are disrupted, innovative thoughts emerge and these may be embodied in new actions. In the process we recognize ignored elements from previous conversations and reinterpret the past in the light of the future we are creating.

> The significance of the past may be recast, a new sense of where to go from here materializes, there may be a shift in people's sense of self and their relations to others, [and] what can be envisaged takes on a fresh shape. The patterning of our social identities shifts spontaneously. (Shaw, 2002, p. 68)

### Conversations bring change

For complex responsive process theorists, this is how organizations change. Conversations bring clarity to a situation, novel ideas form when different ideas unite together, and these are taken forward into future conversations through which plans are formed and enacted. The future is co-created through conversations. The future is not 'there' to be discovered. It is imagined and brought into being as people converse with one another, combine thoughts to produce fresh thinking and offer the fruits of their conversations to others through the future they create. 'We use language to build things in the world, to engage in world building, and to keep the social world going' (Gee, 2014, p. 31). Language changes what already exists.

So it should be no surprise that in the Gospels the incarnate Word uses speech to still the storm, heal the sick, describe the kingdom and challenge the authorities, which precipitates his death and resurrection. His words create the future in the present. As the church converses generously with the planet on God's behalf it continues Jesus' ministry of transformation. Not least, newness is in the grammar of offering communion in Christ. New Christian communities are conceived in a conversational womb of believers and the people around them. A Christian group may have a series of conversations with people who don't attend church. Perhaps the exchanges begin with the Christians asking whether the groups might collaborate in bringing fuller life to the context. The interactions move on to how this might be done, next to the planning of specific actions, and then to the sharing of lives as relationships deepen. A hybrid community, centred on the two groups' joint activity, possibly emerges.

Later maybe, some of the conversations have a spiritual tint. These stimulate further discussion, perhaps in a separate group, for people wishing to enrich their lives by exploring the Christian faith. In time, some of these conversations are with God directly in prayer, study and worship, others are within the group itself, others are with the wider church, and still others are with people outside the church. The latter may include conversations through which the process repeats itself. A new Christian community, a wedding of church and world, has come to birth and unsettled the status quo. The people directly involved are never quite the same again. Further, just as a household is changed when a new baby arrives, the context where the community is born is for ever different, though perhaps not so dramatically. Finally, as we have seen, the tradition passed on is disturbed by the community's return gifts to the church at large. These may include an innovative form of church, such as a novel combination of sport and church, which adds to and maybe challenges the Christian heritage. As with conversations in general, God's conversation with the world through the church generates fresh thinking and new action.

## Storytelling

Sharing stories about reality is a conversational practice that can perhaps best promote transformation. Storytelling is so ubiquitous in human talk (think of gossip) that offering the church will inevitably be framed by stories. These will include 'the key, compelling elements of narrative: setting, protagonist, opponent/predicament, plan/battle, transformation, and resolution' (Enfield, 2022, pp. 150–1). For example: 'In St John's School (setting) are families (protagonist) who want to hang out together and experience a fuller life (predicament). So let's do this by watching a film together once a month and then eating together the next week to discuss it from a spiritual and ethical perspective (plan). As we do this, let's be open to how our lives could be enriched by one another and by the "higher spiritual power" to which we shall try and connect (transformation). Maybe in time we can invite people to explore this power from a Christian perspective (resolution).'

# A CONVERSATIONAL MANNER

In their conversations with people they seek to love, Christians will pepper the trivial but meaningful stories they naturally exchange with mini stories that demonstrate concern for the other, reveal something of the teller's spiritual life and contribute to a larger narrative about God. The stories will be shared, of course, in the manner of good conversational practice – receiving others' stories first, offering an appropriate story, letting it go, telling the story in a way that helps it to be accepted, and welcoming a return story. As people engage with these stories, they may be changed by receiving new information, by seeing an issue in a new light, or by experiencing a change in their emotions. Gradually, we pray, they will be drawn into the larger story of the church as a gift to others.

## Implications

All this means that if you start with the church as God's conversationalist, you end up at the same place as if you start with the church as a gift. The Christian community is to gratefully join the Spirit in offering gifts to the world through processes akin to good conversation. The example of new Christian communities illustrates how the gift exchange framework, which I suggest is applicable to the church's giving in general, not only has the goal of liberation but also the character of conversation. This goes beyond the obvious point that action is necessarily accompanied by talk. The exchange of gifts has a conversational nature, and for this 'conversation' to be wholesome it must be supported by good conversational practices.

The herald model is thereby protected from authoritarian connotations. Describing the church's witness as proclamation can be misconstrued as a town-crier, us-to-you approach. The emphasis is on what the church communicates to others (Dulles, 2002, p. 81). 'Conversationalist', on the other hand, italicizes that a two-way interaction is involved. As a conversation partner with the world on God's behalf and a conversation partner with God on the world's behalf, the church listens as well as speaks. This chimes with the current interest in ecumenical dialogue, interfaith dialogue, mission as 'prophetic dialogue' (Bevans and Schroeder, 2011), and with calls for the church to be more dialogical in its institutional processes (for example, Mannion, 2007).[11]

In particular, to open a chest that our final chapter peers into, the church is to be offered in the manner of conversation *whose outcome the Christian community cannot control*. When the church invites others into its conversations, it opens itself to challenge. When it ensures that people

## GIVING THE CHURCH

to whom the church is offered are fairly heard, it allows the possibility that they will take the conversation in an unexpected direction. When it gives space for recipients to process what they hear and to receive the church's contributions in their own way, the church accepts that the outcome may not be what it prayed for. When church members welcome others' distinctive contributions to the conversation, they permit themselves to be transformed through the exchange. The church therefore cannot dictate the flow of its conversations with the world. And since every gift of the church, not just communion in Christ, is shared through talk, this must be true of all the church's external conversations. In which case, might we define mission as the church's *open-ended* conversations with the world on God's behalf?[12]

Going further, might the conversationalist church have something to offer those who are suspicious of managerial approaches to church leadership, approaches seemingly informed more by secular management theory than by theology? Alison Milbank has called for a return instead to 'virtuous hierarchy', which is the opposite of command-and-control 'in that every level assists and exalts the one below' (Milbank, 2023, p. 99). Might this be achieved through an 'emergent' alternative to managerialism? This would see the church as a divine gift, called pre-eminently to a life of giving to others. Preserving the church's integrity, people invited into the community would experience a consistency between the open-ended conversations of the gift's outside life and the conversations to be found within. The latter would start – and supremely lie – in the gift exchanges of healthy conversations. These conversations, modelled and supported by the church's leadership, would be the sea in which 'virtuous hierarchy' swims and management theory is judiciously weighed. As discussed in Chapter 10, talking's unpredictability would challenge command-and-control, give space for dispersed leadership to emerge throughout the institution and create room for the Spirit to generate new forms of spiritual energy to guide the church in uncharted terrain. Management church would be subsumed within the conversational church.

Indeed, might part of the church's vocation be to show other organizations what good conversations are like? This would add urgency to reflections on the quality of the church's conversations. Do church members' internal conversations, for instance, shape them in habits of speech that are life-giving and kind? Are principles of *communicative action* well embedded in all the councils of the church? How much thought is given to healthy conversation in Christian formation? Can the church become God's school for fruitful conversation, a model and a guide for good conversational manners in other walks of life?

## A CONVERSATIONAL MANNER

Maybe the (overlapping) conversational practices outlined in this chapter can begin to point the way. I discussed them in relation to new Christian communities, but surely they apply to all aspects of the church's generosity? These practices include:

- *Self-awareness*. Church members must pay careful attention to their own conscious and unconscious conversational strategies. Are their words, facial expressions and so forth welcoming or excluding? Critical self-listening is the fundamental conversational practice that enables the empathetic receiving of others and their views.
- *Self-surrender*. Yielding to one another is fundamental to 'empathetic dialogue' through which the church's gifts are offered in a form appropriate to recipients, givers and the relationship between them. By surrendering the platform to its conversational partners the church ensures the latter have an equal opportunity to be heard. This is the starting point for conversations based on *communicative action*.
- *Self-restraint*. Holding back enables the gift to be released. Recipients are not pressured to accept what is offered, nor to receive it in a way that the church thinks best. They are given time to ponder the gift, consider whether they want to accept it and decide the manner in which it will be received.
- *Speech accommodation*. Speech that reaches out to potential recipients smooths the way for the gift to be accepted, while taking the gift solidifies the relationship between givers and receivers. A shared community forms or deepens.
- *Speech divergence*. Alongside the practice of speech accommodation, those who bring the church's gifts will encourage recipients to talk about these gifts in their own way and to develop their own thoughts about them. When applied to new Christian communities, this will cultivate habits of discourse that foster innovative understandings and expressions of the Christian life. In time these new insights and practices may become return gifts to the wider church.
- *Story telling*. Church members who share in God's generosity have a great story about Christ to tell! Their hearers can be drawn into this story through a multitude of tiny stories about organizing practical love together, creating community and exploring Christian spirituality. Stories are the microchips of spiritual transformation.

How might these and other practices contribute to a theology of conversation?

# GIVING THE CHURCH

## Notes

1 'Conversation' can also be distinguished from 'discourse'. The latter is a series of conversations around the same theme or involving the same people.

2 Ignatius Loyola, *Spiritual Exercises*, p. 230. I am grateful to Maria Herrmann for this translation.

3 These conversations include worship, in which verbal antiphony plays a key role such as saying the psalms at an Anglican Evensong, liturgical responses and speaking in tongues followed by the interpretation of tongues.

4 If space allowed, a fuller discussion would include in this section how conversation itself is a gift, originating within the Godhead.

5 Many elements of the church's previous conversations are necessarily transmitted in the context of community, such as in worship or study groups, and are part of the church's conversations with God and the world. Without the Christian community, these conversations in their fullness cannot happen. Sharing these conversations, therefore, must entail passing on the communal life that fosters them.

6 Beta Course, Session 2. www.beta-course.org.

7 Copenhaver cites two studies suggesting Jesus gave only two direct replies, but thinks that a maximum of eight is more accurate.

8 Indeed, might 'proclamation' in part be recast as questioning? 'What situations do you face?' 'What kind of spiritual resources might support you in that situation?' 'What Christian spiritual resources might you welcome?' I am grateful to Dr Anne Richards for this point.

9 Of course, making these judgements is fraught with difficulty and will often be contested. See Enfield, 2022, pp. 127–48. An ethical starting point may be to speak in ways that the *audience* considers to be relevant and appropriate. If speakers disagree with their hearers' perception of fairness, honest communication will include being transparent about this difference of view.

10 However, 'speech divergence', the opposite of speech accommodation, may occur when the Spirit uses these different perspectives to challenge people who are over-invested in work, for instance, or to encourage those who fear their work lacks meaning.

11 Writing of Vatican II's 1965 Pastoral Constitution on the Church, *Guadium et Spes*, Brandon Gallagher says: 'Indeed, "dialogue" might be taken as one of the main themes of the document, from dialogue with atheism to dialogue concerning socioeconomic disputes' (Gallagher, 2015, p. 122).

12 This can apply even when a missional conversation has a clear end in view, such as a wedding service. As often happens, the minister and the couple co-create the service through a conversation in which they are open to one another's ideas.

# 9

# A Eucharistic Spirituality

If the church's giving follows the ethical logic of gift exchange, has the purpose of liberation and happens in the manner of good conversation, how might it be spiritually supported? Whereas the last two chapters explored the church's generosity in relation to liberationist and herald models of the church, this one does so through 'Eucharistic ecclesiology', which understands the church to be centred on Holy Communion (McPartlan, 2001, p. 15). Paul McPartlan writes: 'Modern liturgical studies have taught us to widen our gaze from the elements of bread and wine on the Lord's table ... to understand the Eucharist as the entire celebration of God's people within which the elements are transformed' (McPartlan, 1995, p. xiv). The linguistic connection between the 'body of Christ' given in the celebration and the 'body of Christ' describing the church denotes a fundamental reality. 'It is in the Eucharist that the community of God's people is fully manifest' (WCC, 1982, p. 19). From this starting point I want to open up a eucharistic understanding of the church's call to generosity, Again, I develop this with reference to new Christian communities, and once more I do this praying that the argument can inform other aspects of the church's giving.

The Eucharist has, of course, been understood in various ways – as originally a Passover meal, as a remembrance of this meal through which Christ is present in worshippers' hearts, as a commemoration in which Christ is present spiritually in the bread and wine, as a celebration in which the people are united with Christ when they consume the elements, and as an event in which Christ is so present that the bread and wine are mysteriously transformed into his actual body and blood. In all these understandings, the Eucharist is the liturgical enactment of a gift exchange. Through the Spirit Christ is offered to worshippers as a gift, the congregation receives the gift, and worshippers offer a return gift of praise, thanksgiving and their lives. The Eucharist is about giving par excellence.

Christians disagree, however, about the place of the Eucharist in the church's life. Some see Holy Communion as the centre of the church. By means of the Spirit the church is formed through the Eucharist. Others say that the church is formed by the gospel and Christ is especially present at the Eucharist as an outworking of the gospel. In an ecumenical spirit, this chapter is written from the standpoint of the first approach to complement the previous, more 'Protestant' chapter. It argues that for those who accept the highest view of the Lord's Supper, an *inevitable* consequence is the church's call to generosity. If the church is formed by the Eucharist, its life should *necessarily* be shaped by the pattern of giving described in Chapter 6; as one aspect of this the church will offer new Christian communities to the world. Those with a 'lower' view, on the other hand, will still find in this chapter a lens through which to view the church's generosity but without this having such a prominent place in their thinking. In addition, on either view the Eucharist is vital spiritual food for offering new Christian communities. Not least, it feeds healthy relationships within them.

My theme is not whether or how offering communion in Christ leads to the birth of fully sacramental communities. As it happens, many new Christian communities meet around food, echoing the shared meals central to Jesus' ministry. Especially if remembering the latter is explicit, they can be said to have the beginnings of a eucharistic life. As a step towards more mature liturgical worship, some introduce an informal 'breaking of the bread' during the meal – an *agape* supper, a 'remembrance of the Last Supper' or 'worship of the Eucharist outside the Mass'. In time, our prayerful hope will be that the community comes to celebrate a recognized form of Holy Communion, which may be led by an ordained minister representing the wider church and perhaps serving the community as 'chaplain'. Or from time to time the community may join with its parent congregation for a combined Eucharist. Or new believers may worship in their community and also periodically in another eucharistic congregation, as has traditionally happened with the Church of England's Evensong. Or there may be some combination of these sacramental events.

Rather than discussing these possibilities, the chapter starts with the missional logic of the Lord's Supper. It then extends eucharistic theology by describing the Supper's gift structure – receiving, giving appropriately, letting go, accepting the gift, giving back and transformation. Using new Christian communities as an example, I argue that the church's giving flows naturally out of the Supper. In particular, Holy Communion in the parent congregation breeds habits that help founders grow wholesome relationships within their new communities as the latter begin to emerge. Thereby communion in Christ can be given to others for the goal of justice, in the manner of healthy conversation, and with sacramental support for forming healthy community.

## A gift to the world

In his *Sociology of Giving*, Helmuth Berking suggests that giving has its origins in the hunt. The animal was killed and the meat was given to the women and children who had stayed at home. Later, this was ritualized into a ceremonial killing after which the food was distributed. First comes the killing (the mission, if you like), then the distribution – to the gods (the sacrifice) and to the worshippers. Giving was based upon the distribution. 'In this way, gift-giving is structurally interwoven with the sacrifice' (Berking, 1999, p. 63). The distribution follows the hunting, giving follows the 'mission'. These beginnings are transformed in the Eucharist. A lamb is not killed and offered to the gods; God in Christ is killed and then repeatedly offered to worshippers in the bread and the wine. 'Whoever eats my flesh and drinks my blood abides in me, and I in them' (John 6.56). Those who consume are joined to Christ, who was sent by the Father into the world (verse 57). Being united with Christ, therefore, co-opts worshippers into Christ's mission of love. Far from being a separate event after the mission, the distribution propels worshippers into the mission.

### *The missional logic of the Eucharist*

Notwithstanding different understandings of the Eucharist, it is in Holy Communion that Christ supremely nourishes the world. As we receive the bread and wine we are fed not by assimilating Christ into our bodies, which happens when we eat normal food, but by being assimilated into him; 'the one who feeds on me will live because of me' (John 6.57). As traditional liturgies assert, we become the body of Christ.[1] Joined to Jesus, we become with him food for the world, to be broken, given away and consumed. Congregations can become this food in numerous ways, as I have emphasized. Through the Spirit they can share their resources and practise pastoral care, for example, and when they do so they are appropriately similar to many other groups and organizations. But there is one form of sharing that no other entity can offer. Only the church can share what is at the heart of the Eucharist, communal life in Christ. For communion in Jesus is vital to the celebration. Church members gather round the bread and wine as a single body centred on Christ – 'we, who are many, are one body'. The Supper is Holy *Communion*.

So when the Spirit makes the church available to others in the form of new Christian communities, the kernel of the church's eucharistic life is offered – communion in Christ. This communion can properly be shared

# GIVING THE CHURCH

by inviting people to an existing congregation. However, as we saw in Part 1, especially in today's society this invitation will often be inappropriate because for many people the congregation is out of reach. In such cases, communion in Christ must be offered in the form of new Christian communities. This practice receives support from the very nature of Holy Communion. As Julie Gittoes points out, at the Last Supper Jesus *dispersed* himself as a gift to his followers. Rather than being single entities, his body and blood became multiple entities – pieces of bread and sips of wine that were consumed by each person present. If the church is to live consistently with this dispersal of Christ's body and blood, the gathering itself must disperse as a gift to the world (Gittoes, 2008, pp. 92–3). It must go out to the world, as well as inviting the world in.

However, Gittoes sees this as the dispersal of individuals. The congregation scatters as individuals and families. Now of course, when this happens it remains a communion. In McPartlan's words, 'we are never to imagine Christ acting as an isolated individual. The Church is always associated with him, clustered around him' (McPartlan, 1995, p. 7). But as stressed in Chapter 4, often this communion is not visible. People outside the church encounter believers as individuals rather than as persons-in-community. The communal reality that the Eucharist celebrates and makes possible is unseen. Yet this reality need not remain hidden. Just as the invisible Christ is made visible in Holy Communion's everyday bread and wine, so the Spirit can make communion in Christ visible in ordinary day-to-day existence.

Accordingly, instead of being dismissed as individuals the congregation will be visibly faithful to both the communal and the distributive aspects of the Eucharist by being sent out, wherever possible, as small communities. These communities will combine gathering (into community) and dispersing (into the world), just as gathering and dispersing are connected in the celebration. Empowered by the Spirit, these missional units will become an icon of the church's communal mode of existence. They will be a sacrament – an outward sign that makes real the inward presence of Christ, for whom being-in-communion is his way of life. They will enable organized forms of love for the world, as Chapter 1 described. Going beyond what individuals can achieve on their own, believers together will paint life in the medium of the self-giving love their worship celebrates and thereby enlarge the church's tent (Isa. 54.2).

Dispersing in the form of small communities gives enriched symbolism to the Roman Catholic practice of dipping into the chalice a piece of consecrated bread from the previous Mass. This can be a reminder that every Eucharist leads to the next, and the next and the next (Irwin, 2005, p. 76). In a corresponding way, new Christian communities are called to birth further communities, so that every community leads to another and another. Thus the church is dispersed throughout society in a testament to the dispersal at the heart of the Lord's Supper. The missional logic of the meal 'makes the church', in de Lubac's phrase, but in the form of a gift that keeps on giving.

## A sacramental map

How does the Eucharist shape the congregation's behaviour? Theologians have long understood that the Lord's Supper has ethical implications for those who consume. St Paul urged his readers to behave in a fashion worthy of the meal (1 Cor. 10.14–22). But it is not enough to say, 'Because we have done this in the Eucharist, we should behave in a corresponding way.' We need to understand how this ethical link is made. Some theologians suggest that the Eucharist imprints Christian behaviour on the world. Through baptism and Eucharist 'We learn who we are. Instead of being motives or causes for effective social work on the part of Christian people, these liturgies *are* our effective social work' (Hauerwas, 1983, p. 108; italics in original). Ethics is learned behaviour that becomes part of our identities, like a language. This behaviour is acquired through worship, in which the Spirit forms us in Christ so that we naturally behave like Jesus. That is why worship *is* our work in daily life. But the danger with this view is that the Spirit becomes coercive. Through the Spirit, the influence of the Eucharist is so strong that humans have little say beyond deciding whether or not to participate.

Gordon Lathrop likens the Eucharist to a map. It is a cultural construct that enables worshippers to interpret and navigate their worlds. As the sacramental geography unfolds around them, their view of life is reconstituted. Christians find their way by reading the map that worship creates. They are still formed in worship, but there is more space for human contributions. Worshippers have to read the map, for which they must acquire map-reading skills (Lathrop, 2003, pp. 56–94). Developing this further, however, there is not just one map. The Eucharist can generate a fistful of maps for different people in different contexts, with new maps for new situations. How do these maps emerge? We might say that the prayer for the Holy Spirit over the bread and wine is partly answered when the Spirit inspires worshippers to reflect on the contexts in which they find themselves, to adapt an existing eucharistic map or find a new one to navigate the context, and to describe these maps to others. The maps are created and continually updated as the church reflects on its vocation during Holy Communion. Worshippers are formed in Christian character as they read the sacramental maps the Spirit brings to their attention.

This chapter proposes one such map. It argues that the church's call to generosity, exemplified in new Christian communities, mirrors a theological logic that can be discerned in the Eucharist – its nature as a gift that is received from the world (as well as from Christ), the appropriate sharing of the gift, the eucharistic action of handing the gift over, the incorporation of worshippers into the whole church as the gift is 'consumed', the return gift to God in thanksgiving, and the dying-and-rising transformation the gift makes possible. The church's summons to join the Spirit in thankfully giving communion in Christ to others has a eucharistic shape.

As communicants become aware of it, this map does not only guide the practice of offering new Christian communities. Of particular importance, it helps to build Christ-like community while the initiative develops. As people gather around an outreach activity, the Christian core will face a series of relational challenges – how to empower members of the community, for example, how to reconcile different preferences and learning styles, how to include individuals who have a disruptive influence, how to grow *mutual* relationships between the strong and the weak, and more. As founders of new Christian communities meditate on the Eucharist's map for giving, the Spirit can foster in them habits of generosity that help them bring community members together.

## A gift to be received

We have seen that founders of Christian communities first go into the world with hands outstretched, eager to receive the divine blessings others have to offer. This includes listening especially to people on the edge and involves critical self-listening. Receiving first also echoes the logic of the Eucharist, in which communicants gather round the Lord's table to receive. In fact Christ, the prime giver, is himself a recipient at the meal. The eucharistic discipline acknowledges this. Traditionally, worshippers come to Holy Communion having prepared for Christ's welcome through fasting, prayer and repentance. The Spirit readies their hearts and minds to approach the meal in a manner worthy of the gift. The gift – feasting with Christ – comes into being because Christ graciously receives these human preparations.

This underlines an essential aspect of the Eucharist. Christ receives from the world in order to create the gift. At the Last Supper, Jesus received the upper room and all the ingredients of the meal. Ever since, God has gathered up human contributions to the meal – not just communicants'

## A EUCHARISTIC SPIRITUALITY

spiritual preparations but also the bread and wine, and typically today the building, heating and lighting, the interior decor, candles and more.[2] These inputs are part of creation groaning for redemption, prepared by people who are sinful at heart. It is not the purity of these contributions, therefore, that makes possible the Eucharist. Only through grace are they accepted and transformed into fitting vehicles for worship.

This eucharistic reception of the world reinforces the point that the church's generosity will often start with the receipt of gifts from others. In particular, underlining Chapter 4, it means that there is a place for Holy Communion to be celebrated in the midst of every dimension of human existence. It follows that Christian communities where the Supper is remembered should spread through all the capillaries of society. The more widely the Eucharist is present, the more it can receive from the multiple soundtracks of life. The paradigm for this is Luke 24.13–35. In the midst of a commonplace journey – to Emmaus – the two disciples gather with Jesus. The Scriptures are expounded as they walk. During an everyday meal bread is taken, prayed over in thanks, broken and given. Then the participants disperse. Jesus is encountered through an implicit Eucharist in everyday life.

Some prefer the Eucharist to be staged some distance from life's front-of-house. For example, the Anglican Archbishop Michael Ramsey rightly maintained that the Eucharist 'is not an exercise of piety divorced from common life, rather it is the bringing of all common life into the sacrifice of Christ' (Ramsey, 1990, p. 119). Even so, he argued that the Eucharist 'had to be set apart from common meals in an awe and mystery whereby its nearness to common life was to be realized more deeply' (p. 108). Stepping back from ordinary life avoids the celebration being tainted by the sinful aspects of existence (see 1 Cor. 11.17–34). Holy Communion can then draw in and transform day-to-day reality.

However, although distance from life may sometimes be helpful, why should it always be so? If the Eucharist is persistently celebrated on the outskirts of work, media, networks and more, might it not fail to receive from and be enriched by these spheres of existence? Might it become too remote from life's hills and valleys to seem relevant to them? Samuel Torvend has worried that worship directed to God often fails to make a difference to daily behaviour (Torvend, 2019, pp. xi–xiii). Keith Pecklers quotes the Franciscan liturgist Regis Duffy, who repeatedly asked his students: 'Despite our liturgical participation week after week, Sunday after Sunday, can we honestly say that we find ourselves longing more for God's reign this week than last week, more this year than last year?' (Pecklers, 2003, p. 169). Surely, the more the Eucharist knocks at life's doors, celebrated amid the familiar, the stronger will be its connection to everyday reality? If a craft group worships where members meet, it can more easily use their half-ready or just-completed creations as liturgical props.

Not only does the Supper's receiving from ordinary experiences encourage new Christian communities to be multiplied within the upstairs and downstairs of life, receiving first also has implications for the internal relationships of new communities. By being attuned to Christ's reception of flawed gifts from every human arena, the Christian core of a new community is correspondingly helped to receive first from other community members. Patterned by the receptiveness of Christ, they will graciously receive the gifts others have to offer. This may require them actively to seek out those gifts – to mentor potential leaders, to gently coax gifts that individuals are hesitant to offer, and to build the community around tasks that members find attractive and easy to undertake.[3] It may require them to welcome offerings that take the community in an unexpected direction; perhaps a newcomer's hobby assumes a prominent place.

Not least, leaders will refrain from strong-arming others into tasks that reflect only the founders' priorities. Rather, the community will arise organically as leaders receive offerings that are valued by those involved. A 'Lego Church' in southern England, for example, invites enthusiasts to build models that illustrate a biblical story. Community emerges as the leaders cherish the interpretations – the gifts – that families offer one another. Instead of others depending on the founders for spiritual wisdom, a eucharistic receiving first sets the stage for leaders to receive the insights of community members. Just as the Eucharist 'belongs' to those whose earthly gifts are received by Christ (and shared with fellow worshippers), the community is owned by members whose gifts are received by their leaders (and shared within the community). Within the community's broad trajectory, people are not invited into the leaders' project; leaders facilitate the people's projects – the bedrock of true community.

## Passing on appropriately

I have emphasized that the church's generosity must always be appropriate – both to the receiver and the giver. 'Empathetic dialogue' butters the gift on both sides. The result is hybridization that subverts the views of each party and which is made possible by conversations based on self-surrender. These elements – appropriate to the recipient, appropriate to the giver, and an accommodation between the two – are patterned in Holy Communion and extend its logic to the church's mission. On the one hand, the Eucharist is given in a manner that fits its recipients.

## A EUCHARISTIC SPIRITUALITY

This is reflected in the diversity of its origins. The Gospels introduce the meal in the feeding of the 5,000 in John 6, in the Passover setting of the Last Supper, on the road to Emmaus and at breakfast beside the lake in John 21. These different inaugurations of Holy Communion suited the particular circumstances.

Subsequently, the church has repeatedly indigenized the Supper, whether during the Reformation for example or more recently in the post-colonial South. Indeed, it is inevitable that repetitions of the celebration will vary because of differences in location, content and outcome. Every celebration differs from the one before and from the one next door – in the hymns, subject matter of the homily, mood of the congregation and much else. Though the legitimate extent of diversity is debated, differences enable the Eucharist to flourish in multiple settings. As Cavanaugh says, 'it is precisely God's transcendence of the world that allows liturgical difference, for where God cannot be fully grasped, a diversity of locations and practices is necessary to imply the transcendent' (Cavanaugh, 2002, pp. 118–19).

On the other hand, vital to the meal is memory. We remember the inaugural Last Supper and the self-offering of Christ, but additionally all God's mighty acts and all Christians who have gone before. Through memory, the church makes contemporary where it has come from. This speaks of identity. In particular, each celebration must in some way be recognizable as perpetuating and participating in the Last Supper. Though traditions differ in their understanding of what is recognizable, they all agree that each celebration must be identifiable as a Holy Communion. Christ gives the meal in a multitude of ways to a multitude of people in a manner that is true to his first giving of the meal.

How are context and tradition brought together? The term 'non-identical repetition', which has influenced a number of recent Anglican reflections on the Eucharist, provides a helpful frame for that debate, although it does not provide specific answers.[4] David Ford notes how non-identical repetition provides a third way between 'aspects of modernity which seem fixated on identical repetition', such as quests for standardization and universal norms, and postmodernity's reaction against this by 'contextualizing or relativizing every apparent universal' so that it appears as unique and particular. He suggests that the Eucharist draws on memory of the past to constantly redraw what is remembered. 'Improvisation is part of this refiguring', which is the process by which non-identical repetition occurs. 'There is an expansive dynamic of non-identical repetition which can take into its flow new people, events and practices' (Ford, 1999, pp. 152–4). Non-identical repetition is the eucharistic counterpart to 'empathetic dialogue'.

# GIVING THE CHURCH

The apt giving of new Christian communities flows naturally from the logic of the Eucharist. Each new community must fit the recipients and the givers, and as this is negotiated through 'empathetic dialogue' the outcome will be non-identical to other Christian communities; the community will be unique. In addition, appropriate giving is central to the new community's internal life. In Paul's teaching, a person's gifts must be suitable for the recipients; they must build up the community, which implies that the gift 'works' for those who receive it (Rom. 12.3–8; 1 Cor. 14.26). Equally, gifts must fit the giver. That is why Paul can say everyone has a gift to bring; these gifts vary greatly, all are of unique worth to the body (unique because the gift is particular to the giver), and none is to be valued above the other (1 Cor. 12.21–26). Edification and building up God's people are the scales on which to balance what is appropriate for the giver with what is appropriate to the recipient – what the giver thinks is a teaching gift, maybe, with what the recipient feels is boring (see 1 Cor. 14.12).

As gifts are exchanged, a flexible rhythm to the community's life will develop. Routines will emerge – perhaps once a month the community eats together and discusses a spiritual theme – but these will have the character of 'non-identical repetition': new people may join and add their particular gifts; as existing members become more confident in sharing their gifts they may bring new offerings; an existing gift may evolve in a Christlike direction. Gift exchanges will not feel mechanical and automatic. Without being chaotic, they will have an unexpectedness that brings giving alive. By sharing in, noticing and reflecting upon the non-identical repetition of the Eucharist, founders will be encouraged to keep drawing out people's perhaps surprising gifts so that exchanges are kept on the move and the new community stays fresh. Founders may think, 'If the gift of the Eucharist can be a surprise because it is different each time it is celebrated, should not the circulation of gifts within our community also bring constant surprise?'

## Handing over

Previous chapters have underlined that a gift is not a gift unless it is handed over. This applies to the church's generosity in general; whenever the church gives it must be prepared to let go. In particular, new Christian communities must be allowed in the Spirit to pull their own strings. This should give rise to 'local theologies', which are made possible through conversational habits in which founders restrain themselves and give elbow room to others. A corresponding letting go happens in

# A EUCHARISTIC SPIRITUALITY

Holy Communion. Once Christ has received from the world and offered himself appropriately, he releases himself into the hands of communicants. This echoes the handing over that the New Testament frequently associates with his death. Of the 33 times the role of Judas is mentioned, for example, he is described as 'handing over' Jesus on 31 occasions. In Galatians 2.20 Paul referred to Jesus as the one 'who loved me and handed himself over for me'. In Romans 8.32 he wrote of God 'who spared not his own Son but handed him over for us all'. In 1 Corinthians 11.23, Paul associated the Lord's Supper with this same handing over. 'I received from the Lord that which I also handed over to you' (Vanstone, 1982, p. 14).

Handing over is central to the meal. When Jesus broke the bread and shared the wine in the Upper Room, he handed over his body and blood to the disciples. He placed his life in their hands and let go. The disciples consumed the bread and wine at their own pace, in their own way and with their own thoughts, taking the food and drink into their bodies and making them their own. Jesus

> so surrenders himself into the hands of his Father and into the hands of his people that his flesh is given over so that the breaking and distribution of the bread becomes a symbol for the fact that Jesus himself is distributed. He is no longer master of his fate. He lets himself be consumed by the others in a mystery which does not come to an end on Calvary but which continues eucharistically until the end of time. And here too we are at the heart of a paradox. Jesus lets himself be disposed of, but this action is no passivity, for it is in its depths the active handing over of himself for our sakes in love. (O'Donnell, 1992, p. 43)

By continuing to hand himself over in the Eucharist, Christ takes a risk – that by letting go of his body he will be misused or even abused.

> [A] person's body is that person's availability, indeed vulnerability, to those others whom she or he addresses. And there is never a guarantee that they will not use such availability to the person's injury. If the risen Christ has a body, and if the bread and the cup are that body, then we can steal Jesus and try to use him as a charm ... It is not that such acts are impossible; it is that they are violations of the present Lord. (Jenson, 1992, pp. 32–3)

Christian founders assume a similar risk when they let their community go by drawing others into the leadership and in time relinquishing the leadership to them. They risk the community being 'used' in the wrong way, as happened at Corinth after Paul left. Yet just as Jesus does not shrink from this risk in Holy Communion, neither – as Paul demonstrated – will Christian leaders wishing to be faithful to the meal. Indeed, if handing over risks that the gift will be abused, accepting that risk is to adopt an attitude of forgiveness. The Latin verb 'to give', *dono*, also means to pardon, forgive, remit. What connects the two thoughts is letting go (Horner, 2001, pp. 213–14). In letting go of the new community, those who offer the gift let go of their right to seek retribution if, in their view, the recipients damage the gift. No reckoning would be due to them because the gift is no longer theirs.

Handing over the community, with the dangers involved, follows therefore the logic of Holy Communion. But going further, might founders meditate especially on the risk taken by Christ in the Eucharist? And might this free them to release more readily into the new community their practical and spiritual gifts, their gifts of possessions and money and their offerings of time and talents? For these gifts may not always be received in the way the givers hoped. Contributions may be spurned, then accepted with irksome conditions, next taken for granted and later criticized. When this happens, founders may be tempted to hold back in their giving. Instead, as part of Christian discipleship, they must learn the habit of forgiveness, a habit that oils the practice of letting gifts go, a practice that is fundamental to the healthy exchange of gifts within the emerging community.

## One with the whole

Offering a gift is a sign of welcome. It signifies that the giver appreciates the other person enough to want to cultivate some sort of relationship with them. The relationship then forms and deepens once the gift has been accepted, which lays a platform for the exchange to continue. In particular, receiving the gift of a new Christian community involves accepting not just the immediate community but a world of foreign countries joined to Christ and to each other. A liberationist approach highlights relationships with other Christians who share a justice agenda, while speech accommodation is a key practice for forging these relationships. Again, this forming of community can be seen as a eucharistic process. Community is established and strengthened when Christ receives his people at the altar and when the gift of Christ, his body and blood, are in turn received and consumed. Being received by Christ and receiving Christ opens worshippers' hearts to embrace his entire community.

On this view, accepting the whole church when receiving new Christian

# A EUCHARISTIC SPIRITUALITY

communities is eucharistic par excellence because receipt of the whole is enabled by the sacrament. In Henri de Lubac's oft-quoted phrase, the church makes the Eucharist and the Eucharist makes the church. The church makes the Eucharist when it celebrates the Last Supper. The Eucharist simultaneously makes the church by creating 'an inner reality. By its hidden power, the members of the body come to unite themselves by becoming more fully members of Christ, and their unity with one another is part and parcel of their unity with the one single Head' (de Lubac, 2006, p. 88). The community's unity with the whole body, accomplished unseen when the elements are consumed, is also expressed visibly at other points in the celebration. Worshippers remember the saints, include the universal church in their prayers and pray for the unity of the church (as well as all people) in the sign of peace. Then after the Supper, enabled by the sacrament, the community continues to receive the whole church by deepening relationships with it.

The latter happens, for example, when leaders of a new Christian community invite members to an ecumenical prayer retreat, a Christian festival, or to connect with the wider body online. They become conduits to the bigger church. These connections echo the practice in some traditions of passing the bread and wine from one member of the congregation to the next, who then consumes. Through the Spirit each communicant is a means by which Christ's body and blood are made available to others in the congregation. In a not dissimilar way, members of a new gathering can pass on the whole church to one another through the connections they establish with the church at large. Thereby we glimpse the beginning of an answer to the early Christian prayer, 'As this broken bread was scattered over the mountains, and when brought together became one, so let the Church be brought together from the ends of the earth into your kingdom.'[5]

The eucharistic action of receiving the universal church ensures that celebrations of Holy Communion in the multiple arenas of life – among people with a common interest, for example – can be faithful commemorations. Holy Communion does not require the presence of a great diversity of people with different ages, social backgrounds and so on, as some claim.[6] In the Eucharist, the Spirit unites a segment of the church, however narrow, to the whole Christian family. The church's catholicity is secured spiritually by worshippers invisibly joining all others in Christ, not physically by gathering diverse people around the same conspicuous altar. No gathering will be diverse enough to reflect the full miscellany of the body. On the other hand, any worshipping community will contain some diversity. A Christian community of film buffs may attract people of different ages, for instance. And this variety, however limited, will point to the much greater heterogeneity of the church as a whole. Thus a new community with a precise demographic focus can still be an expression of catholicity.

But might the multiplication of such communities be a threat to unity? Instead of joining together in one assembly, might Christians in a locality fragment into multiple gatherings? The answer lies once more in the eucharistic-enabled acceptance of the gift. The entire church is received and made present when the elements are consumed. This reception is symbolized by the 'open table' of most Protestant churches. Worshippers from different churches are invited to share in the one bread. This necessarily includes worshippers from new congregations. Their inclusion makes clear that these new communities are as much part of God's one family as individuals, with their different looks and personalities, are members of their own biological families. The extension of the family meal to all believers, old or new, expresses concretely the oneness of all Christians in Christ – a unity achieved in the Eucharist however numerous and varied the celebrations.

The importance of reception in Holy Communion challenges the frequent over-emphasis on giving in gift exchanges. The very offer of a gift, as we have seen, denotes receiving – the desire to receive the other person. And of course the gift itself must be received for the desire to be fulfilled. This double reception, by the giver and the recipient, are the shoulders on which the internal life of a new Christian community stands. This goes beyond accepting a person's gifts to accepting the person as a gift. For the Christian founders it involves the whole-hearted acceptance of other people in the community, however irritating, unappreciative or disruptive they may seem.

Christ first accepts the founders in the parent congregation's Eucharist. By melting the defences they erect around their egos, defences that keep others at bay, founders are enabled to bring undefended selves into their new community and thereby receive others as they are. Further, having been accepted themselves, founders accept the gift of Christ at the mother congregation's altar. They then echo this in the new community. They receive other participants as 'little Christs' (see Matt. 25.31–46). Thus the sacramental grace of being received and receiving flows into the community. Members feel accepted, which lowers *their* defences and makes them more accepting of others. They also see in founders a model of acceptance which they copy themselves. Through the founders the community becomes a living Eucharist with the sacramental reception of one another at its core.

## Giving back

After people outside the Christian community have accepted the church's gifts, they will offer, we pray, return gifts to the church. As the to and fro of gifts continues, the church will forge closer relationships with the world, perhaps establishing a platform on which to offer the church's most precious gift, communion in Christ. In the case of new Christian communities, I have suggested that for recipients of the community the appropriate return gift will be first to pass the church on to others in gratitude; this sharing of the church will encompass a wide range of gifts, including the formation of further new communities. In addition, by their lives and missional priorities new Christian communities will offer a second type of return gift – that of 'evangelizing' the church in paths of justice. Speech divergence is a conversational practice that creates space for this prophetic innovation to emerge.

As with the other dimensions, giving back has its counterpart in Holy Communion and brings a eucharistic logic to the church's generosity. The initiative, as always, lies with Christ. Christ gives his life on the cross. Worshippers respond with their offerings of bread and wine. The elements are received and transformed by the Spirit, who returns them to worshippers as Christ's body and blood. Worshippers again respond by giving back. In particular, the people's return gifts are *appropriate* expressions of gratitude. Just as Christ offered himself, the people bring their offerings. Just as Christ speaks to the congregation through the liturgy, the people reply in prayer. Just as the congregation's return gifts can never match the generosity of divine grace, the people respond by praising – magnifying – God. And just as the Supper celebrates Christ's epic gift of himself, worshippers offer back their own lives to Christ as a gift.

This appropriate giving back has its equivalent in a new Christian community's grateful return gifts to Christ's earthly body from which it came. Equally important, as we have seen, giving back involves transmitting to others the heart of the new community, communion in Christ, in the shape of a further Christian community. This passing on is more than a dutiful correspondence to the dispersal of Christ in the bread and wine; it too is a way of giving thanks. And it is a suitable form of gratitude because joyful thanks often include sharing one's gifts. A newly engaged woman shows off her ring; a child invites a friend to join him in playing with his birthday present. Recipients express their delight in the gift of the Christian community by gratefully making the church available to others.

Crucially, however, thanksgiving in the Eucharist should be mingled with regret that many are not yet receiving Christ's gifts. 'Were we to be content with thanksgiving, it would be as if we were saying that God approves of the arrangement whereby we have such food and others do not' (Lathrop, 2003, p. 81). Paradoxically, the Eucharist leaves us satisfied (we've been fed), but also dissatisfied (others have not). Tension between the two spurs mission, vital to which is passing on communion in Christ. Thus in the *epiclesis* we hand the elements and *ourselves* over to the Spirit, to be made use of in advancing God's redemptive purposes.[7] Gratitude is not excessive, allowing satisfaction with the status quo. It is temperate, provoking resistance to today's state of affairs.

This has implications for the new community's internal life. As founders reflect on the dissatisfied gratitude the Eucharist evokes, the sadness at who is absent from outside will have its equivalent within the community. Founders will notice which members are absent from significant moments in the community's life. A conversation may be so rich that founders wish others could have been involved. Or the mutual giving in a fellowship meal may have been such fun that they wish the whole community could have taken part. Or the joy of a close friendship may spark sadness that some in the community seem to lack close friends. These qualms have the potential to challenge the formation of cliques, including self-absorbed families with no room for the vulnerable. Fed by the eucharistic concern for absent ones, founders will encourage social islands to connect with others in the community, just as the community looks outward to the world.

## Transformation

Having breathed in (accepted the gift) and breathed out (returned it), recipients of the church's generosity are transformed. In particular, when this generosity is geared to the most vulnerable in society, recipients may be drawn into the radical movements of justice for which liberationists pray, using story telling as a vital tool. Once more, this transformational aspect of giving is rooted in the Eucharist. The bread and wine are transmutations from wheat and grapes. During the celebration, in a manner that Christians debate, they are changed again into the body and blood of Christ. Those who receive are reshaped by being joined to the dying and rising of Jesus. In him they die to old habits so that new ones can come alive. This happens through the Spirit who implants a model of Christian behaviour, the self-giving of Christ, in worshippers' minds by reminding them of what Jesus has done, and in their hearts by inspiring and enabling them to imitate the model. Self-centredness is turned into gift-centredness.

# A EUCHARISTIC SPIRITUALITY

Just as Jesus died and was raised as a gift to the world, recipients of his body and blood die to self so that they, too, can be gifts to others. Giving is expanded from the giver, the gift and the recipient to include a fourth element, the beneficiary for whose sake the giving is performed. This fourth element is crucial to charitable giving. The giver offers the charity a donation for the benefit of those the charity serves (Saarinen, 2005, p. 51). In a not dissimilar manner, through regular celebrations of the Lord's Supper members of the church are repeatedly transformed so that they can offer themselves as a gift to others for the sake of the world.

When this gift takes the form of a new Christian community, the parent congregation may have to bear a kind of death in its shared life so that it can become a source of transforming life to others. The departure of the leader to start a new community, the going out of a church-planting group, the partial withdrawal of two people from the congregation so that they have time to grow an all-age gathering, the division of an ecclesial cell for purposes of mission, the splintering of a congregation into missional communities that meet together only once a month, the closing of a church activity to free up resources for mission – all these may feel like losses or threats to a congregation. An aspect of its life dies, which changes the congregation. And the pain may be increased by the risk involved: that what is given is not reciprocated.

Yet these 'deaths' need not be the last word. A believing community may fragment to a degree as it multiplies, but through the Spirit these fragments can be stitched together around Christ. A new gathering can become an additional congregation within a local church, or perhaps a new church connected to the wider body. As relationships are forged between the new and the old, the whole church will be enriched. Disintegration (however small) will be followed by reintegration, a kind of death by new kinds of life. By breaking off little communities, offering them as gifts to the world and welcoming people who receive these gifts into the wider body, the congregation will echo the eucharistic gift of Christ's body, which is 'broken for you' so that recipients can be united with Christ. Transformation involving death and resurrection will spawn new insignia of God's approaching reign.

Christian founders of the new community become further agents of transformation by dying to their expectations of what the tradition will look like in their context. This is not dying to the tradition itself, but to expectations of how the tradition will be expressed. Space is given for the Spirit to bring change to people through new forms of the tradition. For instance, at a Messy Church in South London, parents and children absorbed Christian songs and Scripture, which were sung and talked about at home and which impacted them in small but significant ways (Watkins and Shepherd, 2014, p. 104). Through good conversations 'local theologies' can emerge from the context and address it. One example is a community of classic car enthusiasts. Its leader is seeking to develop a Christian spirituality based on classic cars to enrich the lives of the people involved. By such means, just as the Eucharist celebrates life through death, new Christian communities can become celebrations of fresh life. By dying to an existing spiritual imagery, founders can rise to a new spiritual imagination.

Dying to live, the heart of Holy Communion, is also central to the community's internal life. As founders are joined to Christ in their parent congregation's celebration of the Eucharist, they are united to the person who died and rose for them. Enfolded in Christ's death and resurrection, they are empowered to die to self so that their new community might live a fuller life. Dying to self is not the loss of identity, just as Jesus did not lose his identity on the cross. It is a refashioning of identity so that believers can give what they are and what they have to others. But: how pure is the generosity of founders? How far is it a giving of love? How much, in fact, is it a giving like Christ? And for those who fall short, to what extent is their giving redeemed through the grace that comes via apologizing for mistakes, reparation where appropriate, and forgiveness? These spiritual habits, nourished in the Eucharist for example through confession and the exchange of the peace (properly understood), are a prerequisite for true community. They are a sign that the community is becoming a spiritual academy for founders to die to self so that others can become more completely alive.

## Implications

Here, then, is the eucharistic empowerment of the church's call to generosity. To throw some light on this, I have suggested that the logic of the Christian family's much-loved meal underpins the logic of offering others new Christian communities in thankfulness to God. Thus through the Spirit:

- The church receives from the context before giving to the context, just as Christ's gift of the Eucharist draws from the world.
- The church's offer of communion in Christ is appropriate to the recipients and to itself as the giver, just as the Eucharist is faithful to context and tradition by being a 'non-identical repetition'.

# A EUCHARISTIC SPIRITUALITY

- Christian founders hand their new community over to those who receive the gift, just as the bread and wine are handed over to those who consume.
- People who come to faith are connected to the wider church, just as they are united to the whole body when they receive the eucharistic elements.
- Just as in Holy Communion worshippers give their lives back to Christ in thankfulness, new Christian communities gratefully give themselves back to God by offering their gifts to the wider church and passing themselves on to people beyond it.
- New communities should be apotheoses of transformation, just as dying to self and rising to the dispossession of self bring transformation within the Eucharist.

## Enriching the self-donation model

This logic does not follow the sequence of the liturgy as normally understood (gathering, word, meal, sending) but echoes the framework of gift exchange – receiving, appropriate giving, letting go, accepting, giving back and being transformed. However, this giving logic is by no means foreign to the flow of the liturgy. Christ receives the worshippers as they gather with the One who is already present ('The Lord is here'). He gives to them the word and the sacrament in a manner they can understand. These gifts are released as recipients reflect on how the word applies to them personally and as they consume the bread and wine in their own way. The people are joined to Christ and all other believers as they receive his body and blood. They give themselves back to him in their praise, the intercessions, the offertory, and afterwards in their daily lives. They leave having been transformed into a living sacrifice, 'holy and pleasing to God' (Rom. 12.1).

As founders of new Christian communities attend to this rhythm of giving and return giving, they create space for the Spirit to implant in their hearts the eucharistic map of receiving, giving appropriately and the rest of the gift-exchange framework. The map then reminds, inspires and guides them after the celebration. They are nourished both in offering these new communities and in fostering the gift's communal life. In particular, at the Eucharist the Spirit reminds founders of their desperate need of outside help, mediates grace and tutors them in forming an attractive community. Founders are enabled:

- to seek out others in the emerging community with gifts to offer
- to exchange gifts with community members appropriately
- to release their gifts and forgive when these gifts are misused
- to accept other people sacramentally as gifts from God of 'little Christs'
- to offer back to God the return gift of creating inclusive relationships within the community, and
- to be joined to Christ in a dying-to-live pattern of communal life.

## Enriching eucharistic theology

At the same time this chapter expands our understanding of the Eucharist by suggesting how worship and mission should be integrated. Worship is commonly thought to be the supreme goal of mission, whose end point is worshipping God. The danger is that when people reach this destination they settle down and enjoy it almost too much. They are so blessed in worship that they prioritize the experience; mission slips down the back of the altar. The proper response is not to degrade worship from being a love gift to God to being an instrument of mission: worship merely inspires and equips us to offer the church to others. Rather, the answer is to see the Eucharist as a gift from God during which lives are returned as gifts to God for God's sake. The 'end' of worship is God. But because God's nature is to give, the appropriate response will be lives with an embarrassment of generosity.

This benevolence will include the whole bucket list of mission, such as pastoral care, concern for creation, solidarity with people on the social edge, reconciliation and creativity through the arts. As an important aspect of this, in the Supper the church is given a particular vocational shape, giving away new Christian communities. This sharpens the conventional relationship between worship and mission by bringing the gift of communion in Christ centre stage. In worship, the people offer themselves to God, who sews God's own self-giving character into their hearts. The formation of groups offering new Christian communities to others as a normal part of the church's generosity should be a natural outcome.

This shapes the 'liturgy after the liturgy' that refers to mission following Communion. During the celebration, small groups of Christians will be called ('taken'), they will be supported in prayer ('blessed'), they will go out from the congregation ('break'), and they will be offered as the body of Christ to people outside the church ('give'). People will gather round, hear the word, receive the paschal gift, consume it, be transformed into a new Christian community and be sent out to repeat the process, thereby multiplying all the church's gifts to the world. Communal life in Jesus

A EUCHARISTIC SPIRITUALITY

will be passed from one generation to the next, and from one context to another. Discipleship will acquire a eucharistic hue. No longer will the congregation be sent out at the end of the Supper to witness mainly as individuals who return for sustenance to a further Eucharist, leaving a non-sacramental hole in the middle. Rather, as congregational groups offer communion in Christ to others, ecclesial life between one celebration and the next will take a eucharistic form. Liturgy more literally will continue after the liturgy.

Put differently, offering new Christian communities has a sacramental feel to it. Giving communion in Christ *says* something, 'We love you,' and *does* something by enacting that love. It signifies the depth of the relationship the church seeks with others: 'We are giving you the heart of our life.' And it makes that relationship real. Likewise, offering communion in Christ in a liberationist direction both makes a statement (to God and the world) about the church's ethical focus and makes that statement concrete in daily life. New liberationist communities are signs that enable the church's ethical priority. In the same vein, the conversations through which the church offers new Christian communities are sacramental exchanges. Words both signify and enact a relationship. What is said signifies how givers and potential receivers of the church feel about their relationship and enables the relationship to embody those expectations. Giving communion in Christ, therefore, is a fitting 'liturgy' to follow the sacrament.

Finally, this chapter both extends eucharistic theology to church planting and offers church planters a eucharistic compass to navigate their worlds. This is important because much of today's energy behind church multiplication comes from evangelicals with a 'low church' theology. Yet if giving communion in Christ to others is the vocation of the whole church, other traditions must also be able to identify with the call. A eucharistic script provides a more Catholic story about offering new Christian communities for the sake of the world. It invites the question: if the Lord's Supper is central to the church's existence, should this not also be true of the church's Eucharist-like vocation to give communion in Christ away?

# GIVING THE CHURCH

## *Notes*

1 William Cavanaugh cites St Augustine, who 'envisions Jesus saying, "I am the food of the fully grown; grow and you will feed on me. And you will not change me into you like the food your flesh eats, but you will be changed into me"' (Cavanaugh, 2002, p. 47).

2 In one sense these contributions are not strictly gifts. Heating and lighting, for example, are likely paid for through a commercial contract. However, they will often have a gift dimension. The heating and lighting will be paid for from the financial giving of the congregation.

3 For example, the professional leaders of an initiative in an area of poverty deliberately left loose ends in their organization of events. They wanted participants to feel they could contribute by improving on what the leaders had begun.

4 For a recent discussion, see Catherine Pickstock, *Repetition and Identity* (Oxford: Oxford University Press, 2013).

5 The *Didache* IX in Jasper and Cuming, 1990, p. 23.

6 John Zizioulas, for instance, argues for celebrations 'in one place', embracing people of different ages, ethnic groups, class backgrounds and so forth, to echo New Testament practice and to be a visible anticipation of the one gathering of the saints around the Messiah when the Lord returns. See Zizioulas, 2011, pp. 14–19, 46–7. But this is hard to imagine in practice. Can one place be small enough to be accessible yet also large enough to produce the diversity Zizioulas has in mind? And if it is often not possible, does this theological ideal have much practical traction (see Healy, 2000)? Furthermore, did New Testament Christians celebrate the Lord's Supper in one place? As mentioned in Chapter 5, in Jerusalem believers broke bread in their homes, which were scattered across the city (Acts 2.46).

7 The Catechism of the Roman Catholic Church (§1105) declares that the *Epiclesis* 'is the intercession in which the priest begs the Father to send the Holy Spirit, the Sanctifier, so that the offerings may become the body and blood of Christ and that the faithful by receiving them, may themselves become a living offering to God'.

# 10

# Becoming an Attractive Gift

When Alice stepped through the looking glass, she entered a completely different world. *Giving the Church* invites you to pass through a theological looking glass and reimagine the Christian community. It is a thought experiment: what would be the effect on our doctrine of the church if we took the notion of gift from the theological attic and brought it into the room? As the church enters a seemingly new theological era in which the Christendom mode of following Jesus is being pushed to the edge globally and within 'Western' societies, might this be a help to the church? Might generosity make the church less toxic, resonate with Christians who are seeking to express their life together in new ways, and assist the church to love others more fruitfully?

Recognizing that there is too much church to describe in a few chapters, might we still tell a story that addresses today's widespread suspicion of the church?

- The church is summoned to a life of generosity, which can take many forms. One aspect makes the church stand out. The Christian community is the only human institution that is called to offer communion in Christ, its very self, to others. Rightly this can comprise an invitation to an existing congregation, but often today such an invitation will be inappropriate because the church is culturally and sometimes physically inaccessible to many people. In these cases, in gratitude for grace the Christian community is to offer communion in Christ in the form of new Christian communities. This giving is not for the prime benefit of church members but for the sake of the world. Just as someone gives to charity so that it can support a third party, the Spirit gives communion in Christ away so that recipients can enrich others through a host of further gifts.
- The ecclesial self that is given is relational by nature. It consists of four overlapping sets of relationships with God directly, with the world, with the wider church and within each gathering of Christians. These relationships are enabled to grow into Christ by the Spirit working through the word, sacraments, ministry and disciplines. Since gifts in

general arise from, express and deepen relationships, to offer a gift whose essence is relationships is to make available a gift par excellence.

- As they are drawn into Christ, the ecclesial relationships increasingly resonate with humanity's longings for connection to others (oneness), identity (holiness based on self-giving), inclusion (catholicity), and for connection through time (apostolicity). These marks are particularly present whenever the church gives away new Christian communities. Prioritizing the latter has the potential to prompt reform so that the church displays these marks more fully in its internal life and becomes a more attractive gift.
- The church is a gift for a fuller life. So it should not be an esoteric gift removed from the trenches of life but on the front lines. The more the church is present *with* people, the more it can be a present *to* them. And the more the present is accessible, the more likely it is to be received, be passed on and circulate more widely.
- This passing on must be appropriate. Far from being a one-size-fits-all gift, the church should be bespoke. Recipients' unique cultures are to be fulfilled in Christ. But this is not a licence for cultural fragmentation. Following New Testament practice, the church is to gather in culturally specific congregations that also intermingle and cross-pollinate each other. In a world struggling to combine diversity and unity, the church should be a gift by demonstrating both.
- Likening the church to charitable giving should sound the alarm at morally suspect forms of generosity. In response, Chapter 6 described the mutuality that should be involved in the church's giving, using new Christian communities as an example – receiving first, giving appropriately, letting go, accepting the gift (which builds community), giving back and transformation. Illustrating how the church's generosity can be taken in a variety of theological directions, this framework was then integrated with three influential models of the Christian community – the church as a liberating, proclaiming and eucharistic community. The Spirit offers new Christian communities within an ethical framework of gift exchange for the purpose of liberation, in a conversational manner and with the support of eucharistic spirituality.

All this jolts our thinking about the church into a different orbit. If generosity is central to the church's life, how the church gives should have as important a place in theology as sacraments, ministry, church governance and other aspects of the Christian community. In particular, *Giving the Church* challenges inward-looking spiritualities, anti-institutional expressions of faith and quests for Christian community without the church. 'I like Jesus but not the church' is not an answer to the church's sinfulness but a refusal to take up the challenge. It misunderstands who Jesus is. Jesus is not a single human; he is one with his earthly community. So to imagine you can have Jesus without the church is akin to severing the body and hoping to retain a living head.

The church mobilizes generosity by multiplying Christian communities as part of a giant ecclesiastical honeycomb – more church if you like, not less; but better church compared to today's defective church. This final chapter describes some of what this multiplication looks like. It suggests several ways in which the very practice of offering these communities can help cleanse the church from sin. Part of the answer to the church's failings is for the church not to retreat from being a gift but to join the Spirit in continually offering communion in Christ to others as a normal part of its generosity. Again, a number of the reflections that follow will apply to other dimensions of the church as a gift.

## The church's vocation

First, offering new Christian communities will invite church members to see themselves as givers. Just as spouses behave differently when they focus more on giving to the marriage than receiving from it, so church members will act more generously if they seek to give communion in Christ away. If they see themselves as a potential gift they will have reason to reflect on whether they are a welcome one. In particular, the call to offer the church's self, communion in Christ, rewires consumerist attitudes. Instead of members asking 'Is the church satisfying my needs?' they will ask, 'Are we a gift people would want to receive?' Might there be something winsome about a church that is serious (though not obsessed) about critiquing its own life?

Second, the ethical framework for offering new Christian communities can help repair the church's moral fabric. Receiving first, for example, includes careful listening, especially to those on the social edge. The church can best receive from God's activity in the world by paying attention to what the world has to offer. And as we have seen, the world's gifts may include painful criticisms of the church. These can move church members to repentance, reform and to sacrificial forms of service that others recognize as reparation. The church is provoked to make itself a more acceptable gift.

Offering communion in Christ appropriately invites the Christian community to consider what kind of gift it might be. What form of communal life in Christ would be received with joyful thanks, especially by those who are socially excluded? It also invites the church to ask 'What is a suitable gift for *us* to offer?' Christians will look at themselves – who they are, what they know, who they know and what they have (Moynagh, 2017, p. 65) – from the standpoint of generosity. 'What interests, resources and contacts do we have that can make us a gift?' Appropriate giving also includes what is proper to both sides' investment in the relationship, to how much the relationship means to them. So before offering the heart of their life, communion in Christ, church members will ask whether this is a fitting gift at that stage. Have they poured enough love into the relationship and has this love been sufficiently reciprocated for such an offer to be suitable? Sensitive giving, with recipients uppermost in mind, cultivates an attractive church.

In a similar vein, letting the gift go calls for non-coercive church leadership. If the church is to be released into the hands of its recipients, the ecclesial hierarchy cannot take the gift back by controlling how it is used. Instead of chaining the new community to others' expectations, leaders must release members to be themselves in Christ. This does not mean an abdication of leadership. It suggests a particular type of leadership, based on communal discernment with 'small mouths' and 'large ears'. Recognizing that God's word is too immense to be uttered by one mouth or even one group of mouths, leaders should encourage the community to listen to the Spirit through its relationships with God directly, with the world, with the wider church and within the community itself. By questioning, correcting and holding one another to account in healthy forms of conversation, a variety of distributed voices can disperse influence within the church, liberate people at the church's base and so limit the ecclesial abuse that may arise from pyramids of power.

When the gift is accepted, recipients are drawn into the entire body of Christ. For giving the church to others is more than the offer of one particular Christian community. It is an offer to taste life with the whole communion of saints. Failure to offer the complete gift would limit the church's generosity, which would be at odds with the total self-giving of the church's head. So the Christian community must make the fullness of church a practical reality. It must lay down accessible pathways from the congregation to the church at large. It must ask: how well does our diocese, denomination or network help new Christians flourish in their faith? Where are the opportunities for new believers to contribute to the wider church? How welcoming are the church's structures and processes, especially to vulnerable people short of confidence? Is the greater church being made a pleasing gift to people on society's edge?

Receivers of the church will offer return gifts that include experience, wisdom, expertise and knowledge of 'good practice' in education, safeguarding, governance and much else. These gifts will not be accepted unthinkingly, aping 'managerialism' outside the church, but in the context of prayerful theological reflection. They will be seen as contributions to the church's conversation with the world on God's behalf and with God on the world's behalf. In particular, by challenging harmful habits of thought and behaviour new Christian communities can be prophetic voices to the rest of the church, enhancing the gift especially on behalf of the poor.

When God's people and the world draw together through their exchange of gifts, but without the church losing its distinctiveness, the Spirit enables the two to bring out the best in each other. The church's gifts of solidarity with the weak, care for creation, contributions to the creative arts and more help the world enjoy a fuller existence, just as the world's gifts help the church repair its internal life and become more attractive. Giving the church becomes transformative. Thus, by containing the seeds of ecclesial reform, each phase of the framework of giving creates opportunities for the church even to become – maybe, just possibly – a choice gift.

## A methodology for self-donation

Third, beyond this ethical framework is a gift-based methodology for offering new Christian communities, which makes the *process* of giving away communion in Christ more inviting. One approach to multiplying the church has been, in effect, to follow the apostles, who made up their team (Acts 1.21–26), proclaimed the resurrection (Acts 2.14–41), and the church then emerged (Acts 2.41–47). Verbally announcing the gospel dominates the process. Broader aspects of mission, from pastoral to creation care, happen once the new Christian community is formed. Examples include John Wesley's eighteenth-century preaching missions and recent evangelism-based forms of church planting in many parts of the world.

This approach was affirmed in the Vatican II document *Ad Gentes* (§6), which sees preaching the gospel as the chief means by which new churches are established. However, in the same section, *Ad Gentes* recognized that

> circumstances are sometimes such that, for the time being, there is no possibility of expounding the Gospel directly and forthwith. Then, of course, missionaries can and must at least bear witness to Christ by charity and works of mercy, with all patience, prudence and great confidence. Thus, they will prepare the way for the Lord and make Him somehow present.

## The missional journey

Circumstances in which 'there is no possibility of expounding the Gospel directly and forthwith' are now widespread in the 'global North', where Christianity is largely in retreat. They also exist in many parts of the South, such as urban contexts beyond the shadows of the church. Growing numbers of people have had little, if any, contact with the church and have little awareness of Christ. To address this, a variety of innovative forms of Christian community have emerged. 'The missional journey', portrayed below, describes the gift-based methodology that teams starting these new communities have frequently employed. Usually teams have adopted the methodology intuitively, but a growing number have done so explicitly as the journey has become more widely recognized. In consultation with others, the journey was conceptualized in 2006–2010 by members of the UK Fresh Expressions team, a small ecumenical body established in 2005 to encourage 'fresh expressions of church' in Britain.

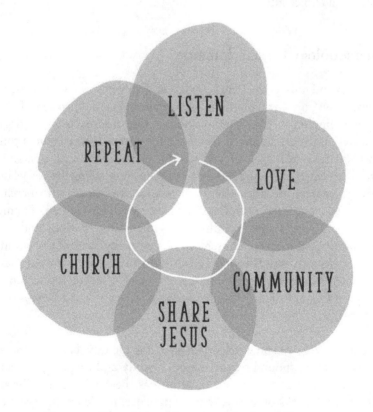

*Figure 1.1: The missional journey, underpinned by prayer and continuing connection to the wider church*

The journey describes what practitioners were seen to be doing as they birthed new forms of Christian community. Aldous and Moynagh (2021) briefly describe the journey's emergence and provide a case study from South Africa.

Just as in Jesus the divine Son went into the world and gathered a human community, so a group of Christians comes together 'in life' to gather a new congregation. In the first instance the team meets not primarily to worship but to offer practical love to people outside the church; members pray and worship in the slipstream of their missional love. The Christians *Listen* lovingly to God directly, one another, the wider church and to the people they feel called to serve, deepening relationships with them. They prayerfully discover how to offer organized *Love*, which is more than forming loving relationships (the latter happens during *Listening*). Organized love involves activities of love, such as arranging a language cafe, a craft group or a keep-fit class. It creates a watering hole around which people gather to form *Community*. These three stages 'prepare the way for the Lord and make Him somehow present'.

As trust deepens, the Christian team uses natural opportunities to *Share Jesus* as part of a fuller life. A new Christian community with the character of *Church* takes shape among those coming to faith, where they are. The community is connected to the wider body (normally the parent congregation) but is not a bridge to regular worship in an existing church; the new community is in effect a congregation in its own right. Then, in the ideal, the new believers *Repeat* the cycle in their own way – leaders puff the dandelion. Of course, life is messier than a diagram! So the circles may overlap, pile on top of each other and sometimes happen in a different order. Each continues when the next ones are added. Not infrequently, teams refocus on an earlier stage.

The stages are not means to an end, making disciples. Each has value in itself. Even if an initiative does not complete the journey, the circles it travels through have their own intrinsic worth. The journey integrates the goal of making disciples with the path the community travels. Community building and Christian formation can be seen 'as two sides of the same soteriological coin' (Paas and Schaeffer, 2021, p. 330). On one side is the journey to being church. On the other is personal growth in Christlikeness. It is one coin because people are enabled to expand their Christian commitment as they participate in and contribute to the community. Being born again is a communal process in which some come to accept Christ, while others don't but remain part of the initiative.

Various pathways lead from the first three circles to the next. Sometimes a separate group enables people to explore Jesus and morphs into a worshipping community alongside the *Love* activity, which continues.

Or enquirers join the leadership team in eating together, having fellowship, planning, Bible study, prayer and worship.[1] The team organizes its worship and study flexibly around the visitors to make them feel welcome. The team grows as visitors return, others join them and the visitors encounter Christ. The planning group becomes the community's worshipping hub. Or third, the whole community travels together. 11 Alive, in England's East Midlands, met cafe-style once a week. Atheists and agnostics helped to plan and lead a short act of worship at the end, which greatly accelerated their journey to faith (Moynagh, 2017, pp. 49, 290).

## An example

Wildwood United Methodist Church, Florida, illustrates some possibilities. In early 2020, the US church had 14 *potential* new Christian communities, each aspiring to be a community in Christ connected to the original congregation. Some were well on the way to being *actual* new Christian communities; they had reached the *Church* stage of the journey. These potential and actual congregations included:

- *Arts for Love.* Art enthusiasts gather to pray, worship and create art together.
- *Blessing Bags.* A group worships and prays as members collect and distribute necessary items for homeless people.
- *Burritos and Bibles.* Seekers gather in Moe's Southwest Grill for burritos, prayer, Scripture and Holy Communion.
- *Church 3.1.* Young professionals run 5km (3.1 miles), pray and have a conversation about some verses from Scripture.
- *Connect.* A church for children involves fun activities, breakfast, Jesus stories and worship in the local community centre.
- *Faithfully Fit.* Health enthusiasts meet in the park for prayer, devotions and walking the track.
- *Higher Power Hour.* Spiritual seekers explore spiritual practices including prayer and poetry.
- *Mascara Mondays.* A handful of women gather in the local coffee shop for prayer and Bible reflection.
- *Paws of Praise.* Dog lovers gather in the local dog park for prayer, worship, Scripture and play.
- *Shear Love at Soul Salon.* A pop-up salon offers free haircuts, prayer and a Bible reflection.
- *Skate. Pray. Repeat.* A group of friends gather at indoor rinks and outdoor tracks to skate, pray and share their faith.

## BECOMING AN ATTRACTIVE GIFT

- *Tattoo Parlor Church*. Seekers receive faith-based tattoos and worship Christ with Holy Communion.
- *Trap Stars for Jesus*. Ex and current drug dealers learn how to start legitimate businesses, with prayer and Scripture mixed in.[2]

Eight years before, Wildwood was struggling with few resources and a broken past in an area of poverty. By 2020 it was a hub with multiple emerging congregations on the rim, its original congregation revitalized and a web of connections between them all. This missional thrust has given the church the confidence and capacity to reach out to more affluent white believers on 'the other side of the tracks' and challenge systematic racism. Together they have held prayer walks for racial unity, organized weekend interracial revivals and jointly started potential new Christian communities that cross racial divides. Offering communion in Christ has not been at the expense of other types of mission. Rather, due to the collective energy of these new communities, the church has been able to mobilize wider social change. Around the nucleus of the parent congregation's offer of new Christian communities a cell of generosity has emerged.

The result is a 'mixed ecology' or 'blended' church. Existing and new forms of church live alongside each other as intersections rather than parallels, in mutual love and support. Old expressions of church are not prioritized over the new. The new is not valued more than the old. Both, in relationship together, are gifts of God's kingdom. The new re-energizes the old, while the old gives birth to the new, nourishes it and passes on the church's spiritual treasures. The future can be different, while the present can stay roughly the same. What brings about this future is the Spirit's initial activity through *Listening*, organized *Love* and building *Community*. Thus in terms of our theme, through listening, loving and community, the Spirit makes the church an attractive gift. God's people become credible by devoting themselves to others. This softens people's hearts and opens them, without pressure, to a richer life in Christ.

### An ancient practice

The *missional journey* is not new. I was brought up by missionary parents who worked in Burundi for what was then known as the Ruanda Mission. The mission was founded by English evangelicals after the First World War. They *Listened* to the local people, especially the chiefs, as they decided where to locate their mission stations. They *Loved* the people by sharing their medical skills and offering them education. They shared their lives (*Community*) and the gospel (*Share Jesus*), and started *Church* when people came to faith. Then they recruited African assistants to *Repeat* the process in the surrounding villages.[3]

Leap back 1,300 years and something similar happened with St Augustine's mission to England. As Bede described it, Augustine and his companions settled in Kent and on the king's instructions were 'furnished with necessities'; they established relationships with the people they were called to serve (*Listen*). They cared for the poor and worked miracles, which presumably included healing (*Love*). They extended hospitality and deepened relationships with people around them (*Community*). And they proclaimed the gospel (*Share Jesus*). All these aspects overlapped. As the number of worshippers grew (*Church*), churches in the surrounding villages were built or repaired, a sign that the process was being *Repeated*.[4]

Race back another 700 years and in Luke 10 Jesus sent 72 disciples on mission. In verses 8–9, they were told to receive hospitality (*Listen*), heal the sick (*Love*) and announce the kingdom (*Share Jesus*), all in the context of *Community* (v. 7). After the disciples left, villagers or townsfolk must have met to prepare for Jesus' arrival since this was the purpose of the visit (v. 1), and presumably in some places they continued to meet afterwards to discuss Jesus' teaching (*Church*). Again, it is important to stress the fluidity of the different stages. The order of *Love* and *Share Jesus* is reversed in Luke 9. Presumably they very much overlapped.

The missional journey represents an intuitive method of founding congregations among people who have little or no background in the gospel. Historically, has this methodology implicitly prevailed whenever the church has been offered without coercion? And if so, has it proved fruitful because *Listening* allows the approach to be widely adapted through learning-as-you-go, and because *Love* and *Community* are the priorities? Might the journey be one of God's special gifts for mission?

### Generous mission

One of the journey's striking features is its dynamic of gift exchange. Each circle is a gift, which elicits a further gift that becomes the basis of the next gift. So, for instance, *Listening* is a gift. It spurs involvement by calling forth further gifts of information, ideas and a willingness to help. These responsive gifts form the basis of the next gift, *Love*, which evokes gifts of engagement, relationship and trust that form the basis of community. The gift of *Community* draws out the gifts of shared enjoyment, gratitude, increased trust and deepening relationships. These encourage an openness to Jesus and lay foundations for exploring him. The gift of

*Sharing Jesus*, we pray, leads to accepting the kingdom, which is a return gift to those who shared the gospel; they are enriched by the joy and insights of new believers. This response enables *Church* to be offered, which elicits further gifts of enthusiasm and gratitude. These encourage the cycle to be *Repeated*, but in a different way to fit the new context; the dynamic of gift exchange is transmitted from one setting to another. The methodology of giving the church thereby echoes the theology behind it. It helps make the gift attractive by engaging people, if they wish, in an ongoing process of reciprocal generosity.

Especially in the early stages, the initiative lies with the team who brings communion in Christ. Potential recipients who have not experienced the gift may be wary or suspicious. They are not unlike consumers who are offered a novel product and wonder if they can trust it. Entrepreneurs have to develop strategies to build consumer trust (Godley, 2013, pp. 11–19).[5] The missional journey's stage-by-stage sequence of gift exchanges performs an equivalent function. The team shows its trustworthiness by taking seriously what it hears from potential recipients and offering back something created with them – organized love. Recipients who respond are offered a further gift, *Community*. Recipients of this gift are offered yet another, fuller life in Christ. So long as they are welcomed and valued, gifts at each stage increase recipients' trust. At the same time, stage by stage recipients give something back to the team – feedback in *Listen*, participation in *Love*, contributions to *Community* and so on. This builds the team's trust in *them*, making it easier for the team to progressively hand over their initiative. Gift exchanges are trust-building handshakes that bring givers and recipients together.

The founding team will best extend their hands by following the Satnav of generosity described in the last few chapters. It will receive first by initiating a process of *Listening*, which should never stop. It will offer its gifts of *Love, Community, Share Jesus* and *Church* by discerning at each stage what is appropriate for recipients, for the team and for the relationship between the two. It will release these gifts into arms outstretched to receive them. It will not be surprised when recipients accept these gifts in their own way. It will welcome receivers' return gifts, even though – inspired by the Spirit – the form of the gift may come as a surprise. And team members will expect themselves to be transformed ('converted') by these exchanges, as well as to see transformation in others. Might all this lay the foundations of a bounteous theology of church planting, a theology very different to market-like approaches that stress efficiency ('follow the manual'), managerialism ('measurable outcomes') and success ('growth is the bottom line') – church planting as lavish generosity rather than a thrifty formula?

GIVING THE CHURCH

In particular, founders will be witnesses to some of the allurements of God's reign. *Listening* shows respect, a kingdom quality; it affirms the other by valuing their contribution. *Love* can be expressed in initiatives that promote pastoral care, environmental concern, social justice, reconciliation or artistic creativity for example – all kingdom traits supported by the gifts and ministries of the Spirit. *Community* is integral to the kingdom. *Sharing Jesus* requires conversations about the person who announced the kingdom. *Church* and the kingdom will become one when Jesus returns. *Repeat* speaks of the expansive nature of the kingdom, which is like a seed that grows into a vast tree (Matt. 13.31–32).

Crucially, rather than these kingdom fruits ripening only *after* a new congregation has emerged (start the congregation and then it bears fruit), they are present also in its birth. The kingdom is expressed in the process, not just the outcome. Which means that offering communion in Christ is a gift whether or not the initiative completes the missional journey. On the one hand, as Chapter 1 argued, the offer can support any missional agenda. A Christian ecology group, for instance, can join others outside the church, explore spirituality to support their campaigns and through the Spirit grow the initiative into a new congregation. On the flip side, if the venture never completes the journey this would not be failure. It would be a new Christian activity: an expansion of the church's missional generosity. Either way, giving wins. Thus new congregations can be welcome gifts to the world through, yes, the breadth of their mission once they are established – supporting charities, campaigning for justice and other initiatives for a fuller life. But this breadth is also enabled by unfurling divine generosity while bringing the community to birth. The church becomes an attractive gift through the very manner in which it is offered.

## Reshaping the church's internal life

My claim is that the church can become a more inviting gift when, as one aspect of the church's generosity and for the sake of the world, the Spirit offers communion in Christ to others in the form of new Christian communities. First, taking this vocation seriously challenges consumerist attitudes among church members. Instead of 'Is the church satisfying my needs?' they ask, 'How can we be a gift others would want?' Second, each phase of the gift exchange Part 2 has described can help the church become a better gift. Third, the very process of offering communion in Christ, if followed faithfully, can make the gift welcome. My fourth reason picks up a theme in Chapter 3: giving Christian community away makes no sense unless its internal life is appealing. Why offer the church if the gift is an unpleasant experience?

In 2019 I witnessed an example of what making the church attractive could mean when visiting a Roman Catholic diocese in Germany. The diocese has many church-run kindergartens, hospitals and charities. Several ordained and lay theologians were encouraging these to be seen as 'places of blessing' that can also birth new Christian communities. But they were running up against an institutional mindset that imagines the church only through the lens of the Mass. So their challenge was to create, in conversation with others, a new ecclesial imaginary – a new theoretical world – that would enable the diocese to be an attractive gift to people who were unbaptized or not regular worshippers.

Their approach was to assume the current ecclesiology and structure of the church. The local church is the diocese gathered around the bishop, who shares his ministry with priests, most of whom serve a parish. Can the parish be re-imagined as a mini-diocese, which effectively it once was? By analogy with the bishop, might the priest's pastoral oversight extend from the congregation to all the ecclesial organizations and communities within the parish, including new types of Christian community? Lay people would lead these new communities, following a long Catholic tradition of lay-led communities, but the priest would have active pastoral and spiritual oversight.

Might this new imaginary build on the widely shared view that the Church's sacramental life is not confined to the seven official sacraments? Much else has a sacramental quality, not least the folk liturgies so important in the Church's life.[6] God works through the material world of processions, for example, to enable people to taste the exuberant joy of God's reign. In a similar vein, might not grace also be experienced within a new Christian community through a shared meal in which food and wine are blessed at the beginning? And might this not become a step towards an experience of grace in the Mass?

Indeed, these theologians were asking, might eucharistic grace extend to these non-eucharistic acts of worship? Lay leaders would receive this grace when they participate in their parish Eucharist. Through the Spirit they would carry this grace with them into the rest of their lives, not least the new communities they lead, and something of this grace would be transmitted when they serve these communities. In particular, eucharistic grace would be present in the communities' informal worship, covering the worship so that participants shared to a degree in the parish Mass. When lay leaders returned to the Mass, they would bring with them, as it were, the community in which they served, which would both nourish the Eucharist and be nourished itself through the leaders' participation.

## GIVING THE CHURCH

Such a view would testify to the Eucharist's fruitfulness, which bursts the banks of the celebration to cover non-eucharistic expressions of worship. Rather than legitimizing the latter as an alternative to the Mass, the centrality of the Eucharist would be affirmed.[7]

These theologians were taking seriously the multitude of conversations that have produced the Church's existing imaginary. In terms of gift exchange, they were first receiving as gifts the fruits of these conversations. They were then offering their own gifts in a manner they thought appropriate to the diocese and to themselves. They were engaging in 'empathetic dialogue'. Constrained by their Church's corridor of history, these theologians sought to keep faith with their tradition while re-imagining it for a new context. The challenge, as they saw it, was for their Church to become a welcome gift to the growing number of people distant from it.

More generally, if the church's internal life is to serve the church's offer of new Christian communities, ministry must almost certainly be re-imagined within the tradition of the denomination, Church or network. Might ministers see themselves as enablers of the church's generosity to others? And might this include helping the church to become an attractive gift? Might ministers become, for instance:

- *Catalysts*, encouraging and equipping lay people to start new Christian communities?
- *Chaplains* to the new community, supporting its leaders, helping them navigate ecclesiastical assault courses and providing pastoral care for community members bruised by life? Being an attractive gift includes being a home for emotional convalescence. Especially where only ordained ministers are authorized to baptize and preside at Holy Communion, ministers can exercise liturgical leadership as representatives of the wider church, reminding new communities that they are part of a greater whole.
- *Connectors*, especially where the new community is led by lay people in their spare time? If lay leaders are too busy, ministers may have to connect community members to the church at large so that the whole church becomes the gift. Connectors are vital in transmitting return gifts from new communities to the wider church and in enabling gifts to be repeatedly exchanged thereafter.

Likewise, the church's worship may need to adapt so that newcomers from different cultural backgrounds are made welcome. In the Church of England, for instance, the Liturgical Commission has encouraged diocesan liturgical groups to seek out and promote good practice. It suggests that congregations invite a skilled person or small group to observe their worship and make suggestions.[8] Under the authority of the bishop and drawing on central guidance, these groups could foster local innovation, facilitate the cross-fertilization of good practice between churches, encourage the latter to visit and learn from each other, and make available to them liturgical expertise and resources from the Anglican heritage. New liturgies could emerge that are faithful to tradition and responsive to context. It is a further example of how the church can become a more enticing gift by turning its internal life outward in self-donating love.

## Emergent change

Finally, and space prevents more than a sketch, the church's attractiveness can be enhanced by the emergent manner in which its life is shaped around generosity. Stephen Pickard has helpfully highlighted the emergent role of divinely inspired human agency in church structures (Pickard, 2012, pp. 160–4). Though he relies on the sociologist Anthony Giddens, his point can be made more strongly by drawing on complex responsive process theory. As touched on in Chapter 8, for example, Patricia Shaw (2002) argues that organizations are networks of conversation – in-person, virtually and inside people's heads. Take away the conversations within an organization and with people outside and organizational life would evaporate. Once it was not uncommon for managers to urge 'Less talk, more work', but in today's 'network society' (Castells, 1996) talk *is* the work. Actions emerge from conversations and are accompanied by them. Think of all the chatter on a building site.[9]

### *Organizations as conversations*

Now, of course conversations take many forms. Some are highly controlled, in a committee for instance. The chair douses embers of energy by sticking rigidly to the agenda, inviting some people to speak but not others, cutting off unwelcome contributions (perhaps with a menacing stare) and steering the committee towards a predetermined outcome. This epitomizes, we might say, a mechanical view of organizations. The organization is a machine directed by senior managers, who pull certain levers to exercise control (the stare). However, this approach comes at a cost. People feel manipulated, even bullied, and energy drains from the room. Creative conversations, often the ones that really matter, occur outside around the coffee machine and are frequently not connected to the official

# GIVING THE CHURCH

discussions. The committee's decisions are subverted by people elsewhere in the organization, who re-interpret or ignore them.[10] The trouble is that organizations, including the church, are far from being machines that leaders can command top down. They are a vibrant morass of relationships, messy, unpredictable and often with a will of their own.

Recognizing this, Shaw and other complex responsive process theorists argue that organizations are not entities 'out there' that managers can act upon, design and direct. Managers are not like a general and his staff on a hill, surveying the battlefield, developing strategies and commanding the troops (Shaw, 2002, p. 140). Rather than standing outside the organization, they are inside, as much influenced by others as influencing them. Managers are more like a general's staff moving through the battlefield, which alters as they go, changes unexpectedly, sometimes responds to their commands and sometimes doesn't and appears different to each of them. *'The territory of exploration ... is formed by the exploration itself'* (p. 141; italics added). It is as people talk that the organization comes to life, that it exists at all. Instead of being fixed external realities, organizations are realities inside people's thoughts, and they are constantly in flux as individuals hold conversations about them in their minds and with others. To understand an organization, therefore – to understand the church – you have to pay attention to the conversations through which it is enacted, both orderly nice conversations and chaotic nasty ones, both public conversations between people and private ones within individuals.

This perspective resonates with the description in Chapter 2 of the relational essence of the church (in which conversations inevitably play a central role) and the portrayal in Chapter 8 of the church as God's conversationalist with the world. In particular, it connects with the claim in Chapter 8 that God's people are called to offer communion in Christ to others not through closed, controlling conversations but through open, liberating exchanges – a communion that is genuinely communal. This can happen when conversations are characterized by the framework of gift exchange that runs through this second part of the book – receiving first, giving appropriately and so on. The church will listen to its conversation partners; it will speak with them contextually; it will allow time for recipients to process and receive the church's contributions in their own way; it will welcome return contributions to the conversation; and it will expect to be transformed through the exchange. Mission becomes the practice of these open conversations and the church's internal life a school for such exchanges.

Open conversations are emergent by nature. These emergent characteristics, which I have described elsewhere (Moynagh, 2017, pp. 21–8), include:

# BECOMING AN ATTRACTIVE GIFT

- *The presence of surprise* rather than predictability. Unless a conversation is tightly reined in, you can never be sure what might be shared and what may emerge. Open conversations don't have a script.
- *The generation of novelty* through the combination of separate ideas. Different contributions build on each other so that a new thought, plan or action emerges bottom up.
- *The key role of feedback.* A positive response to a contribution encourages others to build on what was said (amplification); negative feedback has a dampening effect.
- *Self-organization* rather than top-down control. Through feedback, the conversation gains a direction (known technically as an 'attractor'). Participants filter their contributions to what is relevant to the flow of the conversation, which organizes spontaneously around the theme.
- *The conversation is both stable and fluid.* Contributions are determined by the direction of the conversation ('path dependency'). Yet within that trajectory each person makes their own creative input. If someone contributes at a tangent but in a way relevant to the others, the conversation can change direction completely.
- *When a new theme ('attractor') emerges*, the conversation may follow different rules. Initially, a conversation may be governed by conventions about exchanging personal news. But then participants begin to debate a topic. The logic of news exchange (sharing anecdotes) gives way to the logic of argument (opinions are backed by reasoning). A new level of self-organizing emerges.

## Church as an emergent gift

Here is the key point: at its best, offering communion in Christ to others is also emergent. Because it happens through open conversations, the church's giving necessarily shares the emergent character of these exchanges. For example, the idea for an outreach activity unexpectedly emerged among some young adults who were meeting for prayer and Bible study. The form the initiative took brought together several separate practices to create something new – free canoeing for families, plus food, plus Bible story. The initiative amplified through supporting feedback; families invited their friends, and what started as an experiment became longer lasting. A new 'attractor' emerged, representing the spiritual direction in which the community was evolving. The community was both stable (it met in a familiar rhythm) and creative (interested families were invited to a separate, exploratory Bible study). This additional giving introduced a new level of organization; the previous level,

# GIVING THE CHURCH

regular canoeing, was topped by the Bible study, with its distinctive rules and practices.[11]

If offering communion in Christ is a conversational process and if conversations have an emergent nature, the emergent form of this aspect of the church's giving should not be unexpected. Further, if the same (emergent) conversational framework can broadly guide the rest of the church's generosity and if generosity should be the focus of the church's vocation, we should not be surprised if the church's life as a whole should share in this emergent character. Just as the *missional journey* is a gift-based methodology matching a gift-based theology of the church, so the life of God's people should have an emergent quality that fits the emergent processes by which the church responds to its calling.

What is the punchline? Emergence is a vital way in which the church can become an attractive gift. This is because emergence requires a distributed form of leadership. Leadership is about much more than who are recognized as leaders, their position in the hierarchy, their role description and so on. Leadership is not 'in' or 'done by' a leader. It emerges as people talk together. It is an interactive process, 'within which any particular person will participate as leader or follower at different times and for different purposes' (Lichtenstein et al., 2006, p. 3). The chair of a discussion, for instance, might initially take the lead by raising a problem. The lead passes to someone else who proposes a solution. Several contributions follow, during which leadership hangs in the air as it were. Then someone intervenes decisively with a suggestion for how to take the proposal forward, providing leadership at that point. The chair resumes leadership by summarizing the discussion and checking that this is the group's view. Leadership has shifted within the group. In an emergent church, this shifting pattern of leadership occurs *everywhere*.

This does *not* mean that senior leaders have no role. They can enable or constrain the conditions in which dispersed leadership occurs. They can release the people around them through conversations that are life-giving, affirm participants and are honest. By schooling their colleagues in habits of good conversation, they can help to spread a culture that brings out the best in people. Not least, they can ask questions that set the agenda for conversations elsewhere in the church. When all this happens, others have greater opportunity to exercise leadership through conversations that are open and not controlled. Leadership is dispersed, not unlike the picture in 1 Corinthians 14.26ff., because the priesthood of all believers is dispersed.

Distributed leadership eschews top-down control and articulates a framework of priorities instead. These priorities, generated by emergent means, provide an outline map to guide the institution or network, while also leaving plenty of room for bottom-up improvisation. The latter may give rise to a new attractor that gains momentum and eventually changes the direction of this corner of the church. By means of emergence, the Spirit can be said to guide the Christian community, sometimes unexpectedly, through its members' relationships, and to release gifts, energies, new vision and leadership throughout the church. Rather than bureaucratic or market values, emergence encourages a relational culture.

Clearly this is no guarantee that what emerges will be an attractive expression of the church. Like any organization, the church can never be immune from sin. But the dispersed nature of leadership reduces the opportunity for concentrations of abusive power to persist. Space is left for new attractors to emerge and challenge dominant attractors that are spiritually unmoored. The church can be 'reformed and always reforming' precisely because new centres of influence can confront fifth columnists in the church's midst. As the Christian community prioritizes its call to be a gift, engages with outsiders, sees its life from an outsider's standpoint and responds by seeking to be a more welcome gift, the church can be changed *'from within what it already is'* (Pickard, 2012, p. 92; italics original). The Spirit's work in the world and the church combine to bring fresh tokens from God's future into God's people today. The church is led to perpetual self-correction.

## Conclusion

*Giving the Church* is an extended question: alongside Avery Dulles's six models of the church, might there be a seventh, the church as a gift? In response to grace, the church is called to a grateful life of generosity, expressed in a multitude of ways. As a normal part of this vocation, the church is lovingly to join the Spirit in offering communion in Christ to others in the form of new Christian communities, for the sake of the world. As the church begins to experience life in Karl Rahner's third theological epoch, could this model be a guide to action? Amid post-Christian ashes in the global North and parts of the South, might being a gift help church members to develop a new imaginary that is faithful to their heritage while enabling them to be the church in new ways with new people? Alongside welcoming outsiders into an existing congregation, the church would give away new Christian communities that fit those for whom today's congregations are inaccessible.

In doing so, could the church's giving correct lopsided approaches to mission? On the one hand, might it avoid the frequent neglect of church multiplication by advocates of doing mission on a broad front? Church multiplication would amplify mission ranging from pastoral and ecological care to reconciliation, to making disciples, to other ingredients of a full life. On the other hand, might this happen without the overly narrow focus on evangelism in some forms of church planting? Communion in Christ would be offered in support of any missional agenda, while the methodology of Listen, Love, Community and so on would involve a kingdom breadth of mission. Instead of integrated mission being a second step after the church is born, it would become a first step, part of the very process of birthing the church.

In particular, might giving offer a helpful narrative for church planting? By inviting founders to consider whether their offering is a purified gift, might the story they tell themselves have challenge and self-correction built in? Might a eucharistic version of this story help commend church planting to all sections of the church? Might the herald account contribute to a conversational ethics of church multiplication? And might the liberation perspective encourage multiplication that is driven less by growth and more by justice, by the *passio Dei* as part of the *missio Dei*?

Going further, might giving the church help counter the low view of the church among some Christians today? A high view is implied when the church is brought into the centre of mission and when importance is attached to offering others the whole church. The latter includes the institutional church, whether in the form of traditional structures or new apostolic connections. At the same time, might this ecclesiastical confidence be combined with a humble, questioning stance as the church reaches out to receive gifts from the world, as communion in Christ is offered in a way appropriate to the gift's recipients, as the church is released into the hands of those who receive it, as newcomers' return gifts are welcomed by the church at large, and as the Christian community is transformed by this process of mutual generosity? Might high and humble, exclamation mark and question mark, be faithful to the church's head?

Finally, is all this asking too much of congregations, a daydream on a paradisal cloud? Certainly, offering a new Christian community may not be practical for a small, elderly congregation for example. But it may sometimes be realistic even for congregations whose selves appear too unsure of their faith, too torn by division, or too overwhelmed by life to be given away. Maybe in such cases the process of giving away communion in Christ can actually strengthen Christian identity ('This is what we are about'), provide a goal around which different factions unite and afford opportunities for time-starved and emotionally burdened church members to pray for, and on occasion actively support, people who *are* able to offer new Christian communities; the whole congregation would be involved, even if only a handful take the lead.

Thus the church can turn outward, with everyone taking part. God's people will reorientate their internal life towards external generosity, one aspect of which is multiplying the church to benefit the world. Around the local congregation will spring up new communities, all connected to each other like the rim of a wheel and by spokes to their parent hub, and all spinning out other forms of generosity. 'Incarnational church' with ever more socially diverse gatherings will complement 'attractional church', which invites others on the congregation's cultural terms. Rather than relying on 'Here is church that works for us, please come', the offer will be 'Let us do church together in a form that works for you.' Could this understanding of being a gift release the genie from the church's bottle of love? And if so, in the Persian proverb, might fragrances of kindness remain in the hand that gives the rose?

## Notes

1 This echoes the Last Supper, which combined fellowship, worship and planning – Jesus arranged to meet his disciples in Galilee (Mark 14.28).

2 Might some of these communities be seen as ecclesial satire? Not infrequently satire works through the unexpected juxtaposition of elements previously kept apart in order to expose and challenge accepted realities. Might communities like Paws of Praise work in a missional sense partly because they satirically challenge the separation of church from the rest of life such as dog walking? And might such communities have an important part to play in the church's mission, not by selling out to today's trends but as signs and foretastes of Christ's transforming reign over every trend?

3 For an account of the founding of the mission see Ward, 2017, pp. 11–31.

4 The Venerable Bede, *Bede's Ecclesiastical History of England*, London: George Bell, 2007, chapters XXV, XXVI, XXVII. At roughly the same time, the Celtic missionaries to northern Britain seem to have followed a similar pattern. They lived among the people and learnt from them through listening, found practical ways to love them and build community with them, shared Jesus in ways that connected with them, and gave birth to new Christian communities that multiplied. See Hunter III, 2010, pp. 36–45.

5 These may include disseminating information that allows consumers to judge how they might use the product and offering an after sales service with all the information consumers need after they've bought. In addition to the explicit contract (buy this for that price) there is an implicit contract (we'll provide you with all the information you require). Reciprocity is central.

6 The Roman Catholic Church has three types of liturgy: liturgies authorized by Rome, liturgies authorized by the diocese in consultation with the ecclesial hierarchy, and the people's liturgies, such as processions and devotions to Mary, which emerge from the grass roots.

7 In practice, the theologians recognized, the time required for involvement in these other types of worship may reduce the frequency with which lay leaders attend

## GIVING THE CHURCH

the Mass. But, they maintained, this does not impair the availability of eucharistic grace. Eucharistic fruitfulness cannot depend on the frequency of reception. Two centuries ago in Germany, for instance, people received the Mass just once a year.

8 Church of England Liturgical Commission, 2007, *Transforming Worship: Living the new creation*, pp. 23–4, 26.

9 For some of the evidence that interactions involving conversations were becoming ever more central to the workplace as the network society advanced in the 1990s and 2000s, see Felstead, Gallie and Green, 2002, pp. 123–6 and Johnson, Manyika and Yee, 2005, pp. 25–6. 'Companies thrive on good company' (Starkey and Tempest, 2005, p. 152).

10 Before ordination I worked for an organization whose chief executive arranged with his counterpart in a large bank for the staff to use the bank's sports facilities. When my colleagues arrived at the football pitch, the groundsman greeted them (but in more colourful language), 'I have the keys, I am not letting you in, go away.' Nothing more was heard of the arrangement!

11 Other initiatives may initially copy a template, such as Dinner Church or Messy Church. But as participants are involved in the leadership and ideas well up from within the community, increasingly the initiative will incorporate a variety of different practices and develop its own unique way of life through emergent processes.

# Bibliography

Adams, Edward, 2018, 'The shape of the Pauline churches' in Paul Avis (ed.), *The Oxford Handbook of Ecclesiology*, Oxford: Oxford University Press, pp. 119–46.

Aldous, Benjamin and Michael Moynagh, 'Learning from "Fresh Expressions of Church" and the "Loving-First Cycle" through a case study from Cape Town', *Mission Studies*, 38 (2021), pp. 189–212.

Ascough, Richard H., 'The Thessalonian Christian community as a voluntary professional association', *Journal of Biblical Literature*, 119 (2000), pp. 311–28.

Austin, J. L., 1962, *How to Do Things with Words*, Cambridge, MA: Harvard University Press.

Avis, Paul, 2011, 'Denomination: an Anglican appraisal' in Paul M. Collins and Barry Ensign-George (eds), *Denomination: Assessing an ecclesiological category*, London: T&T Clark, pp. 22–33.

Avis, Paul, 2021a, *Jesus and the Church. The foundation of the Church in the New Testament and modern theology*, London: T&T Clark.

Avis, Paul, 2021b, 'Overcoming "The Church as a counter-sign of the Kingdom"' in Mark D. Chapman and Vladimir Latinovic (eds), *Changing the Church: Transformations of Christian belief, practice and life*, Cham, Switzerland: Palgrave Macmillan, pp. 243–9.

Avis, Paul, 2022, *Reconciling Theology*, London: SCM Press.

Azevedo, SJ, Marcello de C., 'Basic ecclesial communities: a meeting point of ecclesiologies', *Theological Studies*, 46 (4) 1985, pp. 601–20.

Banks, Robert, 1980, *Paul's Idea of Community: The early house churches in their historical setting*, Exeter: Paternoster Press.

Barclay, John M. G., 'Pure grace?', *Studia Theologica*, 68(1), 2014, pp. 4–20.

Barclay, John M. G., 2015, *Paul and the Gift*, Grand Rapids, MI: Eerdmans, 2015.

Barclay, John M. G., 2018, 'Paul, reciprocity, and giving with the poor' in Presian R. Burroughs (ed.), *Practicing with Paul*, Eugene, OR: Cascade Books, pp. 15–29.

Barreiro, SJ, Alvaro, 2010 (1982), *Basic Ecclesial Communities: The evangelization of the poor*, trans. by Barbara Campbell, Eugene, OR: Wipf & Stock.

Barrett, Al and Ruth Harley, 2020, *Being Interrupted: Re-imagining the Church's mission from the outside, in*, London: SCM Press.

Barth, Karl, 1958, *Church Dogmatics, Volume IV, The Doctrine of Reconciliation*, Part 2, trans. by G. W. Bromiley, London: T&T Clark.

Barth, Karl, 2004 (1959), *Church Dogmatics, Volume IV, The Doctrine of Reconciliation*, Part 3.2, trans. by G. W. Bromiley, London: T&T Clark.

Bauckham, Richard, 1993, 'The Acts of Paul as a sequel to Acts' in Bruce W. Winter and Andrew D. Clarke (eds), *The Book of Acts in its First Century Setting*, Grand Rapids, MI: Eerdmans, pp. 105–52.

# GIVING THE CHURCH

Beck, Michael and Michael Moynagh, 2021, *The 21st Century Christian: Following Jesus where life happens*, Richmond, VA: Fresh Expressions.

Belk, Russell W., 1996, 'The perfect gift' in Cele Otnes and Richard F. Beltramini (eds), *Gift Giving. A research anthology*, Bowling Green, OH: Popular Press, pp. 59–84.

Belk, Russell W. and Gregory S. Coon, 'Gift giving as agapic love: an alternative to the exchange paradigm based on dating experiences', *Journal of Consumer Research*, 20, 1993, pp. 393–417.

Bellah, Robert N., Richard Madson, William M. Sullivan, Ann Swidler and Steven M. Tipton, 1996 (1985), *Habits of the Heart: Individualism and commitment in American life*, Berkeley, CA: University of California Press.

Bender, Kimlyn J., 2013, *Karl Barth's Christological Ecclesiology*, New York: Routledge.

Berger, Calinic (Kevin M.), 'Does the Eucharist make the Church? An ecclesiological comparison of Staniloae and Zizioulas', *St Vladimir's Theological Quarterly*, 51 (1), 2007, pp. 23–70.

Berking, Helmuth, 1999, *Sociology of Giving*, trans. by Patrick Camiller, London: Sage.

Bevans, Stephen B., 'Ecclesiology since Vatican II: from a Church with a mission to a missionary Church', *Verbum SVD* 46 (1), 2005, pp. 27–56.

Bevans, Stephen B. and Roger P. Schroeder, 2004, *Constants in Context: A theology of mission for today*, Maryknoll, NY: Orbis Books.

Bevans, Stephen B. and Roger P. Schroeder, 2011, *Prophetic Dialogue: Reflections on Christian mission today*, Maryknoll, NY: Orbis Books.

Bird, Michael F., 2010, *Crossing over Sea and Land: Jewish missionary activity in the Second Temple period*, Peabody, MA: Hendrickson.

Boff, Leonardo, 1986, *Ecclesiogenesis: The base communities reinvent the Church*, trans. by Robert R. Barr, Maryknoll, NY: Orbis Books.

Boff, Leonardo, 2000 (1988), *Holy Trinity, Perfect Community*, trans. by Phillip Berryman, Maryknoll, NY: Orbis Books.

Boff, Leonardo, 2011 (1985), *Church: Charism and Power*, trans. John W. Diercksmeier, Eugene, OR: Wipf & Stock.

Bonhoeffer, Dietrich, 2018 (1954), *Life Together*, trans. by John W. Doberstein, London: SCM Press.

Bonino, José Miguez, 1981, 'Fundamental questions in ecclesiology' in Sergio Torres and John Eagleson (eds), *The Challenge of Basic Christian Communities*, Maryknoll, NY: Orbis Books, pp. 145–9.

Bosch, David J., 1991, *Transforming Mission: Paradigm shifts in theology of mission*, Maryknoll, NY: Orbis Books.

Bourdieu, Pierre, 1990 (1980), *The Logic of Practice*, trans. by R. Price, Stanford, CA: Stanford University Press.

Bourdieu, Pierre, 1997, 'Marginalia – some additional notes on the Gift' in Alan D. Schrift (ed.), *The Logic of the Gift: Toward an ethic of generosity*, London: Routledge, pp. 190–230.

Brueggemann, Walter, 'Pharaoh as vassal: A study of a political metaphor', *The Catholic Biblical Quarterly*, 57(1), 1995, pp. 27–51.

Brueggemann, Walter, 1997, *Theology of the Old Testament: Testimony, dispute, advocacy*, Minneapolis, MN: Augsburg Fortress.

# BIBLIOGRAPHY

Brueggemann, Walter, 2021, *Delivered out of Empire*, Louisville, KY: Westminster John Knox Press.

Bruteau, Beatrice, 2018 (1997), *God's Ecstasy: The creation of a self-creating world*, New York, NY: Crossroad Publishing.

Bulgakov, Sergei, 1993 (1937), *Sophia. The Wisdom of God: An outline of sophiology*, Wylam Northumberland: Lindisfarne Press.

Burger, Coenie, Frederick Marais and Danie Mouton, 2017, *Cultivating Missional Change. The future of missional churches and missional theology*, Wellington, SA: Biblecor.

Caputo, John D., 1999, 'Apostles of the impossible: of God and Gift in Derrida and Marion' in John D. Caputo and Michael J. Scanlon (eds), *God, the Gift, and Postmodernism*, Bloomington, IN: Indiana University Press, pp. 185–222.

Castells, Manuel, 1996, *The Rise of the Network Society. The Information Age: Economy, Society and Culture Volume 1*, Oxford: Blackwell.

Cavanaugh, William T., 2003, *Theopolitical Imagination: Christian practices of space and time*, London: T&T Clark.

Cavanaugh, William T., 2011, *Migrations of the Holy. God, state, and the political meaning of the Church*, Grand Rapids, MI: Eerdmans.

Cheal, David, 2016 (1988), *The Gift Economy*, Abingdon: Routledge.

Choy, Renie Chow, 2021, *Ancestral Feeling: Post-colonial thoughts on western Christian heritage*, London: SCM Press.

Church of England Liturgical Commission, 2007, *Transforming Worship: Living the new creation*, London: General Synod GS 1651.

Clift, Rebecca, 2016, *Conversation Analysis*, Cambridge: Cambridge University Press.

Cole, Neil, 2005, *Organic Church: Growing faith where life happens*, San Francisco, CA: Jossey-Bass.

Colesworthy, Rebecca, 2018, *Returning the Gift: Modernism and the thought of exchange*, Oxford: Oxford University Press.

Comblin, José, 2004, *People of God*, trans. by Phillip Berryman, Maryknoll, NY: Orbis Books.

Congar, Yves M. J., 1983, *I Believe in the Holy Spirit, Volume 1. The Holy Spirit in the 'Economy'*, trans David Smith, London: Geoffrey Chapman.

Copenhaver, Martin B., 2014, *Jesus is the Question. The 307 questions Jesus asked and the three he answered*, Nashville, TN: Abingdon.

Costas, Orlando, 2005 (1982), *Christ Outside the Gate: Mission beyond Christendom*, Eugene, OR: Wipf & Stock.

Cray, Graham (ed.), 2004, *Mission-shaped Church: Church planting and Fresh Expressions of Church in a changing context*, London: Church House Publishing.

Croft, Steven, 2008, 'What counts as a fresh expression of church and who decides?' in Louise Nelstrop and Martyn Percy (eds), *Evaluating Fresh Expressions: Explorations in Emerging Church*, Norwich: Canterbury Press, pp. 3–14.

Davison, Andrew and Alison Milbank, 2010, *For the Parish: A critique of Fresh Expressions*, London: SCM Press.

De Lubac, Henri, 1956, *The Splendour of the Church*, trans. Michael Mason, San Francisco, CA: Ignatius Press.

De Lubac, Henri, 2006 (1944), *Corpus Mysticum: The Eucharist and the Church in the Middle Ages*, trans. Gemma Simmonds CJ, with Richard Price and Christopher Stephens, London: SCM Press.

# GIVING THE CHURCH

Derrida, Jacques, 1992, *Given Time: 1. Counterfeit Money*, trans. Peggy Kamuf, Chicago, IL: University of Chicago Press.

Dexter-Dreis, Joseph, 'Decolonised theology in the North Atlantic world', *Theology* 3 (3) 2019, pp. 1–88.

Dobler, Tamara, 'What is wrong with Hacker's Wittgenstein? On grammar, context and sense-determination', *Philosophical Investigations*, 36 (3) 2013, pp. 231–50.

Drane, John, 2011, 'From one pioneer to another: insights from St Paul' in David Male (ed.), *Pioneers 4 Life: Explorations in theology and wisdom for pioneering leaders*, Abingdon: Bible Reading Fellowship, pp. 149–67.

Dulles, Avery Cardinal, 2002 (2000), *Models of the Church*, New York: Doubleday.

Dunlop, Andrew, 2018, *Out of Nothing: A cross-shaped approach to fresh expressions*, London: SCM Press.

Dutton, Christine, 'Unpicking knit and natter: researching and emerging Christian community', *Ecclesial Practices* 1, 2014, pp. 31–50.

Edwards, Denis, 1999, *The God of Evolution: A trinitarian theology*, New York: Paulist Press.

Emerson, Ralph Waldo, 1907, 'Gifts' in Edna H. L. Turpin (ed.), *Essays by Ralph Waldo Emerson*, New York: Charles E. Merrill.

Enfield, N. J., 2017, *How We Talk. The inner workings of conversation*, New York: Basic Books.

Enfield, N. J., 2022, *Language vs. Reality. Why language is good for lawyers and bad for scientists*, Cambridge, MA: MIT Press.

Enns, Peter, 2005, *Inspiration and Incarnation: Evangelicals and the problem of the Old Testament*, Grand Rapids, MI: Baker.

Ensign-George, Barry A., 2018, *Between Congregation and Church: Denomination and Christian life together*, London: Bloomsbury Academic.

Eriksen, Erik Oddvar and Jarle Weigard, 2004 (2003), *Understanding Habermas: Communicative action and deliberative democracy*, London: Continuum.

Felstead, Alan, Duncan Gallie and Francis Green, 2002, *Work Skills in Britain 1986–2001*, London: DfES.

Fennell, Lee Anne, 2002, 'Unpacking the gift. Illiquid goods and empathetic dialogue' in Mark Osteen (ed.), *The Question of the Gift. Essays across disciplines*, Abingdon: Routledge, pp. 85–101.

Ferdig, Mary and James D. Ludema, 'Transformative interactions: qualities of conversation that heighten the vitality of self-organizing change', *Research in Organizational Change and Development*, 15, 2005, pp. 169–205.

Fiddes, Paul S., 2003, *Tracks and Traces: Baptism identity in church and theology*, Milton Keynes: Paternoster Press.

Fiensy, David A., 1995, 'The composition of the Jerusalem church' in Richard Bauckham (ed.), *The Book of Acts in its First Century Setting, Vol 4: Palestinian Setting*, Grand Rapids, MI: Eerdmans, pp. 213–36.

Finger, Reta Haltman, 2007, *Of Widows and Meals: Communal meals in the Book of Acts*, Grand Rapids, MI: Eerdmans.

Finney, Nissa, Dharmi Kapadia and Simon Peters, 2015, *How Are Poverty, Ethnicity and Social Networks Related?*, York: Joseph Rowntree Foundation.

Flett, John G., 2010, *The Witness of God: The Trinity, Missio Dei, Karl Barth, and the nature of Christian community*, Grand Rapids, MI: Eerdmans.

# BIBLIOGRAPHY

Flett, John G., 2016, *Apostolicity: The ecumenical question in world Christian perspective*, Downers Grove, IL: IVP.

Fong, Bruce W., 1996, *Racial Equality in the Church. A critique of the Homogeneous Unit Principle in light of a practical theology perspective*, Lanham, MD: University Press of America.

Ford, David, 1999, *Self and Salvation: Being transformed*, Cambridge: Cambridge University Press.

Fredrickson, Barbara L., 2004, 'Gratitude, like other positive emotions, broadens and builds' in Robert A. Emmons and Michael E. McCullough (eds), *The Psychology of Gratitude*, Oxford: Oxford University Press, pp. 145–66.

Friesenhahn, Jacob H., 2016 (2011), *The Trinity and Theodicy. The trinitarian theology of von Balthasar and the problem of evil*, London: Routledge.

Frost, Michael and Alan Hirsch, 2003, *The Shaping of Things to Come: Innovation and mission for the 21st-century Church*, Peabody, MA: Hendrickson.

Furbey, Robert, Adam Dinham, Richard Farnell, Doreen Finneron, Guy Wilkinson with Catherine Howarth, Dilwar Hussain and Sharon Palmer, 2006, *Faith As Social Capital: Connecting or dividing?*, York: Joseph Rowntree Foundation.

Gallagher, Brandon, 2015, 'The Christian Church facing itself and facing the world. An ecumenical overview of modern Christian ecclesiology' in Lucinda Mosher and David Marshall (eds), *The Community of Believers. Christian and Muslim perspectives*, Washington DC: Georgetown University Press.

Gee, James Paul, 2014 (1999), *An Introduction to Discourse Analysis. Theory and method*, New York: Routledge.

Gehring, Roger W., 2004, *House Church and Mission: The importance of household structures in early Christianity*, Peabody, MA: Hendrickson.

Giesler, Markus, 'Consumer gift systems', *Journal of Consumer Research*, 33, 2006, pp. 283–90.

Giles, Kevin, 1995, *What on Earth is the Church? An exploration in New Testament theology*, Downers Grove, IL: IVP.

Gittoes, Julie, 2008, *Anamnesis and the Eucharist: Contemporary Anglican approaches*, Farnham: Ashgate.

Glasson, Barbara, 2006, *Mixed-up Blessing: A new encounter with being church*, Peterborough: Inspire.

Godbout, Jacques T. with Alain Caille, 1998, *The World of the Gift*, trans. Donald Winkler, Montreal: McGill-Queen's University Press.

Godelier, Maurice, 1999, *The Enigma of the Gift*, trans. Nora Scott, Chicago, IL: University of Chicago Press.

Godley, Andrew Christopher, 'Entrepreneurial opportunities, implicit contracts and market making for complex consumer goods', *Strategic Entrepreneurship Journal*, 7 (2013), pp. 273–87.

González, Michelle A., 2018, 'Liberation ecclesiologies with special reference to Latin America' in Paul Avis (ed.), *The Oxford Handbook of Ecclesiology*, Oxford: Oxford University Press, pp. 573–93.

Gooder, Paula, 2018, *Phoebe: A story. Pauline Christianity in narrative form*, London: Hodder.

Goodman, Martin, 1994, *Mission and Conversion: Proselytizing in the religious history of the Roman Empire*, Oxford: Clarendon.

Granovetter, Mark, 'The strength of weak ties: a network theory revisited', *Sociological Theory*, 1 (1983), pp. 201–33.

## GIVING THE CHURCH

Greggs, Tom, 2019, *Dogmatic Ecclesiology, Vol. 1. The Priestly Catholicity of the Church*, Grand Rapids, MI: Baker Academic.

Gregory, C. A., 1982, *Gifts and Commodities*, London: Academic Press.

Griffin, Douglas, 2001, *The Emergence of Leadership: Linking self-organization and ethics*, London: Routledge.

Griffin, Douglas and Ralph Stacey (eds), 2005, *Complexity and the Experience of Leading Organizations*, Abingdon: Routledge.

Grindheim, Sigurd, 2005, *The Crux of Election: Paul's critique of the Jewish confidence in the election of Israel*, Tübingen: Mohr Siebeck.

Gutiérrez, Gustavo, 1973, *A Theology of Liberation*, Maryknoll, NY: Orbis Books.

Gutiérrez, Gustavo, 1981, 'The irruption of the poor in Latin America and the Christian communities of the common people' in Sergio Torres and John Eagleson (eds), *The Challenge of Basic Christian Communities*, Maryknoll, NY: Orbis Books, pp. 107–23.

Harned, David Bailey, 1998 (1997) *Patience. How we wait upon the Lord*, Eugene, OR: Wipf & Stock.

Hastings, Ross, 2012, *Missional God, Missional Church: Hope for re-evangelizing the West*, Downers Grove, IL: IVP Academic.

Hauerwas, Stanley, 1983, *The Peaceable Kingdom: A primer in Christian ethics*, Notre Dame, IN: Notre Dame University Press.

Healy, Nicholas M., 'Communion ecclesiology: a cautionary note', *Pro Ecclesia* 4 (4), 1995, pp. 442–53.

Healy, Nicholas M., 2000, *Church, World and the Christian Life: Practical-prophetic ecclesiology*, Cambridge: Cambridge University Press.

Heaney, Robert S., 2019, *Post-Colonial Theology*, Eugene, OR: Cascade Books.

Hebblethwaite, Margaret, 1993a, *Base Communities: An introduction*, Mahwah, NJ: Paulist Press International.

Hebblethwaite, Margaret, 1993b, *Basic is Beautiful: Basic Ecclesial Communities from Third World to First World*, London: HarperCollins.

Higton, Mike, 2018, 'Rowan Williams' in Paul Avis (ed.), *The Oxford Handbook of Ecclesiology*, Oxford: Oxford University Press, pp. 505–24.

Hochschild, Arlie, 1989, 'The economy of gratitude' in David Franks and Doyle McCarthy (eds), *The Sociology of Emotions*, Greenwich, CT: JAI Press.

Holm, Bo Kristian, 2009, 'Justification and reciprocity. "Purified gift-exchange" in Luther and Milbank' in Bo Kristian Holm and Peter Widmann (eds), *Word – Gift – Being*, Tübingen: Mohr Siebeck.

Holmes, Janet and Nick Wilson, 2022, *An Introduction to Sociolinguistics*, sixth edition, Abingdon: Routledge.

Horner, Robyn, 2001, *Rethinking God as Gift: Marion, Derrida, and the limits of phenomenology*, New York, NY: Fordham University Press.

Howson, Chris, 2011, *A Just Church: 21st century Liberation Theology in action*, London: Continuum.

Hull, John M., 2006, *Mission-Shaped Church: A theological response*, London: SCM Press.

Hunter III, George G., 2010, *The Celtic Way of Evangelism*, Nashville, TN: Abingdon.

Hurdley, Rachel, 'Objecting relations: the problem of the Gift', *The Sociological Review*, 55 (1) 2007, pp. 124–43.

# BIBLIOGRAPHY

Hyde, Lewis, 2012 (1979), *The Gift. How the creative Spirit transforms the world*, Edinburgh: Canongate.

Imchen, S. Temjen, 'The election of Israel: a theological critique', *International Journal of Theology* 43 (1 & 2), 2001, pp. 23–9.

Irwin, Kevin W., 2005, *Models of the Eucharist*, New York: Paulist Press.

James, Christopher B., 2017, *Church Planting in Post-Christian Soil. Theology and practice*, Oxford: Oxford University Press.

James, Christopher B., 2018, 'Ecclesiology and missional hospitality' in Mark D. Hinds (ed.), *Essays on the New Worshipping Communities Movement*, Louisville, KY: Witherspoon Press, pp. 15–21.

Jasper, R. C. D. and G. J. Cuming, 1990, *Prayers of the Eucharist: Early and Reformed*, third edition, Collegeville, MN: The Liturgical Press.

Jenson, Matt and David Wilhite, 2010, *The Church: A guide for the perplexed*, London: T&T Clark.

Jenson, Robert W., 1992, *Unbaptized God: The basic flaw in ecumenical theology*, Minneapolis, MN: Fortress Press.

Jenson, Robert W., 'Triune grace', *Dialog: A Journal of Theology*, 41 (4), 2002, pp. 285–93.

Jewett, Robert, 2007, *Romans: A commentary*, Minneapolis, MN: Fortress Press.

John of Damascus, 2003, *Three Treatises on the Divine Images*, trans. Andrew Louth, Crestwood NY: St Vladimir's Seminary Press, II. 23.

Johnson, Bradford C., James Manyika and Lareina A. Yee, 'The next revolution in interactions', *The McKinsey Quarterly*, 4, 2005.

Kaminsky, Joel S., 'Did election imply the mistreatment of non-Israelites?', *Harvard Theological Review* 96 (4) 2003, pp. 397–425.

Keith, Beth, 2014, 'To pluck up and pull down, to build and to plant' in Jonny Baker and Cathy Ross (eds), *The Pioneer Gift*, Norwich: Canterbury Press, pp. 117–40.

Koester, Craig R., 2014, *Revelation. A new translation with introduction and commentary*, New Haven, CT: Yale University Press.

Komonchak, Joseph A., 'Towards a theology of the local church', *Federation of Asian Bishops' Conferences Papers*, 42, 1986.

Komonchak, Joseph A., 1997, 'Catholicity and the redemption of history' in F. Chicca, S. Panizzolo, H. Wagner (eds), *Ecclesia Tertii Millenii Advenientis: Omaggio al P. Angel Antón*, Casale Monferrato: Piemme, pp. 602–13.

Komter, Aafke E., 'Heirlooms, nikes and bribes: toward a sociology of things', *Sociology*, 35 (1), 2001, pp. 59–75.

Komter, Aafke E., 2005, *Social Solidarity and the Gift*, Cambridge: Cambridge University Press.

Koyama, Kosuke, 1979, *Three Mile an Hour God*, London: SCM Press.

Kraft, Charles H., 'An anthropological apologetic for the homogeneous unit principle in missiology', *International Bulletin of Mission Research*, 2 (4) 1978, pp. 121–7.

Kramer, Klaus, 2012, 'Mission in dialogue' in Klaus Kramer and Klaus Vellguth (eds), *Mission and Dialogue. Approaches to a communicative understanding of mission*, Quezon City, Philippines: Claretian Publications, pp. 3–14.

Kreider, Alan, 2016, *The Patient Ferment of the Early Church: The improbable rise of Christianity in the Roman Empire*, Grand Rapids, MI: Baker Academic.

Kristensen, Ragnhild, 2012, 'Missional church – problem or possibility for global mission? Thoughts from a Norwegian perspective' in Beate Fagerli, Knud Jorgensen, Rolv Olsen, Kari Storstein Haug and Knut Tveitereid (eds), *A Learning Missional Church: Reflections from young missiologists*, Oxford: Regnum Book International.

Küng, Hans, 1967, *The Church*, New York, NY: Sheed & Ward.

Last, Richard, 'The neighbourhood (*vicus*) of the Corinthian *ekklesia*: beyond family-based descriptions of the first urban Christ-believers', *Journal for the Study of the New Testament*, 38 (4), 2016, pp. 399–425.

Lathrop, Gordon W., 2003, *Holy Ground: A liturgical cosmology*, Minneapolis, MN: Fortress Press.

Leith, Jenny, 2023, *Political Formation. Being formed by the Spirit in Church and world*, London: SCM Press.

Lévi-Strauss, Claude, 1987 (1950), *Introduction to the Work of Marcel Mauss*, trans. F. Baker, London: Routledge.

Lichtenstein, Benyamin B., Mary Uhl-Bien, Russ Marion, Anson Seers, James Douglas Orton and Craig Schreiber, 2006, 'Complexity Leadership Theory: An interactive perspective on leading in complex adaptive systems', Management Department Faculty Publications, University of Nebraska.

Lings, George, 2016, *The Day of Small Things: An analysis of Fresh Expressions of Church in 21 dioceses of the Church of England*, Sheffield: Church Army.

List, John A. and Fatemeh Momeni, 'When corporate social responsibility backfires: theory and evidence from a natural field experiment', *Management Science*, 67 (1), 2021, pp. 8–21.

Lohfink, Gerhard, 1999, *Does God Need the Church? Toward a theology of the People of God*, trans. by Linda M. Maloney, Collegeville, MN: The Liturgical Press.

Lowrey, Tina M., Cele Otnes and Kevin Robbins, 1996, 'Values influencing Christmas gift giving: an interpretative study' in Cele Otnes and Richard F. Beltramini, *Gift Giving: A research anthology*, Bowling Green, OH: Popular Press, pp. 37–56.

Lupton, Robert D., 2011, *Toxic Charity*, New York, NY: HarperCollins.

Male, David, 2008, *Church Unplugged: Remodelling Church without losing your soul*, Milton Keynes: Authentic Media.

Malo, Antonio, 'The Limits of Marion's and Derrida's philosophy of the gift', *International Philosophical Quarterly*, 52 (2), 2012, pp. 149–68.

Mannion, Gerard, 2007, *Ecclesiology and Postmodernity: Questions for the Church in our time*, Collegeville, MN: Liturgical Press.

Marion, Jean-Luc, 2002, *Being Given. Toward a phenomenology of givenness*, trans. Jeffrey L. Kosky, Stanford, CA: Stanford University Press.

Mauss, Marcel, 1990 (1925), *The Gift: The form and reasons for exchange in archaic societies*, trans. by W. D. Halls, London: Routledge.

McAdams, Dan P. and Jack J. Bauer, 2004, 'Gratitude in modern life. Its manifestations and development' in Robert A. Emmons and Michael E. McCullough (eds), *The Psychology of Gratitude*, Oxford: Oxford University Press, pp. 81–99.

McBride, Jennifer M., 2012, *The Church for the World: A theology of public witness*, Oxford: Oxford University Press.

McGavran, Donald A., 1980 (1970), *Understanding Church Growth*, second edition, Grand Rapids, MI: Eerdmans.

# BIBLIOGRAPHY

McGrath, Mary Ann and Basil Englis, 1996, 'Intergenerational gift giving in subcultural wedding celebrations: the ritual audience as cash cow' in Cele Otnes and Richard F. Beltramini, *Gift Giving. A research anthology*, Bowling Green, OH: Popular Press, pp. 123–41.

McInerny, Brendan, 2020, *The Trinitarian Theology of Hans Urs Von Balthasar. An introduction*, Notre Dame, IN: University of Notre Dame Press.

McPartlan, Paul, 1995, *Sacrament of Salvation. An introduction to eucharistic ecclesiology*, Edinburgh: T&T Clark.

McPartlan, Paul, 'The eucharist as the basis for ecclesiology', *Antiphon* 6 (2), 2001, pp. 12–19.

McPherson, Miller, Lynn Smith-Lovin and James M. Cook, 'Birds of a feather: homophily in social networks', *Annual Review of Sociology* 27 (2001), pp. 415–44.

Madar, Martin, 2019, *The Church of God and Its Human Face. The contribution of Joseph A. Komonchak to ecclesiology*, Eugene, OR: Pickwick Publications.

Malo, Antonio, 'The limits of Marion's and Derrida's philosophy of the gift', *International Philosophical Quarterly*, 52 (2), 2012, pp. 149–68.

Mannion, Gerard, 2007, *Ecclesiology and Postmodernity. Questions for the Church in our time*, Collegeville, MN: Liturgical Press.

Mawson, Michael, 2018, *Christ Existing as Community. Bonhoeffer's ecclesiology*, Oxford: Oxford University Press.

Meeks, Wayne A., 2003 (1983), *The First Urban Christians: The social world of the Apostle Paul*, second edition, New Haven, CT: Yale University Press.

Mesters, Carlos, 1981, 'The use of the Bible in Christian communities of the common people' in Sergio Torres and John Eagleson (eds), *The Challenge of Basic Christian Communities*, Maryknoll, NY: Orbis Books, pp. 197–210.

Metzger, Paul L., 2007, *Consuming Jesus: Beyond race and class divisions in a consumer Church*, Grand Rapids, MI: Eerdmans.

Milbank, Alison, 2023, *The Once and Future Parish*, London: SCM Press.

Milbank, John, 'The Name of Jesus: incarnation, atonement, ecclesiology', *Modern Theology*, 7 (1991), pp. 311–33.

Milbank, John, 'Can a gift be given? Prolegomenon to a future trinitarian metaphysic', *Modern Theology*, 11 (1995), pp. 119–61.

Milbank, John, 1999, 'The ethics of self-sacrifice', *First Things*, March, https://www.firstthings.com/article/1999/03/004-the-ethics-of-self-sacrifice, accessed 3.01.2024.

Milbank, John, 2003, *Being Reconciled: Ontology and pardon*, London: Routledge.

Milbank, John, 2009a, *The Future of Love: Essays in political theology*, London: SCM Press.

Milbank, John, 'The transcendality of the Gift. A summary in answer to 12 questions', *Revista Portuguesa de Filosofia*, 65, 2009b, pp. 887–97.

Miller, Daniel, 2005 (1998), *A Theory of Shopping*, Cambridge: Polity Press.

Milne, Andy, 2016, *The DNA of Pioneer Ministry*, London: SCM Press.

Minear, Paul S., 1960, *Images of Church in the New Testament*, Louisville, KY: Westminster John Knox Press.

Minear, Paul S., 1971, *The Obedience of Faith: The Purpose of Paul in the Epistle to the Romans*, London: SCM Press.

Moltmann, Jürgen, 1967, *Theology of Hope: On the Ground and Implications of a Christian Eschatology*, trans. by James W. Leitch, London: SCM Press.

Moltmann, Jürgen, 1999, 'Hope and Reality: Contradiction and Correspondence' in Richard Bauckham (ed.), *God will be All in All*, Edinburgh: T&T Clark, pp. 77–85.

Moltmann, Jürgen, 2000 (1977), *The Church in the Power of the Spirit: A Contribution to Messianic Ecclesiology*, trans. M. Kohl, second revised edition, London: SCM Press.

Moore, Lucy, 2006, *Messy Church: Fresh ideas for building a Christ-centred community*, Oxford: Bible Reading Fellowship.

Moynagh, Michael, 2012, *Church for Every Context. An introduction to theology and practice*, London: SCM Press.

Moynagh, Michael, 2017, *Church in Life. Innovation, mission and ecclesiology*, London: SCM Press.

Moynagh, Michael and Michael Beck, 2020, *21st Century Christian: Discipleship, mission, church*, Washington DC: Fresh Expressions.

Myers, Fred R., 2001, 'Introduction' in Fred R. Myers (ed.), *The Empire of Things. Regimes of value and material culture*, Santa Fe, NM: School of American Research Press, pp. 3–61.

Myers, Fred R. and Barbara Kirshenblatt-Gimblett, 2001, 'Art and material culture. A conversation with Annette Weiner' in Fred R. Myers (ed.), *The Empire of Things. Regimes of value and material culture*, Santa Fe, NM: School of American Research Press, pp. 3–61.

Nadeau, Kathy, '"Beyond the dumping ground": a critique of the basic ecclesial community model as a strategy for development in an urban site', *Human Organization*, 58 (2), 1999, pp. 153–60.

Niemandt, C. J. P., 'Trends in missional ecclesiology', *HTS Theological Studies*, 68 (1), 2012, http://dx.doi.org/10.4102/hts.v68i1.1198.

Newbigin, Lesslie, 1953, *The Household of God*, London: SCM Press.

Newbigin, Lesslie, 'What is "a local church truly united"?', *Ecumenical Review*, 29, 1977, pp. 115–28.

Newbigin, Lesslie, 1989, *The Gospel in a Pluralist Society*, London: SPCK.

O'Donnell SJ, John, 1992, *Hans Urs von Balthasar*, London: Continuum.

Osteen, Mark, 2002a, 'Introduction: questions of the gift' in Mark Osteen (ed.), *The Question of the Gift. Essays across disciplines*, Abingdon: Routledge, pp. 1–41

Osteen, Mark, 2002b, 'Gift or commodity?' in Mark Osteen (ed.), *The Question of the Gift. Essays across disciplines*, Abingdon: Routledge, pp. 229–47.

Ouellet, Marc Cardinal, 2006, *Divine Likeness. Toward a trinitarian anthropology of the family*, trans. by Philip Milligan and Linda M. Cicone, Grand Rapids, MI: Eerdmans.

Paas, Stefan, 'The making of a mission field: paradigms of evangelistic mission in Europe', *Exchange*, 41, 2012, pp. 44–67.

Paas, Stefan, 2016, *Church Planting in the Secular West: Learning from the European experience*, Grand Rapids, MI: Eerdmans.

Paas, Stefan, 2019, *Pilgrims and Priests: Christian mission in a post-Christian society*, London: SCM Press.

Paas, Stefan and Hans Schaeffer, 'Reconciled community. On finding a soteriology for Fresh Expressions', *Ecclesiology*, 17 (2021), pp. 325–47.

Padilla, Rene, 'The unity of the Church and the homogenous unit principle', *International Bulletin of Missionary Research*, 1982, pp. 23–30.

# BIBLIOGRAPHY

Pangaro, Paul, 'Questions for conversation theory or conversation theory in one hour', *Kybernetes*, 46 (9) 2017, pp. 1578–87.

Pannenberg, Wolfhart, 2004 (1992), *Systematic Theology*, Volume 3, London: T&T Clark.

Parry, Jonathan, 'The Gift, the Indian Gift and the "Indian Gift"', *Man*, 21 (3), 1986, pp. 453–73.

Pasadena Consultation 1978, *The Pasadena Consultation: Homogeneous Unit Principle*, Lausanne Occasional Paper 1, Orlando, FL: Lausanne Committee for World Evangelization.

Pask, Gordon, 'The limits of togetherness' in S. H. Lavington (ed.), *Information Processing 80: Proceedings of IFIF Congress, 80, Tokyo, Japan. October 6–9, 1980, Melbourne, Australia, October 14–17, 1980*, Amsterdam: North-Holland Publishing, 1980, pp. 999–1012.

Pecklers, Keith F., 2003, *Worship: A primer in Christian ritual*, Collegeville, MN: Liturgical Press.

Petrella, Ivan, 2008, *Beyond Liberation Theology: A polemic*, London: SCM Press.

Pickard, Stephen, 2012, *Seeking the Church: An introduction to ecclesiology*, London: SCM Press.

Pickstock, Catherine, 2013, *Repetition and Identity*, Oxford: Oxford University Press.

Pixley, George V., 1987 (1983), *On Exodus: A liberation perspective*, Maryknoll, NY: Orbis Books.

Plaisted, Robert, 'The homogeneous unit debate: its value orientations and changes', *The Evangelical Quarterly* 59 (3), 1987, pp. 215–33.

Potter, Phil, 2009, *The Challenge of Change: A guide to shaping change and changing the shape of the Church*, Abingdon: Bible Reading Fellowship.

Radner, Ephraim, 2012, *A Brutal Unity: The spiritual politics of the Christian Church*, Waco, TX: Baylor University Press.

Rahner, Karl, 'Towards a fundamental theological interpretation of Vatican II', *Theological Studies*, 40 (4) 1979, pp. 716–27.

Ramsey, Michael, 1990 (1936), *The Gospel and the Catholic Church*, London: SPCK.

Rhee, Helen, 2017, *Wealth and Poverty in Early Christianity*, Minneapolis, MN, Fortress Press.

Riesner, Rainer, 2000, 'A Pre-Christian Jewish Mission?' in Jostein Adna and Hans Kvalbein (eds), *The Mission of the Early Church to Jews and Gentiles*, Tübingen: Mohr Siebeck.

Roberts, Robert C., 2004, 'The blessings of gratitude. A conceptual analysis' in Robert A. Emmons and Michael E. McCullough (eds), *The Psychology of Gratitude*, Oxford: Oxford University Press, pp. 58–78.

Rush, Ormond, 2018, 'Roman Catholic ecclesiology from the Council of Trent to Vatican II and beyond' in Paul Avis (ed.), *The Oxford Handbook of Ecclesiology*, Oxford: Oxford University Press, pp. 263–92.

Rusch, William G., 2007, *Ecumenical Reception: Its Challenge and Opportunity*, Grand Rapids, MI: Eerdmans.

Russell, Letty M., 1993, *Church in the Round: Feminist interpretation of the Church*, Louisville, KY: John Knox Press.

Saarinen, Risto, 2005, *God and the Gift. An ecumenical theology of giving*, Collegeville, MN: Liturgical Press.

Sahlins, Marshall B., 2017 (1972), *Stone Age Economics*, Abingdon: Routledge.

Samartha, S. J., 1982, *Courage for Dialogue: Ecumenical issues in inter-religious relationships*, Maryknoll, NY: Orbis Books.

Sanneh, Lamin, 1989, *Translating the Message: The missionary impact on culture*, Maryknoll NY: Orbis Books, 1989.

Schipani, Daniel, S., 1995, 'Liberation theology and religious education' in Randolph Crump Miller (ed.), *Theologies of Religious Education*, Birmingham, AL: Religious Education Press, pp. 286–313.

Schmitz, Kenneth L., 1982, *The Gift: Creation*, Milwaukee, WI: Marquette University Press.

Schnabel, Eckhard J., 2008, *Paul the Missionary: Realities, strategies and methods*, Downers Grove, IL: IVP.

Schreiter, Robert J., 1985, *Constructing Local Theologies*, London: SCM Press.

Schwartz, Barry, 'The social psychology of gift', *The American Journal of Sociology*, 73(1), 1967, pp. 1–11.

Schwöbel, Christoph, 2003, 'A theological ontology of communicative relations' in J. Haers and P. De Mey, *Theology and Conversation*, Leuven: Leuven University Press, pp. 43–67.

Scola, Angelo, 1995, *Hans Urs von Balthasar: A theological style*, Grand Rapids, MI: Eerdmans Publishing Co.

Shaw, R. Daniel, 2018, 'The dynamics of ritual and ceremony: transforming traditional rites to their intended purpose' in R. Daniel Shaw and William R. Burrows (eds), *Traditional Ritual as Christian Worship: Dangerous syncreticism or necessary hybridity?*, Maryknoll, NY: Orbis Books, pp. 1–19.

Shaw, Patricia, 2002, *Changing Conversations in Organizations: A complexity approach to change*, London: Routledge.

Shockley, Grant S., 1995, 'Black Theology and religious education' in Randolph Crump Miller (ed.), *Theologies of Religious Education*, Birmingham, AL: Religious Education Press, pp. 315–23.

Sidnell, Jack, 2010, *Conversation Analysis. An introduction*, Chichester: Wiley.

Smith, Christian and Hilary Davidson, 2014, *The Paradox of Generosity: Giving we receive, grasping we lose*, Oxford: Oxford University Press.

Solomon, Robert C., 2004, 'Foreword' in Robert A. Emmons and Michael E. McCullough (eds), *The Psychology of Gratitude*, Oxford: Oxford University Press, pp. v–vi.

Stacey, Ralph D., 2001, *Complex Responsive Processes in Organizations: Learning and knowledge creation*, London: Routledge.

Stacey, Ralph D., 2010, *Complexity and Organizational Reality*, second edition, Abingdon: Routledge.

Starkey, Ken and Sue Tempest, 2005, 'Late twentieth-century management, the business school, and social capital' in Cary L. Cooper (ed.), *Leadership and Management in the 21st Century: Business challenges of the future*, Oxford: Oxford University Press, pp. 139–59.

Stivers, Tanya, N. J. Enfield, Penelope Brown, Christina Englert, Makoto Hayashi, Trine Heinemann, Gertie Hoymann, Federico Rossano, Jan Peter de Ruiter, Kyung-Eun Yoon, and Stephen C. Levinson, 'Universals and cultural variations in turn-taking in conversation', *Proceedings of the National Academy of Sciences*, 106 (26) 2009, pp. 10587–92.

# BIBLIOGRAPHY

Swete, Henry Barclay, 1919, *The Holy Catholic Church. The Communion of Saints; A Study in the Apostles Creed*, London: MacMillan.

Tanner, Kathryn, 1997, *Theories of Culture: A New Agenda for Theology*, Minneapolis, MN: Fortress Press.

Tanner, Kathryn, 2005, *Economy of Grace*, Minneapolis, MN: Fortress Press.

Taylor, John V., 2004 (1972), *The Go-Between God: The Holy Spirit and Christian Mission*, London: SCM Press.

Taylor, Steve, 2019, *First Expressions: Innovation and the mission of God*, London: SCM Press.

Thompson, Michael B., 1998, 'The holy internet: communication between churches in the first Christian generation' in Richard Bauckham (ed.), *The Gospels for All Christians: Rethinking the gospel audiences*, Grand Rapids, MI: Eerdmans, pp. 49–70.

Tickle, Phyllis, 2008, *The Great Emergence: How Christianity is changing and why*, Grand Rapids, MI: Baker Books.

Torvend, Samuel, 2019, *Still Hungry at the Feast: Eucharistic justice in the midst of affliction*, Collegeville, MN: Liturgical Press.

Uzukwu, Elochukwu E., 2006 (1996), *A Listening Church: Autonomy and communion in African churches*, Eugene, OR: Wipf & Stock.

van den Toren-Lekkerkerker, Berdine and Benno van den Toren, 2015, 'From missionary incarnate to incarnational guest: a critical reflection on incarnation as a model for missionary presence' in Cathy Ross and Jonny Baker (eds), *Pioneering Spirituality: Resources for reflection and practice*, Norwich: Canterbury Press, pp. 216–32.

Vanstone, W. H., 1982, *The Stature of Waiting*, London: Darton, Longman and Todd.

Vanstone, W. H., 1997, *Fare Well in Christ*, London: Darton, Longman and Todd.

Volf, Miroslav, 1998, *After Our Likeness: The Church as the image of the Trinity*, Grand Rapids, MI: Eerdmans.

Volland, Michael, 2009, *Through the Pilgrim Door: Pioneering a fresh expression of church*, Eastbourne: Survivor Books.

von Balthasar, Hans Urs, 1982, *The Glory of the Lord. A theological aesthetics. Volume 1. Seeing the Form*, Edinburgh: T&T Clark.

Wagner, C. Peter, 'How ethical is the homogeneous unit principle?', *International Bulletin of Mission Research* 2 (1), 1978, pp. 12–19.

Walker, John, 2014, *Testing Fresh Expressions: Identity and transformation*, Farnham: Ashgate.

Walls, Andrew F., 2002, *The Cross-Cultural Process in Christian History: Studies in the transmission and appropriation of the faith*, Maryknoll, NY: Orbis Books.

Walter, Gregory, 2013, *Being Promised: Theology, gift, and practice*, Grand Rapids, MI: Eerdmans.

Ward, Keith, 2015, *Christ and the Cosmos: A reformulation of trinitarian doctrine*, Cambridge: Cambridge University Press.

Ward, Kevin, 2017 (2012), 'Revival, mission and church in Kigezi, Rwanda and Burundi' in Kevin Ward and Emma Wild-Wood (eds), *The East African Revival: History and Legacies*, Abingdon: Routledge.

Ward, Pete (ed.), 2012, *Perspectives on Ecclesiology and Ethnology*, Grand Rapids, MI: Eerdmans.

# GIVING THE CHURCH

Warren, Robert, 1995, *Being Human, Being Church: Spirituality and mission in the local church*, London: Marshall Pickering.

Watkins, Clare and Bridget Shepherd, 'The challenge of "Fresh Expressions" to ecclesiology. Reflections from the practice of messy church', *Ecclesial Practices*, 1 (2014), pp. 92–110.

Webster, John, 'On Evangelical ecclesiology', *Ecclesiology*, 1 (1), 2004, pp. 9–35.

Weiner, Annette B., 1992, *Inalienable Possessions: The paradox of keeping-while giving*, Berkeley, CA: University of California Press.

Wells, Samuel, 2019, *A Future that's Bigger than the Past. Towards the renewal of the Church*, Norwich: Canterbury Press.

Wendebourg, Dorothea, 2018, 'The Church in the Magisterial Reformers' in Paul Avis (ed.), *The Oxford Handbook of Ecclesiology*, Oxford: Oxford University Press, pp. 217–37.

Wesley, John, 1988, 'Sermon 16, "On the means of Grace"' in *Wesley's 52 Standard Sermons*, Salem, OH: Schmul Publishing Company, pp. 149–62.

Wilde, Oscar, 2004 (1891), *The Soul of Man Under Socialism*, Whitefish, MT: Kessinger Publishing.

Williams, Rowan, 1994, 'Mission and Christology', J. C. Jones Memorial Lecture, Church Missionary Society, Welsh Members Council.

Williams, Rowan, 2005, *Grace and Necessity. Reflections on art and love*, London: Continuum.

Williams, Rowan, 2006, 'Theological resources for re-examining church' in Steven Croft (ed.), *The Future of the Parish System: Shaping the Church of England for the 21st century*, London: Church House Publishing, pp. 49–60.

Williams, Rowan, 2007, *Wrestling with Angels: Conversations in modern theology*, ed. by Mike Higton, London: SCM Press.

Williams, Rowan, 2008a, *A Margin of Silence: The Holy Spirit in Russian Orthodox theology*, Quebec: Editions du Lys Vert.

Williams, Rowan, 'No-one can be forgotten in God's Kingdom', *Anvil*, 25 (2), 2008b, pp. 117–28.

Williams, Rowan, 2014, *The Edge of Words: God and the habits of language*, London: Bloomsbury Continuum.

Williams, Rowan, 2018, *Christ the Heart of Creation*, London: Bloomsbury.

Wittgenstein, Ludwig, 2009 (1953), *Philosophical Investigations*, fourth edition, Oxford: Blackwell.

World Council of Churches, 1967, *The Church for Others: Two Reports on the missionary structure of the congregation*, Geneva: WCC.

World Council of Churches, 1982, *Baptism, Eucharist and Ministry* (Faith and Order Paper 111), Geneva: WCC.

World Council of Churches, 2013a, *The Church: Towards a common vision*, Geneva: WCC.

World Council of Churches, 2013b, *Together Towards Life. Mission and evangelism in changing landscapes*, ed. Jooseup Keum, Geneva: WCC.

Wright, Christopher J. H., 2004, *Old Testament Ethics for the People of God*, Downers Grove, IL: IVP.

Wright, Christopher J. H., 2006, *The Mission of God: Unlocking the Bible's grand narrative*, Nottingham: IVP.

Wright, Robert, 1996 (1994), *The Moral Animal: Evolutionary psychology and everyday life*, London: Abacus.

# BIBLIOGRAPHY

Yoder, John Howard, 2014, *Theology of Mission: A believers church perspective*, Downers Grove, IL: IVP.

Zizioulas, John D., 1985, *Being as Communion*, London: Darton, Longman & Todd.

Zizioulas, John D., 2006, *Communion and Otherness*, ed. Paul McParlan, London: T&T Clark.

Zizioulas, John D., 2011, *The Eucharistic Communion and the World*, ed. Luke Ben Tallon, London: T&T Clark.

# Index of Names and Subjects

Abraham 42, 123, 141
absolution 175
abuse ix, 2, 3, 10, 18, 57, 67, 76, 175, 178, 189, 242
Acts 25, 26, 30, 43, 69, 99, 101, 127, 128, 129, 131, 132, 140, 238n6, 243
advocacy, advocate 19, 112, 115, 171, 185, 257
altruism 13–15
Antioch 128–9, 130, 131
apostles 43, 65, 69, 87, 89, 90, 91, 93, 94, 96n12, 115, 134, 144n12, 243
Augustine 105, 238n1, 248
Avis, Paul 133–4

Balthasar, Hans Urs von 51n1, 51n8, 111, 193
baptism vii, 12, 28, 34, 43, 56, 62, 64, 65, 105, 149, 221
Barth, Karl 34, 35, 47–9, 91, 111, 112, 116n1, 121, 135, 193
Bede 248
being 8, 34, 64–5, 67, 83, 87, 99, 111, 163, 211, 220
Bible 5, 66, 107, 171, 182, 201, 208
 Burritos and 245
blessing(s) 10, 35, 37, 42, 67, 88, 101, 118, 122, 126, 177, 196, 222, 251
 Blessing Bags 245

Boff, Leonardo 7, 91, 172, 186, 187
Bonhoeffer, Dietrich ix, 27
Bosch, David 5, 43–4
Bourdieu, Pierre 16, 21n12
Brazil 182, 184, 186
Brueggemann, Walter 176, 190n4
Burundi 247

called 1, 8, 10, 18, 19, 25, 33, 36, 43, 50, 53, 57, 75, 113, 119, 142, 167, 181, 191, 193, 214, 220–1, 236, 239, 244, 248, 254, 257
Calvary 39, 227
catholicity, catholic 75, 76, 85–9, 92, 93–4, 95n5, 139, 147, 229–30, 240
Cavanaugh, William 87, 103, 117, 225
Chalcedon 76
challenge 16, 44, 78, 83, 131, 137, 180, 213, 241, 251, 252, 258
chaplain, chaplaincy 142, 171, 218, 252
charity 14, 15, 44, 63, 110, 149, 160, 163, 170, 233, 239
Cheal, David 14, 143n1, 156
Christendom 9, 10, 91, 152, 239
Christianity 9, 21n4, 79, 90, 175, 190n3, 244
 Jewish 9, 69, 123, 136

*Christianity Today* 9
Christmas 16, 21n12, 27, 127
church 7, 12, 31, 43, 46, 47, 55,
  63, 65, 69, 70, 72, 79, 86, 89,
  103–4, 110, 115, 117n10, 120,
  127–31, 134–6, 139, 144n12,
  160, 172, 180, 234–5, 239, 248
  as community 4, 114, 159,
  161–2, 170–2, 181, 182, 209,
  219, 241
  as conversationalist 191–202,
  203–6, 207–10, 211–12,
  213–15, 216n5, 242, 254
  as gift *see also* gift, giving 1, 2,
  5, 8, 9, 11, 18–20, 21n2, 25,
  26–7, 28, 29–30, 32–42, 44,
  45, 49, 50, 53, 55, 57, 60, 62,
  75, 76, 82, 83, 88, 91, 92, 97,
  98, 99–102, 105, 107, 109–10,
  113, 118–19, 120, 123, 126,
  138, 140, 147, 149, 152,
  153–4, 162, 169, 170, 175,
  177, 186–7, 191, 202, 214,
  231, 236–7, 240–2, 247, 252,
  255–6, 257
  Christ as head of 4, 26, 28, 59,
  67, 137, 229, 242, 258
  Church of England 9, 19, 20n1,
  40, 48, 57, 112, 218, 252
  'dinner church' 45, 74, 143n11,
  260n11
  four marks of *see also* catholic,
  catholicity 76–94, 106, 147,
  229
  fresh expressions of *see also*
  Fresh Expressions 49, 95n5,
  112, 189, 244
  Lego church 224
  Messy Church 41, 233, 260n11
  and mission 5–6, 11, 20, 35, 42,
  48–9, 50, 59, 61, 72, 75, 84,
  85, 87, 90, 93, 113, 125, 136,

  141, 147, 166–7, 173, 186,
  189, 224, 244–8, 257
  nature of 54–74, 154, 161, 178
  new forms of 9, 19, 52n19,
  73–4, 245–7
  Orthodox 132
  Roman Catholic 3, 6, 64, 105,
  132, 144n14, 170, 250, 259n6
  self-giving of 3, 8, 11, 30, 34,
  35–40, 42, 44, 53, 78, 84, 85,
  88, 94, 148, 151–2, 163–4,
  165, 170, 174, 187, 197, 241
  six models of *see also* Dulles,
  Avery 25, 257
  Methodist Church of Great
  Britain 9
  world 8–9, 132, 169
church plants, planting 3, 12,
  19, 20, 49, 73, 79, 115, 148,
  188–9, 190, 233, 237, 243,
  249, 258
Common Awards programme viii
communication 15, 124, 141,
  153, 155, 191, 192–3, 194,
  201, 206, 207, 216n9
communion in Christ 1–2, 4–6,
  11, 18, 25, 27–30, 33, 35, 37–9,
  40–1, 45, 46, 49, 53–5, 57, 60,
  67, 72, 76, 79, 84, 87, 92, 97,
  104, 106–7, 109, 113, 123–4,
  126–8, 131, 140, 147–8, 152–4,
  157–8, 160–3, 165–6, 170, 176,
  180, 183, 185, 187–8, 189,
  191–2, 194, 196–7, 199, 202–4,
  205, 208, 211, 214, 218,
  219–22, 231–2, 234, 236–7,
  239, 241–2, 243, 247, 249–50,
  253–4, 255–6, 257–8
congregation 10, 39, 40–4, 45,
  46, 47–9, 50, 56–8, 59, 61,
  63–4, 65, 69, 79, 85–8, 92, 94,
  107–9, 112, 118–19, 123, 124,

## INDEX OF NAMES AND SUBJECTS

134–7, 138, 140, 159, 184,
217, 219, 221, 225, 229, 231,
236–7, 240, 242, 251, 253, 258
established, existing 9, 25, 40–2,
49, 73, 147, 220, 239, 245, 257
for the Doctrine of the Faith 68,
184
homogenous 120–1, 128, 133,
143n3
micro- 9
new 12, 44–5, 48, 49, 72, 73,
79, 94, 115, 527, 137, 142,
177, 188, 230, 244, 250
parent 12, 69, 137, 139, 163,
218, 230, 233, 234, 244, 247
conversation 36, 37, 54, 61, 100,
153, 155–6, 191–2, 194–6, 198,
199, 200–12, 217, 218, 224,
232, 234, 237, 242–3, 250–2,
253–6
Corinth 130, 131, 228
covenant 16, 43, 61, 183, 185
creed 196
Nicene 66, 68, 76
culture 8, 9, 11, 13, 42, 61, 73,
82, 91, 93–4, 115, 120, 123,
133, 139, 149, 164, 171, 180,
185, 201, 203, 240, 256–7

Derrida, Jacques 14, 31
Deuteronomy 124, 143n5
disagreement 56, 68, 70–1, 74n6,
207
discernment 54, 67–70, 72, 136,
177, 181, 191, 210, 242
discipleship 1, 25, 45, 46–9, 112,
126, 147, 189, 228, 237
disciplines 54, 56, 62–6, 67–8,
72–3, 84–5, 105, 137, 147,
172, 191–2, 239
diversity 10, 76, 86, 87, 88, 93,
125, 131, 132, 134–5, 138–9,

143n7, 177, 187, 208, 209,
201, 225, 229, 240
doctrine 2, 3, 6, 18, 19, 20, 25,
34, 49, 71, 94, 121, 135, 147,
148, 239
Dulles, Avery 1, 257

Easter 91, 137
ecclesiology 93, 20, 49, 58, 217,
251
communion ecclesiology 3–4, 8
ecclesiogenesis *see also* Boff,
Leonardo 7, 187
new 114–15
education 137, 164, 242, 247
Egypt 90, 173, 174, 176, 183,
190n4
Emmanuel 111
Emmaus 223, 225
England 41, 46, 95n10, 110,
190n7, 224, 245, 248
ensign 87
Eucharist *see also* Holy
Communion 4, 28, 55, 64–5,
66, 84–5, 140, 195, 217–37,
251–2
evangelism 1, 45, 50, 147, 153,
175, 189, 201, 243, 258
'Affirmation on Mission and
Evangelism' (World Council of
Churches) 125
Evensong 216n3, 218
Exodus 169, 173, 176, 179, 183,
186

faith 1, 7, 9, 28, 47, 48, 55, 59,
60, 73, 77, 79, 83, 90, 108,
112, 115, 120, 122, 135, 136,
157, 165–6, 171, 174, 180,
186, 209, 212, 235, 240, 242,
244, 245, 246, 248, 252, 258
family 8, 26, 27, 28, 37, 40, 47,
48, 55, 59, 71, 78, 79, 86, 89,

100, 101, 102, 103, 104–5,
    107, 110, 113–14, 118, 121,
    129, 130, 131, 136, 141–2,
    156, 157–8, 159, 183, 190,
    197, 202, 229, 230, 234
fellowship 4, 29, 30, 34–6, 38,
    46, 48, 49, 55, 59, 60, 71, 92,
    108, 112, 129, 165, 193, 245
fidelity 66, 92, 93
forgiveness 80, 164–5, 175, 228,
    234
formation 11, 46, 47, 49, 85,
    113, 137, 147, 214, 245
Francis of Assisi 206
Fresh Expressions 52n19, 244
friendship 14, 17, 48, 55, 56, 86,
    118, 119, 129, 140, 198, 232

generosity
Gentiles 9, 69, 127, 129, 130,
    136, 143n6, 202
gift, giving 1, 2, 3
    acceptance of 16, 20, 32, 33,
        39, 51, 81, 83, 99, 114, 148,
        158–9, 165, 183, 185, 188,
        206, 208, 215, 218, 228, 230,
        231, 240, 242, 249
    appropriate 10, 11, 15, 20,
        32, 40, 51, 80, 88, 98–9, 121,
        148, 151, 152, 153, 155, 161,
        165–6, 167, 167n4, 169, 176,
        186, 187, 195, 204, 215, 218,
        222, 224, 226, 231, 235, 236,
        240, 241, 249, 252, 254
    attractive 2, 20, 44, 75–6, 94,
        148, 149, 239, 240, 247, 249,
        250, 251, 252, 256
    available 41, 97, 99, 100, 105,
        108, 109, 148, 166, 178, 188,
        240
    Christian 15
    inappropriate 147, 161

Jesus Christ as 98–100, 103–5,
    111, 113, 116n5, 116n7, 124,
    162, 217, 228, 230
nature of 13, 19, 33, 53, 77, 98,
    147, 148
of God 1, 5, 6, 15, 16, 17, 19,
    25, 26, 28, 29–30, 32, 34, 36–7,
    65, 70, 83, 116n4, 121, 149,
    156, 160–1, 173, 185, 236
of the Spirit 1, 4, 30, 152, 158,
    191, 250
Sociology of Giving (Helmuth
    Berking) 219
unattractive 30, 102
Gift, The (Marcel Mauss) 13, 16,
    156
givenness 117n9
giver, givers 1, 13–17, 18, 32, 37,
    53, 54, 98–9, 100, 103–5, 111,
    113, 115, 126, 149, 150–2,
    153, 154, 155–6, 158, 159,
    160–1, 162, 163–4, 167n4, 170,
    172, 173, 175, 176, 178–9,
    186, 194–5, 200, 202, 204,
    208, 201, 215, 222, 224, 226,
    228, 230, 233, 237, 241, 249
God 2, 7, 18, 31, 34, 36, 41, 42,
    46, 57, 59, 62, 63, 66, 68, 69,
    71, 81, 84, 97, 98, 100, 105–8,
    109, 111, 119, 122, 138, 141,
    152, 158, 165, 173, 174, 176,
    179, 181, 183, 188, 194, 197,
    199, 212–13, 222, 225, 231–2,
    235, 239, 244
grace of 15, 77, 78, 103, 106,
    107, 124
holiness of 94
kingdom of 1, 26, 27, 29–30,
    38, 43, 44, 58, 74, 76, 93,
    94, 101, 104, 114, 115, 132,
    164, 170, 185, 202, 211, 247,
    248–9, 250

## INDEX OF NAMES AND SUBJECTS

love of 17, 18, 44, 72, 82, 88,
  162
mission of, *missio Dei* 5–6, 30,
  35, 54, 58, 64, 72, 85, 113,
  123, 167, 248
nature of 4, 32, 34
people of 3, 7, 9, 25, 26–7,
  28–9, 30, 33, 35, 37, 38–9,
  42–3, 46, 50, 55, 60–1, 67,
  68, 75, 76, 80, 83, 87, 88,
  90, 92–3, 100, 101–2, 103,
  108, 109, 114, 115, 120, 128,
  133, 135, 136, 139, 142, 150,
  154, 166, 177, 182, 183–4,
  204, 217, 226, 243, 247, 254,
  256–7, 259
reign of 1, 2, 29, 38, 39, 76, 78,
  87, 104, 114, 126, 170, 223,
  233, 250, 251
word of 28, 181, 191, 193, 195,
  198, 201, 208, 242
Godhead 33, 51n1, 53, 77, 82,
  92, 93, 162, 194
gospel message 25, 38, 41, 44,
  66, 70, 72, 80, 90, 105, 106,
  108, 109, 112, 114–15, 120–2,
  132, 134, 136, 153, 157, 171,
  175, 181, 182, 185, 189, 202,
  203, 205, 207, 201, 218, 243,
  248–9
grace 10, 15, 18, 25, 26, 28, 29,
  30, 33, 35, 36, 66, 67, 72, 74,
  92, 93, 107, 120, 124, 141,
  169, 223, 230, 231, 234, 235,
  239, 251, 257
gratitude 10, 33, 104, 106, 147,
  152, 160, 161–4, 231, 232,
  239, 248, 249
Great Emergence *see also* Tickle,
  Phyllis 8
growth 9, 50, 72, 119, 147, 245,
  249, 258

guest 17, 125, 126, 153, 154,
  156, 167
Gutiérrez, Gustavo 7, 171

Habermas, Jürgen 203
Hauerwas, Stanley 114
healing 33, 36, 40, 164, 248
heritage 64, 95n10, 134, 185,
  209, 212, 253, 257
holiness 76, 81–2, 83–4, 85, 86,
  92, 93, 94, 101, 240
Holy Communion *see also*
  Eucharist 12, 55, 56, 62, 217,
  218, 219–20, 221–3, 224–5,
  227, 228, 229, 230, 231, 234,
  235, 245, 247, 252
Holy Spirit 1, 3, 4, 16, 25, 58, 63,
  65, 84, 98, 99, 149, 191, 198,
  221
homogenous unit principle *see
  also* McGavran, Donald
  119–20, 139
homophily 119
hope 2, 3, 12, 14, 15, 77, 80, 85,
  174, 186, 187, 189
Hosea 18
hospitality 28, 125–6, 131, 150,
  167, 248
hybridity, hybridization 178, 224

identity 5, 28, 54, 62, 81, 86, 89,
  93, 111, 122, 124–5, 126–7,
  133, 134, 139, 160, 184, 198,
  202, 225, 240, 258
of the church 19, 34–6, 57, 67,
  81, 112, 177, 202, 203
God-given 26, 162
of God, Jesus 81, 83, 90, 99,
  100, 152, 234
Ignatius of Loyola 194
imagination, imagine 2, 10, 17,
  20, 80, 87, 88, 123, 139, 149,

155, 164, 177, 180, 189, 204, 234, 239, 251, 252, 257
Incarnation 7, 25, 60, 111, 123, 162
inclusive 87, 94, 118, 139, 236
Industrial Revolution 110
innovation 134, 190, 209, 210, 231, 253
International Missionary Council 5
Israel 5, 42, 43, 61, 79, 84, 90, 122, 123, 131, 139, 174, 179, 183, 184, 185, 198, 201, 202, 209

James 98, 132
Jerusalem 43, 69, 79, 87, 90, 92, 128, 129, 130, 131, 140, 141
Jewish people, culture 60, 61, 123, 129, 130, 131, 140, 156, 159, 192, 202
Jonah 122
Judaism 174, 209
Judas 227
justice 7, 37, 43, 44, 50, 53, 72, 92, 108, 136, 166, 170, 171, 173, 188, 189, 218, 228, 231, 232, 250, 258

knowledge, knowing 7, 69, 82, 161, 163, 190, 199, 242
Komter, Aafke 118
Küng, Hans 75, 77, 78, 81, 85, 90

language 2, 7, 12, 18, 26, 28, 61, 115, 141, 142, 173, 191, 193, 197, 198, 200, 202, 203, 204, 207, 208, 210, 211, 221
lay ministry, leadership 9, 48, 251, 252
leaders, leadership 26, 45, 55, 56, 60, 63–6, 67, 73, 74, 76, 89,

107, 131, 135, 137, 157, 170, 172, 175, 179, 180, 181–2, 200, 205, 214, 224, 227–8, 229, 233, 234, 242, 244, 245, 252, 254, 256, 257
learning 9, 62, 150, 163, 222, 248
Lego 77, 83, 224
LGBTQ+ 7, 177, 184
liturgy, liturgical 35, 46, 56, 66, 113, 133, 187, 190, 196, 218, 219, 221, 231, 235, 236, 237, 251, 253, 259n6
Liturgical Commission (Church of England) 252
love see also God, love of 12, 14, 16, 17, 18, 27, 31, 36, 37, 40, 43–4, 45, 46–7, 48, 54, 59, 71–2, 79, 82, 88, 92, 94, 99, 105, 112, 115, 120, 124, 136, 142, 147, 150, 157, 162, 165, 194, 197, 206, 207, 213, 215, 219, 220, 227, 234, 236, 237, 239, 242, 244, 245, 246–50, 253, 258, 259

management 214
marriage 39, 40, 53, 55, 62, 63, 78, 95n8, 110, 119, 241
McGavran, Donald 119–20
meal 33, 37, 47, 54, 56, 140, 150, 156, 218, 221, 222, 223, 225, 227, 228, 230, 232, 234, 235, 251
Passover 217
Milbank, John 16, 22n13, 139–41
Minecraft 224
ministry 11, 20, 48, 54, 55–7, 62, 63, 64, 67, 68, 70, 72, 73, 84, 85, 94, 99, 105, 109, 147, 148, 239, 240, 251, 252

## INDEX OF NAMES AND SUBJECTS

Jesus' 149, 159, 199, 201, 211, 218
of the word 10, 195
*missio Dei* 5, 6, 8, 30, 167, 258
mission *see also* church and mission, *missio Dei* 3, 5, 6, 9, 11, 19, 20, 26, 29, 35, 36, 39, 43–4, 45, 47–51, 54, 55, 61, 64, 69–70, 75, 79, 80, 87, 90–1, 92, 98, 113, 115, 121, 122, 123, 125, 126, 135, 136, 147, 150, 152, 158, 166–7, 186, 189–90, 193, 197, 213, 219, 232, 233, 236, 243, 247–8, 250, 254, 257–8
five marks of 42
theology of *see also* theology 6, 72
missionaries 90, 95n10, 125, 185, 243, 247
*Mission-shaped Church* (Church of England) 57, 58, 95n5, 112
Moltmann, Jürgen 5, 75, 77, 78, 87, 91, 95n8, 154, 170
Moses 179, 183

Nazareth 156
network 11, 12, 40, 50, 55, 67, 89, 108, 121, 123–4, 128, 129, 130, 133, 135, 136, 137, 141, 142, 159, 164, 188, 223, 242, 252, 253, 256
Newbigin, Lesslie 112
Nicene Creed 66, 68, 76

obedience 34, 43, 51n1, 58, 100, 185
otherness 117n9

paradigm 55, 152, 173, 223
paradox 20, 150, 206, 208, 227, 232

parish 110, 136, 139, 140, 144n14, 170–1, 184, 251
pastoral care 10, 36, 43, 45, 50, 53, 110, 159, 166, 219, 236, 250, 252
patience 31, 47, 69, 142, 243
Paul 4–5, 26, 28, 69, 71, 82, 101, 124, 127, 129, 130–2, 138, 160, 202, 221, 226–8
Pentecost 30, 79, 87, 90
perspective 27, 60, 81, 88, 89, 97, 105, 106, 123, 138, 155, 166, 175, 180, 814, 191, 254
Christian 173, 212
ecumenical 19, 65
liberation, liberationist 169, 174, 176, 187, 188, 189, 258
Peter 69, 129
philosophy 180, 181, 191
Phoebe 131–2
post-Christendom 3, 8, 10, 19, 73, 142, 180, 257
post-colonial 7, 10, 178, 180, 185, 225
postmodernity 225
poverty 14, 44, 50, 53, 95n8, 109, 135, 149, 150, 171, 184, 247
power 10, 13, 31, 62, 79, 82, 95n10, 114, 116n1, 138, 150–1, 152, 158, 170, 178, 179, 187, 190n1, 200, 205, 212, 229
abuse of 2, 3, 175, 189, 242, 257
prayer 29, 35, 41, 45, 46, 47, 58, 59, 64, 66, 69, 72, 93, 104, 107, 108, 126, 133, 137, 173, 181, 191, 194, 195, 212, 221, 222, 229, 231, 236, 245, 246–7, 255
psychology 191

Rahner, Karl 8–9, 257

reciprocity 13, 22n14, 159, 259n5
reconciliation 10, 35, 43, 50, 77, 80, 88, 120, 147, 236, 250, 258
redemption 25, 223
reflection 7, 11, 20, 29, 45, 53, 58, 66, 171, 174, 214, 225, 241, 243, 246
Reformation 162, 191, 193, 225
relationships 4, 5, 14, 15, 18–19, 30–1, 37, 47, 51, 54–6, 63, 64, 67, 71–2, 73, 76–7, 80, 84, 89, 93, 105, 108, 118, 119, 123, 131, 134, 138, 141–2, 151, 152–3, 154, 155, 160, 163–6, 176, 183, 200, 203, 205, 215, 218, 222, 224, 228, 231, 233, 236, 237, 247, 249, 254
abusive 107
building, developing, deepening 12, 86, 112, 139, 152, 156, 158, 167, 212, 244, 248
dense and thin 137–8, 201
four sets of 58–62, 66, 68, 69–70, 72, 74, 75, 147, 239–40
healthy 16, 62, 148, 218
human 11, 16, 60, 122
of solidarity 15
supportive 2
with God 16, 17, 32, 52n16, 54, 57, 59, 69, 72, 99, 100, 147, 159, 179, 195, 242
repentance 18, 30, 84, 103, 104, 150, 164, 175, 222, 241
Revelation 58, 132
rituals 62, 120
Romans 70, 130, 131, 227
rootedness 89, 93

sacrament 1, 10, 20, 54, 55–7, 62–7, 72, 73, 84, 85, 86, 104,

105, 106, 115, 147, 148, 220, 229, 235, 237, 239, 240, 251
sacrifice 167n4, 219, 223, 235
salvation 26, 29, 49, 100, 121, 123
safeguarding see also abuse 12, 137, 242
Scripture 5, 34, 45, 55, 56, 59, 64–6, 68–9, 90, 98, 157, 191, 193, 194, 195, 196, 208, 210, 223, 233, 245, 246–7
Jewish 42, 122
silence 205, 206
slavery 78, 122, 188
society 7, 8, 14, 25, 42, 48–9, 50, 80, 93, 94, 110, 112, 114–15, 119, 131, 163, 164, 165, 166, 170, 171, 174, 180, 182, 185, 187–8, 190, 220, 221, 223, 232, 242
sociology 191
solidarity 2, 7, 10, 15–16, 53, 71, 78, 80, 83, 113, 118, 119, 134, 171, 174, 184, 199, 207, 208, 236, 243
soul 48, 139, 164, 188
Shear Love at Soul Salon 246
storytelling 212, 215, 232
syncretism 178

Tanner, Kathryn 15, 16
Tertullian 43
testimony 133, 175
theology 5, 7, 15, 49, 53, 73, 115, 180, 182, 187, 189, 210, 214, 218, 236, 237, 240, 249, 256
Black 7, 169, 182
of conversation 215
feminist 7, 169
liberation 6, 7, 8, 20, 149, 169, 170–2, 182, 184, 186

## INDEX OF NAMES AND SUBJECTS

local 182, 226, 234
mission 6, 72
post-colonial 7, 169, 178, 185, 190n1
Tickle, Phyllis 8
transformation 1, 20, 38, 43, 51, 115, 148, 162–6, 169, 186–7, 195, 210, 211, 212, 215, 218, 222, 232, 233, 235, 240, 249
Trinity 1, 4, 5, 6, 25, 27, 28, 31, 53–4, 58, 59, 72, 85, 98, 99, 100, 147, 162, 187, 194, 198

Vatican II 3, 6, 7, 8, 44, 243
vision 3, 9, 114, 121, 122, 139, 160, 190, 257
vocation 11, 12, 20, 25, 35, 36, 38, 42, 48–9, 75, 90, 92, 106, 114, 147, 148–9, 162, 172, 214, 221, 237, 241, 250, 256, 257
volunteer 43, 48, 110, 137, 144n11, 160, 190

wisdom 40, 69, 70, 73, 81, 82, 135, 166, 208, 224, 242
witness 27, 29, 38, 41, 44–7, 48, 64, 91, 108, 110, 112, 114–15, 120, 126, 136, 149, 165, 193, 194, 197, 213, 237, 243, 250
World Council of Churches 1, 4
*The Church for Others*
report 45, 112
worship 11, 12, 29, 32, 36, 46, 47, 56, 58, 59, 60, 61, 64, 69, 72, 92, 98, 108, 126, 134, 137, 140, 157, 173, 176, 191, 194, 210, 212, 216n3, 218, 220, 221, 223, 224, 236, 244, 245–7, 251, 252–3

Yahweh 61, 122, 174, 176, 179, 183, 185, 186
youth club 12

Zacchaeus 150
Zizioulas, John 4, 238n6

www.ingramcontent.com/pod-product-compliance
Lightning Source LLC
Chambersburg PA
CBHW032013040325
22965CB00007B/32